Minders *of*
Make-Believe

BOOKS BY LEONARD S. MARCUS

A CALDECOTT CELEBRATION
Seven Artists and Their Paths to the Caldecott Medal

GOLDEN LEGACY
How Golden Books Won Children's Hearts, Changed Publishing Forever, and Became an American Icon Along the Way

THE WAND IN THE WORD
Conversations with Writers of Fantasy

WAYS OF TELLING
Conversations on the Art of the Picture Book

DEAR GENIUS
The Letters of Ursula Nordstrom

MARGARET WISE BROWN
Awakened by the Moon

MINDERS OF MAKE-BELIEVE
Idealists, Entrepreneurs, and the Shaping of American Children's Literature

Minders *of* Make-Believe

IDEALISTS,
ENTREPRENEURS,
AND THE SHAPING
OF AMERICAN
CHILDREN'S LITERATURE

Leonard S. Marcus

HOUGHTON MIFFLIN COMPANY
BOSTON   NEW YORK   2008

www.houghtonmifflinbooks.com

Library of Congress Cataloging-in-Publication Data

Marcus, Leonard S., date.
Minders of make-believe : idealists, entrepreneurs, and the shaping of American children's literature / Leonard S. Marcus.
p. cm.
Includes bibliographical references and index.
ISBN 978-0-395-67407-9
1. Children's literature — Publishing — United States — History. 2. Children's books — United States — History. 3. Children — Books and reading — United States — History. 4. Children's literature — Publishing — United States — History — 20th century. 5. Children's books — United States — History — 20th century. 6. Children — Books and reading — United States — History — 20th century. I. Title.
z480.c48m37 2008 070.5083 — dc22 2008000589

Printed in the United States of America

QUM 10 9 8 7 6 5 4 3 2 1

The author wishes to express his appreciation to the copyright holders for granting permission to quote from the following original source materials: Kate Stephens to Frank Stockton, March 19, 1898; Louise Seaman to Elizabeth Coatsworth, December 8, 1919; Louise Seaman to Elizabeth Coatsworth, October 1919; Louise Seaman to Elizabeth Coatsworth, November 1919; Louise Seaman to Elizabeth Coatsworth, November 27, 1931: Correspondence by Louise Seaman, Editor for Elizabeth Coatsworth, reprinted with the permission of Simon & Schuster, Inc. All rights reserved. Elizabeth Coatsworth to Louise Seaman, undated (spring/summer 1920); Elizabeth Coatsworth to Louise Seaman, May 18, 1922: reprinted by permission of Kate Barnes and Elizabeth Gartner. May Massee to Charles Buckle Falls, March 7, 1924: reprinted with the permission of Doubleday, a division of Random House, Inc. Anne Carroll Moore to Louise Seaman Bechtel, January 10, 1934: reprinted by permission of the New York Public Library. May Massee to Bertha E. Mahony, undated (spring 1933); May Massee to Bertha Mahony Miller, July 2, 1943; Gertrude Shafer to Robert McCloskey, August 29, 1974: used by permission of Viking Children's Books, an imprint of Penguin Group (USA) Inc. All rights reserved. Frances Foster, unpublished 2002 Ethel Heins Memorial Lecture, Children's Literature New England: excerpted by permission of Frances Foster. Grace Allen Hogarth to H. A. Rey, November 4, 1940: used by permission of Houghton Mifflin Company. Bertha Mahony Miller to May Massee, July 13, 1945: excerpted with permission of The Horn Book, Inc., www.hbook.com. Katharine S. White to Louise Seaman Bechtel, September 12, 1961: excerpted with the permission of Martha White, White Literary LLC. Johanna Hurwitz, interview with the author, May 2, 1997, used by permission of Johanna Hurwitz. Reminiscences of Michael Simon Bessie, July–December 1976, on page 192: used by permission of Columbia University Oral History Research Office Collection. Reminiscences of Thomas H. Guinzburg, December 10, 1979, vol. 1, on pages 95–96: used by permission of Columbia University Oral History Research Office Collection. Richard Jackson, interview with the author, May 8, 1995: excerpted by permission of Richard Jackson. Ursula Nordstrom to Katharine S. White, October 27, 1966: used by permission of HarperCollins, Publishers, Inc. Marilyn E. Marlow, interview with the author, April 22, 1994: excerpted by permission of Curtis Brown Ltd.

The author is also grateful to the owners and repositories of manuscripts and other original source materials for permission to quote from the following: Kate Stephens to Frank Stockton, March 19, 1898, Macmillan Company records: courtesy of Manuscripts and Archives Division, New York Public Library, Astor, Lenox and Tilden Foundations. Elizabeth Coatsworth to Louise Seaman, undated (spring/summer 1920); Elizabeth Coatsworth to Louise Seaman, May 18, 1922; Macmillan Department of Books for Boys and Girls catalog, 1930; Anne Carroll Moore to Louise Seaman Bechtel, January 10, 1934; Katharine S. White to Louise Seaman Bechtel, September 12, 1961: courtesy of Special Collections, Vassar College Libraries. Louise Seaman to Elizabeth Coatsworth, December 8, 1919; Louise Seaman to Elizabeth Coatsworth, October 1919; Louise Seaman to Elizabeth Coatsworth, November 1919; Louise Seaman to Elizabeth Coatsworth, November 27, 1931: courtesy of the Maine Women Writers Collection. May Massee to Charles Buckle Falls, March 7, 1924; May Massee to Ingri and Edgar Parin d'Aulaire, undated (late 1932); May Massee to Ingri and Edgar Parin d'Aulaire, undated (late 1932): courtesy of May Massee Collection, Emporia State University Archives, Emporia, Kansas. May Massee to Bertha E. Mahony, undated (spring 1933); May Massee to Bertha Mahony Miller, July 2, 1943: Bertha Mahony Miller to May Massee, July 13, 1945: excerpted by permission of The Horn Book, Inc., www.hbook.com. Grace Allen Hogarth to H. A. Rey, November 4, 1940, call number bMS Am 2105 (213): used by permission of the Houghton Library, Harvard University.

For my son, Jacob
& in memory of my uncle, Jacob Feld

Contents

FOREWORD

"What Shall the Children Read?"

— *Title of an advice book for parents*
by Laura E. Richards (1939)

CHILDREN'S BOOKS have had a three-hundred-year-long history in America, and for nearly all that time there has been scant agreement as to the books that were best. Publishers, religious and moral leaders, literary critics, educators, librarians, booksellers, psychologists, and parents have all had a say in the matter, alongside the writers and illustrators of the books, and each of these groups have at times expressed their views with such ferocity as to put to rest — or so one might have thought — the persistent notion that a children's book is an entirely innocent proposition. Children have made clear their preferences too, most often by the choice of the books they purchased with their own money. Yet overall it has been a defining feature of children's publishing, as contrasted with other kinds, that the people who buy the books have not been the people for whom the books were intended.

Some readers will be surprised at the notion that children's books have had a "history" at all. The reasons for this surprise are themselves historical. For most Americans growing up during the last century, it was common wisdom that children's literature comprised a vast repository of "timeless" tales awaiting their discovery. The idea that this was so was not entirely without merit and had been nurtured over many years. For decades the chief arbiters of American children's literature had come primarily from the ranks of children's librarians. Their specialized work, a turn-of-the-century American innovation, was predicated on the essentially Romantic conviction that in a world of rapidly changing moral and social codes innocent childhood was in urgent need of protection. The librarians made it their responsibility to provide that protection by surrounding young people with books that fed their sense of wonder and imagination without also exposing them to the world's cares. Hence, the children's rooms at the nation's public libraries were created as much to keep children at arm's length from reading matter deemed potentially harmful to them — the racy adult fiction of Balzac and Dreiser, for example, and the highly colored dime novels sold at the nation's newsstands — as they were to give children ready access to the books librarians thought suitable.

Even timeless books, however, are books of their time. If it took historians some long while to realize this about children's literature, it was perhaps due to the abstracted circumstances in which they, like most people, had first met the books in their own lives: if not in the safe haven of a library children's room, then in dimly lit bedtime encounters shared with a parent or during daydreamy hours of reading alone while other, supposedly happier children played outdoors. Children's books may well have mattered so little to historians of past generations precisely because the books mattered so much to children. With their place firmly fixed in the foreground of young people's intimate lives, few scholars thought to look further or to ask what the books might possibly mean as commercial or cultural artifacts, much less as works of literature and art.

Leaders of the pioneering generation of American children's librarians did attempt to view children's literature historically. But they did so through the lens of their professional vision of themselves as childhood's moral and cultural guardians. As a result, broad swaths of the literature were omitted from the historical record (the Tom Swift, Rover Boys, and other popular series books from the turn of the last century, for example, and later, Golden Books and many books inspired by progressive education) in large part because they were thought not to serve the librarians' more immediate purposes as childhood protectors.

It is hard not to admire those dedicated early librarians for their high-minded intentions. As I took up the study of children's literature, however, first as an undergraduate during the early 1970s and later as an independent scholar, and as I became aware of the gaps in the librarians' histories, I realized that the story they had fashioned about children's literature's timeless tales was part of a larger story in which the librarians themselves had played a part, as had many others with a passionate concern for children, for books, and sometimes also for making money.

During the more than thirty years since I first wondered about these matters, I have come to know other writers and scholars in the United States and elsewhere who were asking some of the same questions at more or less the same time. History has its own history, and it is oddly exhilarating finally to locate oneself midstream in it all.

My own work began with an undergraduate history honors thesis written at Yale in 1972 on early nineteenth-century American children's books considered as signposts of a young nation's emerging values. I was curious about power relationships: how Americans' recent rejection of the autocratic rule of kings might have affected the tone of adult-child relationships in American families. It occurred to me that the children's books of the period — Yale's Beinecke Library, it turned out, had an extraordinary collection — might provide the kind of evidence I needed to begin to answer my question.

Notwithstanding the Beinecke Library's riches, Yale offered no courses on children's literature or the history of childhood, and the first history professors I approached about serving as my adviser made it clear that my topic held no great interest for them. I was most fortunate that David Brion Davis, an authority on American slavery, agreed to take on my project.

Not all children's books are children's literature, as I was reminded as soon as I began plumbing the depths, such as they were, of the formulaic works of Jacob Abbott, Oliver Optic, and other popular antebellum juvenile authors for traces of the influence of the great modern democratic philosophers of childhood led by John Locke and Jean-Jacques Rousseau. In much of my own subsequent work, I have focused on the writers and illustrators who have done the most to make children's books a legitimate literary genre and art form. I have also remained fascinated, however, by the closely related historical phenomenon of children's books as messages passed down between generations — messages forged at the crossroads of commerce and culture. To understand the thoughts and actions of the people responsible for the creation and dissemination of children's books is to glimpse the inner machinery of one of literate society's primary means of self-renewal. In writing now about these "minders" — the publishers, critics, librarians, booksellers, and others who have shaped American children's literature over the last three centuries — I have tried to tell one of American culture's lesser-known yet pivotal stories.

Minders *of* Make-Believe

1

PROVIDENCE AND PURPOSE IN COLONIAL AMERICA AND THE YOUNG REPUBLIC

> Why came we unto this land? Was it not mainly with respect to the rising Generation?[1]
>
> — ELEAZAR MATHER, Northampton, Mass., 1671

> It is for the books of early instruction, in a great degree, to lay the foundation on which the whole superstructure of individual and national greatness must be erected.[2]
>
> — WILLIAM CARDELL, *Story of Jack Halyard* (1825)

NEW ENGLAND PURITANS reverenced reading as the key to living the godly life. Reading made possible the intimate knowledge of the Bible thought necessary to salvation, which every Christian had both the capacity and the obligation to seek. To grow up as an illiterate was a matter of dire consequence, for, as the General Court of Massachusetts noted on providing for the establishment of reading schools for the colony: "One chief project of that old deluder, Satan, [is] to keep men from the knowledge of the Scriptures."[3] With a view to commencing their children's spiritual training at the earliest possible moment, many Puritan families did not wait for school but taught their four- and five-year-olds to read at home.

In 1642 the first of several colonial New England laws mandated that children, servants, and apprentices living in Massachusetts acquire the ability to "read & understand the principles of religion & the capitall lawes of this country." A Connecticut statute of 1650 obliged parents to catechize their children and servants weekly. The New Haven colony made it mandatory for children and apprentices to "attain at least so much, as to be able duly to read the Scriptures, and other good and profitable printed Books in the English tongue." While it took nearly fifty years for the Massachusetts colony's elders finally to make good on the legal requirement, enacted in 1647, for towns of fifty households to hire a teacher responsible for ensuring the reading and writing skills of the community's children, and for towns of twice that size to open a public school, literacy rates seem to have been high before then anyway.[4] As formal education took hold, Latin language and literature studies introduced young people to a second, more worldly experience of reading — one that, offered in the name of the time-honored tradition of the classical education, did not seem incompatible with their Bible studies.

The faithful understood that reading in a sinful world might indeed be turned to sinful ends. "To the seventeenth-century Puritan," writes historian Gillian Avery,

> fiction did not only deflect the reader from more profitable occupation[;] there was an additional, very grave objection. It was untrue, therefore a lie, and therefore damnably wicked. Puritans customarily divided lying into three categories: the pernicious lie, made for evil intent; the officious lie, intended to prevent some danger or procure some good; and the sporting lie, "which is to make one merry, or to pass away Precious Time."[5]

While the first New Englanders had scant opportunity for distraction by fiction, concern over the consequences of the "sporting lie" would far outlast colonial days, when invented tales, in particular those published for young people, had no appreciable place in the cultural landscape. The Puritan belief that indulgence in fiction represented a fateful misuse of the essential life skill of reading set the pattern for what was to remain the central debate about juvenile literature through the time of the Civil War, with reverberations lasting well into the next century.

North America's first printing press began operation in Cambridge, Massachusetts, in 1639, nineteen years after the *Mayflower* landing. The Cambridge Press issued one or more broadsides before producing its first full-fledged book, the *Bay Psalm Book*, in an edition of 1,700 copies.[6] Fifty years later, the first children's book of American origin issued from Boston. *The New-England Primer* was aimed at teaching young people their letters and setting them on the path to the good Christian life. Although few details of the book's creation are known, it is generally believed to have been the work of an English bookseller, publisher, journalist, and staunch antipapist named Benjamin Harris, who fled London for Boston in 1686 following the ascent of King James II to the British throne. Harris is thought to have compiled *The New-England Primer* between 1687 and 1690 and to have offered it for sale at his London Coffee House in Boston. The little book must have sold satisfactorily. In 1691 Harris advertised a second printing. The oldest surviving copy of the *Primer* dates from 1727 and was published in Boston by Kneeland & Green. Whether or not it is quite the same book as the one devised by Harris is unknown.[7]

From the first, *The New-England Primer* served as a much-needed unifying force for the northern colonies' community of pious folk, who, as historian Paul Leicester Ford observed, "very quickly [showed] a tendency . . . toward the individualism implied by all dissent and especially Congregationalism."[8] In the absence of copyright protection, bookseller-printers in towns and later cities from New England to the South reprinted the book well into the nineteenth century. By 1830 the *Primer* had passed through 450 editions, with an estimated total sale of between 6 and 8 million copies.[9]

While an illustrated alphabet in rhyme, the shorter catechism, and selections of prayers and Bible verses remained the unchanging core of *The New-England Primer,* variations in the text from edition to edition were common and became a barometer of changing cultural codes and priorities. The *Primer*'s alphabet rhyme, being the text element that was easiest to alter, displayed the most variation. In the 1727 Boston edition, the "K" verse read: "Our King the good/No man of blood." But seventy years and a revolution later, the equivalent rhyme in a 1791 edition printed in the same city declared: "Kings should be good/Not men of blood." Not to be outdone, a Philadelphia edition of six years later stated: "The British King/Lost states thirteen."[10] Between 1740 and 1760, a span of years that overlapped with the evangelical revivalism of the Great Awakening, the *Primer* alphabet changed to reflect the trend, with the 1727 "C" rhyme ("The Cat does play,/ And after slay") making way for: "Christ crucify'd/For sinners dy'd."[11] After 1790 the emphasis shifted decisively from salvation to worldly concerns, as witness this "K" rhyme from a New York edition of 1819: "Tis Youth's delight/To fly their kite."[12] It was a triumph for secularism that, as Paul Leicester Ford wrote only half in jest, "should have made the true Puritan turn in his grave."[13]

The *Primer* was first published at a time of dramatic change in New England life. By the end of the seventeenth century, church membership in New England had undergone a startling transformation, with women for the first time finding themselves in a substantial majority. With this fundamental shift came others: a diminishment of the father's role as spiritual leader of the household; and a new way of approaching the spiritual care and training of the young that replaced the "emphasis on a vengeful God the father, demanding obedience and submission to his laws" with a less stern, more affectionate "emphasis on the figure of Christ, protecting his followers."[14] These changes within the family and community may help to explain the immense popularity in the colonies of James Janeway's *A Token for Children, Being an Exact Account of the Conversation, Holy and Exemplary Lives and Joyful Deaths of Several Young Children,* the first volume of which appeared in England in 1671, and which booksellers imported to America a decade later. Janeway's tales of the brave and pious deaths of thirteen Christian boys and girls were nothing if not heartrending. Even more remarkable to young readers of the time, however, would have been the mere fact that this was a book — the *first* children's book — whose central protagonists themselves were children. What was more, the boys and girls Janeway described were better Christians than the adults in their midst. Well before Wordsworth, the narratives seemed to suggest that in strength of religious conviction and sheer heroism, the child might indeed be the father of the man.[15]

Historian Bernard Wishy has noted that as paternal rule in the New England household faded in reality, it flourished a good while longer in story and myth. In popular advice books for parents of the 1830s written by Jacob Abbott, Samuel Goodrich, and others, "it was the mothers who were at the center of home life, [but] in books for children written by the same authors, the father was clearly in control of the family. This difference," according to Wishy, "is not surprising for it had not been decreed that the mother formally replace the father. She had, for the sake of practicality, stepped into roles in the nurture literature that the American father could not play well." Under the new regime, not least of the mother's primary duties was "to teach the child that he owed supreme respect, love, and obedience to his father."[16]

The New-England Primer's first edition antedated by less than a half-dozen years the publication in Britain of John Locke's *Some Thoughts Con-*

cerning Education (1693), a wide-ranging essay on child-rearing practices that highlighted children's capacity for reason and their susceptibility to being molded for life through judicious exposure to books and other influences suited to their capacity. Locke must have shuddered at the thought of Janeway's bestseller, however inspirational others found it. By recommending that children be introduced to reading by means of some "easy pleasant book," Locke pointed the way for the creation by England's John Newbery two generations later of a new type of illustrated children's book in which, unrepentantly, amusement shared pride of place with instruction as the publisher's stated goal. By the 1770s, Newbery's groundbreaking books were in circulation in the colonies in both imported and pirated editions.[17]

Before 1800, the American colonists depended on Britain for most of the books they owned and read. Bookseller-printers living in the colonies and their successor states faced daunting technical, financial, and legal barriers to the formation of a book culture independent from that of England. In the 1720s, when young Benjamin Franklin worked in the Philadelphia print shop of Samuel Keimer, North America lacked even a single type foundry, and type imported from England came at considerable cost. When Keimer's stock of letters proved insufficient — "out of sorts," in the terminology of the trade — to meet the shop's workload, it fell to his nimble assistant to improvise a method for molding type with which to increase their stock.[18] Because the colonies had so few paper mills of their own, much of the paper needed for printing had likewise to be imported from England, and paper remained the single greatest production cost for books and other publications well into the first half of the nineteenth century. Most printer's inks, another costly commodity, also had to be imported.

Throughout the colonial period and afterward, the books most commonly found in American households included almanacs and English-language Bibles. Franklin's *Poor Richard's Almanack*, launched in 1732, was the best known of the many homegrown contributions to a burgeoning genre that mixed bits of folk wisdom with a mass of useful information. But prior to the Revolution, a monopoly held by the Crown's printers on the production of English Bibles barred their colonial counterparts from sharing in the lucrative Bible trade.[19] Rampant government censorship made the printer's lot all the less predictable, and harder to bear. Further complicating not just printing but all commerce carried out beyond one's locality were the erratic transportation system and the fact that each colony and new state issued its own paper currency. As Benjamin Franklin soon learned, in respectable society even an accomplished printer was counted a poor marriage prospect.[20]

Burdened by these and other impediments, colonists wishing to enter the book business often saw their best chance of doing so as booksellers. In contrast to later times, when publishing houses maintained flagship shops in prime urban locations for the purpose of trumpeting their imprints and showcasing their wares, in eighteenth- and early nineteenth-century America publishing more often than not was a bookseller's sideshow — a part-time enterprise by means of which a bookseller might, by acting to fill in perceived gaps in his inventory, also supplement his income. The older arrangement, with the importation of books from Britain as its centerpiece, worked perfectly well for a long time. The years of discord between the colonies and the Crown that culminated in the American Revolution finally spurred the growth of printing for publication on American shores. The leader of this parallel struggle for cultural independence was a capable New Englander in the Benjamin Franklin mold named Isaiah Thomas.

Born in Boston in 1749 (the year Benjamin Franklin turned forty-three), Thomas came from a family with no money or social connections. His father had a reputation as a shiftless man, and when Moses Thomas died, leaving behind a wife and five children, Isaiah, at six years old the youngest of them, was apprenticed to the shop of a second-rate Boston printer named Zechariah Fowle. The boy, it turned out, had a brilliant knack for the trade and as time went on Fowle entrusted more and more of the work to his talented and energetic assistant.[21] By age eight, Thomas had already acquired the knowledge and skill to do the casework for a complete book. For his first such job, he produced a ten-thousand-copy edition of *The New-England Primer.*

Thomas's self-assurance only increased with age, and following a "serious fracas" with his employer when he was in his midteens, he set out to make his fortune in print shops as far afield as Nova Scotia and South Carolina. He returned to Boston in 1770 and launched the triweekly *Massachusetts Spy,* a tabloid that steered clear of politics at first but later won a large and devoted readership as a forum for fiery pro-revolution sentiment. All the while, Thomas prudently spread his risk by publishing a variety of pamphlets, books, and almanacs. In April 1775, just days before Paul Revere made his famous ride, the radicalized and by then notorious Boston printer quietly packed up his press and fled inland in the dead of night to safer ground in Worcester, Massachusetts. There, after a brief period of readjustment, Thomas prospered as the official printer for Congress, and he went on to preside over an ever-expanding enterprise that in thirty-odd years published some nine hundred books, one hundred of them juveniles. At the peak of his career, Thomas and his partners operated print shops and bookstores in seven cities and towns stretching from Concord, New Hampshire, to Baltimore, owned a paper mill and a bindery, and had as many as one hundred fifty employees.[22] He died in 1831 one of the nation's wealthiest men, admired as much for his philanthropies as for his far-reaching success as eighteenth-century America's most important publisher and bookseller.

Benjamin Franklin called Thomas the "Baskerville of America."[23] Bibliophiles revered him (and still do) as the founder, in his adopted town of Worcester, of the American Antiquarian Society and as the author of *The History of Printing in America, with a Biography of Printers & and an Account of Newspapers*. But perhaps Thomas's greatest claim to glory was as the "American John Newbery" — the publisher who popularized in the new republic Newbery's Enlightenment view of what illustrated books for young children might aim to achieve.

In 1744 John Newbery, London bookseller and printer, published *A Little Pretty Pocket-Book*, the first of the illustrated "toy" books whose resounding success served equally to define the terms of a new literary genre and to confirm the emergence of a brisk middle-class market for juveniles. The frontispiece of Newbery's first offering bore the motto "Delectando monemus. Instruction with Delight" — words by which the ebullient, hard-driving Newbery ("Jack Whirler" in Samuel Johnson's approving *Idler* sketch) proceeded to publish for the next twenty-two years (while carrying on a second business in patent medicines). Acting on John Locke's prescription of a half-century earlier, Newbery mixed entertainment and instruction in the books he printed and sold, showing by example that the two goals might indeed be made to dance to the same tune. He published serious-minded books for the young as well. Wading cautiously into the colonial market's uncharted waters, he advertised an assortment of the latter, more traditional little volumes as early as 1750 in the *Pennsylvanian Gazette*.[24] Newbery and his successors continued to market their books in the colonies into the 1770s, until Revolutionary embargoes made doing so impossible. By then, colonial bookseller-printers had already begun, if at first only in a small way, to make Newbery's books their own.[25]

In 1779 Isaiah Thomas acquired copies of several Newbery toy books to be sold in his shops and, on exhausting his stock in them, began issuing pirated editions of the books under his own imprint. In the absence of international copyright agreements, it was his legal right to do so. In the overheated political atmosphere of the time, he may well have felt it to be a minor act of rebellion as well. Thomas made small adjustments as he saw fit to suit the American market. A ride in the Lord Mayor of London's coach (in the Newbery original) became, in the Thomas edition of *Nurse Truelove's New Year's Gift*, first published in Worcester in 1786, a ride in the Governor's coach.[26] In a printed message to "young [American] Gentlemen and Ladies who are good or intend to be good," Thomas told the readers of *Little Goody Twoshoes* (1787) that the book they held in hand was the work of "their old Friend in Worcester" — not (as in Newbery's original) "their old Friend in St Paul's Church-Yard."[27] As illustrations (or "embellishments," in the term of the day) for his American editions, Thomas commissioned new woodcuts copied from the originals. Originality, in short, had little to do with Thomas's major contribution to juvenile publishing — the American Newbery was not even the first colonial publisher to pirate the British toy books. Rather, what he did was to build a substantial American readership for the juvenile books that represented the most dramatic alternative until that time to *The New-England Primer*, James Janeway's *A Token for Children*, and other such works of sober religious instruction then to be found in American shops and homes.[28] Not that Thomas himself was a committed ideologue: he published editions of the *Primer* and Janeway's perennial seller as well.

During the Revolution, the importation of books to the colonies from England temporarily came to a halt, but the flow of books had been considerable prior to that time, and book imports seem to have resumed at a lively pace during the postwar years. The latter development might have served to undercut the impetus to foster a homegrown literary culture, but in fact did not.[29] As a first step toward establishing the favorable conditions for such a culture to develop, Congress passed the Copyright Act of 1790, granting protection to American authors over their work for fourteen years from the time of publication. In the emerging economy of the new federal republic, gentleman-bookmen agreed that an author should be free to sell rights to a book region by region, with each bookseller-printer-publisher entitled to offer the work exclusively within his territory. Under this arrangement, Noah Webster, later of dictionary fame, sold rights to his immensely popular three-volume schoolbook, *A Grammatical Institute of the English Language*, to seven different regional booksellers.[30] By the 1790s, Isaiah Thomas, after first attempting to compete against Webster with a schoolbook series of his own, reversed course and became one of the latter's more trustworthy publishers.[31] Both in Europe and North America, print culture was entering a period of rapid, exciting change. Industrial Revolution–era improvements in printing and papermaking technologies were bringing down the manufacturing costs and retail prices of books just as the rapid spread of literacy was creating a vastly expanded book market.[32] In 1772 William Haas of Basel had built the first all-iron press, the first fundamental improvement in press design since the time of Gutenberg. In England at about the same time, wood engraving emerged as an effective new technique for creating finely nuanced illustrations for mass reproduction. The common theme of the innovations was durability for the long haul and the possibility of larger press runs to accommodate the demand from an expanding reading public.[33]

Bookseller-printer-publishers of this formative period typically published for local readerships and counted their successes not in bestsellers but rather, in the historian David D. Hall's apt phrase, in "steady sellers . . . books that remained in print for several decades."[34] Serving a market of relatively limited geographic scope, such publishers did not have the costs associated with the production of large print runs and maintenance of large inventories that would become issues for the national firms of later generations. The use and reuse of traditional and pirated texts also served to hold down costs. Over time, a steady seller might be reprinted in numerous iterations, with changes in text, illustrations, and page count introduced as the economics of the moment or fashion dictated.

Thomas was exceptional for his time in the geographical reach of his operation, and he had only one American rival in this regard, Mathew Carey of Philadelphia. A well-born Irish émigré and political firebrand, Carey, in 1785, had set up shop in Philadelphia as a printer and publisher, casting a wide net with the reading public by offering a newspaper, English Bibles, and the nation's first successful magazine, the *American Museum*.

Carey had defied his father's advice by entering the risky trade he felt passionately about, the pursuit of which had, by the age of nineteen, already forced him to flee Ireland for political exile in Paris, where Lafayette had befriended him and Benjamin Franklin had taken him under his wing.[35]

Carey had put down roots in Philadelphia when, around 1793, he met the man whose professional destiny would become closely tied to his own: Mason Locke Weems, the "Parson Weems" of American legend. The real Weems — "patriot, pitchman, author and purveyor of morality to the citizenry of the early United States of America" — was a man with a thumb in many pies. He had approached Carey as a client with a printing job he wanted done.[36] Trained in Britain as a doctor and cleric, Weems regarded literacy as a spiritual tonic for the world and the dissemination of books as a spiritual calling. During the course of a long and colorful career, he would travel the South as the Philadelphia publisher's indefatigable sales agent, performing marriage ceremonies and dispensing nostrums as he went to those in need while gathering literary intelligence on his employer's behalf as to the gaps in book buyers' libraries. Weems often filled the gaps himself, in thirty-odd years authoring numerous pamphlet essays and a series of hagiographical biographies of great Americans, the latter intended primarily for children.[37]

Ever the impresario, Weems savored, as a kind of sporting victory, his success in persuading the Catholic Carey to publish a Protestant Bible, a project that for a time repaid the effort with the lion's share of the house's profits. As Weems wrote triumphantly to his employer: "'Tis a good thing to be on the back of a good whale, that will keep us up and, after all, land us Jonah like, safe on heaven's dry shore at last."[38]

In the waning days of December 1799, Weems had another great whale in his sights. No sooner had George Washington been solemnly laid to rest than the good parson set about memorializing the nation's most admired man in a book intended for a general readership including but not limited to young people. Writing breathlessly to Carey, he announced:

> I've something to whisper in your lug. Washington you know is gone! Millions are gasping to read something about him. I am nearly primed and cocked for 'em. Six months ago I set myself to collecting anecdotes of him. You know I live conveniently for that work. My plan! I give his history, sufficiently minute — I accompany him from the start, thro'

the French & Indian & British or Revolutionary wars, to the Presidents chair, to the throne in the hearts of 5,000,000 people. I then show that his unparrelled [*sic*] rise and elevation were owing to his Great Virtues: 1. His Veneration for the deity *or* religious Principles, 2. His Patriotism, 3. His Magnanimity, 4. His Industry, 5. His Temperance & Sobriety, 6. His Justice &c &c. Thus I hold up his great Virtues . . . to the imitation of our Youth. . . . We can sell it with great rapidity for 25 or 37 cents, and it would not cost 10. . . . I am thinking that you could vend it admirably; as it will be the first. I can send it on, half of it, immediately.[39]

Fearful of not being first out of the gate, Weems produced for Carey a hastily written eighty-page manuscript featuring a heart-grabbing dedication to Washington's widow — from "her sincere though unknown friend" — and dated "February 22, 1800," the late president's birthday.[40] The little book sold briskly, and Weems, having planted his flag in lucrative territory, proceeded to expand the life over nine editions in as many years, in incremental bursts of embellishment that culminated in the far more substantial and even stronger-selling "definitive" biography of 1809, titled *The Life of George Washington; with Curious Anecdotes, Equally Honourable to Himself and Exemplary to His Young Countrymen.* In the meantime, between 1805 and 1807, John Marshall published his magisterial five-volume official biography of Washington. When the massive work went on sale by subscription, Weems himself, not to be shut out entirely from a rival venture, canvassed the southern states on its behalf by special arrangement with Carey.

It was in his own 1806 edition that Weems offered up to the world the singularly compelling anecdote about the six-year-old plantation owner's son, the cherry tree, and the hatchet — the Washington exemplum against which American children would for generations afterward measure their own moral worth. It mattered not at all to the ebullient sermonizer-salesman that the episode rested on little more than hearsay.[41] With some prompting from the author, Rufus King, a signer of the Constitution and a U.S. senator from New York, commended Weems's biography "to the nation as the best book for children."[42] Among the readers known to have found it inspirational was the young Abraham Lincoln.

Buoyed by the success of his *Washington,* Weems ventured onward in the biographical vein. Typical of the later volumes was his *Life of Benjamin Franklin,* a mongrel work comprising a paraphrase of part 1 of Franklin's

Autobiography and an original narrative of the great man's more eventful later years in which Weems deliberately overplayed Franklin's piety with a view to "correcting" his shortcomings.[43] In this way Weems did his part in Franklin's canonization even as he watched in awe as his life of Washington — the copyright to which he now rued having sold outright to Carey — took its place as second only to Franklin's *Autobiography* as the quintessential Federal-period statement on American character. Weems by then was well on his way to becoming a legend, the American Pied Piper of the printed word who, in his later years, reluctantly granted himself the luxury of a driver as, filled as ever with the "glow . . . of book vending enthusiasm," he careered about the South in a light coach or wagon. As his biographer has recaptured the scene:

> The arrival of his "Flying Library" in a country town was a public event, especially in Georgia where there was less competition for sales than in Charleston or Columbia, where bookshops were beginning to abound. He heralded its coming in the newspapers, offering "Books, Wisdom & Virtue to Georgia forever," and he gave public lectures reminding listeners that in "a happy republic like ours, where the prize of Fame and Fortune all start fair and fair alike, where every thing depends on merit, and that merit is all dependent on Education, it is hoped that wise & generous parents will need no persuasion to give their children those very great advantages that books afford." He promised a liberal allowance "to those benevolent characters who take several copies . . . for Christmas books to their young relations."[44]

When he died in 1825 in Beaufort, South Carolina, the *Raleigh Register* reported that Weems had "been instrumental in circulating nearly a million copies of the scriptures and other valuable books. That in this laborious calling he was actuated by an expanded philanthropy, is proved by his entire neglect of the means of accumulating a large fortune and dying in comparative poverty. His very eccentricities, for failings they could not be called, were the eccentricities of genius and benevolence."[45] The immediate spiritual heir to Weems's brand of morality-laced showmanship and blarney would be P. T. Barnum.

Few writers who came of age in the Revolutionary War era responded with more fervor than Noah Webster to the rising demand for original books by and for Americans or worked harder for their copyright protection. Notwithstanding the progress made in the latter matter, in the rough-and-tumble marketplace in which Webster was obliged to do business more than half of the estimated 20 million copies sold of his bread-and-butter work, *Blue-backed Speller* (1783), appeared in pirated editions for which he received nothing.[46] Webster's campaign to foster an authentically American literature, language, and even orthography met with a mixed response that ranged from chauvinistic approval to Brahmin-like disdain. On the strength of the popularity of his *Speller*, Webster handily won the argument about dropping the vestigial "k" in "mimick" and "u" in "honour." And he drew no criticism when, like Weems before him, he contributed to Benjamin Franklin's enshrinement by incorporating an eleven-page reduction of the great man's life into his popular *Biography for the Use of Schools* (1830).[47] For a time, the Americanisms that Webster favored — "lengthy," "cog," "demoralize," "crock," and "caucus" — met with resistance from those Americans who remained stoutly Anglophile in their cultural allegiances. In the end, Webster was fortunate despite himself that the compilation of his masterpiece, the *American Dictionary of the English Language*, took as long to complete as it did. By the time the impressive two-volume work finally appeared in 1828, the Anglophile Whig Party had been driven from power and the Jacksonian Democrats who replaced them were far more sympathetic to such a project. The new clamoring for American books went beyond demand for spellers and dictionaries. The moment of Webster's triumph coincided with the first flowering of a distinctively American children's literature.

While Thomas in Massachusetts and Carey in Pennsylvania operated regional businesses, the majority of early nineteenth-century bookseller-printer-publishers continued to serve a primarily local trade. Representative of the latter group were the handful of industrious New Yorkers who made a specialty of printing and selling juvenile chapbooks (cheaply produced, illustrated little books) in their Lower Manhattan storefront establishments. Samuel Wood led the way in a shop he opened on Pearl Street, then the heart of the city's book trade, in 1804, originally as a secondhand bookstore. A Quaker, former schoolmaster, and father with strong convictions about the moral education of the young, Wood installed a small printing press in the back of his shop after concluding that the books then available to the city's children were all of inferior quality. He published his first juvenile, a primer called *The Young Child's A B C, or, First Book*, in 1806.

Over the next thirty-two years, he published hundreds more, remaining the leader of his specialty, after 1815 in partnership with his sons. In 1818 Wood established a second shop in Baltimore, which during the six years of its operation produced a great many juveniles as well.[48] Under the influence of his son and partner, William, Wood later made a second specialty of medical books, at first importing British titles for sale and later publishing original works by American authors.[49]

Wood must have cared deeply about the look of his books. He secured the services of America's leading wood engraver to illustrate a great many of them. Alexander Anderson had been a medical doctor in New York before deciding in 1798, while still in his twenties, to abandon his practice in order to pursue the art of wood engraving professionally. During a long and active career as an artist, he created, as he recalled in his memoirs, "an infinity of cuts for [the] excellent set of small books published by Wood, among others."[50] In the cultural accounting of the post-Revolutionary period, Anderson would achieve enshrinement as the "American Thomas Bewick," the "father of woodcutting in America."[51]

Mahlon Day was the second specialist in the juvenile trade to open up shop in New York during this time. He did so in 1820 after first establishing himself as a printer of financial publications, and he proceeded at his Juvenile Book Store (located first on Water Street and later on Pearl Street) to build up the second most important citywide trade in children's chapbooks. That same year Day joined the Society of Friends, an affiliation that may have been useful in gaining a foothold in the school market for juveniles. Like Wood, he sold a selection of titles published by others as well, including a selection of Parson Weems's biographies, books both written and published by the entrepreneurial Boston powerhouse Samuel Goodrich (as "Peter Parley"), and an assortment of primers. Day's own books tended to mimic those published by Wood, except that Alexander Anderson illustrated only occasionally for him, so that more often than not Day had to make do with second best. He continued all the while to maintain his list of business publications, led by *Day's List of Altered, Counterfeit, and Spurious Bank Notes* and the semimonthly update that he sold by subscription.[52] In 1844 Day handed over his shop to his son-in-law, Stephen M. Crane, and devoted himself to charitable work on behalf of the New York Institution for the Blind, the Society for the Reformation of Juvenile Delinquents, the Association for the Benefit of Colored Orphans, and other charities. In September 1854, the publisher of cautionary tales for children perished, along with his wife, daughter, and more than four hundred others, when the steamship *Arctic*, on which they were passengers on a return voyage from England, collided with a bark in a dense fog off Newfoundland and sank.

Solomon King established himself as a New York City juveniles bookseller and publisher one year after Day, in 1821. Less well capitalized than his rivals, he seems not to have owned his own press but rather to have jobbed out the printing of his books to others.[53] Yet he managed to set himself apart from his competitors — like them, King too belonged to the Society of Friends — by his use of copperplate engraving for illustrations, sometimes with the addition of color, and by the more playful spirit of much of his list, which also featured some titles for adult readers. In his first year of operation, King released two juvenile entertainments unlike any to be found in the shops of Wood or Day: *The Art of Making Fire-Works* and *Old Mother Shipton's Universal Dream Book*. King died in 1832, at the age of forty-one, a victim of that year's citywide cholera epidemic.

The little books issued by Wood and Day, to some extent by King, and by the scores of other bookseller-printer-publishers in New York alone who made occasional forays into juvenile publishing adhered to a loose repertoire of conventions that rendered their lists more alike than different from one another, or for that matter from the similar publications of their counterparts in Burlington, Boston, Hartford, Albany, New Haven, Philadelphia, Baltimore, and elsewhere.[54] Surveying 130 titles that bore the Day imprint, one historian offered the rough calculation that "25 per cent can be classed as moral tales and fables, 15 per cent as school books, readers, primers, etc., 50 per cent as dealing with knowledge in general, such as natural history, biography, amusements, etc., and 10 per cent can be classed as religious, such as Bible stories, hymns, etc."[55] One would like to know what percentage of Day's total output was represented by the 130 surveyed volumes, but this information, along with much else that one might wish to know about the ephemeral books of that formative time, appears past knowing.

By the 1820s, John Locke's contention that children responded best to books with pictures had long since become accepted wisdom, and the imperative to enliven children's books with quantities of suitable embellishments necessarily loomed large in the cost of production. The wood engravings for a book might be newly commissioned for the work. Or, as often happened, they might simply be recycled from the stock of engravings commissioned for earlier titles, purchased from another printer's inventory, or assembled from some combination of all these alternatives. All but the first of these practices was bound to result in books whose uneven if not slapdash appearance must have seemed curiously out of place to some in a work exhorting young children to a life of industry, diligence, and honest dealings. Short of the requisite number of engravings needed for a thirty-two-page collection of street merchants' chants, *The New-York Cries, in Rhyme*, Mahlon Day opted to insert four pages of supplementary text describing the architecture of New York's City Hall and the business conducted in the nearby courthouse. In all likelihood, the availability of an engraver's block had dictated the subject of the filler, from which the agile Day took pains to extract a moral by admonishing readers newly inculcated with respect for the city's humble, hard-working scissors grinders and orange men that misdeeds, whether of a criminal or merely childish nature, rarely went unpunished in this world. Day perhaps was reminding his middle-class readers as well of the rewards of aiming higher for themselves on the economic and social ladder.[56]

Day issued his book of cries to compete with a strikingly similar *Cries of New-York* first published by Samuel Wood in 1808. Wood's *Cries of Philadelphia*, issued in 1810, was largely a rehash of his own New York material. Both men's contributions to what was by then a well-established genre owed much to older British chapbooks.[57] A chimney sweep or match girl's honesty was one matter; a publisher's pirating of preexisting works from near or far was another.[58] In the shape-shifting world of these morally upright but commercially opportunistic entrepreneurs — men whose business addresses and partnership arrangements changed almost yearly — illustrators typically did not receive book cover or title page credit. Neither, for that matter, did authors. (Had the latter practice been otherwise, it would have been revealed that Day and his wife often took pen in hand themselves with a view to keeping the presses rolling.) The book-buying public appears to have been indifferent to such questions, at least where ephemeral books purchased for children for between a penny and twelve and a half cents each were concerned. In the New York of Wood, Day, and King, the latter sum would also buy a pound of cherries or a bushel of sand.[59]

As busy and as prosperous as they sometimes were, Wood, Day, and King represented the last vestiges of the era when bookseller-printer-publishers with a local market collectively made up American publishing. A new era was by then already in the making, an era dominated by a new publishing structure that would result in a stunning expansion of the scale and scope of the book business's operations. Thereafter, the remaining small, traditional establishments would only occasionally be in a position to compete effectively.

As if to illustrate the transformation, sometime around 1825 the Boston shop of Munroe and Francis published its *Mother Goose's Quarto, or, Melodies Complete*, a landmark work in that it represented the first American appearance in print of a great many of the now-standard English nursery rhymes. At 128 pages, it was also the largest such collection then readily available in America. Nonetheless, the bibliographer and historian Everett F. Bleiler concluded, this innovative work was not an "important book in itself" because, as far as could be determined, it "was not reprinted, and it left no perceptible trace in the popular memory." Less than a decade later, however, the same shop's *Mother Goose's Melodies* (1833), a distillation and refinement of the earlier book, achieved an "almost national . . . distribution, . . . and it set off a chain of imitations, piracies, and similar collections that continues to the present. It was largely responsible for the adoption of Mother Goose in America as the supreme children's poet, as opposed to her early British rivals, Gammer Gurton, Tom Thumb, Nurse Lovechild, or others."[60] By the mid-1830s, David S. Francis's sons, Joseph H. and Charles S. Francis, had both entered the book trade, the former joining his father in Boston and the latter setting up as a bookseller-printer in 1826 in New York City; perhaps the benefits of youth and a New York base helped to ensure the far-reaching impact of the latter Mother Goose book.[61]

The future, in any case, belonged to larger, better-capitalized firms, such as Harper & Brothers. Begun in 1817 as a print shop, its proprietors — two brothers, James and John, later joined by younger brothers Wesley and Fletcher — quickly parlayed their reputation as top-quality printers and their modest early successes as occasional publishers into something quite grand. Taking the long view, the brothers invested heavily in advanced stereotyping equipment, a bold decision that allowed them both to firm up their position as New York's premier printer to the book trade and to pursue their dream of publishing to the nation.

The Harpers came into their own just as New York City emerged as the clear victor in the competition with Philadelphia and Boston to be nineteenth-century America's preeminent commercial city. In the time before international copyright agreements, the publisher able to purchase the first American shipment of unbound copies of the new novel by Jane Austen or Charles Dickens had the upper hand. As the historian Henry Walcott Boynton has written: "Physically the Harpers had the advantage, as most of the books from England passed through New York. Her position as a seaport had much to do with the New Yorkers' later supremacy over Philadelphians in the book and other markets." On more than one occasion when the race was on to capture the lucrative first-out American sale of the latest prized British import, the Harpers bested not just Mathew Carey but also fellow New Yorkers who were slower to the docks.[62] The opening of the Erie Canal in 1825 further ensured the New York houses' national dominance by providing unparalleled access to the rapidly expanding western frontier market for books.

During the 1830s, with a view to fueling sales and streamlining their marketing efforts, the nimble Harper brothers organized much of their publishing efforts around a number of uniform series, including one for young readers called the Boy's and Girl's Library. The Library offered an eclectic mix of fact and fiction. Among its first titles were two works of nonfiction, *Indian Traits* and *Tales of the American Revolution*, commissioned from a recent Harvard Law School graduate and up-and-coming historian named Benjamin B. Thatcher. *The Swiss Family Robinson* made its first American appearance as another title in the series.[63]

It was also at this time that Harper signed its first important American writer for children. The Reverend Jacob Abbott came to his lifework with just the background that had become typical of a juvenile author of his generation. A born and bred New Englander, Abbott had graduated from Bowdoin College in 1820 (five years ahead of Longfellow and Hawthorne) and had trained for the ministry at Andover Seminary. Uncertain of his calling, he had tried teaching, first at Amherst College and then as cofounder (with his younger brother John, another Bowdoin graduate who also later wrote for children) of a private girls' school in Boston. Then, in 1834, Abbott accepted the pulpit of the Eliot Congregational Church in Roxbury, Massachusetts. He began writing books for the spiritual improvement of young people as an extension of his pastoral work. A timely pursuit it must have seemed in the heyday of the Sunday school movement, whose two major organizational hubs, the Sunday-School Union of Philadelphia and Boston's American Tract Society, both published and distributed numerous such books for children.[64] The American Tract Society published Abbott's second juvenile, *The Young Christian; or, A Familiar Illustration of the Principles of Christian Duty*, in 1832. On the strength of the success of that book, he decided to abandon his ministry, return to his childhood home in Hallowell, Maine, and take up writing full-time. For the next four decades, Abbott produced an average of four books a year. Perhaps as a matter of convenience, he at first favored Boston publishers. Between 1848 and 1861, however, Abbott was a mainstay of the Harper brothers, whose list included more than thirty titles in two of his most popular series for young readers, the "Franconia Stories" and the "Makers of History" biographies.[65]

By the time Abbott made his Harper debut, he was already a favorite with American children as the amiable author of a long run of storybooks about an upstanding young lad named Rollo Holiday. From the original *Rollo Learning to Read; or, Easy Stories for Young Children* (John Allen, 1835), the series had grown to include *Rollo at Play, or, Safe Amusements* (Carter, 1836), *Rollo at Work; or, The Way for a Boy to Learn to Be Industrious* (Thomas Webb, 1837), and *Rollo's Museum* (Weeks, Jordan, 1839), among many others. Abbott's hero, when put to the test by a wide assortment of less praiseworthy youngsters, invariably proves himself to be a child of uncommon sense and moral probity. When in one of the first series volumes a young temptress named Dorothy invites Rollo to listen as she tells him a story, she begins by asking her friend what sort of story he would prefer to hear:

> "Well, Rollo," said Dorothy, "shall I tell you a true story, or one that is not true?"
>
> "Oh, true," said Rollo; "true by all means."
>
> "But true stories are not generally quite so interesting as those that are made up."
>
> "Why not?" said Rollo.
>
> "Oh, because, when people are making up a story, they can tell more wonderful things than those that happen in true stories."
>
> Rollo paused a moment, and then said, "I think, on the whole, Dorothy, I would rather have it true."[66]

By the 1850s, when Abbott wrote the "Franconia Stories," his convictions about the relationship of storytelling to truth-telling had changed. One catches a revealing glimpse of the author's transformation from moralist to literary man when, in *Beechnut: A Franconia Story*, a small group of playmates find themselves in a situation identical to the one faced by Rollo. The question for these children, as it was for Rollo, comes as a test of their moral mettle: they too must decide how to respond to a tempting offer of a story that they might or might not feel right about hearing. Like Dorothy, Beechnut, these children's older friend, gives the youngsters a choice:

> "Shall I tell the story to you just as it was, as a sober matter of fact? Or shall I embellish it a little?"
>
> "I don't know what you mean by embellishing it," said Malleville.
>
> "Why, not telling exactly what is true," said Beechnut, "but inventing something to add to it, to make it interesting."
>
> "I want to have it true," said Malleville, "and interesting, too."
>
> "But sometimes," replied Beechnut, "interesting things don't happen; and in such cases, if we should only relate what actually does happen, the story would be likely to be dull."
>
> "I think you had better embellish the story a little," said Phonny. "Just a *little*, you know."[67]

The Harpers, who were now New York City's largest employer, liked to keep Abbott busy.[68] After a devastating fire in December 1853 swept through the firm's impressive headquarters, destroying everything in its path, it took the brothers only eighteen months to rebuild in grander style than ever. On realizing that the public considered their new fireproof, cast iron–fronted offices and printing facilities on Franklin Square and Cliff Street not only an architectural wonder but also a tourist destination, the Harpers commissioned Abbott to write a book about the building — *The Harper Establishment*.[69] Of far more consequence than this guidebook, however, was the series of biographies of historical personages — Alexander the Great, Julius Caesar, Queen Elizabeth — that Abbott was engaged in coauthoring just then for Harper in collaboration with his brother John. The Abbotts' "Makers of History" books found a readership that crossed generational lines. Not only did older children embrace them, but so did many adults who, lacking in advanced formal education, turned to the straightforwardly written biographies for a catchup course. Late in his presidency, Abraham Lincoln composed a letter to the Harpers in which he expressed his gratitude for the Abbott books: "I have read them," Lincoln wrote, "with the greatest interest. To them I am indebted for about all the historical knowledge I have."[70] Lincoln was a freshman U.S. congressman from Illinois in 1848, the year that Harper published the first title in the series, *The History of Charles the First.*

Jacob Abbott's chief rival, Samuel Griswold Goodrich, had as stormy a career as the genial Maine reverend's career was even-keeled. Born in Ridgefield, Connecticut, in 1793, Goodrich belonged to a distinguished New England family of lawyers and clergymen but grew up in a household of extremely modest means. His grandfather, Elizur Goodrich, is recalled as the friend who urged Noah Webster to write an American dictionary. His cousin Chauncey later married Webster's daughter and succeeded his father-in-law as editor of the *Unabridged.*[71] Further darkening the cloud that hung over Goodrich's formative years was the knowledge that while the Goodrich men of past generations had gone off to Yale, Samuel's father, a minor Congregationalist minister and schoolteacher with a large family to support, would not be able to manage the tuition for his younger son. Instead, arrangements were made for the eighteen-year-old to take a clerkship at a Hartford dry goods store. The job held no interest or future for him. Determined to better himself, the young man embarked on a rigorous program of self-education, in the course of which he mastered the French language, damaged his vision, and secured for himself the friendship and guidance of a well-read man two years his senior named George Sheldon, who was employed as a clerk at a Hartford publishing house. Within a few years' time, the friends had become partners in a bookselling and publishing firm, a high-minded venture dedicated (in the spirit of Noah Webster) to championing American writing and developing innovative schoolbooks written by recognized authorities. There followed a string of calamitous reversals that, to judge by the outcome, served mainly to steel Goodrich's resolve to rise above his humble beginnings once and for all. First, George Sheldon died, a man still in his twenties, leaving Goodrich in charge of a business he was just learning. Then Goodrich himself suffered a fall from a horse that lamed him for life. (His literary alter ego, Peter Parley, would walk with a limp as well.) He married a Vermont senator's daughter only to be left a widower four years later. Then the small publishing firm of Sheldon and Goodrich, of which he was now the sole proprietor, went bankrupt. Out of sympathy for this avalanche of ill fortune, rich Uncle Chauncey financed the earnest young man for a year's sojourn in Europe — the first of the sixteen white-knuckle Atlantic crossings that Goodrich would eventually endure for the sake of his business and his sense of national purpose, as well as for the stalwart delight he took in exercising a restless curiosity that seemed to know no bounds. The trip proved to be not only recuperative but also providential, as it was as an immediate consequence of an audience, at her estate near Bristol, with Hannah More, the grand dame of British moral tract and ballad writers for children, that Goodrich set himself on a path to fame and glory as an American writer for children.

Apart from Holy Scripture, which his father had read to his family daily, the first book that Goodrich cared for as a child had been Hannah More's *Moral Repository.* When he came to it as a twelve-year-old, he later recalled, "the story of the Shepherd of Salisbury Plain, was to me only inferior to the Bible narrative of Joseph and his brethren."[72]

More's inspirational "Cheap Repository Tracts" series reached millions, and there was no end to the pilgrimage of the grateful who made their way to the seventy-nine-year-old's door. Goodrich's own cordial interview with "Holy Hannah" — the irreverent epithet was the handiwork of Horace Walpole, coiner of "serendipity" — seems instantly to have cleared the thirty-year-old's head: "It was in conversation with that amiable and gifted person," he wrote, "that I first formed the conception of the Parley Tales — the general idea of which was to make nursery books reasonable and truthful, and thus to feed the young mind upon things wholesome and pure, instead of things monstrous, false, and pestilent."

As a child, Goodrich had reacted with distress to a book of fairy tales that a friend had put into his hands. As he recalled in his memoirs:

> Some children, no doubt, have a ready appetite for these monstrosities, but to others they are revolting, until by repetition and familiarity, the taste is sufficiently degraded to relish them. At all events, they were shocking to me. . . . I felt a creeping horror come over me, as the story ["Little Red Riding Hood"] recurred to my imagination. As I dwelt upon it, I soon seemed to see the hideous jaws of a wolf coming out of the bedclothes, and approaching as if to devour me. . . . At last I became so excited, that my mother was obliged to tell me that the story was a mere fiction.
>
> "It is not true, then?" said I.
> "No," said my mother, "it is not true."
> "Why do they tell such falsehoods, then?" I replied.[73]

The nightmarish intensity of the experience colored the whole of his publishing and writing career. After his return to the United States, Goodrich in 1826 married the daughter of a wealthy Boston manufacturer and ship owner. The couple moved to Boston later that year, and as Goodrich considered his options he secretly worked on a book for young readers called *The Tales of Peter Parley About America.* To his delight, the Boston firm of Carter, Hendee, & Company published his chatty first effort in February 1827.

The vagaries of authorship were soon brought home to him. "Untrumpeted, and for several months seem[ing] not to attract the slightest attention," Goodrich later wrote, the book had appeared to be an utter failure when fortune once again smiled on him. As he recalled with pride: "Suddenly I began to see notices of it in the papers, all over the country, and in a year from the date of its publication, it had become a favorite."[74]

In the unfussy, avuncular manner that was to endear his writings to young readers on both sides of the Atlantic, Goodrich, artfully mixing fact and fiction from the opening page, had his narrator introduce himself with a friendly flourish:

> Here I am! My name is Peter Parley! I am an old man. I am very gray and lame. But I have seen a great many things, and had a great many adventures, and I love to talk about them.
>   I love to tell stories to children . . .[75]

Setting the future pattern, the book featured a generous complement of illustrations by Abel Bowen, Boston's leading engraver, and by Bowen's protégé, George Loring Brown. In short order, Goodrich met the call for an enlarged second edition tailored (by the addition of study questions, chapter divisions, and supplementary illustrations) for classroom use. By 1828 he had a sequel ready as well, *The Tales of Peter Parley About Europe.* His entrepreneurial fervor having now shifted back into high gear, he chose to re-enter the trade and publish the new Parley under his own Boston imprint. Thoughts now turned to what else he might publish. While in England, Goodrich had admired the festive juvenile gift annuals — handsomely bound illustrated miscellanies — that he had seen in the shops. He now made plans to launch a similar series. *The Token, A Christmas and New Year's Gift for 1828* was the first annual volume in a fifteen-year-long run whose contributors would include Hawthorne, Longfellow, Oliver Wendell Holmes, and the historian George Bancroft.

Goodrich first met Nathaniel Hawthorne in 1829, a year after the failure of the latter's self-published first novel, *Fanshawe*.[76] At their initial meeting, Hawthorne told Goodrich about a short story collection he hoped the latter would consider for his list. The Salem writer's "unsettled . . . views" and devastated manner seem to have put off the other man, who later declined the book but offered vaguely to help place it elsewhere.[77] Despite their shaky start, they began working together, with Goodrich settling into a cynical routine of plying the emotionally brittle author with praise as he paid him poorly for each of ten stories that ran, unsigned, in *The Token* between 1831 and 1833.[78] As Goodrich's health declined, he also gave Hawthorne freelance ghostwriting work that helped maintain the breakneck pace of Parley production.[79]

Goodrich occupied second-floor offices in the Old Corner Bookstore, a downtown Boston building that within a few years' time would also be the headquarters of Ticknor & Fields. With Emerson, Thoreau, Longfellow, and eventually Hawthorne on the Ticknor list, the firm's ground-level bookstore soon became the city's literary hub. If Goodrich regretted that the greater glory he had once aspired to had gone to others — the glory due the publisher of the new American literature — he had, at any rate, created a sort of American empire. Daniel Webster, on his return to the United States from England in 1839, would remark that two Americans excited the greatest curiosity and interest in the people he had met on his journey. English lawyers all inquired about the eminent legal scholar and Supreme Court justice Joseph Story. British children begged for news of Peter Parley.[80]

Webster's own high regard for Goodrich went well beyond his patriotic pride in a fellow countryman's renown abroad. The two men shared a vision of the historical moment in which they had come of age. An oration on the subject by Webster could just as well have served as Goodrich's declaration of faith in the bedrock convictions in which he, and Peter Parley, believed:

It is an extraordinary era in which we live. It is altogether new. The world has seen nothing like it before. I will not pretend, no one can pretend, to discern the end; but everybody knows that the age is remarkable for scientific research into the heavens, the earth, and what is beneath the earth; and perhaps more remarkable still for the application of this scientific research into the pursuits of life. . . . We see the ocean navigated and the solid land traversed by steam power, and intelligence communicated by electricity. Truly this is almost a miraculous era. What is before us no one can say, what is upon us no one can hardly realize. The progress of the age has almost outstripped human belief; the future is known only to Omniscience.[81]

The fact that Peter Parley's fame had swiftly crossed the Atlantic was thanks principally to pirated editions of his work and counterfeit "Parleys" written by others and published without the author's sanction. As early as 1832, a scheme had come to Goodrich's attention whereby Thomas Tegg, a London publisher of cheap editions, was hiring writers to imitate the American sensation's rambling, conversational style and publishing the books as the work of Peter Parley. Discerning an opportunity in the outrage, Goodrich in 1832 sailed for England, purchased copies of whatever "spurious Parleys" he could lay his hands on, and, once back in the United States, republished the better ones himself. To keep a clear conscience, he inserted a disclaimer in *Parley's Rambles in England, Wales, Scotland, and Ireland* when it appeared under the Goodrich imprint in 1838: "This work is chiefly copied from the London work, which was got up in imitation of the several books which have appeared in this country."[82] The ragged affair suggested that Americans' long-standing cultural dependence on Mother England might at least be starting to become something more nearly resembling an even exchange.

From his Boston offices, Goodrich kept the Parley machine churning while also publishing books by other authors. For a time he undertook the editorship of the *American Journal of Education*. In March 1833, he launched *Parley's Magazine: For Children and Youth*, a biweekly intended to promote his books and extend the reach of his deep-seated convictions about juvenile literature and education. When ill health forced Goodrich to relinquish the editorship of the magazine after just one year, he chose as his successor William Alcott, a medical doctor and a cousin and friend of the controversial New England educator Bronson Alcott.

Goodrich outlined his ambitious plan for the magazine in the inaugural issue, indicating that readers could expect:

I. Geographical Descriptions, of manners, customs, and countries; II. Travels, Voyages, and Adventures, in various parts of the world; III. Interesting Historical Notices and Anecdotes of each State, and of the United States, as well as of foreign countries; IV. Biography, particularly of young persons; V. Natural History, as birds, beasts, fishes, etc.; VI. A familiar description of the Objects that daily surround Children in the Parlor, Nursery, Garden, etc.; VII. Original Tales, consisting of Home Scenes, Stories of Adventure, etc., calculated to stimulate the curiosity, exercise the affections, and improve the judgment; VIII. An Account of various trades and pursuits, and some branches of commerce; IX. Cheerful and Pleasing Rhymes, adapted to the feelings and comprehension of youth.[83]

Elsewhere in the issue, Goodrich expressed the then-unconventional view that education ought to encompass training of the body as well as of the mind. In this opinion, as in others, he (like Alcott after him) revealed an affinity with the pedagogical theories of the Swiss educator Johann Pestazzoli (1746–1827), who emphasized firsthand experience and direct observation as the basis of early education and whose age-graded sequence of "gifts" or educational toys prefigured the exciting work of twentieth-century progressive educators.[84]

Goodrich chose not to publish *Parley's Magazine* himself, and the periodical changed houses three times in as many years before settling in under the imprint of the Francis brothers — Joseph H. of Boston and Charles S. of New York. Meanwhile, the Panic of 1837 sent Goodrich headlong into bankruptcy for the second time. Thereafter, he never again risked publishing his own books. He could not resist altogether, however, reentering the magazine business, which was then on the cusp of a major expansion, and in 1841 he launched *Robert Merry's Museum* in association with the New York publisher I. C. and J. N. Stearns, in an undisguised bid to reclaim the readership of the still-flourishing *Parley's Magazine.* In true Goodrich fashion, later that same year Peter Parley himself began writing for the new magazine. Goodrich, however, did not intend to rely entirely on the tried and true. For the September 1842 issue, in what must then have seemed a breathtaking innovation, the editor who had always cared so much about the quality of the illustrations associated with his publications experimented with a tinted frontispiece for the magazine.[85]

For printers and publishers of the 1840s and 1850s, the attainment of color reproduction in illustrated books and magazines was the next great technological hurdle. Until then, a woodcut or engraving, when not offered to the public in black and white, had to be individually hand-colored, typically by a small group of women or girls arrayed along a workshop table. The colorists took turns overlaying a series of stencils on the line art, each time applying a different-colored pigment to areas of the image. The shops of bookseller-printer-publishers like Samuel Wood and Mahlon Day in New York and Munroe and Francis in Boston were the places to go for hand-colored picture books of this kind, which held special allure for their owners. Certainly this had been the case for Hartford's great nineteenth-century librarian Caroline M. Hewins, who recalled that as the daughter of a prosperous Boston merchant she had been fortunate enough to own several such volumes: "Many of the picture books of the fifties were published in Albany by Sprague or by Fisk and Little, hand colored or rather hand daubed, and in pasteboard covers. The best of them," she wrote in her memoirs, "was *The Alderman's Feast* because it told so much about London."[86]

Scrambling for cultural validation as the nation approached mid-century, Anglophile Americans spoke with pride of their own "John Baskerville" (bookseller-printer-publisher Isaiah Thomas) and of the "American Thomas Bewick" (engraver Alexander Anderson). By the late 1830s, an "American Cruikshank" had joined the pantheon of reflected glory in the person of a New York illustrator and printer named Robert Henry Elton. An artist who worked in something like the same vein of sprightly magpie wit as the satiric illustrator Cruikshank, Elton welcomed (and encouraged) the comparison. From his shop on Canal Street, he proceeded to put before the New York book-buying public energetically illustrated picture books that, as the historian Michael Joseph has remarked, presented a striking alternative in sensibility and visual makeup to those published by Wood, Day, and their contemporaries. Whereas the bookseller-printer-publishers farther downtown "continued to valorize rural eighteenth-century life and art, and infuse American children's books with a sense of rustic sentimentality," Elton, according to Joseph, "countered with crude exaggeration and parody. His images were rough, cartoon-like, and appealed to the imagination of an increasingly urban population that had already embraced burlesque."[87]

As a skilled illustrator and entrepreneur, Elton might well have been expected to seek novel ways to showcase the pictorial elements of the books he both decorated and published. Yet the extent of the technical virtuosity and innovation he achieved — his use, for example, of shaped and multiple blocks within a single illustration frame to create sophisticated compositions of baroque complexity — could not have been predicted.[88] Around 1850, apparently with a view to his early retirement from the book trade in order to pursue other business interests, Elton took in a younger partner, John McLoughlin Jr., and formed Elton & Co. Within five years' time, references in advertising to "John McLoughlin, successor to Elton & Co.," signaled a changing of the guard, and the name most closely associated during the decades after the Civil War with the application of chromolithography to the large-scale production of inexpensive illustrated juvenile books, puzzles, and games decked out in flamboyant carnival colors made its own first appearance in print. Two decades later, McLoughlin Brothers (John Jr. having been joined in the firm by his brother Edmund) would open the nation's largest color printing plant in Williamsburg, Brooklyn.

Over the years, Samuel Goodrich and Daniel Webster had come to know each other, and in 1850, when Webster became secretary of state under Millard Fillmore, he arranged for Goodrich's appointment to a choice diplomatic posting as U.S. consul to France. Goodrich's tenure in the French capital proved to be a far stormier one than he might have wished. Soon after his arrival, a bloody coup brought about the overthrow of President Louis Napoleon. The untested diplomat finessed the change of regimes well enough to remain in the government service until 1853, when the election of Franklin Pierce brought a fresh round of patronage appointments and the writer received word, as he would later describe this bittersweet time, that he had been "restored to the privileges of private life."[89] The news came as Goodrich's one-time protégé, Nathaniel Hawthorne, sailed for England as the newly appointed U.S. consul in Liverpool.

As consul, Goodrich had found the time to write three books in French, including two for young readers, aimed at acquainting the French with the American people and their history.[90] On being relieved of his official duties, the writer, in a wistful, valedictory mood, decided to stay on for a time in the country he had come to love, to rent a cottage just outside of Paris, and to write his memoirs. Goodrich began his discursive *Recollections of a Lifetime*, which eventually ran to two volumes, with a lengthy discussion of his family history, then went on to describe his rural Connecticut youth, and finally the (in his view) insignificant but hectic circumstances of his professional life. He took the occasion to wax eloquent about his lifelong hero Benjamin Franklin, whose *Autobiography*, also written in France, had exercised such a powerful influence over him — quite apart from the good use Goodrich had put it to years earlier as fodder for his own young reader's *Life of Benjamin Franklin* (1832).[91] His assessment of his own career was blunt: "I have written too much," Goodrich declared, "and have done nothing really well."[92]

For Goodrich, the chief value of his life's story resided in its unremarkable nature.

> I must again apologize for, or perhaps rather explain, the introduction of these commonplace details [concerning his initial encounter, as a poorly educated eighteen-year-old, with his future business partner George Shelton]. Were I writing for the popular favor, and sought success only through the current taste of the day, I should choose for the exercise of my pen a subject very different from that which gives birth to these pages. I know that the public crave high-seasoned meats. Romance must be thrilling; biography startling. History must be garnished with the lights and shadows of vivid dramatic representation. Who, then, of the great excited public would condescend to these simple memorials of apprentice boys in the middle ranks of life?[93]

In a later passage in *Recollections*, which Goodrich completed in New York, he answered his own question, noting that in a career that had spanned nearly thirty years he had written or edited 170 books (116 published for children as Parleys), for a total sale of 7 million copies. Whatever the depth of his self-doubts, the garrulous old schemer had somehow not quite failed to impress himself after all. As usual, Goodrich was content to let the facts (at any rate his version of the facts) speak for themselves.

Yet "Peter Parleyism" had by then entered the language as a term of derision invoked by critics who, having been touched by Romanticism's wing, argued that books for the young should have the power to instill sympathy with "the invisible."[94] The title that Nathaniel Hawthorne chose for the children's storybook he published in 1852 with Ticknor & Fields summed up the changed sensibility: *A Wonder Book for Girls and Boys*. Even Hawthorne's one-time taskmaster, Goodrich himself, had apparently begun to moderate his lifelong opposition to fantastic tales. Under his editorship, *Merry's Museum*, starting in 1848, published (or rather pirated) several fairy tales by Hans Christian Andersen. (However Goodrich had come by the stories, it was certainly not with Andersen's cooperation.)

At Christmastime in 1852, a reviewer for the *New York Daily Times* marveled at the wealth and variety of juvenile books available to shoppers for holiday gift giving — books "ornamented so profusely, and gilded and silvered so prettily, to say nothing of the variegated contents, stories, facts, and fables."[95] The sheer profusion of offerings published expressly for the young would have been enough to inspire wonder in any man or woman of Goodrich's generation, the last Americans to have come of age in homes where typically the Bible, a few well-thumbed almanacs, and a volume or two of old sermons were the only reading matter. What was more, in a near-complete turnaround of the situation of twenty-five years earlier, a very substantial portion of the books being offered for sale were American books for American children.

Growing up in privileged surroundings on the outskirts of 1850s Boston — her father cofounded the store that became Filene's — Caroline M. Hewins had the complete run of the new bounty of juvenile fare. The Hewinses' home library boasted an illustrated edition of Aesop's *Fables*, a three-volume illustrated *Arabian Nights*, the Munroe and Francis *Mother Goose's Melodies* and *Marmaduke Multiply*, chapter books by Jacob Abbott, Lydia Maria Child, and others, story collections by Maria Edgeworth, volumes of the Grimms' and Andersen's fairy tales in English-language translation, a variety of juvenile magazines, and more. "*The Wonder Book*," Hewins recalled, "was on my pillow when I opened my eyes on the morning of my seventh birthday."[96]

The supremely well read little girl from West Roxbury would not, in the long run, be content to keep her store of literary treasure to herself. After graduating in 1862 from the Girls High School and Normal School in Boston, Hewins taught school for a time and then spent a year at the Boston Athenaeum working under that private library's esteemed librarian, William Frederick Poole. The experience proved to be a life-changing one.[97] In 1875, at the age of twenty-nine, Hewins became the librarian of the Hartford Men's Institute. Three years later, when the Hartford Library Association absorbed the Institute, Hewins was placed in charge of the new entity, which had been established to provide free library service to the city. In her new role, and with little by way of either precedent or administrative support to guide her, Hewins made work with children a priority and organized one of the world's first circulating collections of children's books. Publishers at the time scarcely took note of the quixotic venture. But in the decades to come the force of the idea that Hewins had seized upon would compel nearly every publishing house with an interest in the juvenile trade to rethink its business.

2

WONDER IN THE WAKE OF WAR
Publishing for Children from the
Gilded Age to the Dawn of the
New Century

> Therefore we say, — and it is a big "therefore," — do not be afraid of
> interesting books, even if they do not contain information on all top-
> ics; do not be afraid of excitement, so long as it is healthy; do not keep
> young minds always on the high pressure system of instruction.[1]
>
> — WILLIAM T. ADAMS, in *Oliver Optic's Magazine* (1872)

THE UNSPEAKABLE BRUTALITY of the Civil War left American authors and publishers for young people, once so boldly prescriptive in their
pronouncements about right and wrong, less confident in their moral authority — yet certain that children's books would, if anything, play a more
vital role in young Americans' lives during the postwar years than ever before. Writing in the December 1865 issue of the *Atlantic Monthly*, Samuel
Osgood, a Unitarian clergyman and scholar and member of the Transcen-
dental Club, argued that juvenile literature had the power to foster the intellectual development and to preserve the spiritual well-being of the nation's younger generation. Yet, he noted with regret, as "fruitful as America
has been and is in children's books, we have not yet apparently added a single one to the first rank of juvenile classics." Osgood speculated that the
reason for this failure could be laid at the door of a fundamental imbalance
in the rhythm and pace of American life, stemming from the widespread
tendency of adults to exert undue pressure on the children in their care to
grow up too soon:

Reading begins very early with us; and the universal hurry of the
American mind crowds children forward, and tempts them in pleasure,

as in work and study, to rebel at the usual limitations of years, and push infancy prematurely into childhood, childhood into youth, and youth into maturity. . . . Our heads are apt to be much older than our shoulders, and English critics of our juvenile literature say that much of it seems written for the market and counting-room rather than for the nursery and playground.[2]

The war and the unprecedented news coverage and parade of books that brought home its grim consequences to young and old alike had done nothing to right the imbalance. The children's magazines published in the North, such as *The Student and Schoolmate*, *Merry's Museum*, and *Our Young Folks*, vilified the Confederate enemy.[3] Battlefront adventure novels by Oliver Optic, popular dime-novel thrillers sold at newsstands, serious commentaries addressed to the young on the evils of slavery, and sober tales that emphasized children's added responsibilities at home while their fathers served on the battlefield all made the Civil War an absorbing reality for the North's young readers. While most children's books and magazines offered somewhat softened and idealized stories of heroism meant to inspire patriotic fervor and a comforting confidence in the righteousness of the Union's cause, the raw horror of war also occasionally broke through, as in Harry Castlemon's *Frank on a Gun-Boat* (1864), which described a sea battle that leaves "the deck . . . slippery with blood and the turret . . . completely covered with it."[4] A great many children, of course, also scanned the newspapers and illustrated magazines that came into their homes, led by *Harper's Weekly* with its powerful engravings based on actual battlefront sketches. The South, which suffered far more than the North from materials shortages and from a generally more fragile economy, concentrated its wartime publishing efforts for children on educational materials such as *The Confederate Spelling Book* and *The Dixie Primer*.[5]

In Samuel Osgood's estimate, one of the war's major impacts on America's children had been to intensify their natural tendency to rebel against their elders, as if the War Between the States had spawned a home-front war between the generations. Writing as a northerner for northerners, he pondered: "What shall we do with our children? . . . The Slaveholder's Rebellion is put down; but how shall we deal with the never-ceasing revolt of the new generation against the old? And how to keep our Young American under the thumb of his father and mother without breaking his spirit?"[6] For Osgood and a growing number of others, the answer lay in the creation of a new juvenile literature that while morally responsible was also adamantly nonprescriptive, a literature that showed respect for young readers' intelligence and trust in their already having acquired a basic understanding of right and wrong, and that on occasion might serve up tales of rebellion to satisfy vicariously the urge for the real thing. It would not be long before critics were remarking on the coming of just such a sea change in the literature. An essay in *Putnam's Magazine* for December 1868 proclaimed:

> Verily there is a new era in this country in the literature for children. It is not very long since all the juvenile books seemed conducted on the principle of the definition of duty "doing what you don't want to," for the books that were interesting were not considered good, and the "good" ones were certainly not interesting. Most Sunday-school books were stories of unnaturally good and pious boys and girls, who, however, were not attractive enough to rouse a desire of imitation in the youthful breast.
>
> But now we have a different order of things, and books for children are about as varied in their scope as those for grown people.[7]

Three years later, a writer for the *Overland Monthly*, the San Francisco journal edited by Bret Harte, was, if anything, more sanguine about the juvenile literary renaissance that appeared to be under way:

> The old-fashioned stories, with a moral or pious reflection impending at the close of every sentence, or the clumsily adjusted mixture of didactic truth and saccharine rhetoric administered like sulphur and treacle for the moral health of the unhappy infant, are happily long since abandoned. The idea of pleasing children by writing down to their suppositious level and flavoring the work with bland imbecility, has also exploded.[8]

Reports of the explosion, however greatly exaggerated, nonetheless captured the gist of a fundamental change in attitude about the role of literature in a child's life. This change, in turn, was but one aspect of a broader generational shift that was both prompted and reinforced by the realization that the United States had at last become a single nation. Whatever the residue of hatred and bitterness left over from the war, American society stood unified by weblike systems of rail and telegraphic communication, by the sense of "manifest destiny" that continued to impel the nation's westward expansion, and not least by the broadly based elaboration of a national print culture, which in the first burst of renewed prosperity that followed the end of hostilities found one of its most vivid expressions in a great flowering of new magazines.

By 1865 nearly every major American book publisher of the era — Harper, Putnam, Appleton, and Scribner, among others — published, or would soon publish, at least one magazine. No new house with the ambition to rise to the top could afford not to participate in the trend. Prestige accounted for only part of the allure of an inherently ephemeral medium. There was good money to be made in magazines as well, with the potential to do so rapidly increasing in direct proportion to the growth of the American middle class. Favorable postal rates for periodicals in concert with the spidering forth of the rail network helped to put even the most far-flung enclaves of potential subscribers within easy reach of East Coast publishing firms, whose managers made good use of their magazines both to advertise the books they also published and to promote the good name of their houses. For book publishers, the magazines functioned as a proving ground for as yet untested authors and as opportunities for rewarding best-selling authors with well-paid serializations and assignments. In the case of printer-publishers such as Harper & Brothers and Hurd & Houghton, magazines also served as a stopgap for maintaining the presses at maximum capacity even when demand for other printing work slackened. For their part, readers everywhere welcomed the chance to indulge the new national fascination with illustration, the appetite for which had been greatly sharpened by the pictorial reportage of the Civil War by *Harper's Weekly* featuring daring fieldwork by Winslow Homer and others. For untold thousands of Americans, illustrated magazines were a compelling new way to experience the world. As the fashion — and hunger — for periodicals spread, literary monthlies, advice magazines for homemakers and parents, and children's magazines emerged as thriving concerns.

No publisher wished to miss out on the golden opportunity. Thus, in January 1865, with the end of the war in sight, Ticknor & Fields, Boston's preeminent literary house and publisher of the *Atlantic Monthly*, introduced a sister publication for young readers called *Our Young Folks: An Illustrated Magazine for Boys and Girls*.[9] In the spirit of the times, the new monthly proudly announced itself as a new kind of magazine dedicated to placing literary excellence above moral instruction. The editors, John Townsend Trowbridge, Lucy Larcom, and Gail Hamilton (the last was the pseudonym sometimes used by Mary Abigail Dodge), each a well-known writer, were unblushing in their assertions that theirs was the "best juvenile magazine ever published in any land or language." What was more, they had good reason to think so, at least for the first two years of the magazine's nine-year run, after which competition from a handful of rivals cracked the market wide open.[10] In the meantime, as word of *Our Young Folks* spread, circulation grew to exceed 75,000, with subscribers mailing in their money from as far away as Alabama, California, and Ontario.[11]

Those who did so were most likely not disappointed. Lucretia P. Hale's madcap "Peterkin Papers" stories made their first appearance in the magazine's pages, as did Thomas Bailey Aldrich's *The Story of a Bad Boy* and the short story that Charles Dickens later retitled "The Magic Fishbone." Other notable contributions, drawn in part from the incomparable Ticknor stable, included work by Longfellow, Whittier, Harriet Beecher Stowe, Louisa May Alcott, Edward Everett Hale, and Elizabeth Agassiz, wife of the eminent Harvard scientist. The magazine took equal pride in its illustrations, with even the great Winslow Homer joining the lists.[12] In the late fall of 1866, on the eve of his departure for France, Homer sold the magazine a group of five freestanding sketches of children, to be used as the editors saw fit. The Homer images appeared one or two at a time, as wood engravings, between June of the following year and August 1868, in each instance with a caption in verse written to order. Editors Larcom and Trowbridge penned four of the five rhymes themselves; to edit a magazine in those postwar years very often meant to write it.[13]

In January 1867, the five-year-old Boston publishing house of Lee & Shepard introduced its entry into the juvenile periodicals sweepstakes with *Oliver Optic's Magazine: Our Boys and Girls*. The firm, like so many others, had gone into business first as a bookseller, setting up shop at 155 Washington Street in central Boston, just across from the Old South Church and a short distance from Little, Brown (at 112 Washington Street) and Ticknor & Fields (at the corner of Washington and School Streets). William Lee came to the new enterprise with impressive credentials in both bookselling and publishing, having risen to a partnership at the Boston literary house of Phillips, Sampson — founders of the *Atlantic Monthly* and the first book publisher associated with Emerson and his circle — and, following that company's bankruptcy, having continued for a time as a partner at Crosby, Nichols, Lee and Company. Lee's partner, Charles A. B. Shepard, had many years of experience as a local bookseller. Both men had the respect of the trade and a popular touch in book selection. As if to prove the latter point, following Phillips, Sampson's demise in 1857, Lee had had the good sense to purchase the stereotype plates for eighteen juveniles first published by the firm, all the work of a writer named William Taylor Adams but known to readers as "Oliver Optic." Lee's acquisition that day would go a long way toward putting the firm on a solid financial footing for years to come.

The son of a tavern keeper and descendant of two U.S. presidents, Adams had worked for twenty years as a Boston schoolteacher and principal when, in 1865, at the age of forty-three, he turned to writing full-time.[14] By then he had made his name as the author of more than twenty-five juvenile novels and as the editor (from 1858) of *The Student and Schoolmate*, a monthly intended at the outset primarily to help children improve their rhetorical skills. Adams had a sure hand for crafting adventure stories for boys that combined colorful incident with just enough underlying high moral purpose to satisfy a wide readership. It was almost entirely on the strength of the outsized success of his many boys' novels that, by the end of its first decade in business, Lee & Shepard earned its place as one of the nation's most important publishers of juveniles.[15]

The indefatigable Adams poured out fiction under a dizzying array of pen names — as Irving Brown, Gayle Winterton, Brooks McCormick, and Clingham Hunter, M.D., among others.[16] By far the best known of his literary monikers was Oliver Optic, his designation for a knowing, avuncular narrator not unlike Samuel Goodrich's once-ubiquitous Peter Parley. But where Parley's main purpose was the presentation in palatable form of cartloads of useful (if not necessarily accurate) information about history, geography, and the natural sciences, Optic — the memorable name was a variant on that of a character in a popular play performed at the Boston Museum — specialized in fiction that freely blended moral sentiment and raucous adventure.[17] As Adams explained in the preface to his first commercial success, an early work called *The Boat Club* (1855): "The author . . . has endeavored to combine healthy moral lessons with a sufficient amount of exciting interest to render the story attractive to the young; and he hopes he has not mingled these elements of a good juvenile book in disproportionate quantities."[18] Critics' divergent opinions as to his success in this last regard fueled the controversy that continued to swirl around him for the rest of his long career.

None could deny Adams's shrewd grasp of the market or his Midas touch for profiting from it, whether as author or editor. It was Adams who in 1867 introduced the world to the rags-to-riches inspirational fiction of Horatio Alger Jr. in the pages of *The Student and Schoolmate*.[19] With the launch of *Oliver Optic's Magazine*, a weekly begun in a twelve-page format and soon expanded to sixteen, Adams had at his disposal an attractive new platform from which to promote (by serializing) his own books, to scout for talent on behalf of his publisher, and, in the last-page editorials he addressed to parents, to air his views on juvenile literature and, on occasion, take aim at his enemies.

Adams's writings enjoyed the kind of outsized popularity that serious-minded literary folk struggle not to feel bitter about, even if his bombastic style made it easy enough for contemporaries like John Townsend Trowbridge and Lucy Larcom to regard their own work as differing not merely in quantity but in kind. The menu from which Adams served up his magazine had little in common with *Our Young Folks'* loftier fare. In December 1866, however, just days before the launch of *Oliver Optic's*, a direct challenge to *Our Young Folks'* position suddenly appeared on the horizon, the exquisite handiwork of a soft-spoken but fiercely competitive son of a Boston merchant family with Winthrop, Saltonstall, and Manwaring underpinnings named Horace E. Scudder.

The youngest of seven children, Scudder was an earnest New Englander who had reached manhood determined not to rely on his family either for financial support or for social advantage. His parents were both devout Congregationalists, yet in a sign of changing times, they had raised him on Hans Christian Andersen as well as the Bible. After attending the Boston Latin School as a classmate of Henry Adams, Scudder had entered Williams College, a school chosen for him by his father over Harvard as the more religiously orthodox institution. While there, however, he had paid more attention to literature than to religion, immersing himself in the Greek poets and editing the *Williams College Quarterly*. After graduation, having concluded that teaching, the career best suited to his temperament, was barred to him on account of a chronic hearing problem, he turned to writing as the closest alternative, and he met with enough initial success as a literary essayist and an author for children as to begin to feel right about calling himself a literary man.[20]

The idea of writing for children had occurred to him casually, out of a good-natured impulse to amuse a niece. In making the effort, Scudder had found he had the knack. What was more, the experience rekindled fond memories of his childhood reading of Andersen. The two strands of his fledgling career as essayist and fantasist first converged in a piece about Andersen that Scudder published in the September 1861 issue of the *National Quarterly Review*. The following year he published a collection of his own children's stories, *Seven Little People and Their Friends*, followed by a second collection two years later.

Amid this welter of activity, Scudder, still in his midtwenties, happily bowed to the judgment of his fellow critics, who had taken to calling him the "American Hans Christian Andersen" and who regarded him as an essayist of moment.[21] Fatefully, it was just then, as the world was opening itself to him professionally, that word came from India of the death by accidental drowning of his beloved older brother, David, who had gone there as a missionary. Moved to respond as a writer to the loss, Scudder reread his brother's letters, composed a memoir based on them that he intended only for private distribution, and went to discuss the matter with the finest printer he knew, Henry Oscar Houghton, owner of the Cambridge-based Riverside Press. Scudder had first met the distinguished older man when as a student editor at Williams during the mid-1850s he had engaged the press to print the *Williams College Quarterly*. The Riverside Press was New England's preeminent printing establishment, with a roster of top-drawer clients that included Little, Brown, Ticknor & Fields, Roberts Brothers, and G. and C. Merriam Company, publisher of a popular new dictionary.

The printing industry just then, much like publishing, was sliding headlong into a volatile period of high-stakes expansion. When Little, Brown abruptly shifted its lucrative account to a rival printer, the Riverside Press, notwithstanding Houghton's responsible stewardship, was just as swiftly thrown into financial difficulties. The crisis impelled Houghton to take in a partner who could bring fresh capital to the business, and the result of his search would alter forever his relationship to the world of books, for the first time making Houghton a publisher as well as a printer.

Scudder and Houghton had met at a critical moment in both their careers, and the lively dialogue that now unfolded between them ranged well beyond the original purpose of their meeting. The editors of *Our Young Folks* had lately been courting Scudder to contribute a regular monthly story to their magazine, and he had decided to add this assignment to his part-time duties as literary adviser to E. P. Dutton, a young Boston house known primarily for its books on religion. What had begun for Scudder as a kind of gentleman's speculation was rapidly taking on the shape of a real career. The time now seemed right to bring greater unity to the busy patchwork of his professional activities.

For his part, Houghton, who was not quite old enough to be Scudder's father, needed swiftly to come to grips with his new role as a publisher. The conversation peaked when, unbidden, Houghton made the astonishing offer to Scudder to publish his memoir not as a keepsake for a job printer's fee but rather as a commercial venture for sale to the trade. Henry Houghton, it turned out, had much more in mind for the industrious young man. Knowing of Scudder's association with Dutton, he proposed to the young man that he undertake comparable work as the editorial adviser of Hurd & Houghton. Again, Scudder said yes to what looked to be a part-time assignment that would entail reading incoming manuscripts and corresponding with their authors. By the end of 1864, however, his first year with the house, it had become clear that the responsibilities Houghton intended for him far exceeded all the others in his eclectic portfolio, and that what Henry Houghton really had it in mind to do was to hand Horace Scudder, on publishing's nearest equivalent to a silver platter, the all-consuming and utterly absorbing work of a lifetime.

The new business partner whose financial stake had made this possible was Melancthon Montgomery Hurd of New York City. A tall, elegant man about town with a family fortune made in railroading and land speculation, Hurd brought to the partnership an ample supply of bankable social connections, a solid knowledge of the book trade, and a flair for salesmanship.[22] Hurd, who had served an apprenticeship of sorts with a Bridgeport bookseller, reveled in European travel and the whirl of gas-lamp New York society. Under the two men's partnership arrangement, Hurd was to preside over Hurd & Houghton's imposing new headquarters on fashionable Broome Street in Lower Manhattan and cultivate the firm's literary contacts abroad. Houghton would remain in Cambridge (where he was a leading citizen and eventually served as mayor) to oversee the printing operation, which, its recent reversals notwithstanding, remained a megalith. Houghton would also have a hand in the publishing side of the enterprise, visiting New York from time to time for consultations. It was soon decided that in addition to the Cambridge plant, the firm would need a centrally located Boston outpost. With this in mind, Houghton took space in the upper reaches of the Old Corner Book Store, just down the hill from Boston Common, the State House, and the Athenaeum, a dormered, colonial-era, brick house-and-shop brimming with literary associations.

The street-level bookstore had long served as home to Ticknor & Fields and as a gathering place for the cream of New England's literary writers. The firm's two founders had started out there as booksellers and had until recently owned the entire building, managing their publishing business from behind a green curtain in an unprepossessing ground-floor office. Just ahead of them, Samuel Goodrich had established his second-story perch on the premises. From 1839 to 1855, the shop's customers, when not attended to personally by the jittery but gentlemanly William D. Ticknor, received the benefit of knowledgeable service from an ardent young clerk named Thomas Niles Jr. As devoted a book man as his mentor, Niles went on to an important editorial career at Boston's Roberts Brothers, where he published Louisa May Alcott, Christina and Dante Gabriel Rossetti, Robert Louis Stevenson, and Emily Dickinson.[23]

The quintessential antebellum figure, Samuel Goodrich died in 1860, just as the Boston publishing world was undergoing a wholesale changing of the guard. When Hurd & Houghton moved into the Old Corner Book Store, it was on a lease signed with the building's first new owner in more than thirty years, E. P. Dutton & Company. As Dutton's editorial adviser, it must have been easy enough for Scudder to broker the deal for his new employer.[24]

Anxious during the early months of 1865 for his house to gain a foothold in the burgeoning market for illustrated magazines, Henry Houghton began to weigh the options for doing so in consultation with Scudder. It was decided that Scudder would edit the new magazine, whatever it might be. For the American Hans Christian Andersen and his employer and patron, the decision to enter the juvenile market must have seemed a natural one.

The new challenge fired Scudder's competitive instincts. In preparation for the launch of the *Riverside Magazine for Young People*, Scudder undertook a close study of *Our Young Folks* and decided to hold in reserve a story of his own that he had promised the latter magazine. Meanwhile, with a view to expanding the young editor's horizons on the eve of the glorious venture, Melancthon Hurd instructed Scudder to pack his bags for a six-month business trip to England. The two men traveled in style, and when Scudder returned to Boston in November 1865, he was exhilarated, having made the rounds of British publishers and, among other adventures, dined with and acquired a new manuscript for the house from the voluble Algernon Swinburne. By the following spring, with a contract of his own in hand that guaranteed him "absolute control" of the magazine, a generous salary, and even a modest royalty on retail sales once profitability was achieved, Scudder turned his sights on the heady work of securing contributors. His double-barreled appeal to writers emphasized his quest for quality and his willingness to pay for it: "Mr. HO is heartily engaged in the matter! So is Mr. Hurd. There is capital enough to give a cheerful boldness and now all that I want is a spirited corps of contributors."[25] *Our Young Folks* printed an average of 650 words of prose and paid its writers four dollars a page; the *Riverside Magazine* would run one thousand words and pay six dollars per page for stories sold outright by the author and five dollars if the author chose to retain copyright. The gist of these arrangements was to offer more value to reader and writer alike. Illustration was to be managed with the same high regard for quality and the same willingness to outspend the competition. As a result, Scudder had the pick of American illustrators and secured work from Thomas Nast, F. O. C. Darley, and John La Farge, among others.[26] It went without saying that under Henry Houghton's supervision the printing would be first-class. Scudder was twenty-eight when, on December 20, 1866, the inaugural issue of the *Riverside Magazine for Young People* finally went on sale.

In an effort to set the new magazine apart from *Our Young Folks* (and doubtless also to fire a shot across *Oliver Optic's* bow), Scudder himself penned a column of musings addressed to parents, with advice about their children's literary education. He called the page "Books for Young People," and in his inaugural piece the American Andersen issued a bold forecast:

> A literature is forming which is destined to act powerfully on general letters; hitherto it had been little disturbed by critics, but the time must soon come, if it has not already come, when students of literature must

consider the character and tendency of Children's Letters; when all who have at heart the best interest of the Kingdom of Letters must look sharply to this Principality.[27]

To a striking degree, Scudder's prophecy would indeed become reality in a few short years, with some of the nation's most distinguished writers (led by Mark Twain and William Dean Howells) opting to write for young readers on occasion, and with such leading magazines as the *Atlantic Monthly* and *The Nation* devoting regular review space to the genre. In the United States, several of the most widely read books of the last decades of the nineteenth century (as gauged by sales) would be children's books: from 1865 to 1869, *Hans Brinker, Little Women,* and *Innocents Abroad;* from 1870 to 1879, *Little Men, The Hoosier School-Master,* and *The Adventures of Tom Sawyer;* from 1880 to 1889, *Uncle Remus, Heidi, Treasure Island, The Adventures of Huckleberry Finn,* and *Little Lord Fauntleroy;* and from 1890 to 1899, *Black Beauty.*[28] Scudder's prediction had more than wishful thinking behind it. Of all the factors driving the upsurge, the new magazines were the greatest single force.[29]

In his first column, Scudder swiftly got down to brass tacks by admonishing parents not to consider as worthy of purchase for their children only the latest fashionable books to be found in the shops, nor to assume that young people should read only the books published expressly for them. Scudder's comments epitomized his broad-minded and unwaveringly noncommercial outlook. As *Riverside*'s editor, he would, it seemed, have his chance to teach after all. In subsequent issues, he compiled lists of books he deemed suitable for summer reading, offered a comparative evaluation of several nursery song and poetry collections for children, invited readers to reconsider the works of Shakespeare and Sir Walter Scott as literature for the young, and gave a thoughtful appraisal of the genre of the family story.[30] Evenhanded to a fault, he lavished praise on a volume of poetry published by the rival house of Ticknor & Fields while taking exception to verse collections partly comprising contributions to his own *Riverside Magazine.* As the monthly solidified its reputation, Scudder began to cede his space from time to time to the growing roster of top-flight contributors he had writing for him. By May of the first year, the column had become an occasional feature. So enthusiastic had been the response to the magazine of writers and artists that before the year was out Scudder had more than enough material in the well to fill all twelve issues for 1868.[31] Critics likewise had nothing but praise for the venture, with the *American Literary Gazette* proclaiming that "the *Riverside Magazine*, with its beautiful cover, its charming illustrations, and its capital prose and verse, is one of the most attractive magazines which we have. It is edited in good taste, and published with a liberal, enterprising determination to excel."[32]

Yet, by the end of 1867, Scudder's employers were already grumbling about the high cost of keeping the magazine going. Hurd and Houghton's reaction laid bare the frenzied speculative atmosphere that primed the era's publishers to anticipate a greater return on their investment in magazines, and to expect it sooner, than was at all reasonable. Scudder responded by stoically volunteering to accept a 50 percent pay cut while at the same time writing substantially more of the magazine himself. In addition, he offered to help trim other expenses to the extent feasible — provided that he could continue to pay his contributors top dollar. He loved *Riverside* and was prepared to do whatever was necessary to keep it alive. For their own part clearly ambivalent, Hurd and Houghton refused, as gentlemen, to reduce Scudder's salary but accepted his offer to take over more of the writing work. They then slashed his operating budget by substantially more than the editor thought wise.[33] In the face of these troubling developments, Scudder had no choice but to soldier on — and to pray for the miracle of a sizable jump in circulation.

The editor who would later write that "to say there is humor is to say there is real life" could still afford to laugh at one consequence of *Riverside*'s undeniable succès d'estime.[34] During the postwar years, the genteel dream of earning one's literary laurels as an author for children had grown so fashionable as to send armies of mid-Victorian women to their writing tables. Grousing to his friend Charles Eliot Norton at the *North American Review*, Scudder gasped at the poor quality of the unsolicited manuscripts that crossed his desk:

> You know of course how much has to be rejected . . . but do writers for reviews send *bosh*? I suppose you have tedious, lumbering papers, but I hope you have no contributors answering to the great herd of writers for the young, who make me daily wonder how they could suppose I should print their work: but I suppose that the mind which conceives such trash has a depth which appreciates it. If I were to make a Swamp

Magazine for People who never will be Young out of my rejected articles, I think my friends would begin to wonder how the Riverside was even as good as it is.[35]

Hard work and good fortune had, however, put much more than "bosh" on Scudder's plate. The stellar group of writers he had drawn around him included Lucretia P. Hale, who also published in *Our Young Folks;* Mary Mapes Dodge, justly famous by then as the author of *Hans Brinker, or, The Silver Skates* (1865); Frank R. Stockton, whose first work for children appeared in *Riverside;* Sarah Orne Jewett of Maine; and, most famously, Hans Christian Andersen.[36] In all, seventeen of Andersen's fairy tales made their first appearance in the *Riverside Magazine,* starting in late 1868. In that same year, in his capacity as Hurd & Houghton literary adviser, Scudder also negotiated the right to publish the sole authorized American edition of all Andersen's works. The exemplary deal Scudder struck showed how, in the best of circumstances, a publisher's book and magazine interests could work hand in glove to the firm's greater benefit.

The agreement with the world's most famous author for children had not come about easily, or without much persistence by Scudder, whose first three letters to the great man, written between 1862 and 1866, had each gone unanswered. In all likelihood, Andersen replied to Scudder's fourth letter, dated March 13, 1868, only because of the highly advantageous business proposition Scudder had outlined in it. Although by the 1860s Andersen's fairy tales were well known to two generations of American children, their author had not yet received a penny in income from their sale in the States. With the lack of international copyright agreements, Andersen had no right, from a purely legal standpoint, to expect otherwise. Among gentleman publishers, however, a moral issue was also at stake, as was the degree of risk that a hypothetically unlimited number of editions of the same author's work added to an industry already vulnerable to sudden swings in popular taste and fashion. To address the latter problem, some publishers offered royalties or other payments to foreign authors in return for the right to publicize their editions as the only authorized ones. Scudder was the first American publisher to make such a proposal to Andersen, and for that, Andersen, a child of poverty who never learned to take his later success for granted, was to remain deeply grateful for the rest of his life.

Scudder had maintained his resolve throughout the years of Andersen's silence as much thanks to the worshipful high regard in which he held the Danish writer, whom he had long since made a literary role model, as because of the starch in his New England spine. Enclosed with his first letter to Andersen, dated March 8, 1862, had been a copy of Scudder's adulatory *National Quarterly Review* essay, published only a few months earlier — a piece that had served to burnish the twenty-four-year-old's own literary reputation even as it added greater luster to Andersen's. When Scudder next wrote to Denmark, on November 14, he enclosed a copy of his *Seven Little People*. Andersen's failure again to respond may have shaken Scudder, as he allowed nearly four years to pass before his next attempt. His third letter, a long one, opened with a methodical review of his previous communications, then proceeded to the dramatic revelation that an unsigned appreciation of Andersen that had appeared some time before in the respected Danish newspaper *Dagbladet* was in fact a reduction of Scudder's own *National Quarterly Review* essay.[37] Although Scudder did not say as much, it was in all likelihood he who had arranged for the *Dagbladet* article, for the express purpose of making sure that one reader — Andersen — would see it and be favorably impressed: such was the measured but relentless campaign that Scudder waged to capture Andersen's attention.[38] He followed this ingratiating disclosure with the news that he, Horace Scudder, was moving up in the publishing world and was now "engaged in establishing a new magazine for the young." Hoping by this to at last pique Andersen's interest, and with absolutely nothing to lose, Scudder finally leapt into the breach with an ambitious proposition: "And now, am I too bold in asking whether you will not contribute from your store?" He then outlined a plan for Andersen to submit twelve original tales for publication in the *Riverside Magazine* in return for a substantial sum.[39]

This letter, however, met with silence as well. Scudder now resolved to bide his time as he shepherded his new magazine into print and marshaled his employers' support for a still grander plan he had in mind for Andersen. By March 13, 1868, Scudder was at last in a position to write again. Once again he invited Andersen to contribute, on liberal terms, to *Riverside*, but with the added promise of publication by Hurd & Houghton of a "complete edition of your *Märchen*," a substantial volume that, by carrying the author's authorization, would be likely to drive pirated editions from the American market and result in significant royalty income.

On April 21, Andersen made his reply. Wading warily into the exchange, he began by gently poking a few holes in Scudder's representations about the nature of his high-minded juvenile monthly while at the same time thanking the American for his friendly overture and intimating that he might indeed be willing to contribute new tales to the *Riverside Magazine*. None of the Danish writer's misgivings — that *Riverside* appeared, for example, to be aimed primarily at readers much younger than those for whom he intended his fairy tales — could mask the fact that Scudder's latest gambit had at long last done the trick. Having warmed to the prospect of a well-prepared complete edition of his fairy tales, Andersen must have stunned Scudder by upping the ante with a proposal of his own: if Hurd & Houghton would also agree to publish his memoir, Andersen told Scudder, he would happily update the work with several new chapters written expressly for the authorized American edition.

Scudder was thrilled, and in the cordial exchanges that followed at one- and two-month intervals (communication was slowed by the need for each correspondent to have a translation of his latest reply prepared in the other man's language for mailing and by Andersen's relentless travel schedule), the grand scheme grew to encompass a projected edition of all the writer's published works, including not only his fairy tales and autobiography but also his novels and plays. Setting aside his first impression that his tales might not find themselves "entirely in their right place" in the *Riverside Magazine*, Andersen agreed, as well, to contribute original fairy tales to Scudder's monthly, as inspiration and his travels allowed.[40] For a magazine whose potential readership lay with the growing ranks of educated, middle-class families who, in the new spirit of American Romanticism, appreciated imaginative literature as a worthy element of a young child's education, the news could not have been more heartening, or better timed. If *Riverside*'s sad tale of lagging subscription figures was to end happily, Andersen was the man for the job.

In 1868 Louisa May Alcott, at thirty-six the author of a labored literary novel called *Moods* and of the well-received Civil War memoir *Hospital Sketches*, became the third editor of a juvenile magazine launched twenty-seven years earlier by the late Samuel Griswold Goodrich. The magazine was *Robert Merry's Museum*, whose eponymous presiding spirit had begun life as the second of Goodrich's fictive alter egos. As a gouty, peg-legged storyteller and amiable guide to children, Merry bore an all too striking resemblance to Goodrich's first such creation, Peter Parley. Readers of the new magazine did not seem to mind, and Goodrich, always a Barnum-esque master of self-promotion, proceeded to exploit the new periodical, as he had the old one, as an engine for cross-marketing his books. With *Merry's* successfully launched, he conceived the neat trick of having his two imaginary gentlemen "meet," an event heralded by an announcement in *Merry's* that Peter Parley had agreed to become a "contributor."[41]

After Goodrich left *Merry's* for good, two far less colorful editors came and went before the job passed into Alcott's capable hands.[42] Alcott accepted the post at the start of what was to prove the most fateful period of her life. In the same diary entry dated September 1867 in which Alcott noted the job offer from *Merry's*, she also recorded a momentous piece of advice that her editor at Roberts Brothers, Thomas Niles Jr., had offered her: that she consider writing a novel for girls.[43] Alcott had bristled at the suggestion of a "girls' story," a genre that she claimed held no interest for her. Indeed, she went so far as to say that apart from her own three sisters she knew very little about girls — and cared even less. She told Niles that if she were going to write a book for young readers, she would much prefer to write a "fairy book." When the editor responded coolly to that idea, Alcott, high-strung but ever the pragmatist, let the matter drop. At the same time, she saw that the editorship of *Merry's*, which came as such jobs generally did with the expectation of substantial writing work, would give her ample time to mull over the prospects for the type of book that Niles had said he *was* willing to publish, and that she would be paid for her efforts.

Alcott had long since shouldered the burden of her family's financial support. As *Merry's* editor, for which she received an annual fee of $500, she wasted no time.[44] Alcott rented a room within walking distance of the magazine's office on Washington Street in downtown Boston and for the first issue published under her supervision produced a sketch for what was to become the breakfast scene in *Little Women*.[45] In May 1868, she returned home to Concord to begin writing her novel in earnest. She wrote at breakneck speed, without stopping to revise. On July 15, she finished the first half of *Little Women*, a manuscript long enough to be published as a book. That fall, after the first printing of two thousand quickly sold out, Niles urged the author to proceed immediately with the second and final installment, which she began in November and completed on January 1, and which Roberts Brothers published in March 1869. By then it was already clear that Alcott and her publisher had an overwhelming commercial success on their hands. Having quite suddenly found a means of earning previously unimaginable sums, and with no pressing need to remain in the employment of others, Alcott resigned the editorship of *Merry's Museum* in 1870, the year in which Roberts Brothers published her second juvenile novel, *An Old-Fashioned Girl*.[46]

Thomas Niles Jr. did Alcott a great service when, just as her fortunes were about to take a spectacular upward turn, he advised her to retain the copyright to *Little Women* rather than sell it outright to Roberts Brothers for $1,000. As Alcott's star continued to rise, however, and as her actions came less often to be governed by bare-knuckle necessity, Niles revealed a less attractive side of his personality as he shored up his firm's long-term interests by preying on the author's well-known vulnerabilities. A literary scandal was brewing in Boston just then as Mary Abigail Dodge, the witty Ticknor & Fields romance author and *Our Young Folks* magazine editor, was deeply engaged in publicizing her suspicion that James T. Fields had cheated her out of royalties due her. Dodge's *A Battle of the Books*, which she published as Gail Hamilton under the imprint of Ticknor's archrival Hurd & Houghton, issued a clarion call to authors to exercise greater vigilance in their dealings with the slippery men who called themselves publishers. When Alcott, taking a leaf from Dodge, approached Niles about raising the royalty rate for her new book above the 10 percent on retail sales that she had accepted for *Little Women*, the publisher, knowing well the low esteem she had for girls' books (including her own), petulantly dismissed the idea. Playing mercilessly on Alcott's self-doubt and grimly forecasting the worst for *An Old-Fashioned Girl*, he reminded her that as a "second class story teller" she "ought not to expect more. . . . Surely you don't want an additional percentage on a failure." Then, when sales of the novel swiftly passed the thirty-thousand-copy mark, circumstances compelled Niles to change tack. Without a trace of embarrassment, he next resorted to a shrill appeal to her sense of gratitude and loyalty: "But you, I am quite sure, *without ample reason*, would never desert those who both by their brains and their money have *helped* you to achieve the position you hold today." Niles held his ground for the time being but raised Alcott's royalty to 12 percent in 1871 for *Little Men*.[47] The next year he saw his crucial contribution to Roberts Brothers' success rewarded with a partnership.[48]

As the long-distance friendship between Hans Christian Andersen and Horace Scudder waxed ever more cordial, the latter took up the challenge of mastering Danish with a view to translating the authorized edition himself. Scudder had other plans in mind as well. In a letter to Andersen dated October 28, 1871, he invited the writer, whose appetite for exotic travel was legendary, to come to the United States for a lecture tour. Such a trip, he assured Andersen, might be organized on the same lavish scale as the two triumphant American tours made by Andersen's old friend Charles Dickens. The latter of these still belonged to recent memory, having taken place over the winter of 1867 and on into the next year, under the sponsorship of Ticknor & Fields. Scudder doubtless reveled at the prospect of bringing home comparable glory to Hurd & Houghton as Andersen's American host. While the thought of fresh rounds of public adulation, gilded encounters with solicitous dignitaries, and leisurely stays in the new nation's great homes could only have appealed to the incurably vain and limelight-besotted author, growing concern for his health and for the perils of a transatlantic voyage proved, in the end, to be obstacles too powerful even for Scudder to overcome. The editor renewed his invitation on several occasions. Time and again, Andersen graciously declined, leaving the New World as a place to dream about.

For Scudder, Andersen's response was the latest in a series of recent major disappointments. On November 21 of the previous year, he had grimly written his Danish friend to inform him that

> the December number of the *Riverside*, which goes to you to-day, contains the announcement that the magazine is to be discontinued after this year. The Publishers have decided that it will not be expedient to go on with it, and I have ventured to make provision for the publication of such of your stories as you may be pleased to send me, to be published first in magazine form. Our good friends, Messrs. Scribner & Co.[,] have begun the issue of a magazine, called *Scribner's Monthly*[,] with which the *Riverside* is incorporated.[49]

Scudder had swallowed the bitter pill as best he could. In December 1870, the *Riverside Magazine* became a department of *Scribner's Monthly*, a new general interest magazine fielded by the eponymous New York book publisher.[50] The transfer of Scudder's editorial services to the new owner was not part of the new ownership agreement, a scenario that would have required that he move to New York. What Scribner did acquire — along with the inventory that Scudder had built up in reserve for *Riverside* —

was, as the letter to Andersen demonstrated, the editor's full cooperation and the promise of his own continued contributions as a writer.

The launch of *Scribner's Monthly* marked a bold attempt by a mid-sized, old-line New York house to join the first rank of the nation's trade publishers. In its early years, Scribner had grown and prospered primarily on the strength of its books devoted to religious philosophy, particularly those authored by the leaders of Presbyterianism. A second strength of the list was the long string of bestsellers that Charles Scribner had such a knack for acquiring — crowd-pleasing books by the flamboyant New York newspaperman and essayist Nathaniel Parker Willis and by Donald Grant Mitchell, who, as Ik Marvel, had produced one of mid-nineteenth-century America's most cherished volumes of lyric musings, *Reveries of a Bachelor, a Book of the Heart.*[51] For the founder of the house, the launch of *Scribner's Monthly* represented the fulfillment of a long-held dream — a dream, however, whose realization he lived only just long enough to see. Charles Scribner died of typhus while traveling abroad a year later, whereupon ownership of the house passed to his son, Charles Jr., and to two partners, Dr. Josiah Gilbert Holland and Roswell Smith. These three men, caught up like so many of their contemporaries in magazine fever, decided in 1872 that rather than merely build on the remnants of the *Riverside Magazine*, they would instead create an impressive new freestanding juvenile magazine under the Scribner banner.

As a first step, Smith asked Mary Mapes Dodge, then the associate editor of the weekly *Hearth and Home*, to set down her thoughts for such a magazine. Dodge's prospectus, which ran as an unsigned article in the July 1873 issue of *Scribner's Monthly*, did double duty as a dress rehearsal for her editorship of the magazine and as a teaser of sorts for the *Monthly*'s subscribers, who would soon learn that the ideal juvenile magazine they had had described for them was about to assume tangible form — just in time for Christmas.

Dodge had written that a magazine for young readers should have the atmosphere of a child's "pleasure ground," a safe harbor where children could both find delight and feel in charge. Tedious moralizing of the kind that generations of youngsters were accustomed to from their Sunday school publications and so many of the other books and magazines published for them could have no place in such a magazine. Leading authors and artists would eagerly contribute, she predicted, knowing that the editorial standards brought to bear on their work would, if anything, surpass those of the adult magazines with which their names were already associated. Nor would parents have anything to fear from a monthly that so deliberately shut the door on the old-fashioned style of moralizing. "Doubtless," Dodge wrote, "a great deal of instruction and good moral teaching may be inculcated in the pages of a magazine; but it must be by hints dropped incidentally here and there, by a few, brisk, hearty statements of the difference between right and wrong." It was all a question of balance, of taste, and above all of art. "Harsh, cruel facts — if they must come, and sometimes it is important that they should — must march forward boldly, say what they have to say, and go."[52]

It had not been long before Henry Houghton realized that in Melancthon Hurd he had cast his lot with a dilettante and that to ensure the long-term prosperity of the house they had cofounded he would need to find other, more responsible men of means with whom to share the burdens of management. In 1872 he turned yet again to Horace Scudder, offering him a junior partnership in the firm where he already functioned as editor in chief.[53] Scudder's heart was in his writing by then, but he accepted the partnership anyway. Houghton brought two other partners into the firm that year as well, a wealthy investor named Edmund Hatch Bennett and a Boston scion intent on making his mark in the book trade, George Mifflin. Henry Houghton, the quintessential self-made man, was understandably fearful just then of becoming entangled with another spoiled aristocrat, and he had put the young Boston Brahmin to the test by scheduling one of their first interviews for seven-thirty in the morning. Much to Houghton's astonishment, Mifflin had arrived on time. Nor had he failed afterward in his attention to detail during an apprenticeship period spent in the counting room copying bills and in the bindery. When all was said and done, the bold strokes of 1872 had accomplished Houghton's purpose exactly. At Christmastime the following year, he and his colleagues had more than usual to rejoice about, having just acquired from James R. Osgood & Company (the last remnant of their archrival Ticknor & Fields) the nation's premier magazine, the *Atlantic Monthly*.[54]

That holiday season, few Boston businessmen had half as much to celebrate. Little more than a year earlier, on November 9, 1872, what came to be known as the Great Boston Fire had swept through the city's downtown business district, destroying much of it, including the offices of James R. Osgood and the warehoused stock of Lee & Shepard, Horace B. Fuller, and several of the city's other publishers. Then, on September 17, 1873, the failure of Jay Cooke & Company, a major underwriter of the Northern Pacific Railroad, triggered a nationwide financial panic that severely undercut the Boston publishers' chances of recovering from the fire.

As always, there were winners as well as losers. The publishing firm of Lee & Shepard was badly compromised both by the fire and by the panic; the demise of *Oliver Optic's Magazine* and Lee & Shepard's declaration of bankruptcy both followed in 1875.[55] For the remnants of the once-proud Ticknor & Fields, the dramatic reversals of the early 1870s accelerated the decline. The turmoil at that house had begun with the death, in 1864, of its cofounder, William D. Ticknor. Four years later, the firm reorganized as Fields, Osgood & Company. Then the nasty public dispute that erupted following Mary Abigail Dodge's accusations of financial improprieties on the part of the house damaged James Fields's reputation and prompted his early retirement in 1871, whereupon the house reconstituted itself as James R. Osgood & Company. Then came the Great Fire, followed by the Panic of 1873. The publisher had been slipping steadily even before the twin catastrophes lined up to bring about the end. Before the decade was out, Osgood & Company had merged with Hurd & Houghton's Riverside Press division, thence to become, in 1880, one of the key constituents of a new Boston literary powerhouse, the Houghton Mifflin Company.

Amid all the chaos in Boston, the larger New York houses pressed their advantage. For East Coast publishers in a position to expand, the completion of the Transcontinental Railroad in 1869 enabled them for the first time to ship their books at a reasonable rate as far west as California. Prior to the completion of the monumental rail project, the cost of shipping books to the more far-flung parts of the country had been high enough that regional bookseller-publishers, such as Anton Roman of San Francisco, had been able to undersell even the nation's biggest house, Harper & Brothers, notwithstanding Harper's aggressive discount policy. A. Roman and Company, publisher of the *Overland Monthly*, tried a variety of tactics to remain competitive, the most effective perhaps being that of specializing to some extent in books with a distinctly regional flavor, including some, such as May Wentworth's "Golden Gate" series, that were intended for children. Roman, however, like so many others, fell victim to the

Panic of 1873 and the seemingly unstoppable trend toward consolidation in publishing, finally declaring bankruptcy six years later.[56]

In May 1873, Mary Mapes Dodge sailed for Europe with her son Harry to catch her breath and to call upon writers she hoped might contribute to the new magazine she had agreed to launch for Scribner. The first issue of the magazine to be called *St. Nicholas* was ready for the typesetter and Dodge's capable assistant, Frank R. Stockton, was at home and on hand in case of emergency. In England, George MacDonald, the Rossettis, and the Reverend Charles Dodgson were among those who played host to Dodge, the celebrated author of *Hans Brinker*. On the Dutch leg of the trip, young Harry had the odd experience of wandering anonymously into a bookstore thousands of miles from home and having a copy of his mother's novel urged upon him.[57] Dodge returned to New York to the astonishing news that her employers, Messrs. Holland, Smith, and Scribner, had seized the opportunity created by the turmoil in Boston to buy out *Our Young Folks* from its beleaguered parent company, James R. Osgood, and to merge that magazine's subscription list and other assets with those of *St. Nicholas*. It had been decided in her absence that the Boston-based magazine would take its valedictory bow in October and that *St. Nicholas* would launch the following month rather than in January 1874, as originally planned.[58] Thanks to this extraordinary coup, the only remaining serious competition for Dodge's magazine had suddenly moved to the other — her own — side of the equation. Horace Scudder had already extended his good offices to her. Now, in a comparable gesture of gentlemanly goodwill, John Townsend Trowbridge, one of *Our Young Folks'* triumvirate of editors, endorsed the new magazine and agreed to write for it too.[59] Flush with cash, the house of Scribner would cement its relationship with Dodge herself by publishing, and heavily promoting, a new edition of *Hans Brinker* in 1874.[60]

It was as though all of Dodge's life had been an apprenticeship for her new job. Her father, James Jay Mapes, had been an intellectually gifted (and financially guileless) polymath: a magazine publisher, inventor, artist, agriculturalist, and chemist. Both he and Mary's mother, Sophia Furman Mapes, had taken a keen interest in their five children's educations, which were conducted at home during the early years with the help of tutors and governesses. Learning also took place around the dinner table, where the illustrious guests, all friends of the children's father, included Horace

Greeley, William Cullen Bryant, and John Ericsson, the nautical engineer who later gained lasting fame as the designer of the Union navy's ironclad gunship *Monitor.*

In 1851 Mary married another friend of her father's, a New York lawyer named William Dodge. The couple had two sons and were enjoying their comfortable life in New York when, overwhelmed by sudden financial reversals and the life-threatening illness of their elder child, William disappeared one night in 1858 and was subsequently found drowned. In the aftermath of these terrible events, Mary and her two sons went to live with her parents on the experimental farm her father had established years earlier in New Jersey. In the hope of distracting her, James Mapes offered his widowed daughter magazine work. Giving herself over to the assignment, she honed her skills both as an editor and also, in regular, unsigned contributions to *Working Farmer* and *United States Journal,* as a writer. Expanding her literary horizons, in 1863 she published her first short story in *Harper's New Monthly Magazine* and, the following November, her first book, a collection of juvenile tales called *Irvington Stories.* Once again her father had extended a guiding hand. Knowing that her sons found her a captivating storyteller, James Mapes had encouraged her to capitalize on the swelling wartime demand for heroic boys' fiction and arranged an introduction to his New York publisher friend James O'Kane. *Irvington Stories,* as it turned out, contained only one tale of the kind urged upon her by her father. Cheek by jowl with "Capt. George, the Drummer Boy" there appeared others — fantastic, moralistic, religious — that by their sheer variety perhaps reflected her magazine editor's instinct for appealing to the widest possible range of tastes. The book sold just well enough for O'Kane to agree to publish a second book by the author. This time Dodge indulged a long-standing wish to write a work of fiction set in Holland.

Dodge's *Hans Brinker, or, The Silver Skates,* appeared in December 1865 to enthusiastic reviews and unexpectedly strong sales. A bestselling book of the era was defined as one with a sale of at least 300,000 copies. In 1865 only two books published in the United States had achieved that pinnacle of success: Dodge's *Hans Brinker* and Charles Dickens's latest novel, *Our Mutual Friend.*[61]

Unlike Louisa May Alcott, with whom she was soon to form a close friendship, Dodge lacked the ability to swiftly write book after book. As a widow with two children to support, the dependable income attached to the editorship held out immense appeal. Dodge remained on the job for the next thirty-two years, easily weathering a change in ownership when in 1881 Roswell Smith bought out his Scribner partners' interests in *St. Nicholas* and assumed control of the magazine as head of the newly formed Century Company. Not surprisingly, Dodge's relationship to Scribner's book division cooled in the months that followed. She brought her next juvenile novel, *Donald and Dorothy* (1883), not to Scribner but to Roberts Brothers, Louisa May Alcott's house, after first serializing the book in her own magazine.[62] She published all her remaining few books with the Century Company.

It was about this time (1873) that, according to one of his biographers, Hans Christian Andersen received two guests in his Copenhagen rooms: the Danish author Vilhelm Bergsøe and a twenty-five-year-old Norwegian-born American who was a university professor and the editor of the *Atlantic Monthly*, Hjalmar Hjorth Boyesen.

"So you've come all the way from America, Herr Boyesen?" Andersen is said to have remarked. "Well, nowadays the distance is a mere trifle. I have many friends in America. Do you know Horatz Scooder?"

The visitor thought for a moment before replying that regretfully he did not happen to know Andersen's friend.

"How strange," said Andersen in return. "I heard that his books were supposed to be both charming and popular, and besides, he's translating most of my fairy tales into American English."

"Oh, you mean Horace Scudder!" Boyesen did indeed know the man well. The American editor then brought up yet again the possibility of a visit by Andersen to the United States, even volunteering to serve as his guide. Andersen seemed to demur, saying that if he could avoid the long voyage by being telegraphed across the ocean, he would certainly come, adding: "It's odd how distant America has become for me. I can easily imagine myself up on the moon, and I can picture all sorts of amusing things taking place there. But in the great, cold, and prosaic land to the west, the poetic imagination must starve to death from lack of material."[63]

As Horace E. Scudder was to Boston during the last quarter of the nineteenth century, Mary Mapes Dodge, with her ascension to the editorship of *St. Nicholas*, now became to New York: the "dominating influence . . .

affecting for good the production of children's literature in America."[64] Dodge came to the job not only with a lifetime of immersion in American literary culture but also with a large circle of literary friends, starting with those she had first met in her parents' house. She now added immensely to her store of contacts by taking advantage of the opportunity left open to her to publish writers and artists who also worked for *Scribner's Monthly.* The key to it all, as Scudder had also known, lay in producing a magazine in which any writer would be proud to appear and in being able to pay top dollar. In this, Scribner's partners happily stood in absolute accord. From the first, Dodge had at her disposal impressive sums even for a talented newcomer. In 1876, when unpublished twenty-year-old Katherine D. Smith (later to become famous by her married name of Kate Douglas Wiggin) submitted a short story called "Half a Dozen Housekeepers" to *St. Nicholas,* she received by return mail a letter and a check for $150.[65]

Established authors and artists were just as pleased to have their work showcased. The serialization of *Eight Cousins,* Louisa May Alcott's story of a rich orphan girl named Rose Campbell who is sent to live with her Boston maiden aunts, was sure to stir interest in the book to come after it first appeared in installments in the magazine starting in the January 1875 issue. The August installment, however, also ignited a literary firestorm over Alcott's scathing references to the reading matter that two of the heroine's male cousins favored. Leaving no doubt as to the target of her scorn, Alcott dubbed the offending books "optical delusions," a phrase meant to heap disapproval on the sensational writings of William Taylor Adams and his imitators and the distorted view of life that Alcott implied they imparted to young readers.

By 1875 *St. Nicholas* had seventy thousand paid subscribers and a total readership that doubtless far exceeded that number as copies were passed around within families and among friends. Roberts Brothers planned to publish *Eight Cousins* in book form in late 1875 in time for the Christmas trade. Any new book by the author of *Little Women* was sure to be widely read. To Adams, all this was reason enough not to allow Alcott's attack to go unanswered.

Adams had friends in high literary places, and they swiftly rose to his defense. *Appleton's Journal of Literature, Science, and Art,* a smart new monthly that associated itself with the more relaxed postwar attitude toward juvenile literature, cattily observed:

We wonder, by-the-way, if Miss Alcott realizes the risk she runs in deviating from her own proper field of story-telling and "dropping into" criticism? She devotes a couple of pages of "Eight Cousins" to denouncing the methods of her co-workers and disrespectfully characterizes certain well-known ornaments of current literature as "optical delusions." It is fortunate for her peace of mind, perhaps, that she has put the Atlantic between her and that din of warfare the first notes of which, as we understand, have already sounded.[66]

The magazine's parent company, D. Appleton & Company, was a leading New York trade house and had demonstrated its advanced views a few years earlier, in 1866, when it had seized the chance to purchase the rejected sheets for the first printing of a new British work of nonsense fantasy called *Alice's Adventures in Wonderland* and published the first American edition.[67]

Scribner's Monthly took Alcott to task for condemning Adams's liberal use of slang when she herself made use of the same technique in her own books. Alcott's complaint, moreover, betrayed an unbecoming immaturity on her part, calling to mind, as the *Scribner's Monthly* writer put it, the "'hazed' Freshman [who] retaliated upon Freshman when he became a Sophomore."[68]

Adams himself responded to the charges in *Oliver Optic's Magazine*, arguing, reasonably, that Alcott's accusations were themselves more sensational than anything he had ever put into a story for children. "She seems," he wrote

> to have deliberatively misrepresented the books she writes about. Her citations indicate that she had the book in hand from which she quoted, and we hardly think she could have made a tooth-pick out of the true cross without intending to do so. She could not have put that bar-room illustration into "Sunny Shores" without meaning to be untruthful. In a word, she has said enough to identify the Optic books, and then charged them with the faults of all the juvenile books published, her own included.
>
> Ah, Louisa, you are very smart, and you have become rich. Your success mocks that of the juvenile heroes you despise. Even the author of "Dick Dauntless" and "Sam Soaker," whoever he may be, would not dare to write up a heroine who rose so rapidly from poverty and obscurity to riches and fame as you did; but in view of the wholesale per-

version of the truth we have pointed out, we must ask you to adopt the motto you recommend for others — "Be honest and you will be happy," instead of the one you seem to have chosen: "Be smart and you will be rich."[69]

Why had Alcott left herself open to such a charge? She was scornful of the obvious relish with which Adams produced volume after volume of the type of formula fiction that she herself had resorted to only out of stark necessity, and with no illusions as to its merits. She regarded the other author and herself as members of two very different tribes. While it would have gratified her no end had her first book, the contemplative novel for adults called *Moods*, received anything like the acclaim that greeted *Little Women*, Alcott welcomed the latter book's very considerable success only inasmuch as it had allowed her to fulfill what she took to be her duty to her family. To the extent that Alcott regretted having set aside her true literary ambitions for the sake of expediency, Adams hovered like a ghost at the very doorstep of her literary conscience. In the months before she commenced work on *Little Women*, Alcott's editor at Roberts Brothers, Thomas Niles Jr., had not simply urged her to write a "girls' book." Knowing of her family circumstances and desire to make money, Niles had been blunt: "Do something," he had told Alcott, "like Oliver Optic."[70]

As though to absolve herself of the guilt she felt at continuing to write sequels to the book that had made her fortune, Alcott cast herself increasingly in the role of social reformer, becoming active in the women's suffrage movement and, in October 1875, the year of *Eight Cousins'* publication, attending the Women's Congress in Syracuse, New York, albeit only as an observer. As Alcott's biographer Martha Saxton has commented, the author conceived *Eight Cousins* not so much as a novel as "a series of lessons, . . . an exercise in discussing girls' education."[71] In condemning Adams, the high-minded reformer in Alcott had conveniently forgotten what Alcott the storyteller was herself capable of. By singling out her rival in this way, she had all but guaranteed that the ridicule she privately considered her due would come down on her head in the most public way imaginable.

Perhaps the sorry affair owed something as well to the frenzied atmosphere of American juvenile publishing just then. To judge by the high failure rate of Boston houses that made a specialty of the genre, a boom-or-bust mentality prevailed as the ambition to capitalize on a growing market collided with rapid changes in the standards and tastes by which such books were evaluated. Looking back at the careers of her predecessors of a century earlier, Little, Brown's Helen L. Jones, writing in 1969, noted that of the twenty Boston houses known for their juvenile lists at the time of the Civil War, fewer than a handful remained in business by the turn of the century. Brown, Taggard and Chase, later known as Brown and Taggard and later still as Taggard and Thompson, passed from the scene sometime after 1876, as did Crosby, Nichols, Lee and Company. T. O. H. P. Burnham; Andrew F. Graves; J. E. Tilton and Company; Walker, Wise and Company, and its successor, Walker, Fuller and Company — were likewise all gone before 1890.[72]

From the 1870s onward, the story of American trade book publishing would primarily be a story set in New York.[73] Harper & Brothers held pride of place as the nation's — and, after 1850, the world's — largest trade house, publisher of Richard Henry Dana's *Two Years Before the Mast*, Henry Ward Beecher's *Sermons*, authorized editions of much of the later work of Charles Dickens, and substantial "libraries" of literary classics, juveniles, and titles in other categories, many of them low-priced and all highly profitable.[74] When Fletcher Harper, the last of the four original brothers, died in 1877, the leadership of the house simply passed into the waiting hands of the founders' five sons (and an ever-growing roster of cousins), leading citizens all of the gilded city and age in which their printing and publishing concern, housed in two colossal, ironclad buildings on Franklin Square, ranked with the industrial world's legendary businesses.

Harper & Brothers entered the hotly contested juvenile magazine market in November 1879 with an eight-page weekly called *Harper's Young People: An Illustrated Weekly*.[75] While the brilliant launch of *St. Nicholas* presented an immense challenge to the editor assigned to the new venture, Kirk Munroe, himself an author of boys' adventure stories, no publisher was in a better position to mount the counterattack that would be required. To jump-start the new magazine's circulation, Munroe's employers devised a clever plan for piggybacking on the company's three active subscription lists. Within six weeks, as subscriptions and first-rate material flowed in, the editor was able to double his page count and enlarge both the page and type size to what was to become the weekly's standard format. In the years to come, Munroe would serialize James Otis's *Toby Tyler*, William Dean Howells's *A Boy's Town*, and Howard Pyle's *Men of Iron*, all prior to their publication by Harper in book form; obtain contributions from Mark Twain, Sarah Orne Jewett, Louisa May Alcott, and John Townsend

Trowbridge; and in general create what would have been judged, had *St. Nicholas* not existed, a magazine of singular breadth and literary merit. As it was, *Harper's Young People* always remained somewhat in the shadow of the dynamic monthly that had planted its flag first.

Because illustration played such a crucial role in the success of the new national magazines, the art directors at the major publishing houses became figures of immense prestige and influence. Richly paid, they basked in the glow that a generation or two later would gather about the heads of Hollywood directors like D. W. Griffith and Cecil B. DeMille. At Harper & Brothers, art director Charles Parsons trained and championed generations of illustrators. Howard Pyle recalled his shaky start with Parsons, who responded favorably from the first to the young man's pictorial ideas for *Harper's Weekly* but found his draftsmanship wanting. In 1877, fearing he might be pegged for good as the kind of lower-rung illustrator whose sketches were purchased for final execution by their creative betters — the "young Olympians" of Parsons's brilliant stable — Pyle braced for a do-or-die test of his prospects and poured his heart and soul into a preliminary sketch for a drawing that he proposed to call "A Wreck in the Offing." Pyle later recalled the moment of truth when, six weeks after presenting his work to the great man, Parsons rendered his verdict:

> I think it was not until I stood in the awful presence of the art editor himself that I realized how this might be the turning point of my life — that I realized how great was to be the result of his decision on my future endeavor. . . . I can recall just how the art editor looked at me over his spectacles, and to my perturbed mind it seemed that he was weighing in his mind (for he was a very tender man) how best he might break the news to me of my unsuccess. The rebound was almost too great when he told me that Mr. Harper had liked my idea very much and that . . . they were not only going to use it, but were going to make of it a double-page cut. . . . My exaltation was so great that it seemed to me that I knew not where I was standing. . . . I found a friend and I took him to Delmonico's, and we had lunch of all the delicacies in season and out of season.[76]

A young illustrator's life was nothing if not unpredictable. The previous year, as a new arrival in New York, Pyle had enjoyed a heady run of acceptances from *St. Nicholas's* Mary Mapes Dodge. Then came the chilling news that *St. Nicholas* had in hand all the artwork it required at present and would not be accepting more work anytime soon.[77] The art directors at both Harper and Scribner seem to have sympathized to some extent with the lot of their freelance illustrators and apparently did not object when an artist plied his trade at both houses. Pyle occasionally worked under exclusive contract for Harper, although never for more than a year at a time. Notwithstanding the uncertainty, a talented, agile artist stood to reap substantial rewards for his efforts, with the most sought-after illustrators earning princely annual incomes. As Pyle quickly learned, more than one road might lead to lasting fame and fortune. It was in part through his early association with Parsons, the overlord for all the Harper magazines, that he later became a Harper juvenile book author. It was thanks in part to his early association with a juvenile editor, *St. Nicholas*'s Mary Mapes Dodge, that Pyle achieved comparable success at Scribner, although by the time Scribner published his *Merry Adventures of Robin Hood* (1883), Dodge and *St. Nicholas* had both moved on to the Century Company. Pyle's editor for books at Scribner was none other than Charles Scribner Jr. himself.[78]

Across the East River, in a vast red brick printing plant in Williamsburg, Brooklyn, McLoughlin Brothers was engaged in producing a great many of the most elaborately illustrated children's books of the postwar years. The publisher, which also had offices in Lower Manhattan, valued the reputation for innovation in printing and design that it had inherited from its precursor, Elton & Company. During the 1860s, McLoughlin Brothers was quick to exploit the new technique of two-color wood block illustration, an advance that brightened and regularized the appearance of children's books and picked up the pace of production over what had previously been possible using the traditional hand-coloring stencil method. In the following decade, the company committed itself to the far more fluid — and flamboyant — possibilities presented by the perfection of chromolithography, a process entailing the meticulous application of individual colors onto a series of printer's stones with a grease-based crayon. What resulted from this latest retooling of their operation was the creation of a myriad of children's picture books, novelties, and games of unprecedented visual appeal, the best exhibiting the same raucous energy and hyperbolic showmanship seen in the great circus posters of the day, and all unabashedly designed for the amusement of children, often with a dollop of "instruction" tossed into the kettle as well for the paying grownups.[79]

Larger in format than traditional chapbooks and offered at prices that most people could afford, McLoughlin books were typically unsigned either by the author or by the illustrator. Some of the more recognizable books on the list, including editions of the work of Kate Greenaway, Walter Crane, Randolph Caldecott, and Lewis Carroll, were merely pirated editions, created without the author's or artist's consent or involvement. On some occasions, however, the house engaged illustrators whose names had the value of a selling point, the most notable among them being Thomas Nast.[80] Movable books, cloth books, tabletop theater books — all emerged from the company's helter-skelter Brooklyn plant, which, in its heyday during the last two decades of the nineteenth century, employed seventy-five artists. The house prospered until the death of John McLoughlin Jr. in 1907, after which the two sons who inherited the business allowed it to drift. Milton Bradley bought out the company in the 1920s and succeeded in reviving it for a time.[81]

To many Americans, McLoughlin Brothers stood for good value, technological wizardry, and a suitably indulgent attitude toward the young. Not everyone loved the books, however. Incensed over the inferior quality of the American printer's work and by the bitter fact that he stood to earn nothing from it, English illustrator Walter Crane wrote in 1877 to the editor of *Scribner's Monthly* entreating him to inform his readers of the injustice he had suffered. The editor obliged by publishing, in the September issue, both Crane's letter and a message of his own in which he urged a boycott of the McLoughlin pirated edition of Crane's *The Baby's Opera. St. Nicholas* weighed in on the matter in November, urging a boycott as well.[82] By the end of the century, a new set of critics would arrive on the scene, including some who would look down on McLoughlin Brothers books as garish rather than cheerful and bright, sing the praises of the Crane, Greenaway, and Caldecott originals, and yearn for the English masters' as yet undiscovered American peers — critics, what was more, who would need no prompting to say all these things in public.

In 1876, just over two decades after Boston, the city that prided itself on being the Athens of the New World, opened America's first free public library, the U.S. Commissioner of Education compiled the first detailed survey of public library service around the nation. The Commissioner's findings were impressive in the extreme: as of that centennial year, Americans enjoyed free access to 2,500 libraries and a total of 12 million books. Over the next twenty years the number of libraries would double and their collections triple in size, in a second great advance that preceded by just a few years the truly historic surge in library construction spurred by Andrew Carnegie's philanthropy.[83]

It was by no means obvious at the outset that public library service should include special provisions for work with children. The 1876 Commissioner's report made no reference to young people or their needs as readers or as potential library patrons. The omission was not an accident. Rather, it reflected the majority view among library professionals — isolated experiments in the East and Midwest to the contrary — that children were noisy nuisances better left to their own, their parents', or their teachers' devices.

In 1887 the first librarian to set aside a corner of her reading room for children, Minerva Sanders of Pawtucket, Rhode Island, was regarded warily as a radical by the local citizenry, in part for having opened her library's doors to children. Three years later, the Brookline, Massachusetts, public library made over its basement as the nation's first children's reading room. In 1893 Cleveland's librarians found a place for their city's young people in a corridor.[84] By then, the debate over the matter — as carried forward at the annual meetings of the American Library Association, an organization founded in Philadelphia during the nation's centennial year, and in the pages of the Association's journal Booklist — had tilted decisively in favor of ministering to the young, at least to those aged twelve and older. More and more of her colleagues now sided with Milwaukee's Lutie E. Stearns and Hartford's Caroline Hewins, who throughout the 1880s and for decades to come remained steadfast advocates of service to children.[85] In 1890, at a time when professionalism was increasingly taken to be synonymous with specialization, the Pratt Institute Library School in Brooklyn, New York, introduced the nation's first specialized course of study in children's librarianship, directed by Mary Wright Plummer. A decade later the options of aspirants widened with the opening in Pittsburgh of the Training School for Children's Librarians.[86] One 1896 Pratt graduate, Anne Carroll Moore, would achieve worldwide influence over the new profession from her high perch just across the East River as the New York Public Library's first director of work with children, starting in 1906.

Moore had come to Pratt from Limerick, Maine, where, as the youngest of seven children and the only daughter, she had developed the unusual goal for herself of becoming a lawyer like her father. Luther Moore, who admired his daughter's keen intellect, approved of the plan and had just taken the twenty-one-year-old in at his office to read law when the influenza epidemic of 1891–92 suddenly took his life, followed days later by that of the young woman's mother. In the aftermath of this family tragedy, Moore regrouped and with the help of a Brooklyn minister and family friend rethought her future. Whatever else she may have had in mind when she traveled south to enroll in the Pratt Institute library program, a life spent working with children had no part in it.

Moore entered Pratt with the idea of preparing for research and reference work. Halfway through the two-year course of study, however, the director of her program, Mary Wright Plummer, asked her to serve as the first head of the school's demonstration library for children. Cheerfully or not, Moore accepted the job and, once immersed in her new specialty, found that work with children could indeed be rewarding. She stayed on to run the demonstration library for a full ten years, during which time she also began to realize greater ambitions. In 1900 the young librarian from Maine traveled to Montreal to attend the American Library Association's annual convention and was elected president of the first roundtable of librarians specializing in work with children. It was her first national leadership role, and she found that the limelight suited her.[87]

During Moore's years at Pratt, a complex series of negotiations were under way in Manhattan aimed at consolidating the city's sprawling patchwork of private and neighborhood libraries into a unified public system. As planning proceeded, Moore's advice was sought about how service to children might best be organized for such a vast institution. The chance to preside over the New York Public Library's Office of Work with Children, when it was offered to her in 1906, came when she was fully prepared to meet the challenge. Intensely competitive and acutely aware of the unique opportunities that lay open to her as the person in charge of children's library service in the capital city of publishing, Moore dashed off a letter to her niece with the extraordinary news of her appointment: "It's the only place that I have ever felt I might be induced to consider if I could have right of way, for taken in a big way it would knock the spots out of any other like position in the country."[88]

From an analysis of the data compiled for the U.S. census of 1890, the superintendent of the census arrived at the dramatic conclusion that the

American frontier, long imagined by Americans as a place of limitless possibility, had become so populous as to have effectively passed out of existence.[89] The idea of the frontier, however, remained very real for readers of the mighty torrent of dime novels that Americans — primarily boys and men — purchased in great quantities at newsstands around the country. The colorful dime-novel genre had made its first appearance in 1860, and in the decades that followed an estimated 557 such books had featured the exploits of Buffalo Bill Cody alone. (To the less attentive reader, the number of Buffalo Bills would have seemed even greater, as the rascally publishers of pulp fiction often merely retitled an old book each time they reissued it at ten-year intervals.) In 1901, with the flamboyant frontiersman-turned-showman's popularity at its peak, the New York publishing house of Street and Smith introduced a weekly series of paperbacks, the "Buffalo Bill Stories," devoted entirely to his adventures.[90] Frontiersmen and pioneers may have "won" the real West on the fruited plains and lonesome prairies that stretched west of the Mississippi, but the West of legend was largely forged at the ink-spattered copy desks of Lower Manhattan.

Just a year after the census, in 1891, the boundaries of intellectual property underwent an equally radical redefinition with the final passage by the U.S. Senate, and the signing into law by President Benjamin Harrison, of the 1891 International Copyright Act, which for the first time permitted foreign authors to obtain copyright protection for their work in the United States. The measure, long opposed by Harper & Brothers (among others), whose deep pockets had allowed the company swiftly to purchase unbound sheets of important British books ahead of the competition and thus to be first out with a long list of bestsellers from abroad, served to level the competition in a way that favored smaller, less well capitalized houses. Because the bill bound American publishers to pay royalties to foreign authors, the measure also created a powerful incentive to lavish more attention on American writers, whose proximity to the centers of publishing suddenly seemed an advantage. Publishers reevaluated the operational structures of their houses in part with this new imperative in mind. In time, this led to the creation at several firms of specialized editorial departments, including some devoted entirely to juveniles.

The 1890s, a time of increasingly violent gyrations in the business cycle, saw dramatic reversals of fortune for some members of the publishing pantheon. Boston's Roberts Brothers did not long survive the loss of its visionary editor Thomas Niles Jr., who died in 1894 while traveling in Italy. Four years later, the house to which Niles had brought such literary distinction sold off its stock, printer's plates, and other assets to Little, Brown and Company, a house once known primarily for publishing law texts and for its elegant Boston bookshop. The purchase had a transformative effect, making Little, Brown the new — and sole — serious rival north of New York of Houghton Mifflin.[91]

Meanwhile, in New York the unthinkable was happening. Against the backdrop of the decade's financial panics and spiraling trail of commercial bankruptcies, several members of the far-flung second generation of Harpers opted to retire or else to liquidate their shares in the family-owned firm. Adding to the unaccustomed instability at the house was the overconfidence of those within the second-generation group who continued to run it. Greatly misjudging the house's strength, these younger managers overexpanded, with disastrous consequences. On *their* departure, the Harpers who remained woke up one day to find themselves seriously short of cash.[92]

In urgent need of a substantial loan, the publisher approached J. P. Morgan about the delicate matter, making contact through an associate who usually advised Morgan on art purchases. Under the terms of the loan negotiated in November 1896, Harper & Brothers for the first time ceased to be a family-owned enterprise and was transformed into a stock company. The publisher's troubles did not end there, however. Three years later, when it became apparent that the publisher lacked the funds even to meet its interest payments, Morgan ordered a total reorganization of the house under the supervision of S. S. McClure, a magazine publisher well known for muckraking and sensationalism, and on both counts an utterly distasteful choice to the Harpers themselves.[93] In 1899, as one of many consequences of the housecleaning, *Harper's Young People*, which had already been suffering from a decline in circulation, ceased publication.

That same year, *St. Nicholas*, with its circulation holding steady at seventy thousand, introduced a beguiling new department dedicated to publishing examples of its young readers' own writings, artwork, and puzzles. "The St. Nicholas League," as edited by Albert Bigelow Paine (later to become Mark Twain's official biographer), conducted a monthly competition for which readers submitted entries in response to an announced theme. Winners not only saw their work and names in print but also received gold or silver badges and on occasion even cash prizes. The extraordinary list of League contributors who grew up to become luminaries of American arts and letters would eventually include F. Scott Fitzgerald, Ring Lardner, Rachel Field, Cornelia Otis Skinner, E. B. White, Katharine S. White, Robert Benchley, Deems Taylor, Stephen Vincent Benét, Edmund Wilson, Bennett Cerf, Norman Bel Geddes, Henry Steele Commager, Elinor Wylie, Eudora Welty, and Rachel Carson. Here, as Anne Carroll Moore and other admiring critics would never tire of saying, was proof indeed of the impact for good made on young readers by the best that literature and art had to offer them. A valedictory letter published in the magazine's October 1910 issue expressed one eighteen-year-old's thanks to the editors for having done so much to nurture her talent:

> Camden, Maine
>
> Dear St. Nicholas: I am writing to thank you for my cash prize and to say good-bye, for "Friends" was my last contribution. I am going to buy with my five dollars a beautiful copy of "Browning," whom I admire so much that my prize will give me more pleasure in that form than in any other.
>
> Although I shall never write for the League again, I shall not allow myself to become a stranger to it. You have been a great help and a great encouragement to me, and I am sorry to grow up and leave you.
>
> Your loving graduate,
> Edna Vincent Millay[94]

In Chicago toward the end of 1897, a writer and an illustrator were introduced one day at the city's Press Club and became fast friends. The writer, L. Frank Baum, was then employed as the editor of *The Show Window*, a national trade magazine for retail shop and department store window dressers. The artist, William Wallace Denslow, was a well-known newspaper illustrator and graphic designer. The two men soon began to see themselves as collaborators. The first major book project they undertook together was an entertainment for children smartly titled *Father Goose: His Book*.

Thinking at first to self-publish *Father Goose* in partnership with Baum, Denslow went to see Chicago's George M. Hill, a printer and publisher for whom the illustrator had done some work, about preparing sample mockups of his layouts.[95] As a publisher, Hill was known for cheap editions of the Bible, reference works, Dickens, and other standard fiction and for its talented staff.[96] When George Hill surveyed the material Denslow had in hand, he proposed instead to publish it under his imprint in an arrangement, not uncommon at the time, that would substantially limit the publisher's risk. Hill would pay for the printing, binding, and distribution of the book, and Baum and Denslow would pay for everything else, including the cost of making printer's plates for the illustrations and of producing advertising posters. *Father Goose* was published in September 1899 and proved to be a notable success. By Christmas it had sold more than seventy-five thousand copies.[97]

Baum, who had suffered demoralizing business reversals in the past, was eager to capitalize on the triumph. He quickly produced more juvenile manuscripts, not necessarily intending them for illustration by Denslow, with whom he had quarreled about the credit due each man for the work now enjoying such success. Before these bad feelings soured their relationship, however, the collaborators had already joined forces again in the creation of a storybook fantasy that the author had been working on for years and that, once published, would immortalize both men — *The Wonderful Wizard of Oz*.

When Baum and Denslow brought the completed manuscript of their new project to Hill for his consideration, it still had an earlier title, *The Emerald City*. Hill rejected the title but took the book, provided the collaborators would once again shoulder the cost of the plates. Published in August 1900, *The Wonderful Wizard of Oz* received favorable reviews and sold well, though not as briskly in the early going as *Father Goose* had done. Anticipating a great windfall, Hill opened a New York office before the year was out to handle the surge in business. Once again, a publisher had misjudged his situation. In February 1902, the George M. Hill Company went into receivership and the firm's assets were put up for auction.[98]

In the aftermath of the Hill debacle, Baum began a new, though ultimately unsatisfactory, relationship with an Indianapolis-based publisher, Bowen-Merrill (later Bobbs-Merrill). In September 1902, the company purchased the plates for and secured the rights to *The Wonderful Wizard of Oz*. The following July, Bowen-Merrill reissued Baum and Denslow's masterpiece as *The New Wizard of Oz*. By then, a splashy theatrical production loosely based on the book was enjoying a resounding success, with triumphant runs in Chicago, New York, and elsewhere on a North American tour that continued for eight years.[99] The popularity of the play fed the sale of *The New Wizard of Oz*. In the end, however, it would seem to Baum that Bowen-Merrill had not done nearly enough to promote his work.

In Chicago, meanwhile, two of George M. Hill's key employees, general manager Frank Kennicott Reilly and sales manager Sumner C. Britton, formed a new publishing partnership and approached Baum about writing an Oz sequel to headline their list. In January 1904, the author signed a contract for *The Marvelous Land of Oz*, the first of many such agreements with the firm of Reilly & Britton (Reilly & Lee from 1919), where he finally felt he had found a publishing home. Later that year, Baum made his first appearance in *St. Nicholas* when the magazine serialized *Queen Zixi of Ix*, a fantasy set in two neighboring realms of Oz. The association with the prestigious monthly gave Baum, now a wealthy and much published man, perhaps the one thing he still lacked professionally: the approval of the field's literary establishment, and in particular that of the most respected arbiter and tastemaker of the day.

Mary Mapes Dodge, now in her midseventies, was ailing just then, but the magazine she had founded thirty-five years before continued to advance from strength to strength. Two years earlier, Jack London had sent Dodge a short story — in payment, he said, of the debt he owed her for publishing a magazine that had so moved him during a bad time in his early years that he had felt impelled after reading it one day to give up his delinquent life, pull himself together, and become a writer.[100]

Dodge had always enjoyed the company of younger people. When her first assistant editor, Frank Stockton, left the magazine to write full-time, she had hired as his replacement William Fayal Clarke, a bright fellow who was close in age to her own younger son. Clarke had soon become almost a member of the Dodge family, a friend to Jamie and Harry Dodge as well as to their mother. For a time he and the Dodges all lived in the same boardinghouse. He remained at *St. Nicholas* for fifty years. When Dodge died at her summer cottage at Onteora Park, an artists' colony in upstate New York, on August 21, 1905, it was Clarke who best summed up the meaning of her life: "It is given to few," he said, "to exercise so far-reaching an influence upon young minds, and thus upon the future of the nation. She left the world not only happier, but better than she found it."[101]

3

INNOCENCE LOST AND FOUND
The 1920s

Let the grown person brood over the stern realism of sordid surroundings, abnormal sex problems, hopeless effects of heredity and
environment on character and what not, the healthy boy and girl in-
stinctively rejects all this in favor of the story where industry is rewarded and love comes into its own.[1]

— EFFIE L. POWER, Director of Work with Children, Cleveland
Public Library, in *The Publishers' Weekly* (1923)

"TEN YEARS AGO," wrote Bertha E. Mahony, a Boston bookseller, editor,
and critic, in the summer of 1928, "it seemed that all the best books for boys
and girls had been published. While our hopes centered about Eliza Orne
White, Beulah Marie Dix and John Masefield, the height of our expectations lay with the coming of an attractive new edition of a favorite or classic
book, usually an importation for England, and with Scribner's illustrated
classics as one of the most important annual events. . . . We examined wist-
fully the beautiful German, Swedish, Bohemian and French picture books,
wondering why we could not make beautiful books like these in America."[2]

Mahony recalled that in 1918 she had answered this last question for
herself by pointing to the lack of specialized attention to children on the
part of America's publishers and the fact that none of the major houses
made books for boys and girls the "responsibility of *one* able person." In her
view, such a haphazard approach had been bound to result in the publication of a great many books of disappointing quality, the kinds of juvenile
fare — dime novels, Tom Swift series fiction, and the like — that periodically prompted some librarian or critic to worry aloud that American children read far too indiscriminately and far too much.[3]

Since then, with astonishing speed, a powerful new system for publishing and disseminating children's books had taken shape during the
years immediately following the First World War. For authors, artists, pub-

lishers, booksellers, librarians, parents, and children alike, the consequences of these new arrangements had already proved to be salutory. Elements of the system included a newly created profession — that of the juvenile editorial director — a prestigious new literary prize, a new forum for providing unprecedented review coverage, and, in the enterprising spirit of modern public relations, a new national "week" dedicated to children's books. Having triumphed on distant battlefields of their choosing, with American industry on the rise and Old World empires left in tatters by the hugely destructive war, Americans felt that their own cultural coming of age was at last at hand. In no quarter was this conviction more firmly held than among the growing ranks of professionals concerned with the education and general welfare of the nation's children.

By 1919, public library service to children was an established reality with which publishers were struggling to come to terms. A year earlier, *The Bookman*, the monthly magazine that introduced the bestseller list in America, engaged the New York Public Library's Anne Carroll Moore to contribute a regular column on children's books. Moore wasted little time in highlighting the need for a new set of publishing arrangements to ensure that the exploding demand for good children's books would be met. Several paragraphs into her second annual Christmas holiday roundup for that magazine, Moore complained, half in apology to her readers, of the difficulties she faced as a critic writing about a category of books that publishers often did not take seriously:

> I have been a long time in leading up to the books of 1919, for I have less to say about them than I had anticipated. It has been impossible to see some of the most promising titles, even in galleys. The publishers have endeavored to supply information where text has not been available, but I am impressed with the necessity of securing more adequate information at an earlier date.[4]

In later years Moore would become better known for her bluntness than for the tact more or less demonstrated here. Yet the moral of the tale was clear enough: if the unnamed publishers had only cared more about their children's books and committed the resources necessary to back up that concern properly, the *Bookman*'s readers might have been better served. Moore was not entirely alone in her plight. When the editor of the American Library Association's *Booklist*, May Massee, needed precious advance copies of children's books for review, she traveled all the way from Chicago to New York to secure them — on loan! — from their publishers.[5]

In the same *Bookman* piece, Moore recalled a telephone conversation she had had a year earlier with a Boston publisher. She had placed the long-distance call — always a grand gesture in those days — for the purpose of complimenting the editor for a picture book recently issued by the Atlantic Monthly Press. Excited by the excellence of the book, Moore, having stated her business to the underling at the other end of the line and been told that the editor was currently in Europe, had then ventured to ask whether she might hope for more such books from the firm in the future.

"Does *Jane, Joseph and John*," she asked, "mean that the Atlantic Monthly Press is going to undertake the publication of children's books?"

"Oh, no," had come the oddly cheerful reply, "nothing of the kind." Perhaps sensing Moore's disappointment, the underling added that the house would consider issuing another juvenile if an especially original one happened to present itself. For now, however, the press had no such "plans."[6]

That had been the state of things in 1918. The following year, the Atlantic Monthly Press announced its intention to publish, on a regular basis, "good modern books for children . . . of a high literary standard . . . [and with] special attention . . . given to their illustration, typography, [and] binding."[7] Moore received the news with greater pleasure than surprise.

Leaders of the publishing and library worlds, and of countless other areas of professional life, were just then taking up ambitious projects that the war had forced them to put in abeyance. A team of English scientists' long-deferred expedition to observe a total solar eclipse now yielded the first experimental confirmation of Albert Einstein's theory of relativity. Aviators made the first nonstop transatlantic flight from Newfoundland to Ireland and the first flight from London to Australia. And in the early months of 1919, Moore, then in her twelfth year at the helm of the children's services division of the world's largest public library system, found herself happily immersed in preparations for the nation's first "Children's Book Week" celebration, the proposal for which had first been put forward in 1915 at the annual meeting of the American Booksellers Association by the chief librarian of the Boy Scouts of America, Franklin K. Mathiews.

In 1915, when the scout leader had risen to address the hundreds of booksellers and publishers gathered in New York, he had spoken with passion about the responsibility they shared to advance the moral development of young people, as many as 90 percent of whom, in the late 1910s, were destined to enter the workforce with an eighth-grade education. Mathiews's goal for the special week he envisioned was to have it become an occasion for parents and community leaders to join forces to encourage the young not just to read but to read the "best books" available to them.[8]

The war had put the American publishing community onto a crisis footing, with all thoughts turned to economizing and to supporting the troops. But when booksellers gathered for their annual meeting in May 1919, they were once again eager to hear from Mathiews. In his new address to the members, Mathiews spoke more narrowly about the Boy Scouts' own objectives and about his rapidly growing organization's membership as a promising market for books. "In our efforts to meet the needs of the soldier for books," Mathiews reminded his audience, "we have been telling the public again and again that we had four million men under arms. Let me tell you that, between the ages of ten and sixteen, there are ten million boys, with their parents, who constitute for you a perpetual field for exploitation."[9] President Wilson, Mathiews announced, had just proclaimed June 8–14 to be "Boy Scout Week." The scout librarian urged booksellers to look upon this upcoming celebration as an opportunity to contribute to the nation's well-being while disposing of carloads of volumes on nature lore and crafts.

Ideas for special weeks of one kind or another were not in short supply at the booksellers' convention that spring. A proposal for a "Patriotic Book Week" was put forward (but not approved) as a way to stanch the rise of anarchy, Bolshevism, and other "subversive" influences that had put many Americans in a state of fear for their country's survival.[10] But it was Mathiews's original proposal that in the end captivated the group's imagination. With energetic support from the idealistic young coeditor of *The Publishers' Weekly*, Frederic G. Melcher, the booksellers agreed to pursue the Children's Book Week possibility. Soon afterward, the Girl Scouts of America expressed interest in cooperating with the effort, as did the New York Public Library's Anne Carroll Moore.

That summer, as returning troops marched triumphantly up Fifth Avenue past the New York Public Library lions, Mathiews, Melcher, and Moore met in room 105, Moore's fabled Forty-second Street inner sanctum, to map out plans for the upcoming Book Week festivities. The group agreed that it should serve primarily as a catalyst to the nation, offering inspiration, encouragement, and administrative support as needed to local and regional grass-roots efforts throughout the forty-eight states.

That first year Children's Book Week observances would take the form of Sunday sermons, mayoral addresses, school reading contests, newspaper editorials, and, at the New York Public Library's Central Children's Room, a memorable talk by Kate Douglas Wiggin, the beloved author of *Rebecca of Sunnybrook Farm* (1903). Wiggin had launched her writing career more than forty years earlier as a contributor to *St. Nicholas* magazine and had devoted much of the rest of her life to serving as one of the American kindergarten movement's leading proponents. *Rebecca*, a well-received film version of her most famous book starring Mary Pickford, had recently put Wiggin back in the limelight and helped to renew the optimism of librarians who had been wary about the fate of classic children's books in a nation whose young people seemed all too readily distracted by new forms of mass entertainment.

Unifying the crazy quilt of Book Week activities across the nation was the celebration's official poster featuring an image of two well-groomed, rosy-cheeked youngsters at home — a schoolboy in an Eton suit and his golden-tressed older sister — happily immersed together in stacks of books. Aimed at attracting the notice of the nation's book-buying mothers, the poster was instantly recognizable as the work of America's most celebrated woman illustrator, *Good Housekeeping* cover artist Jessie Willcox Smith. The slogan chosen as a rallying cry — "More Books in the Home!" — had obvious appeal for booksellers, but it also served the purposes of their librarian friends, who considered children's pride in book ownership a boon to their own mission of instilling in the young a sense of enfranchisement in the world of books. Home indeed seemed the ideal place to start, as the Brooklyn Public Library's Clara Whitehill Hunt remarked: "It is a woeful waste to leave to teacher and librarian — that is, to leave until the child, at seven or eight, learns to read — the influencing of the reading tastes of one's boys and girls."[11] Children who owned good books, the argument ran, would reread and treasure them and then turn to the library in search of others about which they might feel similarly. As Franklin S. Hoyt of the Education Department of Houghton Mifflin summed up the point in an address to the American Library Association convention that August: "Especially in the case of children does the value of stimulating individual ownership of books loom large as an important factor in establishing the reading habit. . . . Those children who early learn to love books and reading will certainly have books about them as they grow up."[12]

A week in mid-November was chosen for the celebration to coincide with the start of the holiday book-buying season, then the *only* time of year when most publishers and booksellers featured juveniles on their lists and display tables. For librarians who regarded themselves with pride as bulwarks against the crass commercialism of the age, the plan held risk, but the chance to spur public interest in good books seemed far to outweigh the risk.

Mathiews, Melcher, and Moore (their more whimsical colleagues now spoke of the "Three Ms" or "Three Musketeers") had invited a fourth person, Louise Seaman, to take part in the Book Week deliberations that summer. Moore and her colleagues had recently thrilled to the news of Seaman's appointment by the Macmillan Publishing Company, now the nation's largest publisher, as director of a new editorial department to be devoted entirely to children's books. Macmillan's Department of Books for Boys and Girls was the first of its kind anywhere in the world. Seaman, who had joined the company a year earlier to do promotional work, officially started in her new assignment on June 23, 1919. The meeting in room 105 was the very first she attended as Macmillan's juvenile editor.[13]

Recalling his decision to create the new specialty, Macmillan's president, George P. Brett, would write: "It had occurred to me [that children's] books would benefit more than any others, perhaps, from separate editorial supervision."[14] The editing and design of books in which art often played as large a role as text required special background and skills, of course. But Brett had not acted on that basis alone: "Also," he recalled, "I believed that children's books are perhaps more important than any other kind. Through these books one reaches young minds at the plastic age when moral character is being formed. Hence the importance of their selection and editing cannot be overestimated."[15]

To lead Macmillan's Department of Books for Boys and Girls, Brett had chosen an ambitious twenty-four-year-old staff member with a background in teaching. Born and raised in Flatbush, Brooklyn, New York, and the eldest of four children, Louise Seaman (from 1929, Louise Seaman

Bechtel) came to publishing with a Vassar degree and three years' class-room experience at Miss Glendinning's progressive day school in New Haven, Connecticut. While at Vassar, Seaman had pursued a rigorous course of study, taking challenging classes in literature, history, and economics. She had become passionate about journalism and had served, during her junior year, as the founding editor of the *Vassar Miscellany Weekly*, a campus newspaper. Seaman had also made the most of her time in New Haven, where she enrolled in graduate courses at Yale while teaching school. Although she came to enjoy her time at Miss Glendinning's, teaching did not hold much long-term appeal for her, and at the first opportunity she moved to New York in search of more satisfying work in advertising, in book publishing, or at a newspaper.

Seaman applied for a variety of jobs, including one in the royalty department of a publishing house and another at the advertising desk of the liberal daily *New York Post*, a position she was told might lead to a more "literary" assignment. Meanwhile, a Vassar classmate, Becky Lowrie, had established herself at Macmillan as a valued manuscript reader. It was in part on her say-so that Macmillan's president, George Brett, decided, at a time when few women held positions of any consequence in publishing, to take on Seaman as well.

At Macmillan the ebullient new arrival quickly made her mark by the elegant stunt of composing a "Sonnet to the Catalogue" inspired by the advertising copy she had been hired to churn out. During a brief stint in the Education Department, the division of the house from which trade books thought suitable for children occasionally emanated, she acquired useful experience and contacts that likewise helped set the stage for her selection for the new job.

Seaman's timing also had been good. American workplaces of all kinds were departmentalizing. With modern business becoming a specialist's domain, Brett's experiment conformed to the latest in corporate organizational theory. He had already applied the theory to other divisions of the house, with the goal "so to build up the business that each department, regarded almost as an independent kingdom, should rival and if possible outstrip firms that specialized in its particular field."[16] The creation of the Department of Books for Boys and Girls raised the status of work that in the past had been carried out haphazardly by many hands.

It was not by chance that Brett had chosen a woman for the job. In elevating Seaman, he had acted on the belief — gospel to many employers of the day — that women knew more than men about children and were thus better equipped for work that ministered to children's needs. At least some progressive-minded women were of the same opinion. Bertha Mahony, writing in *The Horn Book* in 1928, commented: "There seems every natural reason why women, properly qualified, should be particularly successful in the selection of children's books to publish and their publishing." Employing an analogy that she may have lived to regret, Mahony continued: "When it comes to deciding upon the format of a book, it is more like dressing a little girl than anything else. One chooses every detail of her wardrobe in harmony with herself. So with a book, its size, type, style of printing, cover material. . . . To this delightful task women would seem to bring particular interest and ability."[17] One can readily imagine Seaman bristling at the suggestion that her work had anything much to do with a game of dress-the-girl. Complicating life around the office for her was the fact that she looked much younger than her age, a circumstance that made it all the harder for her — her decisive and rather prickly manner notwithstanding — to command the unqualified respect of her clubby male colleagues. On offering Seaman her new assignment, Brett had not been able to resist letting her know that he had already tried a man in the job and had found him lacking in the requisite touch. This confidence, if Brett had meant to flatter her by it, backfired miserably. Far from feeling flattered, Seaman had been enraged by the condescending remark. But she had also kept her wits about her and maintained her perfect poise.[18] It was thus that in 1919 the editing of children's books joined school teaching, library service to children, and missionary work in the sisterhood of modern-day "mothering" professions.

During the 1920s, the identification of juvenile publishing with woman's work gave American women their first entrée into the upper reaches of a profession long regarded as an all-male domain, a gentleman's club for Scribners, Putnams, Holts, and Harpers. In 1891 Seaman's employer, George Platt Brett, had succeeded his father as head of the American division of the British house. From early on in his tenure, the younger man had shown a notable openness to the idea of entrusting women with responsible jobs.[19] Kate Stephens, who figures prominently in the house's correspondence files of the mid- to late 1890s, may well have been the first woman to be hired as an editor; her correspondence with Frank R.

Stockton and other authors shows that she edited a wide range of books, including juveniles, essay collections, and popular nonfiction aimed at a mixed readership of young and old.[20] At about the same time, the younger Brett also hired a Wellesley graduate named Jessie Reid as a sales assistant in the Chicago office. Reid was eventually transferred to New York to direct the firm's advertising office and educational publishing division.[21] At other houses, however, such as Knopf, a woman could hope to become an editor or manager only if she also happened to be the owner's wife.

The creation of Macmillan's Department of Books for Boys and Girls was immediately recognized within the industry as a historic initiative. Other trade houses were quick to follow suit by establishing juvenile departments of their own. All of this did little, however, to ensure that the new group of editors, much less their assistants, would be treated on equal terms with their colleagues. Deferring to their expertise in editorial matters, the heads of houses gave the women an enviable freedom to develop their departments as they thought best. But their status within the office and publishing industry hierarchy remained anomalous and always a bit up for grabs. Brett expected Seaman to continue to produce advertising copy for the house on top of all her new responsibilities. Enduring the patronizing slights of the men came to seem the price to be paid for the privilege of holding such a job. Like Seaman, several of the first women to enter the arena arrived with a Seven Sisters degree and the well-honed social skills that implied. A number of colleagues — including a former student at Miss Glendinning's, Eunice Blake, who became Seaman's assistant in 1927 — entered the field with the further advantage of prior experience in acting.[22]

Seaman inherited a backlist of 250 children's titles published by Macmillan's English and American branches. Thanks largely to the company's British patrimony, no house could boast a deeper reserve of bankable classics. Macmillan published the standard American editions of *Alice's Adventures in Wonderland;* Charles Kingsley's *Water Babies;* Mrs. Molesworth's *The Cuckoo Clock,* illustrated by Walter Crane; *The Little Lame Prince;* and a long shelf of gift editions illustrated by Arthur Rackham.

Seaman's first task was to organize and cull the list. Her 1920 inaugural catalog, which ran to eighty-eight pages, made it clear, however, that she did not intend simply to play caretaker. Printed in a tall, narrow, utilitarian trim to fit snugly in a salesman's coat pocket or mailing envelope, Catalog

Number 1 had been designed to make a big impression. A "gay, informal picture book about books," it artfully combined illustrations, promotional copy, and apt literary quotations to give a window onto the editor's publishing philosophy.[23]

Inspiring words by John Dewey — "Growing is not something which is completed in odd moments; it is a continuous leading into the future" — introduced the section devoted to school and college stories "for older boys and girls."[24] A few jaunty lines by E. V. Lucas heralded the list of "Alice" editions:

> The Grownup and the Prillilgirl
> Were walking hand in hand;
> They were as pleased as Punch to be
> Alone in Wonderland:
> "If there were other books like his,"
> They said, "It would be grand."

Satisfied with Seaman's progress during her first year, Brett showed his appreciation by giving his editor a raise. Writing from France in the summer of 1920, her best friend from college, and her future author, Elizabeth Coatsworth, congratulated her on having been granted a "decenter wage." But mindful that the dream job had come with considerable baggage, Coatsworth counseled the classmate she affectionately called "Bob-o-links": "You're both brave and strong, but don't be too eager at the bit."[25]

Meanwhile, a validation of sorts of Seaman's efforts made its welcome appearance several blocks to the north of Macmillan's Greenwich Village offices. The newly opened Children's Book Shop, at 2 East Thirty-first Street just off Fifth Avenue, marked the first commercial venture of its owner, Marian Cutter. Eager to establish herself by winning powerful friends for her enterprise, Cutter, a former Bridgeport librarian, invited Seaman to lunch at the Civic Club.[26] An amateur psychologist of sorts, she took keen delight in sizing up her customers (the very first of whom had pulled up to the shop in a yellow limousine) and in practicing the art of "camouflag[ing] under a leisurely manner a hundred associated ideas . . . [that often made her] feel a bit like a human pencil undergoing the process of sharpening."[27] She and Seaman must have had much to talk about. Cutter's shop, which had a fireplace and an area for the display of original picture-book art, joined Boston's Bookshop for Boys and Girls as a new

kind of specialty bookstore aimed at satisfying the growing demand for juveniles.[28] Before long, Washington, D.C., would have its counterpart, in the
Cinderella Book Shop, as would Los Angeles and San Francisco.[29]

"Soon," Brett recalled, Seaman "was ready to discuss her own programs of publishing with me. These I was personally concerned with, and
extra critical about, since I had had three children of my own and remembered a great deal about their reading tastes."[30] Advice from above, however
well intentioned or wise, might easily have become intrusive, even destructive, and Seaman would not be the last editor in her position to receive
pointers from a male superior who equated expertise in her field with the
mere fact of having a few children of his own at home. Brett, however, genuinely trusted Seaman's judgment and remained as good as his word when
it came to vouchsafing her independence concerning important matters.
Not quite three years into her editorship, she let friends know that the work
still agreed with her. As the peripatetic Coatsworth, writing from North Africa, reported to her in May 1922: "I think you'd like to know that Mary
Mallon [a Vassar classmate] said that of all the people she knew you seemed
most right in your life — for which you might thank heaven and yourself."[31]

By then, Seaman had her third list in hand and could take pride in the
knowledge that a growing audience of colleagues and admirers stood ready
to praise and promote whatever she might choose to publish. It had also
become clear to her that she wished to publish for two readerships: the existing market comprising the children of the better-educated classes and
(more remarkably) the less educated and financially less well off majority
of Americans, whom the publishers of children's trade books, until then,
had largely chosen to ignore. By her later estimate, a mere "10 per cent [of
America's children and adults] would find books under whatever conditions, 10 per cent would never read." She called the remaining 80 percent "hopeful spots . . . worth trying to help find books."[32] In 1923, with
the latter group already in mind, Seaman introduced the Little Library as
an affordable series of lesser-known children's classics. The unprepossessing, pocket-sized, illustrated volumes were priced for the budget-conscious
parent at a dollar each. By the early 1930s, the series had grown to thirty-
two volumes.[33] A few years after the successful launch of the Little Library,
the chance to create a companion series for younger children arose when
Charles Stringer of the Jersey City Printing Company proposed to work

with Seaman on a series of lower-priced picture books that would show-case promising new printing techniques developed by his shop.[34] At fifty cents each, the Happy Hour Books, which made their debut in 1927, cost less than one-third of the standard price of the picture books that an espe-cially fortunate child might hope to receive at Christmastime — elegantly printed, oversized, clothbound volumes illustrated by the French artist Maurice Boutet de Monvel or the Americans Jessie Willcox Smith, Maxfield Parrish, or E. Boyd Smith. Seaman proudly published many such grand books herself, but she remained mindful of the fact that their purchase was an option primarily reserved for the privileged few. It would require con-siderable ingenuity on the illustrator's part, as well as the printer's, to pro-duce fifty-cent picture books that the librarian-critics would not dismiss as "cheap." In Berta and Elmer Hader, an ambitious young husband-and-wife team who had made their initial reputations as contributors to the chil-dren's departments of *Good Housekeeping,* the *Christian Science Monitor,* and *McCall's,* Seaman had found precisely the illustrators the situation called for.

With her customary flair for publicity, Seaman had organized a na-tionwide talent search for the Happy Hour Books, inviting illustrators to submit samples of their work that showed they could work within the stringent guidelines laid down by Charles Stringer. The Haders won with a dummy for *The Ugly Duckling* that, Seaman later recalled, "stood out above all the rest . . . [for being] so simple, so childish, so funny; the colors were so clear and bright; the ducks were well drawn; the layout artistic without be-ing 'arty.'" A practiced public speaker who frequently took to the road to tout her list, Seaman noted with satisfaction, "I have only to throw one of these *Ugly Duckling* pictures on the screen from a lantern slide, to get a rip-ple of appreciation, chuckles all over the audience."[35] When it came time to introduce the first Happy Hours Books in Macmillan's 1927 catalog, the ed-itor, in an effort to disarm the critics, declared: "Although they are both small and cheap, we feel that each volume is an achievement in book-making."[36]

Seaman's reformist zeal for making children's books more affordable conformed to broader cultural trends. With the dramatic expansion during the 1920s of the nation's educated urban middle class, more Americans than ever before recognized reading as an essential means to the char-acteristically American end of self-improvement. The message was clear enough even for those still leading a hardscrabble existence who, like Selina DeJong, the working-class heroine of Edna Ferber's *So Big* (1924), dreamed of sending their children to college. Ferber might well imagine such a mother of the 1920s admonishing herself: "'I couldn't have [an education] myself, and always regretted it. Now I want my boy (or girl) to have a good education that'll fit 'em for the battle of life. This is an age of specialization, let me tell you.'"[37] Americans like those depicted in Ferber's bestseller helped make a resounding success of the Modern Library's sixty-cent "world's best classics," launched by Boni & Liveright in 1917 and later taken over by Random House. They also lifted H. G. Wells's massive *Outline of History* (1920) and Will Durant's *The Story of Philosophy* (1926) to bestseller status, subscribed (starting in 1922) to the *Reader's Digest*, and joined the Book-of-the-Month Club, founded the following year.[38]

Seaman rapidly staked out a public role for herself as well. Starting with a piece she coauthored in the September 11, 1920, issue of *The Publishers' Weekly*, she produced a steady stream of articles for newspapers, popular magazines, and professional journals. Barnstorming the nation, she addressed ladies' clubs, parent-teacher associations, librarians' and writers' groups, and civic organizations at every possible opportunity, setting a personal record during Book Week in November 1925 by delivering nine speeches in Harrisburg, Pennsylvania, in a single day. Three years earlier, as "The Story Lady," she became the first person to read to children regularly over the radio. Her weekly half-hour broadcast, which ran for two years over Newark's station WJZ, was begun at a time when radio was in its infancy and station owners had more airtime than shows to fill it with and were unsure how to make money from the medium. While keen to perform a public service, Seaman gamely kept her company's best interests in mind as well: the books and authors she highlighted on the show always came from Macmillan. Contests of all sorts were a favorite promotional device of the fun-loving, newly public relations–savvy 1920s. Picking up on the trend, "The Story Lady" blithely invited listeners to write in to her. Those who submitted the "most interesting" letters were rewarded by return mail with copies of Macmillan books.[39]

In January 1920, from an office in New York's Greenwich Village, a new juvenile magazine first appeared with the aim of addressing the needs of one of the nation's largest underserved groups of young people, its African

American children. *The Brownies' Book*, as the monthly was called, had begun life as an annual special issue of *The Crisis*, the magazine of the National Association for the Advancement of Colored People, founded in 1910 by educator and author W. E. B. Du Bois. *The Crisis* enjoyed a healthy circulation of over 100,000 when Du Bois joined with his business manager, Augustus Granville Dill, and literary editor, Jessie Redmon Fauset, to launch the new periodical that proudly hailed its readers as the "Children of the Sun" and stated its intention to give them a "thing of Joy and Beauty, dealing in Happiness, Laughter, and Emulation."[40]

The war's end had filled Du Bois with a profound sense of hope. As he wrote in *The Crisis* for December 1918: "The nightmare is over. The world awakes. The long horrible years of dreadful night are passed."[41] The year 1919, however, proved to be a particularly violent one at home. As historian Katharine Capshaw Smith has noted: "Angered by black resistance to discriminatory labor and housing practices, white mobs rioted in Chicago, Washington, D.C., Elaine, Arkansas, and at least twenty other towns and cities across the nation, killing hundreds of African Americans."[42] As Du Bois published one vivid account after another of the terrible events of 1919 in *The Crisis*, it concerned him that children exposed to such disturbing material might react by growing embittered or by developing a hatred of white people rather than striving to cultivate their talents for the benefit of their people. *The Brownies' Book* became Du Bois's vehicle for expressing his high hopes for and to the younger generation.

In some respects, the new magazine resembled nothing so much as the most admired of American children's monthlies, *St. Nicholas*. It was printed on good-quality paper and aspired to excellence in fiction and poetry, photography and graphics. It featured humor, nature lore, adventure, folk stories, biographical sketches, and heroic tales from history. Like *St. Nicholas*, it set out to interest a broad readership ranging in age from six to sixteen.

But Du Bois had no wish to circulate a magazine for young people that, for the sake of maintaining a positive outlook, pretended that racial harmony already flourished in a country where not only segregation but also racially motivated violence remained rampant. When it came to portraying, or even simply referring to, people of color, *St. Nicholas* itself often did no better than to perpetuate the worst impulses and ingrained prejudices of white American culture.[43] While he deemed the entertainment of young readers a worthy goal, Du Bois had additional aims in mind for readers of *The Brownies' Book:* "(a) To make colored children realize that being 'colored' is a normal beautiful thing. (b) To make them familiar with the history and achievements of the Negro race. (c) To make them know that other colored children have grown into beautiful, useful and famous persons. (d) To teach them delicately a code of honor and action in their relations with white children."[44]

The Brownies' Book, which gave Langston Hughes his first publication and featured many more of the writers associated with the Harlem Renaissance, somehow failed to catch hold. By the publisher's own estimate, there were two million "children of the sun" living in America in the early 1920s, and twenty thousand subscriptions — or one for every one hundred of them — represented the minimum number of subscriptions needed to keep the magazine afloat. At its peak, *The Brownies' Book*'s subscription list never reached five thousand.[45] Evidently, Du Bois had miscalculated. Perhaps for those young people whose parents read *The Crisis* each month, it was that magazine that they too felt impelled to read.

In the early pre-sweeps days of radio, the giveaway contest, like the one Louise Seaman set up for awarding Macmillan books to skilled letter writers, was considered the most reliable gauge of the size of a radio program's audience. Prizes of a grander sort were just then being established to lift American cultural pride. Bankrolled by a legacy from one of the nation's great newspaper fortunes, the Pulitzer Prizes were launched at Columbia University in 1917 as annual awards for excellence in journalism, fiction, poetry, musical composition, history, and other cultural pursuits. Frederic G. Melcher, a young bookseller with New England roots who was soon to become coeditor of *The Publishers' Weekly*, thought it regrettable, though hardly surprising, that children's literature had not been included as a category. By 1918, Melcher, in addition to the editorial post that had brought him to New York, had also assumed an industry-wide role as secretary of the American Booksellers Association. Three years later, representing yet another organization in which he stood at the forefront, the National Association of Book Publishers, he attended his first American Library Association convention, in Swampscott, Massachusetts, and took part in a program promoting Children's Book Week. Melcher had been casting about for fresh ways to build on the early successes of the weeklong celebration.

On the day after his scheduled talk, he asked for the chance to address the children's librarians a second time in order to present an idea that had occurred to him overnight. Speaking in the largest available meeting hall — the cavernous, steel-raftered garage belonging to Swampscott's New Ocean House Hotel — Melcher told a rapt crowd that the time had come for children's literature to have its own Pulitzer Prize as a vehicle for encouraging — and publicizing — high achievement in writing for the young, and that librarians, having no commercial stake in the fate of any particular book, constituted "the jury which could give value" to it. "Now," he said with a flourish, was "the time to inaugurate it."[46] With his previous night's reading, Charles Knight's *Shadows of Old Booksellers*, fresh in mind, Melcher proposed a name for the new award: the John Newbery Medal, in commemoration of the eighteenth-century English bookseller-printer-publisher who had popularized the notion that children's books should offer their readers delight and instruction in equal measure. The response to his call to action was wildly enthusiastic. The American Library Association's Executive Committee would have the final say in the matter, but the feeling in the room was that history had just been made — that this was the genesis of the world's first literary prize for a children's book.[47] When the Executive Committee met later that same day, they voted to authorize the awarding of the first Newbery Medal at the next year's conference in Detroit.

Librarians seeking relief that June afternoon from the sweltering heat gathered on the hotel's oceanfront veranda and immediately fell into speculating about what book might have received the Newbery Medal in the current year had there already been a Newbery Medal to win. As the Brooklyn Public Library's Clara Whitehill Hunt recalled, Hugh Lofting's *The Story of Doctor Dolittle* swept the field, leaving those who played the game that afternoon feeling pleasantly satisfied that they and their colleagues did indeed know a superior book for boys and girls when they saw one.[48] The scene on the veranda seemed proof in and of itself that Melcher's plan was likely to accomplish his goal of "securing the interest" of three or four hundred of the nation's librarians "in the whole process of creating books for children, producing them, and bringing them to the children."[49] The librarians returned home exhilarated. "Never was there such a conference as this," *Library Journal* reported breathlessly afterward.[50]

Melcher had not had enough time to work out the criteria of eligibility for the award. He was still unsure, for example, whether any book published in the United States in a given year should be considered regardless of the book's, or the author's, country of origin. It would be another year (nearly six months *after* the awarding of the first medal) before the terms of the prize were formally set, limiting consideration to books written by citizens or residents of the United States.[51] Defining the award in this way amounted to an idealistic gamble, as it was not at all clear just then that America had, or might soon have, enough children's authors of merit to conjure with the likes of Kenneth Grahame, E. Nesbit, and Walter de la Mare. Bemoaning this situation in *The Bookman* in 1919, Anne Carroll Moore had been blunt: "We may as well face frankly at the outset this reluctance to write for children on the part of competent [American] writers. . . . The present indications are that the number of outstanding books for children and young people will be smaller than for 1918."[52] One reason for establishing the new award was, of course, to give more (and it was hoped better) writers another brass ring to strive for. It remained to be seen, however, whether the Newbery Medal would do as much to spur American creativity in the field as it would to honor the literature's British beginnings.

In his September 1921 letter to Clara Whitehill Hunt, Melcher offered to raise the money needed to pay for the design and striking of the medal (in the end he paid for it all himself) and to stand ready to advise the librarians, provided that he could remain out of the limelight. Melcher feared that if his role in the matter were to become better known, his longtime association with the business side of the book world might somehow tarnish the medal's credibility. As to the mechanism for selecting the winners, he was adamant that the librarians should work the procedure out among themselves. A committee was selected to write guidelines for the new award, with Hunt as chair. She and her colleagues decided that any librarian engaged in at least part-time work with children — a 1921 survey found that 472 librarians met this standard — should be eligible to nominate a book. "To give everyone this chance," Hunt noted, echoing Melcher's sentiments, "will create interest and induce good feeling." Hunt, however, had no desire to leave the final decision to majority rule: "It is most important that the final judges of the award be a few of the people of recognized high standards and experience. If a majority vote of all so-called children's librarians determine the award it is entirely possible for a mediocre book to get the medal."[53]

The outcome of the hastily organized first-round ballot for the 1922

Newbery all but mooted Hunt's concern. When the 212 nominating votes cast were tallied on March 8, 1922, it was found that 163 votes had gone to a single book — Dr. Hendrik Willem van Loon's *The Story of Mankind* (Boni & Liveright). So overwhelming had been the vote — the first runner-up, *The Great Quest* by Charles Boardman Hawes (Little, Brown), received 22 votes — that Hunt and her inner circle felt no need to deliberate further.

By then, *The Story of Mankind* was selling briskly to adult readers grateful for a less cumbersome alternative to H. G. Wells's *Outline of History*, and it was enjoying strong sales as a gift book for youngsters as well. The librarians' choice had been more in the nature of an endorsement than a discovery. Under different circumstances, the prior appearance of the Wells bestseller might have doomed the lesser-known van Loon's book as an ill-timed also-ran, at least in the adult trade. But Hendrik van Loon's brash, man-about-town publisher, Horace Liveright, was famously adept at public relations, and when reviewers turned to *The Story of Mankind*, they did so primed with the knowledge that the Dutch-born American historian had been plumbing the depths for his own tome long before Wells's book had made its way across the Atlantic.[54] Critics who might have been expected to question the seriousness of a history book calibrated to appeal, in part, to school-aged readers instead cheered the signal success with which van Loon had managed to craft a complex yet surprisingly accessible work for a dual readership — a volume gaily decorated, what was more, with the author's own witty hieroglyphs. The *New York Times Book Review* reported, in the second of two glowing critiques of the book, that while *The Story of Mankind* was "intended primarily for children," it nonetheless seemed likely that "many people" would "prefer Professor van Loon's work [to Wells's for its] . . . succinct, and yet comprehensive, manner of telling the story."[55]

As to the Newbery, van Loon had done what he could to campaign for the honor. The historian and raconteur who, only a few years earlier, had lost a teaching job at Cornell for cavalierly speaking out in defense of the Kaiser's Germany had shown better judgment in his dealings with librarians. As Anne Carroll Moore's biographer would recall, the author had brought his "*Story of Mankind* . . . to Room 105 and to the Central Children's Room literally chapter by chapter, as he wrote it, the manuscript, rolled up like wallpaper, bulging the pockets of his ample overcoat."[56] Moore's verdict, published for all to see in *The Bookman* — "the most invigorating and, I venture to predict, the most influential children's book for many years to come" — could not have been more enthusiastic, or more helpful to his cause.[57]

At the ALA annual meeting in Detroit that June, Frederic Melcher took to the podium to introduce Clara Whitehill Hunt at a festive afternoon ceremony attended by an overflow crowd of hundreds of librarians. First Hunt formally accepted the gift of the Newbery Medal from Melcher. Then the librarian from Brooklyn presented the first medal to van Loon. Finally, the author made a "very appreciative speech" before being whisked away for a round of press photographs and a newsreel recording.[58]

For those in attendance, it was a moment to be savored, the culmination of more than twenty years of unprecedented nationwide community service, much of it unsung. As Melcher had foreseen, the librarians embraced the medal as much as a validation of their own efforts as an endorsement of the work of an author in their midst. Acknowledging Melcher's signal contribution to the day's events, Hunt had declared from the podium: "We feel strong and proud because you . . . are putting into our hands a weapon, one of the most potent of our times — publicity of the best kind."[59]

Melcher was happy to accept that much public praise, but for the rest of his long, distinguished career he remained as good as his word and safeguarded his creation from even the appearance of its having been contrived as a commercially motivated "book campaign or publishers' idea."[60] Privately, he regarded the Newbery Medal as one of his proudest achievements, and in editorials in *The Publishers' Weekly* and in speeches delivered throughout the country, he continued for the next four decades to affirm his belief in the pivotal importance of children's books to the cultural vibrancy and political well-being of a modern, democratic society. Melcher shared the librarians' hope that the Newbery would also serve as an incentive to the nation's finest writers to turn their hand to writing for the younger generation. Taking the measure of the events in Detroit, he reminded the publishing world at large: "We should not forget that by creating a greater audience, we are also creating literature itself, for the creator of literature is drawn out by the appreciation of literature, the author needs the audience as much as the audience needs the author."[61]

Not everyone shared unreservedly in the euphoria of the moment. Louise Seaman could not help greeting the news of the voting with mixed emotions on learning that while Macmillan titles had garnered three of the five runner-up distinctions (later called "Newbery Honors"), the publisher had failed on that historic occasion to take home the big prize. The pill was made the more bitter by the fact that as of 1921 Macmillan's adult trade division had published twice as many Pulitzer winners as any other house.[62] Was the vaunted new medal to be decided by a popularity contest after all, or as a ratification of Miss Moore's predilections? Among the Macmillan Newbery runners-up had been Padraic Colum, the Irish expatriate novelist, playwright, and storyteller whom Seaman had inherited from an editor in Macmillan's schoolbook division. Colum, to be sure, had long since won the admiration of the New York Public Library staff and — equally hopeful portent — had seen his books praised by Moore in *The Bookman*. Other critics, however, had been cooler to his work, suggesting that Colum's retellings of mythology, folklore, and the epics of classical literature were a bit "special" for "the average American child." Colum would become the first of the writers to win a succession of Newbery Honors — three for him — but not the medal itself. In an oddly defiant essay published in Macmillan's fall 1930 catalog, Louise Seaman Bechtel addressed Colum's detractors head on, declaring him to be "the most important author on the Macmillan list of children's books."[63]

Later in 1922, Louise Seaman's work received an endorsement more powerful, in its way, than a Newbery when Doubleday, Page and Company announced its plans to open a juvenile department patterned on Macmillan's. With this dramatic development, Seaman ceased to be a publishing anomaly and became a publishing pioneer. She welcomed May Massee, her counterpart at the younger firm, as the second member of a professional sisterhood in the making. Massee was unmarried and not quite forty when she arrived from Chicago to begin her new career.[64]

Massee had no experience in book publishing, yet she came well qualified to her new job. Born in Chicago and raised in Milwaukee, she had grown up in a house full of books, the second of four children of transplanted northeasterners "of English Puritan descent" — good stock to those who cared. As a child, she had read *The Youth's Companion* and *St. Nicholas* and had been encouraged by her parents to write and draw. She had attended normal school, taught public school in Milwaukee for one unrewarding year, and then enrolled in the Wisconsin Library School with no thought, apparently, of ever again working with children. While on the staff of the Buffalo, New York, public library, however, Massee had drawn the assignment of manager of the children's room and, quickly hitting her stride, had transformed her new domain into what her author and friend Elizabeth Gray Vining later described as a "center of joy and interest."[65]

Massee earned a reputation as a creative, energetic, and ambitious specialist in library work with children. As to her ambition, a colleague, half out of cattiness and half in admiration, once remarked of the soft-spoken but steely-nerved woman that Massee never attended a national library convention without coming home with a new job. In 1913 she won the plum editorship of the American Library Association's review publication, *Booklist*. From her new office in Chicago, she emerged as a national presence. Wielding the librarian-critic's moral authority with a characteristically light but emphatic touch, Massee wrote quotable copy and made regular trips to Boston and New York not only to scavenge for review materials but also to meet with publishers. It was on one such lightning trip that Massee and Louise Seaman had first met, in Macmillan's offices. Macmillan publisher Brett had authorized Seaman, who was the younger of the two women by more than ten years, to greet the visiting editor in her role as house "publicity slave." As she recalled of the encounter years later, she had anticipated her meeting with the editor of famously strong views with some trepidation. Massee, however, had immediately put her at her ease and shown that she "grasped quickly the implications of my little new side job of editing the Macmillan children's books. I think it was on the same day that both she and Mr. Brett told me that I ought to discard the old English term 'juvenile.'"[66] At Doubleday and later at Viking, Massee would insist that the term "junior books," rather than "juveniles," be applied to the books she published.

As her knowledge of the publishing world grew, so did Massee's appetite for playing a more active role in it. When her Chicago friend the poet Carl Sandburg expressed an interest in writing a series of "tales with American fooling in them" for his own three daughters, Massee did more than simply encourage the effort.[67] In advance of the publication of *Rootabaga Stories* (Harcourt, Brace, 1922), she also aided Sandburg in his pursuit of magazine serialization, acting in effect as his agent. In the small but high-minded children's book world of the 1920s, no one would have read a hint of impropriety into this intimate involvement of an influential critic in an author's commercial fortunes. Participation by an esteemed poet like Sandburg raised the literary standard of books for boys and girls; that was what mattered. Promising his friend one-quarter of the proceeds from her efforts, Sandburg predicted that at the very least they would "have some fun in the handling of 'em [the stories]."[68] It went without saying that Massee would do so. As Frederic Melcher would later say of her: "Few people . . . moved more comfortably in the overlapping territories of publishing, book-selling and library work than Miss Massee."[69]

Massee's career took a fateful turn when, over lunch one day at Chicago's Blackstone Hotel, a visitor from New York, Sam Everett of Doubleday, Page, outlined his firm's plans for a children's book department to rival Macmillan's. Everett gamely asked Massee to suggest a suitable manager for the new enterprise and listened as she gamely named several candidates. Then he offered her the job, and Massee, completing the ritual dance, accepted.[70]

Massee's new responsibilities brought her to New York, where she took up residence in Greenwich Village, the great city's literary heartbeat and hub. She arrived in the year that Scribner published F. Scott Fitzgerald's *Tales of the Jazz Age*, Harcourt, Brace published Sinclair Lewis's *Babbitt*, and Eugene O'Neill's play *The Hairy Ape* (brought out in book form by Boni & Liveright) premiered at the Provincetown Playhouse, just a few blocks from her apartment. In what free time she had, Massee gorged herself on the city's theater scene and art museums and galleries, gathering impressions, honing her editorial eye and ear, and making the acquaintance of booksellers, artists, writers, and others who before long would be drawn into the web of her all-consuming life's work.

Measured in terms of sales, the publishing and printing industry during the 1920s was New York City's second-most important business, surpassed only by ladies' garment manufacture.[71] The city was rapidly becoming a world center for all forms of mass communication and entertainment, from advertising and radio to theater and the popular song. For those who held the levers of culture, it was hard not to feel a bit euphoric. "Culture follows money," Fitzgerald tartly reminded his Anglophile friend Edmund Wilson, who professed to prefer London to the city where he plied the journalist's trade at *The New Republic* and *Vanity Fair*. In 1931, as New York and the nation sank ever deeper into depression, a stunned and chastened Fitzgerald would recall, as though from a long-ago dream, the once-invincible rationale for "jazz age" rapture and jubilation: "We were the most powerful nation. Who could tell us what was fashionable and what was fun?"[72] Who, for that matter, could tell American librarians or their editor sisters what made for literary distinction in a book written for children? As Louise Seaman Bechtel would remark: "The happiest years for children's bookmaking came after the First World War, with the influx of books and also of artists from Europe. Then bookmaking stepped away from its tradition. It was a time of sufficient prosperity for American publishers and public to support experimental bookmaking."[73]

As Doubleday's editor, May Massee reverse-commuted each day between her apartment in the city and the firm's offices on suburban Long Island. Founded in New York in 1900, Doubleday, Page had built its reputation on a list of popular "back to nature" titles for armchair hunters, conservationists, and explorers. In 1910 the publisher had taken its own advice and moved its headquarters from the stone-and-steel metropolis to an elaborately landscaped campus of low-slung white brick structures in Garden City, New York. Laying the cornerstone for the spacious new offices, former president Theodore Roosevelt had conferred his blessing on "everything that gives more chance for fresh air to the men, the women, and above all, to the children."[74] For Massee, the unconventional arrangement held in store another invaluable benefit. The Garden City move had allowed Doubleday the luxury of operating its printing plant alongside its editorial offices. The firm's head of production, Walter Gillies, was a master color printer. Gillies eagerly agreed to tutor Massee as she began to explore new ways of raising the aesthetic level of illustrated books for young readers.

Massee, like Macmillan's Louise Seaman Bechtel, championed the ideal of the "book beautiful" — the picture book as an aesthetically uplifting work of art expressly designed for bedtime and story hour sharing. High on both editors' agendas was the creation of new picture books to rival those of the English masters — Randolph Caldecott, Kate Greenaway, Walter Crane, Beatrix Potter, and L. Leslie Brooke — who dominated the American market, along with a small number of picture books imported from France and elsewhere. Now postwar national pride spurred the new American editors to cultivate homegrown talent. Massee took every opportunity to involve the people around her in the noble effort.

"They must have color, beauty, better illustrations, type, paper, but most of all real color," she had been telling a friend over dinner at a restaurant of the picture books she envisioned publishing when, as though on cue, a man seated at a nearby table had piped up to declare: "I want to make a picture book like that, an ABC book for Bedelia Jane. And I want to make all the wood blocks."

"All right," Massee reportedly told the stranger, who turned out to be none other than the well-known poster artist and muralist C. B. (Charles Buckle) Falls, "we'll make one."[75] In the fall of 1923, Falls's *ABC Book* became the first book Massee published at Doubleday.

During the war years, Falls had won the admiration of his peers for the extraordinary flamboyance (for an American) of his approach to color and design. Yet it was in all likelihood precisely because of the unmistakably European flavor of his work that he had failed to win many lucrative commercial accounts. A writer taking the measure of Falls's achievement at midcareer in 1923 lamented this "instance of a genius not having [had] the opportunity" he so plainly deserved. "And so it is that the man who might become the foremost poster artist of America is allowed to remain a sort of handy man of art, expending his energy in a dozen different directions. This is a tragedy."[76]

Working closely with both Falls and Doubleday production manager Gillies, Massee served her apprenticeship in bookmaking during the creation of the *ABC Book*. As she later recalled:

> The type was all set in galleys and Mr. Gillies came into my office, apologized for taking my time, and brought a cardboard frame exactly the page size of the book-to-be, margins correctly measured, properly proportioned. The galleys were exactly cut and pasted together and rolled so that the first page would come off first. He had signatures, with numbered pages, cut exactly to the size of the book. He showed me how to unroll the galleys, measure off the pages, and plan so that the dummy when finished would be a perfect model of the book-to-be.[77]

The *ABC Book* garnered praise not only as an outstanding example of illustration and design but also as striking proof that American artists were indeed capable of rising to the level of their English peers and elders. Writing in *The Bookman*, Anne Carroll Moore hailed Falls's book as "an excellent rallying point," adding that "we may well feel proud that an ABC book so admirable in design and in color printing has been produced on this side of the Atlantic."[78] Not entirely glossed over in the critical euphoria was the fact that Falls's book did not quite measure up to the British picture book it most closely resembled, Sir William Nicholson's *The Square Book of Animals* (text by Arthur Waugh, 1899). For Massee, who went on to publish the American edition of Nicholson's picture-book masterpiece, *Clever Bill* (1926), Falls's alphabet book was a better than good beginning.[79]

The critical success of the *ABC Book* had been more than enough, in any case, to justify the artist's hopes for better financial times ahead. The wished-for lift failed to materialize, however. And in March 1924, with just under six thousand copies of the first printing of ten thousand having sold during the Christmas season, Massee found herself in the classic position of an editor having to console the author of a much-praised book over its disappointing sale:

"Dear Charles," she began, striking the frank but motherly tone that was to become one of her editorial hallmarks,

> . . . I want to say that I think you have been simply wonderful about the whole thing, and you know how sorry I am that you are disappointed; but I still have faith, which is founded on solid grounds, that in the end you will be very glad you did it. You made the most distinguished children's book of the year and if reputation means anything to you, the name you made with that book is a big one.[80]

Massee's growing mastery of book production and design, and of the economics of publishing, strengthened her reputation both within and beyond the house, and that reputation, in turn, afforded her wider scope for experimentation. Against the backdrop of such disturbing recent events and developments as the Palmer Raids, the resurgence (not only in the South) of the Ku Klux Klan, and America's rejection of membership in the League of Nations, Massee resolutely committed Doubleday to children's book publishing with an internationalist dimension. The national climate was anything but receptive to a sympathetic embrace of the foreign, especially with respect to cultures other than those of northern Europe. With encouragement from her librarian friends, however, many of whom knew firsthand the immense value of library collections planned in part with the needs of immigrant children in mind, Massee persevered. For younger children, she published the graphically vigorous work of Maud and Miska Petersham, a husband-and-wife illustration team several of whose early books — most notably *The Poppy Seed Cakes*, written by Margery Clark, and their own *Miki* — drew inspiration from Miska Petersham's childhood in Hungary. (Maud hailed from Vermont.) The Petershams' books, like the best of Falls's work, were widely praised as touchstones of the new American picture book.

For older children, Massee published novels of everyday life in Russia, Africa, Persia, and Latin America. Elizabeth Cleveland Miller wrote ardently about the people and culture of Albania. Massee encouraged her to do so, telling the author of *The Children of the Mountain Eagle* (1927): "No child who reads these stories and is sensitive enough to be touched by them could ever again be as provincial as most American youngsters are."[81]

In the years that followed, May Massee and Louise Seaman would continue to regard each other as friendly rivals. When they talked, it was most often to exchange information about such practical matters as "costs and profits, estimates and processes."[82] They shared an occasional author (the quixotic Rachel Field, who cavalierly called for sealed bids for the publishing rights to her historical fantasy *Hitty: Her First Hundred Years*, an eventual Newbery winner for Macmillan) and a handful of illustrators (Elizabeth MacKinstry, Boris Artzybasheff, Kurt Wiese, the Petershams). And the two women would later have occasion to console each other when, after years of brilliant accomplishment, each in turn found herself shut out of a cherished job.

In the meantime, they vied for the chance to publish the field's best writers and artists. Charles Finger's *Tales from Silver Lands*, a story collection on Doubleday's 1924 list that introduced young readers to the folklore of South America's indigenous cultures, took the Newbery Medal for the following year, winning out over two runners-up that included one published by Macmillan. For Massee, it was to be the first of a great many such backstage victories. Seaman would have to wait to experience the same satisfaction until 1929, when Eric P. Kelly won the medal for his historical novel set in medieval eastern Europe, *The Trumpeter of Krakow*.

The picture book was Massee's forte, whereas the strength of Seaman's early lists was more broadly based. Cornelia Meigs, a Bryn Mawr writing instructor, was another of the seasoned authors who, like Padraic Colum, had first published children's books through Macmillan's Education Department. Meigs wrote "with distinction from an unusual background," noted Anne Carroll Moore, conferring her blessing on a rising star with one Newbery Honor already in her quiver.[83] Meigs's historical novels would become a staple of the Macmillan list.

An adventurous traveler and accomplished equestrian, Seaman enjoyed the hunt aspect of her work. She prided herself both on her ability to gauge the potential in an unformed book idea and on the finesse with which she harnessed the talents of her far-flung and ever-widening circle of authors. "There's a girl named Frye — Tall, dark, polite," Seaman wrote Elizabeth Coatsworth not long after becoming editor. "Came in for illustrating and submitted a scheme for an anthology which was interesting but impossible."[84]

Writing with the practiced nonchalance of a *New Yorker* "Talk of the Town" reporter, Seaman confided to the readers of her department's 1928 catalog: "We asked [Baroness Dombrowski] to try her hand at true stories of some of the jungle animals she knows so well, and exciting chapters [of *Boga the Elephant*] began to arrive."[85] In the same catalog, she recalled that the Scandinavian artist Hedwig Collin had discussed plans with her for his new folktale collection *East of the Sun and West of the Moon* both "in New York and Paris." Seaman seems to have decided early on that Coatsworth herself, her self-dramatizing best friend at Vassar, should also become a Macmillan author. Within months of Seaman's promotion to editor, Coatsworth, a poet with many irons in the fire, was already flirting with the idea, by turns resisting Seaman's gentle overtures and soliciting her guidance about a genre into which it might not otherwise have occurred to her to venture: "If you want to know what sort of children's book to write for me," Seaman advised her in an otherwise chatty letter about their travels and friends, "go talk to Miss Mahony at the Bookshop for Boys and Girls at the Women's Industrial Union on Boylston Street." Not one to conceal her impatience, least of all from someone about whom she cared so much, Seaman pointedly added, "When are you going to start it?"[86]

When Coatsworth finally did start, it was with an Isadora Duncan–like grand gesture, improvising an amusing fantasy for the editor while she herself posed for her portrait in an artist's studio. The story begun that day grew into Coatsworth's well-received first children's fantasy, *The Cat and the Captain* (1927).

Coatsworth had long before learned to heed her college friend's clear-eyed advice and to value her blunt brand of encouragement. Seaman could always be counted on to say something helpful that was also true: "*I think* the important thing," she would write Coatsworth one day when the latter woman was in deep despair over her literary prospects, "is that you keep on writing: that you have the same interest and eagerness, and that you try new fields — You *can* write plays and stories and essays, and your mind mustn't get fixed in any groove (not that I imagine it ever will). And you're not too *ancient* you know, and you ought to be *pretty* happy, it seems to me, at the actual work you have done, whatever anyone thinks of it."[87] The publication by Macmillan of *The Cat and the Captain* marked the casual start of Coatsworth's sixty-year-long career as a writer for children.

Anne Carroll Moore, self-styled critical voice in the wilderness, continued her *Bookman* column through 1924, when the editors of the soon-to-be-launched Sunday *Books* magazine section of the *New York Herald-Tribune* approached her about conducting a children's feature for them. The new magazine was sure to reach a far wider audience, a prospect that appealed to Moore, but she was not prepared to take the chance unless it could be done on her own terms. After laying down several stiff requirements that she thought might well quash the deal (no advertising to appear on the page; books reviewed not to be limited to current ones; Moore to write a lead review and assign the remainder of the space as she pleased, selecting suitable illustrations as well), Moore accepted the offer and began a six-year run that further broadened the already considerable scope of her influence. Moore called her new column "The Three Owls," the wise birds symbolizing the importance of the writer, the illustrator, and the critic (this third owl to be depicted with ruffled feathers) to the field. Might there not also have been a fourth owl for the editor, or a fifth for the librarian? "Feeding the owls" became her shorthand for the weekly ritual of composing a lead article and effectively editing a magazine within a magazine made up of contributions commissioned by Moore from the many authors, illustrators, publishers, librarians, and booksellers of her acquaintance.[88]

Other critical voices were just then being heard or were about to be heard. In October 1924, Boston's Bookshop for Boys and Girls sent out to a small list of national subscribers volume 1, number 1, of *The Horn Book* magazine, an eighteen-page illustrated quarterly devoted to children's literature and topics of related interest, and as such the first magazine of its kind in the world.

The bookstore that inspired *The Horn Book* was itself a pioneering venture, a project of Boston's progressive Women's Educational and Industrial Union.[89] *The Horn Book* had begun modestly as a store newsletter. Its editor was the shop's smart, entrepreneurial founder, Bertha E. Mahony. As assistant secretary at the Union during the prewar years, Mahony had acquired valuable public relations experience, and by 1915 — she was then thirty-three — she was ready to make her mark. It was then that the idea for a children's bookstore came to her. In the early going Mahony demonstrated both seriousness of purpose and political savvy by asking the Boston Public Library's chief children's librarian, Alice M. Jordan, to instruct her in the literature she intended to sell. Mahony then set out to win the confidence of other powerful library and publishing figures, including Anne Carroll Moore, Clara Whitehill Hunt, Hartford's Caroline M. Hewins, and *The Publishers' Weekly's* Frederic Melcher.

The Bookshop for Boys and Girls opened its doors on October 9, 1916, in second-best quarters one flight up on mainline Boylston Street. Six years later, as *The Horn Book's* inaugural issue went to press, the store remained in business — hardly a negligible achievement — and occupied a larger, better space, with an expanded stock that now included "Books on Many Subjects for Grown-Ups," as the new sign announced. Mahony had added adult titles to her shelves as much for philosophical reasons as for practical ones. As she later wrote: "People want to take care of their own book requirements while shopping for their children, but more important still, the children themselves like the presence of grown-up books in a nearby space."[90] Mahony would not be the last member of the small group who helped to define children's books as a specialty and also questioned the wisdom of isolating the literature from the literary mainstream.

The first *Horn Book* retained much of the idiosyncratic flavor of the store itself. Fall books were recommended in breezily annotated, age-appropriate lists, not in the stately, full-dress reviews of the journal's later years. A few favored titles received more extended treatment. An article about English paper toy theaters aimed frankly at disposing of the store's newly received shipment of the novelty imports. In her buoyant first editorial, Mahony teased subscribers with the promise that publication *might* proceed quarterly: "Lest this horn-blowing become tiresome to you or to us," she vowed, "we shall publish the Hornbook [*sic*] only when we have something of real interest to say; not oftener than four times a year."[91]

An article by the editor's old mentor and friend, Alice M. Jordan, read like a benediction. Mahony, the librarian suggested, had indeed learned her lessons well, her bookshop having long since earned a "worthy place among the recognized Boston institutions." No less, Jordan declared, might now be expected of *The Horn Book*.[92] Anne Carroll Moore and Macmillan's Louise Seaman soon gave their own enthusiastic endorsements, the latter ordering eight subscriptions for friends, while reaching deep into her old copywriter's stash of superlatives to pronounce herself "thrilled, excited, entranced, inspired."[93]

A strong hint that *The Horn Book* might take an open-minded view of books came in the Boston bookstore's response to one of the 1920s' more entertaining publishing phenomena. *The Crossword Puzzle Book*, the first (and for some while the only) publication of the upstart New York publishing house of Simon & Schuster, had not only introduced a new type of word game to Americans earlier that year but also touched off a sort of national crossword puzzle mania. The shop had at first stocked just a few copies of the novelty book (which came with its own "free" Venus pencil). "Very soon," however, as Mahony reported, "the supply gave out and the book was reordered. Its fame spread fast (faster than 'The Plastic Age' or 'So Big')" — two other bestsellers that year. "Would it amuse a friend in the hospital?" Customers came to the store with all sorts of special uses for the novelty book in mind.

Then one day in strode a lively mother whose tongue-in-cheek complaint Mahony recalled with an air of professional triumph:

> "You have no idea," [the mother] said, "what an expense the Crossword Puzzle Book is to us. We have had to get an atlas and a new dictionary, and now I want a good reference book on Greek mythology. It is terrible what deep water we get into, and the children are developing very inquiring minds."

Might it be that *The Crossword Puzzle Book* was also a children's book? Evidently the answer was yes. Clearly unbothered by highbrow critics' dismissal of the book as a nonbook and a fad, Mahony took delight at the extent to which it stimulated children's self-directed learning — a key goal of the progressive education movement.[94]

Although it might thus have seemed logical to assume that *The Horn Book* would champion progressive tendencies within children's literature, any such conclusion would prove to be more than a bit premature.

By the 1920s, librarians had installed themselves as the nation's authorities in the children's book field. Against the backdrop of a publishing industry that historically had treated juveniles as formula literature, whether of the moralizing or sensationalist variety, librarians had, sometimes alone, steadfastly made the case for literary standards. Then, just as their authority had come to seem beyond question, the librarians found themselves — or rather, their point of view — under attack. To some within the group's leadership, it seemed inconceivable that this should be so.

In their path-finding child development studies, William James and John Dewey had raised fundamental questions about the nature of children's intellectual and emotional growth. Implicit in their work was the suggestion that children's books, as distinct from other types of literature, might be understood, evaluated, and perhaps even written and illustrated within a developmental framework. During the 1910s and 1920s, Lucy Sprague Mitchell — the founder of New York's Bureau of Educational Experiments, a friend of Dewey, and a student of James — became the first researcher to explore this possibility in earnest. Working in a crowded honeycomb of offices at 69 Bank Street, a tumbledown Greenwich Village building that had once served as a yeast manufacturer's warehouse, Mitchell exhorted her research staff to "rise" to the heady challenge of crafting fresh approaches to learning along newly discovered developmental principles. Among the Bureau's efforts were pioneering studies aimed at determining the changing significance for children, from year to year, of the spoken and written word, both in and out of books.[95]

The Bureau also set out to train a new generation of teachers for the nation's progressive schools. With a nursery school of its own on the premises, the Bureau was able to offer its researchers and teacher trainees ample opportunity, in the best Dewey-James empirical way, to learn directly from children as well as from each other. Mitchell and her colleagues rarely spent time with the children without notebooks in hand to record the "language data" to be gleaned from the children's "spontaneous utterances." As the stacks of notebooks accumulated, Mitchell sifted the data for developmental patterns and considered the implications of her findings for children's literature at every age level.

Mitchell herself had longed since childhood to write imaginatively. In 1921, in the next phase of her lifelong exploration of the relevance of language development to children's literature, she published *Here and Now Story Book*, a collection of age-graded stories and poems intended as the prototype for a developmentally sound new literature for preschoolers. In her introduction, Mitchell dismissed the very assumptions upon which librarians so confidently based their recommendations of the year's best books.

One basic disagreement centered on the appropriateness of folk and fairy tales for children under the age of seven. For their part, the librarians regarded such traditional tales as touchstone works beside which modern writing for children should be judged. Traditional stories like those retold by the Grimms and Andrew Lang and the literary fairy tales of Hans Christian Andersen and others were the very centerpiece of the New York Public Library's fabled story hours. At Anne Carroll Moore's instructions, every children's room in the New York Public Library system celebrated Andersen's birthday and all staff members, as part of their training, were required to demonstrate competence in storytelling. Librarians considered the "timeless tales" an essential part of every child's cultural inheritance and an antidote to the materialism — and literal-mindedness — of the age.

Writing in *The Bookman* in 1919, Moore had laid down the law for those who would consider tampering with the quasi-sacred texts:

> Let me state here that I am ready to take as strong a stand as need be on the matter of rewriting and reediting the classics for children. Hands off Mother Goose and the old fairy and folk tales, the poetry, and the great traditions of the race, unless the work is signed and there is fair evidence of competent literary treatment.[96]

Imagine, then, the reaction of Moore and her colleagues on coming upon the following passage in Lucy Sprague Mitchell's introductory essay: "To the child the familiar *is* the interesting. . . . It is only the blind idea of the adult that finds the familiar uninteresting. The attempt to amuse children by presenting them with the strange, the bizarre, the unreal, is the unhappy result of this adult blindness. . . . [As] for brutal tales like Red Riding-Hood or for sentimental ones like Cinderella I find no place in any child's world."[97] Mitchell laced her explanatory text with many such high explosives, making no effort to conceal her contempt for what she took to be the librarians' sentimental misjudgments. In attempting to write for children, she freely acknowledged, she might well not have succeeded in producing literature herself. But she *had* at least "tried to ignore what I, as an adult, like" in determining what children at distinctively different stages in their development might find most meaningful.[98] Virginia Haviland of the Library of Congress would later recall the "controversy raging over 'milk bottles' versus 'Grimm' for the pre-school child."[99]

It would be Louise Seaman who most successfully bridged the two largely antagonistic worlds of the librarians and progressive educators. In 1925 she published Anne Carroll Moore's essay collection, *The Three Owls: A Book About Children's Books, Their Authors, Artists, and Critics*. Four years later she published Mitchell's innovative geography book for young readers, *North America: The Land They Live in for the Children Who Live There*. In later years Louise Seaman Bechtel would serve on *The Horn Book*'s editorial board alongside Moore while also participating in Mitchell's children's book workshop, the Bank Street Writers Laboratory.

In 1925 Seaman thrilled her admirers when she published one of the children's gift books of the decade: a lavish, oversized, English-language edition of *The Adventures of Pinocchio* featuring the illustrations of the dynamic Italian modernist comics artist Attilio Mussino. The Mussino *Pinocchio* had made its first appearance in Italy in 1911 to great fanfare and was the sort of special foreign-language volume that the New York Public Library's Central Children's Room took special pride in placing out on open shelves for the public. Seaman's account of her decision to publish the costly American edition hints at the broad scope of the library's influence as both a horizon-expanding resource and an inspiration for publishers. "One day," she wrote years later,

> roaming in the [Central] Children's Room . . . I found a little gang of boys, aged anywhere from six to twelve, their heads clustered low over a book I couldn't see. I asked [the librarian] what was the absorbing book. "Oh, that's our big Italian Pinocchio." "My goodness," said I, "are they reading Italian?" "Oh no, those are not Italian boys. They're just crazy about the pictures." So I waited to see it myself. I felt the way the boys did. So I started negotiating with Bemporad, the Italian publishers, to print that book in Italy with an English translation.[100]

The story of the project's painfully slow and bureaucracy-mired germination was one that Seaman never tired of repeating.[101] Negotiations dragged on for years before arrangements could be finalized. When it was finally published in the fall of 1925, Macmillan offered its Mussino *Pinocchio* at a princely five dollars per copy. As expensive as this was by contemporary standards, the book soon went back to press for a second printing, and then for a third.

The decade of the 1920s unfolded like the early scenes of a play as, one by one, new editors took their places onstage, joining their counterparts from other houses and from the allied realms of librarianship, bookselling, and criticism. In 1925 E. P. Dutton chose Marion Fiery, a member of Anne Carroll Moore's New York Public Library staff, to direct its fledgling juvenile department. The following year, Harper & Brothers hired Virginia Kirkus, a former journalist and teacher, to head its new Department of Books for Boys and Girls. In 1927 Little, Brown engaged author and critic Lucile Gulliver as its founding department head. The American branch of the venerable Oxford University Press established its children's book department in 1928, although evidently only after much soul-searching. As the first Oxford juvenile editor, Winifred Howard, later recalled: "Some thought it beneath the dignity of Oxford University Press to deal in anything so trivial as children's books! Also they said it would spoil the sale of our other books."[102] That same year, Alfred A. Knopf formed its first children's list and became the first publisher to hire away a juvenile editor (Marion Fiery) from another firm (Dutton). And in 1928 Elisabeth Bevier became the first full-time children's book editor at Harcourt, Brace, working closely with company cofounder and director Ellen Knowles Harcourt. When a new publishing house, Coward-McCann, opened for business that same year, its organizational structure provided for a children's book department from the start, and former journalist Ernestine Evans stood at the helm. Few publishing managers by then would have questioned the wisdom of making such arrangements. In a small way, the editors were even becoming celebrities. In 1925 Doubleday became the first house to trade on its juvenile editor's reputation by stressing in advertising that its books had all been carefully selected and prepared by the well-known authority May Massee.

In 1919, 433 new books for children were published in the United States. A decade later the annual output had more than doubled to 931. The dramatic expansion of the field appeared even more impressive when measured in terms of the total number of books printed. Viewed that way, growth had been nearly threefold, from 12 million books in 1919 to more than 31 million less than a decade later.[103]

Still, librarians and the new group of editorial directors led by Louise Seaman Bechtel and May Massee could not take heart from all of the decade's most telling statistics. In 1926 the American Library Association, conducting a survey of children's reading preferences, questioned thirty-six thousand children in thirty-four cities about their favorite books. Fully 98 percent of those responding named a book by a single author, Edward Stratemeyer, the author-entrepreneur responsible for the lion's share of the formulaic, sometimes sensationalistic series books — the Rover Boys, Tom Swift, Hardy Boys, and other series — that librarians reviled as subliterary.[104] Stratemeyer's books were in all likelihood the ones that Franklin K. Mathiews had had in his sights in 1913 when he addressed the American Booksellers Association convention in New York on the theme of "Books as Merchandise or Something More," or the following year when, in an essay in *Outlook* magazine provocatively titled "Blowing Out the Boy's Brains," he condemned contemporary series fiction as destructive to young people's mental and physical well-being.[105] In 1906 Anne Carroll Moore had made it one of her first orders of business as the New York Public Library's director of work with children to purge the library's collection of series fiction — books she considered trash.

By 1920, Edward Stratemeyer had emerged as the undisputed heir to the sensationalist tradition of juvenile fiction that had been perfected and profited from in past generations by Alcott nemesis William T. Adams and by Adams's protégé, Horatio Alger Jr. The son of a prosperous, German-born, New Jersey tobacco shop owner, Stratemeyer proudly pointed to the two American heroes whose fabled careers he strove religiously to emulate, Henry Ford and Alger, the latter of whom he had once worked for. When Alger died in 1899, it was Stratemeyer of all the many writers in his stable who had been given the honor of finishing the master's last several manuscripts (without, as went without saying, the expectation of credit as coauthor). After striking out Alger-like on his own as an author of fiction series aimed (primarily) at red-blooded preteen and teenage boys, Stratemeyer, like his mentor before him, found, by around 1910, that the demand for his stories was such that he would need a small army of freelancers to maintain the frantic pace of series publication.[106] Turning to newspapermen for their proven ability to pound out acceptable copy on a stiff deadline, Stratemeyer formed a syndicate, or "fiction factory," to produce the steady stream of manuscripts called for in his contracts with publishers, for whom he now effectively served as a packager. In 1918 the flourishing Stratemeyer Syndicate left East Orange, New Jersey, for good to move into offices in Manhattan.

Stratemeyer writers, whose individual identities were concealed behind the pen name associated with the series they wrote for, worked from a detailed outline and within a strict set of guidelines supplied by their employer. One seasoned Stratemeyer freelancer referred to the work as "laying the pipes" because so many elements had to be made to fit with some finesse within the prescribed number of pages: the obligatory recapitulation of the previous installment, the basic story line, the cliffhanger chapter endings, and, perhaps most importantly, the well-placed teasers advertising installments yet to come.[107] The whole system worked brilliantly and on a massive scale, with sales of the fifty-cent books measured in the millions. *Fortune* magazine would write of the man behind this controversial publishing phenomenon: "As oil had its Rockefeller, literature had its Stratemeyer."[108] The analogy was apt enough, and it summed up everything that librarians most feared about the intrusion of commercial values into the culture of childhood.

Then, in 1928, a new American picture book by a largely unknown author-artist appeared that would serve as a standard-bearer and rallying point for librarians and their allies. *Millions of Cats* was the work of a young midwestern woman named Wanda Gág, who had come to New York to make her reputation as a printmaker. Gág's lithographs had just begun to be noticed by critics at exhibitions at New York's Weyhe Gallery and in the pages of *New Masses*. It was at a show at the Weyhe that Ernestine Evans of Coward-McCann had first become aware of the artist whose career she would do so much to shape: "All I knew about Wanda Gág," Evans later recalled, "were her pictures. . . . They were beautiful, and very simple, and full of the wonder of simple things. . . . I had always wanted to reach out and touch them. It was this that made me sure that if the new publishing house of Coward-McCann was going to enlist America's artists in the service of children, Wanda should head the list."[109] When Evans contacted her about the possibility of their working together on a picture book, Gág in her diary at first belittled the project as something to be executed rapidly, for the money. She soon would decide otherwise and conclude that she had stumbled onto a major new pathway for her artistry. Many another graphic artist of her generation — including some inspired directly by Gág's example — would come to the same conclusion. The following year, when librarians awarded *Millions of Cats* a Newbery Honor, they chose to recognize the book's distinction while apparently not feeling quite right about giving the literature prize to a picture book. It may well have been then that the idea for a companion award for illustration was born, although it would be another decade before the Caldecott Medal became a reality, through another gift from Frederic Melcher.

The legacy of disillusionment forged by World War I left all but unbridgeable the gap between the nation's leading literary writers and its authors for children. If in 1904–1905 educated men on both sides of the Atlantic wept openly at James Barrie's stage play about a puckish lad who equated the attainment of adulthood with death itself, the next generation preferred a harder-edged, defiantly "smart" and unsentimental outlook. The Lost Boys had grown up to become the Lost Generation. Raymond Chandler spoke of the "terrible honesty" required of writers in his time.[110] The feverish embrace by Ernest Hemingway, D. H. Lawrence, F. Scott Fitzgerald, Edna St. Vincent Millay, and others of erotic experience as ripe material for literary fiction and verse served further to isolate the literature destined for children, as did the modernist impulse to reject most traditional narrative procedures. Freud and his American followers likewise did their best to give Victorian sentiment a bad name, sending novelists — and their adult readers — scrambling to dissociate themselves from the books they themselves had read and loved as boys and girls. The critic Edmund Wilson even put down Algonquin Round Table wit to the acting out of some such compensatory need: "They all came from the suburbs and 'provinces,' and a sort of tone was set — mainly by Benchley, I think — deriving from a provincial upbringing of people who had been taught a certain kind of gentility, who had played the same games and who had read the same children's books — all of which they were now able to mock from a level of New York sophistication." Wilson concluded: "I found this rather tiresome, since they never seemed to be able to get above it."[111] Be that as it may, Dorothy Parker's famously tetchy review of A. A. Milne's *The House at Pooh Corner* (1928) — "Tonstant Weader Fwowed up" — summed up the smart set's acute uneasiness with a type of popular children's book that, not altogether fairly, had become emblematic to many of the status of children's literature as a precious backwater.[112]

The Horn Book devoted its August 1928 issue to a celebration of the first ten years of Louise Seaman's pioneering work in publishing. It was in her introduction to this special number — the first of its kind undertaken by the magazine — that Bertha Mahony remarked on the rueful sense that she and her colleagues had had only a decade earlier that "all the best books for boys and girls had [already] been published" and that nothing new was likely to be written for children in their lifetime to stand beside the classics of old.[113] The issue carried tributes to Seaman by Cornelia Meigs and other Macmillan authors, a poem by Elizabeth Coatsworth, a reminiscence by publisher George P. Brett, and a piece by Seaman herself — ever the promoter of her list — about Berta and Elmer Hader, the illustrators whose first fifty-cent Happy Hour picture books had appeared the previous fall. Interspersed among the homages were pages reproduced in full from the fall 1928 Macmillan catalog, not as paid advertisements but rather as illustrations. Mahony concluded the issue with a note highlighting the many "other children's book departments" that publishers had founded over the last decade in the wake of Macmillan's example. This last gesture proved insufficient to forestall the predictable complaints from the editors of rival houses, who questioned the propriety of a review journal's giving one publisher quite so much free publicity.[114] Although a culture of genteel comportment continued to define the children's book publishing world for decades to come, this awkward episode may be said to have marked the end of the fledgling enterprise's era of good feelings.

A year earlier, writing in the *Atlantic Monthly*, Seaman had offered parents and the literary elite a glimpse into her editorial philosophy. Strikingly, though hardly in favor of undoing the work of the last decade, she made a point of enumerating the adverse consequences of having established children's book publishing as a separate domain. The negative aspects of the new system, Seaman argued, were "numerous: . . . overproduction by the publisher and the author; overinvestment by the bookseller relative to the ability of his staff; overexaggeration of the 'appeal to the child,'" among others.[115] Implicit in the critique was a challenge to the pivotal role played by librarian-critics in the new system. Then, however, as if to mollify her librarian friends with a counterbalancing criticism aimed at her colleagues in the progressive education camp, Seaman declared that child psychology, being as yet an inexact science, could not possibly be counted on to provide reliable standards by which to judge, let alone to write or illustrate, a good children's book. "Our only honest recourse," Seaman concluded, "is to try to treat each new person as a person, the hardest effort in the world, even in adult relations. To foster it, we try to offer it nothing which it will have to outgrow.

"Therefore, no 'childish' books."[116]

All in all, it was a remarkable exercise in editorial self-scrutiny, a measured attempt to discredit the cant on both sides of the contemporary argument about good books for children in a troubled time of smashed illusions. Most of all, Seaman's essay was a plea for an open-minded consideration by the members of her sisterhood of fresh ideas and influences from the larger world. What happened next, however, was, if anything, a turn in the opposite direction as, secret garden fashion, the children's book world detached itself ever further from the cultural mainstream.

4

SISTERS IN CRISIS AND IN CONFLICT: The 1930s

[The Depression] reached children's books a little slower than others, but when it hit them, it hit harder.[1]

— LOUISE SEAMAN BECHTEL, in *The Horn Book* (1936)

We are not dangerously new! . . . Neither [are we] dangerously traditional!

— LUCY SPRAGUE MITCHELL, foreword to *Another Here and Now Story Book* (1937)

THE GREAT DEPRESSION had dramatic consequences for the publishers of children's books. As budget-strapped librarians cut book purchases (by 1932, by an average of 25 percent), publishers responded by sharply curtailing their lists. In 1931, 873 new children's books and 245 new editions of older titles were published in the United States. Three years later the numbers had dropped to 466 new titles and 135 new editions.[2] Publishers had other troubling statistics to reckon with. In 1930, with a view to economizing, the organizers of Children's Book Week reissued Jessie Willcox Smith's original 1919 poster rather than commission a new design. But a slogan — "More Books in the Home" — that in 1919 had sounded like eminently reasonable advice for parents now rang hollow amid growing evidence that as millions of Americans struggled to make ends meet they were choosing to have fewer children and that the national birthrate had entered a period of historic decline.[3] With fewer children "in the home," retail demand for children's books seemed certain to decline alongside institutional demand, hurting publishers' prospects still more.

Faced with these implacable realities, publishers had their commitment to specialized editorial work for children sorely put to the test. Alfred A. Knopf was among the first houses to economize by closing down its fledgling juvenile department altogether. Coward-McCann merged its operation with that of Longmans, Green. At Harper, six years after Virginia Kirkus joined the firm to launch its Department of Books for Boys and Girls, work on children's books was reassigned to the editorial trade division. Kirkus left the house where she had discovered Laura Ingalls Wilder to found the review service that still bears her name.[4]

At some firms, ambivalence prevailed in the form of shortsighted cost-saving measures taken hastily and just as abruptly rescinded. Following Kirkus's departure, Harper named the department head's former secretary, Louise Raymond, to oversee the list, presumably at a substantially lower salary than Kirkus's. Within a year's time, however, Raymond, a Bryn Mawr graduate and the wife of a prominent lawyer, had not only proven her own worth but had also made the case for the Department of Books for Boys and Girls and won appointment as its second director.[5]

As though to underscore the mood of discouragement as the decade began, the Book Week celebration for 1930 coincided with an agricultural promotional event called Apple Week. A national produce shippers' group had arranged for boxloads of apples to be distributed to hundreds of unemployed Americans to sell on street corners during the week of November 22. The scheme generated such favorable publicity that it was soon adopted year-round, furnishing modest employment for some and giving the nation one of its most bittersweet Depression-era memories. At year's end, *The Publishers' Weekly* asked its readers, only half in jest, whether members of their own industry had not missed an important opportunity by failing to organize a plan to sell children's books on street corners at Christmastime.[6]

Fear that the major accomplishments of the past decade might now unravel prompted a vigorous response from some key elements of the book world. In January 1930, the *New York Times Book Review* inaugurated a fortnightly page devoted to books for young readers, under the editorship of Anne Thaxton Eaton, librarian of the Lincoln School, Teachers College.[7] The *Times* feature, later made weekly, aimed at competing with the rival *Herald-Tribune*'s comparable coverage in *Books*, begun six years earlier under the forceful direction of Anne Carroll Moore. In December 1933, Katharine S. White, the fiction editor at *The New Yorker* (and the wife of one of that magazine's principal writers, E. B. White), contributed the first in a long series of annual (and later semiannual) "Children's Shelf" reports to that magazine on the current state of literature for young people. White's critical acumen and sophisticated sense of fun combined with her lack of allegiance to the close-knit library sisterhood to ensure *New Yorker* readers of an outlook unlike any to be found elsewhere. Unimpressed by the pronouncements of the experts, she adopted the pose of an informed but often bemused spectator and, applying her bracing powers of observation and self-scrutiny to the new season's books, proceeded to let the chips fall where they might. As she dryly observed in the preamble to her second column, dated December 1, 1934:

> The hardy, and we sometimes think presumptuous, writers of children's books are back this year covering a spectacular range and sinning in a multitude of covers. We are offered everything from the adventures of a bureaucratic rabbit, by the daughter of our President, to the Lord's Prayer for either a Catholic child or a Protestant child. It was the odd impact of this slice of the Bible on a four-year-old of our acquaintance that made us question the whole idea of juvenile literature: the child, ever since listening to the majestic cadences of "For thine is the kingdom, and the power, and the glory," has been referring in his less beatific moods to a new kind of power boat known to him as a Glory Boat. Even this rather cursory experience with the working of a child mind makes one wonder how any adult has the nerve to prepare any literature for the young whatsoever.[8]

White's clear grasp of the difficulties entailed in writing well for young readers was not enough to deter her husband, who, sitting down at his typewriter months later, batted out a number of the episodes (based in part on stories he had once told his nieces and nephews) that eventually found their way into *Stuart Little*. Later in the decade, while Katharine struggled over her year-end *New Yorker* piece, E. B. White commented breezily in his own "One Man's Meat" column in *Harper's*: "It must be a lot of fun to write for children — reasonably easy work, perhaps even important work."[9] Seeing an opening in this remark by a writer she held in high esteem, Anne Carroll Moore dashed off a letter to White, urging him to pursue his curiosity about the genre for the benefit of children everywhere. In his reply to Moore, White tactfully stepped back from the provocative suggestion that to do so might not be a terribly hard thing to do and informed her that he had "started to write a book for children about two years ago, and I have it about half done. Perhaps with your encouragement," he added, gamely feeding the owls in the most flattering way imaginable, "I will get round to working some more on it. I really only go at it when I am laid up in bed, sick, and lately I have been enjoying fine health. My fears about writing for children are great — one can so easily slip into a cheap sort of whimsy or cuteness. I don't trust myself in this treacherous field unless I am running a degree of fever."[10] Several more years would pass before White completed the manuscript of *Stuart Little;* when he finally did so, Moore's reaction to the unconventional, deliberately open-ended tale more than sufficed to confirm Katharine S. White's disdain not simply for Moore herself but for a system that left the fate of contributions to an entire department of literature largely in the hands of nonliterary people.[11]

As the Hoover administration struggled to come to grips with the economic crisis, the spotlight briefly fell on the plight of the nation's children. On November 19, 1930, the White House Conference on Child Health and Protection convened in Washington's Constitution Hall, bringing together hundreds of experts from a variety of fields to evaluate the current status and future needs of America's young people. A pet project of President Hoover, the four-day gathering featured reports by specialists on nutrition, birth defects and common childhood physical impairments, mental health, orphan care, and juvenile delinquency, among other concerns. The president, in a keynote address that was broadcast on national radio, offered an overview of the scope of the challenge facing those who wished to help "lighten the burdens of children." Of the nation's 45 million children, Hoover noted, "35 million are reasonably normal." Of the remaining 10 million, "more than 80 percent . . . are not receiving the necessary attention" that parents alone were generally not in a position to give.[12] Addressing the conference on the place of books and reading in the contemporary child's life, the American Library Association's executive secretary, Carl H. Milam, praised the path-finding work of librarians and publishers of recent years while also noting that the best of children's literature remained a luxury beyond the reach of a large portion of the nation's youngsters.[13]

According to Milam, nearly half of America's children aged fifteen and under were without ready access to public library service of any kind.[14] The librarians, it was true, conceived their work as that of augmenting, not supplanting, the home efforts of parents to foster a love of reading in the young. Much to the librarians' disappointment, however, the majority of

American parents seemed content to leave the matter almost entirely in the experts' hands. While surveys showed that the "average American family" purchased ten books a year, there were still "thousands of homes without books or magazines suited to children," as well as "indications that home libraries play a relatively unimportant part in the reading experiences of American children."[15]

Parents, Milam added, many of whom had grown up without the benefit of childhood books of their own, did not necessarily bear the major responsibility for this sorry situation. On the whole, the nation's booksellers continued to do too little to meet the special needs of parents interested in purchasing a suitable book for their children. The time had come, Milam said, for booksellers to follow the enlightened example set by the librarians and publishers. "The idea of a separate children's department in a bookstore, under competent supervision, with separate alcoves for little children and for older children, is fairly new and not as yet widespread. And bookstores run exclusively or chiefly for children are so few that they can easily be counted." Were booksellers to take his suggestion, Milam argued, a pleasant surprise would likely be their reward: the discovery that "specialized service to children is profitable."[16]

The White House report had nothing but praise for the "splendid publishing programs of the last ten years[,] which have brought to children some of the best work of the finest present day writers and artists."[17] The challenge lay rather in educating more parents as to the availability and value of the newly created literature, and more booksellers to both the social significance and good business sense of participating in the process. As Louise Seaman Bechtel would sum up the nettlesome matter years later, the good books that she and her colleagues labored so mightily to publish all too often remained "books in search of children."[18]

Not all of the retrenchment forced on publishers by the Depression was cause for regret. Looking back at the previous decade, when juvenile publishing had ranked as the industry's fastest-growing sector, it seemed clear to observers that far too many books had been published.[19] And despite the new strictures imposed on the editors of children's books during the Depression years, memorable work continued to be published. It would become a truism of Depression-era publishing lore that hard times had taught those left in charge of the departments an invaluable lesson in making more with less.

The roster of picture books from the early and mid-1930s that left a lasting impression is impressive: *Angus and the Ducks* by Marjorie Flack and its sequels; *The First Picture Book* by Mary Steichen Martin, photographed by Edward Steichen; *The Little Family* by Lois Lenski; *Men at Work* by Lewis W. Hine; *The ABC Bunny* by Wanda Gág; *The Story of Babar* by Jean de Brunhoff, a French import; *The Story About Ping* by Marjorie Flack, illustrated by Kurt Wiese; and *The Story of Ferdinand* by Munro Leaf, illustrated by Robert Lawson. Of all the picture books of that remarkable era, the one that perhaps struck the most resonant note with contemporary readers was a tale of little-guy courage and determination called *The Little Engine That Could,* whose inspirational mantra — "I think I can, I think I can" — furnished Americans with a lesson in hope three years before the nation's newly inaugurated president, Franklin D. Roosevelt, declared, in a comparable expression of faith in the power of positive thinking, that Americans facing hard times had nothing "but fear itself" standing between themselves and their national destiny.[20]

At Harper, Louise Raymond's emergency strategy focused on efforts to create picture books able to do double duty in the marketplace by meeting librarians' high aesthetic standards while still falling within the price range of budget-minded parents. Raymond saw her chance when Georges Duplaix, a Harper author and businessman from France with a thorough knowledge of color printing processes, devised a new method that allowed the firm to issue American editions of two titles from the much-admired French Père Castor picture-book series, at the modest retail price of one dollar each. The flamboyant Duplaix, a recent émigré to America, also translated the text of the two French books (both of which had been the work, originally, of his wife), created his own printer's plates, and even brokered the arrangement between Harper and the French publisher Flammarion.[21] Acting in his capacity as head of the Artists and Writers Guild, the New York book-packaging outpost of a major midwestern printing concern, the Western Printing and Lithographing Company, Duplaix would continue to send special full-color projects Harper's way while also keeping his thumb in as many other publishing pies as possible.[22]

Western, with its headquarters in Racine, Wisconsin, had established the Guild for the purpose of generating presswork by the innovative method of developing book projects to be sold, more or less ready-made, to publishers, who would then issue the books under their own imprints. In addition to savings of editorial time and effort, publishers reaped the further benefit of the lower production costs made possible by the vast scale of Western's massive printing operation. Although viewed at first as little more than a sideshow by the mainline houses, the Guild would soon become a force to be reckoned with when, in partnership with the upstart New York publishing firm of Simon & Schuster, it launched a line of low-priced picture books that compelled a reevaluation both of the critical standards by which such books were judged and of the economics of making them.[23]

First-rate fiction for older children was published as well, including books that appealed with special force to Depression-era Americans. *Little House in the Big Wood,* the first of Laura Ingalls Wilder's autobiographical novels of American frontier life, held up the struggles for survival of an earlier generation of pioneers as implicit proof that Americans possessed the moral strength and determination to weather any adversity. Wilder's elaborately detailed accounts of campfire building, butter churning, and other (one might have thought tedious) frontier routines and chores highlighted not only the pioneers' bare-knuckled resourcefulness and adaptability but also their capacity for joy even under the most trying circumstances. Here was a close-knit family that had made the most of a rugged, frill-free life premised on hard work, stick-to-it-iveness, and self-reliance; Americans of the 1930s could only hope to do as well. The Wisconsin-born writer's advanced age at the time of authorship (Wilder was sixty-five when Harper published her first novel) added to the mystique surrounding her first book, underscoring as it did the triumphant nature of her family's survival, down to the present day. Strikingly, the 1933 Pulitzer Prize for history was awarded, posthumously, to Frederick Jackson Turner, the University of Wisconsin scholar whose writings on the closing of the American frontier, first published in the 1890s, asserted the pioneering life's pivotal role in the formation of the nation's democratic values. Urbane 1920s intellectuals and writers had had little more than a patronizing smirk for America's buckskin-clad forebears: what a difference a depression made.[24]

Classics in new or revived editions enjoyed renewed attention from publishers and readers alike. By reissuing books already in the public domain, publishers were able to factor out royalty payments from the cost side of the equation and thus to offer the books at more affordable prices to consumers. Book buyers for their part embraced the standard titles for comfort, as good value, and, most poignantly, as a means of "bettering" themselves in anticipation of better times to come. At Macmillan, with its incomparable backlist of perennials by Lewis Carroll, William Thackeray, the brothers Grimm, and others, and with its Happy Hour and Little Library thrift editions, the recently married Louise Seaman Bechtel was in a stronger position than many of her colleagues to maintain business more or less as usual.[25] Each week she and her doughty staff of two passed judgment on the fifty to one hundred manuscripts that came in through the mail, a volume of submissions sharply up from pre-Depression days.[26] Macmillan, already the nation's largest publisher, had the pick of the litter, and with each new Newbery victory that fell into the Macmillan column, the Bechtel legend continued to grow. The 1930 medal went to Rachel Field for *Hitty, Her First Hundred Years*, a doll's "memoir" that the publisher had won in a sealed-bid auction. The following year Elizabeth Coatsworth captured the prize for her Buddhist-inspired fable about immortality and the creative life, *The Cat Who Went to Heaven*. Closing out the publishing year of 1931 in a letter to her old college friend, Bechtel burst with confidence in the future and with satisfaction at Coatsworth's triumph: "I suppose," she wrote,

> this is the time and place for me to say what you have heard so many times already, that is how happy I am that we have done these books together and how very extra proud of having you in particular a Newbery Medal author. This is all a most thrilling and interesting adventure in books, and ideas, as well as in business[,] and I am very hopeful not only for what you may do in the future but for the long life of most of these books both on the market and in libraries and schools in America.[27]

By 1932, however, depression economics had forced Bechtel to dismiss her capable assistant, Eunice P. Blake.[28] The decision came within a year of George Platt Brett's retirement as president and replacement by his son and namesake, George P. Brett Jr. Whether the loss of Blake was more a cause or a consequence, Bechtel's relations with her new employer quickly turned anything but cordial. The younger Brett lacked his father's elegant manners as well as any feeling for the pioneering work that she had done for the house. He proceeded to cut Bechtel's budget and, still more provocatively, to understate (as she later recalled) the financial contribution that her department made to the company as a whole.[29] She remained at her job until an injury sustained in a horseback-riding accident in December 1933 sent her to the hospital for what was projected to be a long and painful recovery. When Macmillan announced her resignation on January 15, 1934, health reasons alone were cited as the cause.

It was a measure of the universal esteem in which Bechtel was held that news of her departure prompted heartfelt messages of farewell from both Lucy Sprague Mitchell and Anne Carroll Moore — two authorities who rarely agreed — with the latter declaring: "You've done a big job superbly. . . . The Macmillan Company have a good deal to live up to in sustaining the tradition you have established and I am writing the President to that effect."[30] In later years, Bechtel herself made no effort to conceal her bitterness at having been forced — more by internal pressure than by health considerations — to step down from her post.

Perhaps the single most spectacular act of administrative shortsightedness, however, had come with the firing in late 1932 of May Massee as director of Doubleday Junior Books, the department founded by her ten years earlier. The dismissal caught Massee completely unawares. As recently as late August, she had written Ingri and Edgar Parin d'Aulaire of the triumph she anticipated, that September, for the couple's grandly conceived new picture book, *Ola*. To make matters worse, Massee had only just moved into larger quarters in a beautiful old carriage house near Washington Square Park and now found herself without the means to cover her expenses. Louise Bechtel would recall this low point in her colleague's career as, "for a time, a personal tragedy."[31]

That November, in a public show of indignation, Anne Carroll Moore selected Massee as the main speaker at the New York Public Library's Children's Book Week celebration, the annual "pink tea" held in the Central Children's Room, where the library's all-important list of "Children's Books Suggested as Holiday Gifts" was unveiled. In a further show of support, Moore chose Massee's protégés, the d'Aulaires, to be the event's honored guests. Moore, who regarded such occasions as command performances, had had the invitations printed without first consulting the d'Aulaires, who, as it happened, were happily ensconced in Paris just then and would have been hard-pressed to return to New York in time for the November 14 tea. The couple finessed the potentially explosive situation by sending, at Massee's prompting, a "special message" to be read to the assembled guests by Moore herself. Satisfied with this act of obeisance, Moore proceeded in her own remarks that afternoon to herald the d'Aulaires' *Ola* as the picture book of the year.[32]

Massee, in the meantime, wrote the artists frankly about her own situation, seeking assurances of their loyalty to her: "I hope you will not promise books to anyone before you come back. I do not know exactly what I am going to be doing but I am sure of some publishing connection and I would like to talk to you about your books before you sign any contracts." Massee went further, suggesting, with a proprietary nonchalance that barely concealed her sense of desperation, that the d'Aulaires would be well served to let her see "whatever contracts" they did sign, with whatever house. "I think it will help you if I do and you can just say that you are not making plans before you have talked with me. This will not be any loss to you and I am sure will be a gain."[33]

That December a dispirited Massee accepted a lunch invitation from Harold K. Guinzburg, president of the eight-year-old Viking Press. Viking had set a course for itself as a firm with Olympian literary aspirations and had already assembled a roster of notable authors that included Sylvia Townsend Warner, Stefan Zweig, and Upton Sinclair. Guinzburg's opening gambit with Massee had been to remark that "he had been thinking about children's books and that maybe we had some of the same ideas." Massee was prepared to believe that they did. During a visit to Viking's offices, she was impressed by the talented, congenial staff Guinzburg and his editor in chief, Ben Huebsch, had gathered around them. Generous terms were offered: "absolute control to build the thing and a good percent of profits — (if any)! And meanwhile a living wage."[34] By the start of the new year, Massee made her triumphant return to publishing as the founding director of Viking Junior Books. Writers and illustrators who had pledged their loyalty to her included the d'Aulaires, Marjorie Flack, Maud and Miska Petersham, Robert Lawson, and Kurt Wiese. From this strong beginning, Massee proceeded to build an incomparable core group led by Ludwig Bemelmans, William Pène du Bois, and Robert McCloskey, among others. No editor of her pioneering generation would touch Massee's record of success, especially in the realm of picture books.

To herald her arrival and demonstrate his long-term confidence in her, Guinzburg engaged an architect-friend of Massee's to design a beautiful new office for her use.[35] The walls and ceiling were paneled with an exquisite honey-colored mahogany. The centerpiece of the ceiling design was an oval relief carving of Taurus: the editor's birth sign and symbol of the creative life. Incised in Latin on the cornice was Massee's jaunty personal motto: *Ne quid nimium, etiam moderatio* (All things in moderation, including moderation).[36]

In the annual competition for the children's book field's most coveted award, Massee proved to be as good as her word. In 1935 Monica Shannon became the first Viking author to win the Newbery Medal, for her novel *Dobry*. Viking authors won again in 1937, 1938, and 1940. By 1940, Massee also had a remarkable eight Newbery runners-up to her credit. A joke began to circulate that it was none other than Massee herself who tallied the Newbery committee's ballots each year in private consultation with her old friend Anne Carroll Moore.[37]

Although no one seriously suspected anything of the sort, the larger meaning of the story was not lost on industry insiders, notwithstanding the special problems publishers faced during the worst of the Depression. To succeed in the specialized library-dominated market for juvenile books, a publishing house did indeed need to field specialists of its own. By 1935, even a house with as solid a reputation in the children's book field as Charles Scribner's Sons (a reputation acquired in its case more than a half-century earlier with its successful involvement in the illustrated magazine trade) recognized the necessity of hiring a full-time editor — its first ever — to oversee the firm's profitable juvenile list.[38] In a classic expression of trade publishers' ambivalence toward the genre, the new editor, Alice Dalgliesh, soon found herself parrying the offhand suggestion of the firm's president, Charles Scribner III, that she might wish to carry out her duties from home. Dalgliesh began her long tenure at a desk set up for her in a hallway. Later, as the editor dryly recalled, a more suitable place was found in a railed-off portion of the house's prestigious fifth floor: "It had the advantage of being almost at the entrance to Maxwell Perkins's office, where the great ones of the adult writing world came and went."[39]

Dalgliesh had come to publishing with a background in the education world's equivalent of the avant-garde: seventeen years' experience as a schoolteacher at the progressive Horace Mann School and instructor in children's literature at Teachers College, Columbia. Her impeccable credentials also included the authorship of several children's books, most of them published by Louise Seaman Bechtel at Macmillan. It was Bechtel who had first urged Dalgliesh to try her hand at writing for young people and who continued, even after the younger woman took the Scribner job, to play the mentor's role for her. Neither woman suffered from false modesty, as Dalgliesh's account of their first encounter confirms. In the exclusive male preserve in which both women operated, absolute self-confidence, or at any rate the appearance of it, seemed a quality worth countenancing in one another:

> As a teacher and a reviewer of children's books, I felt I knew almost all there was to know about books for small children. I would, I decided, write to the Macmillan editor and give her suggestions. I did — brashly enough. Louise Seaman invited me to tea at her apartment, defended her books ably, charmed me by her personality, and that was the end of that. The beginning for me, however, for she asked me to try out some picture-book manuscripts with the Horace Mann children, notably Helen Sewell's *Blue Barns*. Soon I found myself walking into Louise Seaman's office with *The Little Wooden Farmer*.[40]

Louise Seaman Bechtel shared Dalgliesh's interest in the revolutionary research being conducted in both the United States and Europe into numerous aspects of childhood development. Both women felt committed to exploring the implications for children's literature of that growing body of research. In an essay in *The Publishers' Weekly* in 1930, Dalgliesh associated herself in spirit, if not in name, with progressive educators such as Bank Street's Lucy Sprague Mitchell. She noted the recent tendency of publishers to "stop and consider what children really like and to provide material which will keep pace with the modern child's interests." In indicating her approval of this trend, she echoed the central theme of Mitchell's *Here and Now Story Book:* "Modern life," Dalgliesh observed: ". . . is full of interesting, real things, and there is no time for sugary little fairy tales of the type that used to be published by the dozen."[41] In her semiautobiographical novel for young readers, *Along Janet's Road*, Dalgliesh would have her editor-heroine wonder aloud why it was that her submissions pile was always cluttered with "so many silly tales about little fairy Dewdrop or little fairy Rosebud. . . . With stories like this she had little patience."[42] That an educator committed to such views would be chosen to direct Scribner's new department was striking proof that progressive ideas were well on their way to achieving general respectability.

As the editor at a house with a long history of success in the field,

Dalgliesh felt — as had Bechtel at Macmillan — that she could afford on occasion to experiment in matters of format, design, and subject matter. Serious biography and science fiction became hallmarks of her list, and in later years, once Scribner updated its antiquated printing facilities, Dalgliesh made her department a contender in the picture-book arena as well. Among the perennial bestsellers she held in her quiver were the Scribner's "Illustrated Classics" series featuring principally the artwork of N. C. Wyeth; the adventure stories by Wyeth's mentor Howard Pyle; and *The Wind in the Willows*, *Peter Pan*, *Hans Brinker*, *Little Lord Fauntleroy*, and the 1927 Newbery Medal winner, *Smoky* by Will James. *Smoky* had originated on the adult trade list under the editorial supervision of Maxwell Perkins, the daring editor best known for having championed the work of Hemingway, Fitzgerald, and Wolfe. In *Along Janet's Road*, Dalgliesh offered a thinly veiled portrait of James as the "cowboy writer" who regaled his editor with quaintly homespun illustrated letters. "He had always dealt with men editors, however, and was not a little doubtful about trusting his book to 'a lady editor.'" On the whole, she had found her inherited Scribner list an "astonishingly masculine" one, not surprising perhaps for a house whose most important authors — the troika of greats in Perkins's stable — were nearly as renowned for their explosive, bad-boyish behavior as they were for their path-finding work.[43]

A letter from Maxwell Perkins to Marjorie Kinnan Rawlings, written as the latter was struggling with an early draft of *The Yearling*, confirms Dalgliesh's appraisal: "A book about a boy and the life of the scrub is the thing we want. . . . It is those wonderful river trips, and the hunting, and the dogs and the guns, and the companionship of simple people who care about the same things which were included in *South Moon Under* [her first novel, published by Scribner in 1933] that we are thinking about."[44] Perkins grandly suggested that Rawlings's new book might take its place beside such acknowledged classics as *The Adventures of Huckleberry Finn*, Kipling's *Kim*, Davy Crockett's memoirs, *Treasure Island*, and Edward Eggleston's *The Hoosier School-Boy*: "All of these books are primarily *for boys*. All of them are read by men, and they are the favorite books of some men. The truth is the best part of a man is a boy." To which Rawlings replied: "Do you realize how calmly you sit in your office and tell me to write *a classic?*"[45]

It seems never to have occurred to Perkins to turn the project over to Scribner's new juvenile editor, and it was perhaps only a matter of circumstance that Perkins, over the course of his career, did not earn a greater portion of his fame as an editor of "boys' books." In one important instance, an author's resistance conspired against such an outcome. Early on in their relationship, Perkins, it seems, had told Hemingway that if he would be willing to delete the occasional obscenity from his work, older boys might read the books by the thousands.[46] Hemingway had declined to make the necessary accommodations; Perkins recounted the episode to Rawlings, who enjoyed salting her own draft manuscripts with expletives, in a sort of cautionary aside that the author heeded.

The Yearling was finally published in 1938, and the following year it won the Pulitzer Prize in fiction. Dalgliesh in the meantime had carved out a place for herself among the Scribner men — aligning herself with the avuncular Charles Scribner III rather than the hard-drinking, oracular Perkins and building a "peaceful, profitable outpost," as one of her many assistants recalled.[47] Dalgliesh showed no signs of wishing to become known as children's literature's Maxwell Perkins; nonetheless, her department quietly captured the industry's respect and more than a few of its accolades.

By 1935, the Depression had begun to ease for the publishers of children's books. Lists were again expanding, though far more cautiously now than during the 1920s. If a celebratory mood was not yet in order, it had become time to regroup. Taking the measure of the moment, The Publishers' Weekly ran a series of profiles of the current heads of children's book departments in New York and Boston. The honor of leading the parade went to Helen Dean Fish of Frederick A. Stokes, a house notable for, among other things, its fifty-four-year history of publishing children's books as of 1935.[48] Fish was a Wellesley graduate who came to publishing with a background in theater and settlement work. While directing Stokes's juvenile list, it was noted, she also performed a multitude of other tasks at the house, ranging from administering the library department to screening submissions of adult fiction. Another Wellesley alumna, Doris S. Patee, now presided over the Macmillan department founded and directed by Louise Seaman — when she was not carrying out her numerous other duties in the areas of manufacturing, promotion, and advertising.[49] And so it went, as publishers struggled with their priorities.

Even one famously profitable house saw the need, as a condition of employment, to extract the last ounce of productivity from its editorial director of children's books. Grosset & Dunlap's backlist of hugely popular juvenile series books — the Tom Swifts, the Hardy Boys, and others — was as rock-solid a foundation of profitability as any in the field. Nonetheless, Laura Harris was expected to do her own sales promotion work for the entire juvenile list and to edit Grosset's cookbooks and albums for stamp collectors.

Demand for Grosset's fifty-cent series books, aimed at readers ages ten to sixteen, had held firm throughout the worst of the Depression years. In 1934 *Fortune* magazine reported that the company had sold 45 million copies of the books over the previous quarter-century — a staggering quantity that, if stacked volume on volume, would, as the magazine observed, make a seven-hundred-mile high monument. *Fortune* had a clear idea as to where the monument belonged: in Brooklyn's Evergreen Cemetery, on the grave of Anthony Comstock (1844–1915), secretary and special agent of the New York Society for the Suppression of Vice and a relentless critic of series fiction for young people. Comstock's fiery verbal attacks — published in his book-length diatribe *Traps for the Young* and elsewhere — had done little to suppress the far-flung adventures of the likes of the Rover Boys. Neither for that matter had the more high-toned criticisms of the American Library Association. Following the death of Edward Stratemeyer in May 1930, control of the Syndicate had passed directly from the sixty-seven-year-old millionaire to his two grown daughters; just twelve days after his death, Grosset & Dunlap had launched what proved almost immediately to be the Stratemeyer Syndicate's most popular series ever, the tales of a daring girl detective with a smart blue roadster, Nancy Drew.[50] "The series books," as *The Publishers' Weekly* blithely reported in its tribute to Grosset editorial director Laura Harris, "go merrily on."[51]

Whether or not the newer titles were "much improved," as the breezy industry-journal reporter declared, the shadow cast by this publishing phenomenon proved long enough to darken the reception of series fiction of unassailable literary merit. During the 1930s and 1940s, the principal victim in this regard, when it came time for the awarding of the Newbery Medal, was Laura Ingalls Wilder, whose "Little House" books, however praised and admired, somehow always managed to fall short of the required number of librarians' votes.

In the same positive spirit as *The Publishers' Weekly*'s articles on editors, *The Horn Book* devoted its July–August 1936 issue to a celebration of the career of May Massee. With Louise Bechtel now in forced retirement, the tribute amounted to a passing of the torch and a sort of anointment. For the next thirty years, publishing and library colleagues alike would regard Massee as the undisputed dean of her profession. Taking pains to avoid striking a valedictory note in praising an editor whose career was far from over, notable authors and artists long associated with Massee lined up to reminisce or offer assessments of her many achievements. Ludwig Bemelmans recalled their first meeting:

> About seven years ago a typographer brought Miss Massee to my house for dinner. It was a dreary building of six rooms in a noisy neighborhood. The windows of my living room looked out at a cobweb of telegraph wires, a water tank, and a Claude Neon sign that flashed "Two Pants Suits at $15.00." To hide this *mise en scène*, and because I was homesick for my [Tyrolean] mountains, I had painted outside of my windows a field with blue gentians, the foothills around Innsbruck, and a peasant house with a Forester sitting in front of it, on his lap a wire-haired dachshund, and a long pipe dividing his white beard. "You must write children's books," decided Miss Massee. And with her help I started to write.[52]

Luminaries from the publishing and library worlds also contributed to the *Horn Book* tribute. Viking's senior designer and production man, Milton B. Glick, noted with collegial pride that Massee was the first woman to have become a member of the American Institute of Graphic Arts.[53] Frederic G. Melcher of *The Publishers' Weekly* recalled an early encounter at a workshop where Massee had held forth on the usually deadly subject of library book selection. Melcher, who had endured many such lectures by others in the past, was utterly smitten: "I had never known anyone who was so brilliantly able to inject into the mechanics of title winnowing a sense of high crusade of the spirit." A sense, Melcher might have added, so like his own.[54] Massee's fervor, always a surprise at first coming from someone with so tremulous a voice and willowy a frame, assumed a shape-shifting dimension whenever the subject turned to her hopes for the field. The Boston Public Library's Alice M. Jordan, quoting from the Viking catalog for 1933, captured the editor in all her ardor:

"We believe," Massee had declared in a characteristic statement of her publishing credo,

> that when our children's books reflect the best influences from all the people who make this country what it is, they will be most truly American books. We hope to publish such books, we want them to be clear-minded and beautiful, books that will make young Americans think and feel more vividly, make them more aware of the world around them and more at home in the world within, more able to give something to their generation and thoroughly to enjoy the giving.[55]

Had Frank Capra's Mr. Smith gone to Viking instead of to Washington, he would have expressed many of the same sentiments, in more or less the same words.

A gallery of illustrations culled from Doubleday and Viking books filled out the issue's pages. (Still smarting from the accusations of favoritism that had marred the publication of the special Seaman number, Bertha Mahony Miller took care to state that *The Horn Book* had received neither payment nor guidance from the publishers.[56]) Among the images on view was one by Robert Lawson from a picture book due from Viking that fall. *The Story of Ferdinand*, written by Munro Leaf, would confirm Massee's preeminence in the picture-book realm. A critical triumph and an immediate bestseller, it made the reputations of both the author and illustrator and proved to be one of those rare books openly appreciated by adults as well as by children.

As the book's fame grew, it also became a lightning rod for political controversy among adult readers for whom the Spanish Civil War, which had broken out just months before its release, in June 1936, was an issue of passionate concern. Leaf and Lawson's fable, it was noted, was the tale of a young Spanish bull that refused to fight. Critics asked whether such a story was not to be taken as an oblique commentary on the war. "It was attacked by everybody!" the author recalled years later. "It was called 'Red propaganda,' a bitter satire of pacifism, on the one hand, and a pro-Fascist tract on the other."[57] Objections were raised often enough for Anne Carroll Moore to feel impelled to render a verdict in the matter. Writing in *The Horn Book*, Moore sought to settle the controversy once and for all:

"Far be it from the artist, the author or the critic Owl to read meanings into *Ferdinand*, that effortless, happy collaboration of Munro Leaf and Robert Lawson. They have never had any doubt that *Ferdinand* was designed for sheer entertainment of the ageless." Refusing to acknowledge the relevance of Franco's rise to power to the debate, Moore continued: "If it also brings Spain to life in the mind of any one, so much the better."[58] Later that year, Munro Leaf issued his own public rebuttal to the charge. Interviewed in the *New York Times*, the author insisted that Ferdinand's unwillingness to do battle in Madrid signified nothing more (or less) than the young hero's "good taste, and strength of character." Ferdinand, he suggested, was "just a superior soul, a philosopher."[59] The author, who by day served as a director at the publishing firm of Frederick A. Stokes, confessed to having written *Ferdinand* in a mere forty minutes on a rainy Sunday afternoon, and to having done so for the sole purpose of supplying his artist friend, Robert Lawson, with something amusing to illustrate. Lawson, it seemed, had been complaining to Leaf about the creative limitations imposed on him by his publishers. Like Ferdinand, the artist had been feeling unduly reined in. "Rob, cut loose and have fun with this," Leaf had told Lawson at the time.[60] If *The Story of Ferdinand* had any hidden meaning, it lay in the inspiration to be gleaned from the example of a free spirit unleashed against great odds.[61]

The controversy, in any case, only added to the publicity surrounding the already phenomenally successful book. That same year, *The Story of Ferdinand* became the first original story animated by the Disney Studio as a film short for theatrical release. Lawson's Westport, Connecticut, barn became a warehouse for the host of Ferdinand toys and products that the phenomenon spawned. There was even a Ferdinand song.[62]

Ending its 1936 May Massee issue with a flourish, *The Horn Book* made the dramatic announcement that Anne Carroll Moore, whose weekly assignment as the *New York Herald-Tribune*'s children's book review-page editor had come to a sad end in 1930 as another casualty of the Depression, now planned to resume her column in *The Horn Book*'s pages. The new feature, to be called "The Three Owls' Notebook," would debut in the very next issue. To many in the field, Moore's return to print must have seemed a timely and affirming development. Life *would* go on; the Owls *would* be fed.[63] As if to furnish further proof of this, word now came from London that British publishers were beginning to adopt the American model of placing their children's book lists under the direction of knowledgeable woman specialists.[64] Here was a once undreamed-of sort of vindication: mother England — land of Newbery, Lear, Carroll, Caldecott, Greenaway, and Potter — taking its cultural cues from the Americans in matters relating to the production of books for children. Before the decade was out, the juvenile department of one British house, Chatto & Windus, would even be headed by an American, Grace Allen Hogarth.

To a few idealistic Americans with money or access to it, the mid-1930s even seemed a good enough time to set up shop as children's book publishers. In New York two such ventures were launched, in 1935 and 1938, respectively. The first of these, Holiday House, was the creation of three young people with overlapping dreams.

Vernon Ives was a passionate bookman from upstate New York who, following graduation from Hamilton College, had apprenticed himself in the renowned letterset firm known as the Print House of William Edwin Rudge. After just two years at Rudge, and following the founder's death, Ives had become a partner in the firm. The publishing side of the industry held greater allure for him, however, and feeling by then that he had acquired the requisite experience, the self-starting Ives was quick to accept a college friend's proposal to found a publishing house of their own. Ted Johnson's "only qualification" at the time, as Ives recalled years later, "was his father's money."[65] The old friends were soon joined by Helen Gentry, an accomplished designer and printer who had learned her craft at San Francisco's Grabhorn Press before setting out on her own with the noble goal of creating aesthetically pleasing books for children. For Gentry, the move to New York — undertaken more for the sake of her novelist husband's career than for her own — had seemed a risky proposition. How, she recalled worrying during the long, cross-country train ride, would someone with her uncompromising craft approach to bookmaking fare in the epicenter of commerce and the mass media? She had already corresponded with Ives, however, and on meeting him knew at once that she had found a kindred spirit and a professional home. As Gentry wrote not long afterward on behalf of the firm: "Holiday House has been chosen as our name for two reasons. First, because we expect to have fun making the books. Second, because we hope they will have a happy spirit that will make young people fond enough of them to keep them, and to lend them only to careful friends, and to hand them down to their children — and, in some cases, to their grandchildren."[66]

Writing in the *New York Herald-Tribune* about Holiday House's first list, May Lamberton Becker reported: "Books easy to the eye, stoutly made, meant to last. They have the look of rightness a children's book should have. Each is . . . part of the fulfillment of a pledge made . . . by a publishing enterprise trying, in its own quiet way, to make its children's books notable examples of typography and thus to train appreciation of a noble art form from an early age in the way it should go."[67] Becker's grand words gave the flavor of the newcomers' lofty goals even as they hinted at the partners' naïveté, at the start, as to the difference between a fine-press collector's edition and a picture book destined for a young child's sticky hands. Among the company's first productions were "Stocking Book" editions of fairy tales — charming, miniature gift volumes that booksellers were unsure how to display and that librarians feared would be too easily stolen.[68] Ives and the others were quick studies, however. Without sacrificing their keenness for superior design and production, they adjusted their plans with a view to publishing books "less exotic in appearance and far more popular in content."[69]

"What saved us," Ives recalled of the firm's shaky first months of operation, "was the arrival of Glen Rounds, trying to peddle some drawings to anyone for a few dollars."[70] The second Holiday House list featured the debut of this colorful cowboy artist from the Dakota Badlands. A friend of Thomas Hart Benton, Rounds was a Paul Bunyanesque character who had "prowled the country" as a cowhand, carnival barker, and lumberjack and was a tall-tale teller par excellence.[71] In New York, where he took night courses at the Art Students League alongside Jackson Pollock, he cut an incongruous figure as a tall, lanky westerner in a Stetson hat pounding the pavement with an artist's portfolio. Rounds's folksy, flamboyant brand of Americana, so well matched to Depression-era tastes, would remain a Holiday House list staple for the next half-century.

Holiday House occupied makeshift offices in the Rudge plant at 225 Varick Street, in the heart of the city's gritty printing district, where long flatbed trucks rumbled over the cobblestone streets at all hours bearing massive rolls of paper and the acrid smell of printer's inks hung in the air. As Rounds later recalled, on arriving at the Varick Street address with samples of his animal drawings, he found the firm's three principals huddled at "three old desks behind a barrier of wooden boxes in the corner of the press floor, with old Miehle cylinder presses thumping and wheezing on all sides."[72]

A few blocks to the north, on a Greenwich Village byway lined for the most part with tumbledown row houses, the decade's other new, and equally quixotic, publishing company had set up shop in a projection closet in the warehouse building that now served as the headquarters of Lucy Sprague Mitchell's Bureau of Educational Experiments.

The commercial success of Mitchell's *Here and Now Story Book*, the Bureau founder's first attempt at writing for young children, and the intense critical debate that the book had generated in library and education circles had sharpened Mitchell's appetite for new forays into the publishing arena.[73] Mitchell's deep-seated interest in children's literature, and children's writing, had had distressing beginnings. She came of age convinced that her father, Otho Sprague, wholesaler to the nation (the company he cofounded, Sprague and Warner, later became General Foods) and benefactor of the University of Chicago, had all but crushed her powers of imaginative expression. "My father," she recalled decades later in retirement, "was really upset if he found that I had written anything. When I was 7 or 8 I wrote poems by the yard, but my terror in life was that he would find them."[74] In her twenties, as a Radcliffe graduate in search of fulfilling work, Mitchell resolved to find some way to spare young people from the destructive impact of the societal prejudices and pressures to which her father had subjected her.[75] She tried college teaching but concluded that students at that stage were already too old to shed the damage done to them in the form of suppressed childhood creativity. The really important work lay with children of the youngest ages — and, to the extent possible, with the adults entrusted with their care. Having thus found her "focus," Mitchell formulated a plan for working directly with preschool children and their teachers.

Lucy Sprague Mitchell had a genius for planning and a genius for rallying the right people to her cause. In the mid-1930s, as she weighed her next step as an author for children, she concluded that, rather than write a sequel to her *Here and Now Story Book* on her own, it made better long-term sense to involve her best teacher trainees and staff in a collaboration. As always, Mitchell was looking ahead. By encouraging her younger colleagues with a taste of publishing success, she hoped to increase the chances that one of them might one day become the *real* here-and-now writer of whom she dreamed.[76]

Another Here and Now Story Book, with contributions by Mitchell and more than a dozen other writers, appeared from Dutton in the spring of 1937 to far less controversy than the earlier volume, and to as much or greater success. Even *The Horn Book*, in its May–June issue for that year, made an event of its publication, profiling Mitchell and, in praising the book, acknowledging that the library world's initial rejection of her point of view had perhaps been shortsighted. As Bertha Mahony Miller explained: "We feared that, if the boundaries in the content of stories for little children were fixed too tightly to familiar and *seen* things, the element of wonder would be lost."[77] The new open-mindedness may well have owed something to the presence of Louise Seaman Bechtel as one of the anthology's contributors. Bechtel had emerged from retirement to become both a *Horn Book* contributor and a Bank Street adviser: a bridge of reason between warring worlds. Mitchell had done her part too, striking a conciliatory note in a prologue ("A Reassuring Aftermath") addressed to critics.

As the May–June *Horn Book* went out to subscribers, Anne Carroll Moore, as it happened, was in England to tour the countryside, to take tea in Hampstead with her old friend the illustrator L. Leslie Brooke, and, if possible, to score a ticket to the King's coronation. The librarian must have known what was afoot at the magazine. Her "Three Owls' Notebook" for the issue, filed from abroad, closed with a veiled barb aimed at would-be here-and-now converts. While out walking on an English country road, Moore, it seemed, had encountered two brothers, aged nine and seven. Turning to the older of the two, the librarian had ventured to ask what kind of books he liked to read:

"'Witches,' responded George and launched voluntarily into what might be described as a bowdlerized version of 'Toads and Diamonds.' We listened enchanted to George's version, which substituted primroses and violets for the more costly flowers and jewels of the tale as Andrew Lang tells it. The story lasted far down the road and left us" — and here finally was the point of the anecdote — "completely satisfied with Albury Heath's educational opportunities."[78]

Winning *The Horn Book*'s approval had been a victory worth achieving. Mitchell's focus now turned to a far greater prize. As she continued to cultivate the writers around her and to consider how best to put *Here and Now*–style books into the hands of the greatest number of children, Mitchell decided that the time had come for Bank Street to cement a permanent relationship with a publisher committed to her goals. It was about then that a young man with children enrolled in the Bank Street nursery school attracted her notice. A recent Yale graduate, William R. Scott was casting about for a good use of his family inheritance, one that would satisfy his passion for literature while also engaging his skill as a book designer and printer. Like Vernon Ives, Scott was a man of refined sensibilities. As a parent, he felt committed to progressive education's ideals of respect for children's individuality and creative spirit. Mitchell told Scott about her plans and then boldly proposed to him that he use some of his money to found a small publishing house of the kind she envisioned. Persuading him turned out not to be a very hard thing to do.

Scott, his wife Ethel, and his brother-in-law John McCullough formed the enthusiastic core group of the new firm of William R. Scott and Company, which at the outset lacked only one critical ingredient: an editor with a more than casual knowledge of children's literature. Mitchell herself had begged off when asked to assume this pivotal role. But she had assured Scott that she knew the perfect candidate for the job. Once again, she was right in her assessment. Margaret Wise Brown — Mitchell's protégée and assistant for publications-related matters — easily stepped into the newly created position to become, however briefly, the most innovative picture-book editor of her generation.

When Brown had first sailed into the Bureau's headquarters just a few years earlier, no one would have forecast such a future for her. A glamorous, spoiled, and seemingly unfocused young woman, she had struck some staff members as, at best, an unlikely candidate for teacher training. It had soon become clear that "Brownie," as she came to be known around the school, did indeed have no strong desire to teach. Yet, as Mitchell also discerned, the young woman with an apartment on one of the Village's most fashionable blocks possessed an uncanny gift for intuiting the emotional responses of small children and for translating her observations into quicksilver words. The first evidence of writing talent emerged in the course of the standard Bank Street teacher training regime, which stressed trial-by-fire learning from "direct experience." Teacher trainees were expected not simply to read books to the nursery school children with whom they worked but also to write stories of their own for them and to test their creations on the children as a way of learning what really interested preschoolers, and why. It soon became clear that Brown had a poet's feeling for language. She also had a prankish sense of fun and a romantic longing to join what she understood to be, as Mitchell herself did, a literary and spiritual quest. There seemed to be no end to her capacity for thinking of new book ideas and even ideas for new *kinds* of books for the youngest ages. As though all that were not enough, the charismatic ash-blond editor with film-star good looks had a reliable knack for charming the artists and writers she met into working with her. It only added to her mystique that she spent her weekends hunting rabbits on foot with her Long Island society friends. As Scott's editor, she devoted the rest of each week to hunting for authors.

The inaugural Scott list, published in the fall of 1938, consisted of five books, including two written to order by the prolific, mercurial editor for artists she had recently befriended and wanted not to let slip away. Each of the five books was an experiment. There was a "tactile book" — a forerunner to *Pat the Bunny*, printed on cloth, with sewn-on buttons and cotton "tails" for touching and even a little toy metal bell. A spiral-bound board book marked another departure in format, as did two accordion-style panoramas, one about city life, the other about life in the country. The rhythmic, repetitive text of the fifth book, the only one organized in traditional picture-book form, did not, however, tell a traditional story and was illustrated by Russian émigré artist Esphyr Slobodkina with color-saturated geometric collage graphics that drew inspiration from Mondrian and the illustrator's Russian Constructivist contemporaries.

When the books were finally ready to be shown, Brown and Bill Scott made the obligatory pilgrimage to room 105 of the New York Public Library in the hope of receiving Anne Carroll Moore's blessing. One can only imagine what dagger thoughts flashed through Moore's mind as she examined the floppy cloth pages of the impossible-to-shelve, toylike novelty called *Cottontails*, with its jangling bell, and the other storyless books. Predictably, the great proponent of picture books in the once-upon-a-time story hour vein was neither impressed nor amused. Moore leafed through the little stack of books placed before her and pronounced her grim verdict: "Truck! Mr. Scott. They are truck!" *The Horn Book*'s recent change of heart in regard to the here-and-now had apparently done nothing to temper Moore's attitude on the subject. It would be a long time before the New York Public Library gave Scott much in the way of business.

For as long as anyone could remember, American trade houses had published their new titles twice a year, in the spring and fall. In contrast, children's publishing had only a single "season," consisting of the few frenzied weeks toward the end of the year that culminated in Christmas. Publishers had held to the latter pattern even after the advent of library service to children had introduced a substantial new market whose purchasing routines had little to do with holiday gift-giving. In choosing to retain the one-season arrangement, publishers were doubtless influenced by the stiff resistance of booksellers who, as the White House report of 1930 had found, lacked both the willingness and the expertise to cope with a year-round influx of youngsters and parents. Louise Seaman Bechtel and others had argued for years for a second season for children's books.[79]

A major impetus behind these exhortations was, of course, the pragmatic desire to expand the opportunities for bookselling. But advocates also wished to plant the notion in the minds of parents and other responsible adults that books were not relevant to children's lives only once a year. In a sign of the book trade's reviving economic prospects, the two-season idea finally took hold in 1937, following the creation that year by the *New York Herald-Tribune* of an annual Spring Festival of Children's Books. To a jubilant Anne Carroll Moore, the Festival, which came festooned with prizes, posters, a luncheon, a book fair, and an impressive publicity effort, represented "literally a dream come true."[80]

Just weeks later, building on this momentum and in hopes of reinvigorating the industry further, Frederic Melcher announced his intention to endow a new illustration award to complement the Newbery Medal. Thrilled at the news, Bertha Mahony Miller wrote in *The Horn Book* for July 1938:

"For the past fifteen years the number of beautiful picture books . . . illustrated by the [author] has been steadily increasing. It has been hard to have go unhonored such books as Anne Parrish's *Floating Island*, the Petershams' *Christ Child*, the d'Aulaires' *Ola* and Ludwig Bemelmans' *Hansi* and *The Golden Basket*."[81] In past years, apparently in an effort both to cope with their frustration and to give artists their due, the Newbery committee had chosen picture books by Bemelmans, Parrish, and Wanda Gág as Newbery "runners-up."

There was never much doubt what the new medal would be called. Melcher had a keen sense of the past and — rare among men who worked in the higher reaches of the publishing industry — a profound respect for children's literature. A collector of Randolph Caldecott first editions, he knew the history of the genre. In a letter to the Brooklyn Public Library's Clara Whitehill Hunt, he explained his reasons for wanting to associate the new prize with the creator of *The Three Jovial Huntsmen* and *The Diverting History of John Gilpin*. In addition to his unique importance as an innovator in picture-book art and design, Caldecott "supplies us," Melcher wrote, "with a name that has pleasant memories — memories connected with the joyousness of picture books as well as their beauty. Whatever direction new books may take, I think that joyous and happy approach is one thing we should be gently reminded of."[82] The same group of twenty-two librarians from around the country would choose both the Newbery and Caldecott winners, mailing in their ballots for tabulation by the chair.

On June 24, 1937, at a meeting at New York's Hotel Pierre to iron out the details of the award, Anne Carroll Moore surprised her colleagues by proposing that the medal be named for L. Leslie Brooke, a friend of the librarian's, and arguably England's living successor to Caldecott in illustration. In the awkward scene that followed, Moore's motion was put to a vote and, as none of the others present felt up to challenging her publicly, the motion passed unanimously, whereupon the matter was referred back to Melcher.[83] As it was well known that he strongly favored naming the medal for Caldecott, and as Melcher had the final say, the effort by Moore had little chance of success and is hard to understand except as an exercise in mixed emotion in a time of momentous change. For Moore, one aspect of the change was acutely personal: she was facing mandatory retirement from the New York Public Library in 1941. Perhaps she had not been able to resist flexing her muscles one more time as the first among equals, however ineffectually.

And yet with the introduction of the new medal, the greater recognition for the field that Moore herself had fought so valiantly for over the years seemed more nearly within reach than ever. The children's book world was coming of age. One inevitable consequence of the attainment of this new stage, she must have realized, was the rise in influence of institutional authority — in the form of awards committees, magazine editorial boards, book publishing departments, and the like — and the corresponding decline in the influence of the field's pioneering individuals, including Moore herself.[84] With the issue of the name of the prize resolved, Frederic Melcher turned his attention to the design and casting of the medal, the first example of which would have to be ready for presentation the following spring.[85]

For librarians, an award upholding standards of excellence in illustration for children had come not a moment too soon. Moore and her colleagues had long regarded Edward Stratemeyer, whose death in May 1930 had been front-page news in the *New York Times*, as the era's most destructive influence on American children as readers. By the late 1930s, librarians had begun to view Walt Disney as something akin to Stratemeyer's reincarnation. Disney's first full-length feature animation, *Snow White and the Seven Dwarfs*, premiered at Hollywood's Carthay Circle Theatre on December 22, 1937, and immediately opened in theaters around the country. In the now-familiar pattern that Disney himself had helped to pioneer earlier in the decade, an array of variously priced picture books, all with illustrations inspired by the Disney animation originals, appeared in stores in time for the film's general release.[86] Although movie critics greeted *Snow White* with enthusiasm, librarians were predictably less sanguine about the license Disney had taken in adapting one of the most cherished stories in the traditional fairy-tale canon. Leading the charge, Anne Carroll Moore lamented in *The Horn Book*: "The saddest publication of 1937 from the Owls' point of view was the Snow White from Hollywood. It smelt quite as bad as it looked and provides a striking example of the let's have fun with anything we can use in our business state of mind."[87] Moore had not yet seen the movie. The experience of doing so a few months later only hardened her opposition. The crux of her criticism, Moore took care to note, had nothing to do with the film's various "nightmare effects," which some adults had found objectionable. Moore believed that the real violence done by the film lay in Disney's distorted treatment of traditional story material held sacred by librarians on behalf of the children whose cultural legacy it was. "Not in my memory," Moore declared,

> has there been a sharper challenge to libraries, schools, and homes to sustain the integrity as works of art tales which have formed the bedrock of literature for children during the 19th and 20th centuries. The easy acceptance of sophisticated characters and settings with interpretations which derive from the comic strip and music hall rather than from the natural environment of old tales and the simplicity of the characters — whether dwarfs or humankind — is a more subtle danger to the crystal of imagination which is just beginning to sparkle in all children than a nightmare effect upon a particular child.[88]

Nor, from the librarians' point of view, did Disney represent the only new threat. Comic strips — most with a broadly based appeal to both adults and children — had been a circulation-boosting popular feature of American newspapers since the 1890s. Throughout the early 1900s, down-market printer-publishers had been experimenting with new formats in which to package and exploit the lucrative cartoon-panel narratives. During the mid-1930s these efforts culminated in the invention of the comic book — a pulp magazine, really, with a grab bag lineup of features aimed primarily at children and sold at newsstands for a dime.[89] Crude drawing styles, formulaic plotting, wildly exaggerated notions of heroism, and excitable, subliterary writing led the list of offenses cited by librarians in their critique of this new incursion into their domain.

The sharpness of the attack only served to confirm the comic book's rapid rise as a force to be reckoned with. Superman, the fevered dream of two precocious Cleveland teenagers, soon became the musclebound standard-bearer of that force. Appearing on newsstands starting in June 1938, *Action Comics*, with an installment of the Superman saga as its centerpiece, sold at the rate of nearly one million copies per month. In contrast, a picture book published by Viking or Macmillan could rarely boast of a first printing exceeding five thousand copies.

The first Caldecott Medal was presented in Kansas City at the American Library Association's annual convention on June 14, 1938 — within days of the publication of the first issue of *Action Comics*. Dorothy P. Lathrop accepted the award for her illustrations for *Animals of the Bible: A Picture Book*. The text, which comprised excerpts from the Old and New Testaments, had been selected by Helen Dean Fish, who also edited the book for Stokes. The ceremony, at which the Newbery Medal was also awarded, took place on a Tuesday afternoon before a large gathering of members of the American Library Association's Section for Library Work with Children. Both winners' acceptance speeches were broadcast live over national radio. Lathrop, a twenty-year veteran as an illustrator, spoke of her lifelong fondness for animals, her reverence for children, and her sense of responsibility as an artist toward both her subjects and her young audience:

> I wonder if we don't too often forget how new this natural world is to children, how fresh and unjaded their interest in it? Of course, we authors and illustrators are up against tremendous competition in trying to market our wares. No wonder we sometimes strive desperately to at-

tract with novelty the attention of publishers who are adults and of a buying public which is also adult. But to the child himself the most novel invention is not more strange and wonderful than the living creatures of this world.[90]

In a piece that looked back admiringly over the whole of Lathrop's career, Bertha Mahony Miller singled out for praise a second facet of the illustrator's work in addition to her excellence as a nature artist: Lathrop's gift for depicting the poetic realm of fairie. Miller spoke with regret of the marginalization from the cultural mainstream that she believed was the certain fate of imaginative fancy like that exhibited in Lathrop's ethereal graphics. She noted with approval that "of the twenty-nine books Miss Lathrop has illustrated, twenty-four have been directly concerned with the fairy world. . . . Indeed, Miss Lathrop has created a Fairy Academy in these strange times of ours. For this twentieth century, with all its magic in machinery and the coming-true of scientists' dreams of centuries, has seen the blasting of other dreams and much destruction."[91]

Miller made these rueful remarks at a time of alarming news about the wars in Europe and Asia. American children now viewed the latest images of industrial-age destruction in the pages of weekly mass-circulation magazines and in movie-house newsreels. Launched in November 1936 by Time, Inc., *Life* magazine rapidly transformed black-and-white still photography into the dominant illustration medium of the popular magazine. *Life* — and, from 1937, its rival *Look* — were in effect becoming the nation's picture books.[92] Critics like Miller might still argue that photography could never completely satisfy the requirements of imaginative illustration for children, as librarians conceived the matter, and that photographs were instead to be classed as one more instance of Miller's "magic in machinery": image-making at its most literal-minded.[93] Ironically, as this debate was carried on in the pages of *The Horn Book*, *The Publishers' Weekly*, and elsewhere, the overwhelming impact of *Life* was making the most powerful argument yet mounted in modern times for the educational value and sheer drama of all forms of illustration.[94]

Lathrop, as it happened, received the Caldecott Medal just weeks after Houghton Mifflin's American edition of J. R. R. Tolkien's *The Hobbit* arrived in bookstores. Tolkien's eccentric book — a purported prequel to recorded history in which the purposeful deeds of wizards, elves, and dwarfs served to put the folly of humankind in a clarifying perspective — was published as a children's book and won general praise from the field's critics. Anne Carroll Moore hailed *The Hobbit* as a "rich imaginative tale . . . rooted deep in Saxon lore . . . [that] is wonderful to read aloud."[95] The *Herald-Tribune* Spring Book Festival judges awarded it one of the year's best books prizes. Bertha Mahony Miller called *The Hobbit* one of those "rare books which stay in the mind like poetry, revealing always fresh joys and new meaning."[96] To Moore and her colleagues, the Oxford professor's remarkable work, and Lathrop's "Fairy Academy," were not mere escapist literature and picture-making, but rather narrative art with a vital role to play in helping to spare young people from a disenchanting preoccupation with the worrisome spectacle of a civilization on the brink. The accomplishment of that heroic task had become the librarians' central mission, and the medals now theirs to bestow were as shining markers on the path to a better future.

On April 30, 1939, one hundred and fifty years to the day after George Washington took the oath of office as the nation's first president, the New York World's Fair, constructed on swampland in Flushing Meadows, Queens, opened to the public. The fair's exultant theme, "The World of Tomorrow," had been chosen to express modern mankind's supposed faith in the capacity of industrial-age technology to trump ideological and cultural differences and thereby to render war a thing of the past. The fair's planners presented the future as a suavely streamlined, technology-based urban utopia. From the start, however, fair skeptics seemed to have the upper hand. *Life*, which devoted a major picture essay in its July 3, 1939, issue to the World's Fair, summed up the spectacle as a "magnificent monument to and by American business."[97] *The Nation*, while refusing to endorse the fair's rosy premise about technology's transformative power, sang its praises as a Barnum-esque extravaganza that by making science and industry seem as entertaining as a three-ring circus might somehow serve a useful purpose as public education. Before long, fair organizers were left to wonder why, despite the best efforts of a high-powered public relations operation headed by the indefatigable Grover A. Whalen, attendance that first season was falling far short of expectations. In retrospect, as one of the planners concluded, the fair had "opened with overpowering ceremony, great pomp, and with regal splendor. So much so, that the common run of people, especially from small places throughout the country, . . . seemed to become sort of frightened in a way by it all." The fair's grandiose world of tomorrow simply had not had all that much appeal for ordinary Americans.[98]

That same spring, a young Ohio-born artist was hard at work in his Greenwich Village studio on a picture book that presented a far less glamorous yet equally utopian vision of modern America. In *Make Way for Ducklings*, Robert McCloskey proposed that American life always worked best when anchored in respect for time-honored values such as family unity, respect for the natural world, and a fine neighborly concern. The editors of *Life* became interested in what McCloskey was up to when they learned (doubtless thanks to a well-placed telephone call from May Massee) that the artist had recently purchased a crate-load of ducklings at a local market and hauled them up to his West Twelfth Street apartment to serve as live models. The offbeat backstory — squawking birds being given the run of a New York artist's kooky bohemian loft — meshed perfectly with the lighter side of *Life*'s omnivorous, world-at-a-glance style of reportage. A reporter and photographer were dispatched to the fourth-floor walkup, and the piece was put to bed complete with candid shots of ducklings scrambling adorably up and down the artist's sleeve. Then, on September 1, 1939, the German army invaded Poland, and the entire issue for that week was scrapped to make way for the catastrophic news of all-out war in Europe.[99]

By the time the New York World's Fair reopened for its second and final season the following spring, the fair slogan had been changed from "The World of Tomorrow" to "For Peace and Freedom." Guest orators and the organizers' own endless stream of promotional utterances no longer played up the elusive dream of global interdependence. A new folksiness and focus on traditional American themes now dominated a fair that only months earlier had touted itself as the antithesis of provincialism. As one of that season's many promotional events, fair officials selected New York City's "typical American boy," as determined by physical appearance and the results of an essay contest. The winner, an eighth-grader at PS 53, had written: "The typical American boy should possess the same qualities as those of the early American pioneers. He should be handy, dependable, courageous, and loyal to his beliefs." Among this typical lad's sources of enjoyment were "the comics, the movies, outdoor games, pets, and radio programs. He . . . is always thinking up something new to do or make. That is why America still has a future."[100] The pragmatic, house-proud tone of the newly recast "super country fair" doubtless reflected the majority American opinion in the spring of 1940 that the war in Europe was still none of America's business.[101] By the time *Make Way for Ducklings* was published in the fall of 1941, McCloskey's urban idyll, with its quaint views of Boston and story of the "magic in machinery" yielding right of way to a feather-clad mother and her children, suited the nation's mood supremely well.

McCloskey had at least one thing in common with the fair designers across the East River. Trained as a mural painter, he thought in terms of dramatic broad-brush effects and panoramic vistas. As an illustrator, McCloskey liked to work big and favored any device that maximized a feeling of expansiveness in his drawings. With its sweeping aerial views (all the more exhilarating because so novel for readers with little or no experience of air travel) and other equally dramatic double-page spreads, *Make Way for Ducklings* emerged from the artist's drawing table as a monumental structure in picture-book form. The awarding to McCloskey of the Caldecott Medal for 1942 assured the book of a long life. In contrast to that happy ending, and in an ironic surprise twist worthy of O. Henry, the four thousand tons of steel used in the construction of the iconic Trylon and Perisphere of the "World of Tomorrow" fared less well: soon after the World's Fair closed for good, the dazzling white symbolic structures were unceremoniously scrapped for recasting as armaments.[102]

May Massee planned her Viking lists with a view to keeping her medal contenders out of competition with one another. *Make Way for Ducklings* had been ready to go to press for a full year when it finally did so, the editor having concluded (correctly as it turned out) that the Caldecott Medal for 1941 was destined for Robert Lawson.

Had the American Library Association established the Caldecott Medal a year earlier — had it presented the first medal, that is, in 1937 for a book published in 1936 — the inaugural award doubtless would have gone to Robert Lawson for *The Story of Ferdinand*. Four years later, when May Massee telephoned him in March 1940, it was with the good news that he had won the medal for a picture book tracing the story of his own unremarkable but hard-working and morally decent family back several generations, a book whose wistful title summed up the prewar twilight moment perfectly: *They Were Strong and Good*.

5

WORLD WAR AND MASS MARKET
The 1940s

Children emerging from rattles to picture books, children who are to-day living in an upside-down world, need books to make them laugh, to make them feel secure, and above all, to make them believe in the permanence of good and beautiful things.

> — GRACE ALLEN HOGARTH, in *Bulletin of the New Hampshire Libraries* (September 1943)

What is there about Comics that makes children like them so well?

> — OHIO SIXTH-GRADE TEACHER, quoted in *Library Journal* (October 15, 1943)

"THE BLUEBELLS ARE VERY LOVELY and the hawthorn blossom like snow on the green hedges and the cuckoo [is] calling of a world of beauty that will survive — and Freedom will survive, whatever happens to us."[1]

Writing from Hill Top Farm, Beatrix Potter sent this message of resolve to Anne Carroll Moore on May 25, 1940 — the eve of the Battle of Dunkirk. With news of the war growing ever more terrifying, Potter had written that same day to several American friends, first to reassure them that life in the Lake District went on almost as usual, but also to enlist their help should two young cousins of hers need to be evacuated to the United States or Canada. Earlier that May, Hitler's army had swept west from Germany through Holland, Belgium, and France. And on May 14 the BBC had broadcast a special alert to all owners of private pleasure craft to make them ready in the event that an emergency evacuation of Allied troops from Dunkirk should become necessary. "It would be idle to conceal that we are very anxious," Potter told Moore. Yet she had little thought for her own safety. "Personally in old age it does not matter much to us, and we 'will stick it out' whatever happens." As for those belonging to England's younger generations, so very many of whom had grown up on her books, she foresaw "a lot more misery" in the months ahead.

Moore had first met the crusty, publicity-shy author of *The Tale of Peter Rabbit* in 1921 on a visit abroad to aid in the postwar restoration of children's library service in France.[2] Not only had the two women gotten along splendidly on that occasion, but Moore had even managed to persuade the long-retired and famously strong-willed artist-turned-farmer-and-conservationist to illustrate a new children's book, to satisfy the clamoring of her American fans. *Cecily Parsley's Nursery Rhymes* appeared the following year — a picture book that added more luster to Moore's reputation than to Potter's; still, an enduring friendship had been forged.[3] The librarian's third and most recent visit to Top Hill Farm had been in happier times, during the spring of 1937, the festal season of King George VI's coronation.

Writing from Maine in her "Three Owls' Notebook" column for *The Horn Book* for July 1940, Moore quoted from Potter's "wonderful letter" and then, resetting her gaze, declared that "never" had she seen "the New England country more freshly green, more beautiful." If there was a lesson to be gleaned from the glory of her native Maine landscape, it was surely, Moore suggested, the very lesson that Potter had limned in the splendor of the reborn English countryside: "New England and Old England may well mingle memories of beauty after heavy frosts and dark hours as they rebuild once more their common faith in the unconquerable spirit of men and women who have struggled to maintain the world of beauty."[4]

She closed her July column with a eulogy for another of the English friends she had last visited during that long-ago spring of 1937, illustrator L. Leslie Brooke. The artist had died in London on May 1. Such was the high regard in which Moore held his contribution to the picture book that to mark his seventieth birthday, in 1932, Moore, in her best fairy godmother manner, had proclaimed the occasion a "festival day" to be celebrated annually in all the children's rooms of the New York Public Library system.[5] From that year onward, on September 24, Brooke's *Johnny Crow's Garden* and other beloved picture books had been ceremoniously read aloud at library story hours, and a birthday greeting cabled, in the name of the city's youngsters, from the Central Children's Room to the artist at his Hampstead home. Rising diva-like to the solemn occasion, Moore assured her *Horn Book* readers now that, despite the artist's passing, his "day" would continue faithfully to be observed and that his books would last. After reciting the list of beloved Brooke titles, Moore added, in a sort of offstage whisper: "We have laid in a goodly store of these indispensables [*sic*], mindful of the sad shortage of English picture books during the War of 1914–18 and afterward."[6]

Lofty rhetoric ceded to sober fact in the "Three Owls'" ruminations. By the time Moore's latest column reached her readers in early July, the evacuation of Dunkirk had passed into history and the Battle of Britain had begun. That October, Dorothy Lathrop, James Daugherty, Thomas Handforth, and Hendrik Willem van Loon were among the noted illustrators who contributed original artwork to a charity sale organized by the War Relief Society in Manhattan for the benefit of British children living in the war zone.[7] For Americans, even those who had hoped the spreading conflicts abroad would leave their own nation untouched, the air was thick with foreboding. Before the fall was out, as Moore, then sixty-nine, entered upon the final year of her tenure at the New York Public Library, a Baltimore newsboy named Russell Baker, bearing "newspapers with gigantic headlines" that told of the devastating aerial bombardment of London, would share the astonishment of millions as he "marveled at the destruction of a civilization I'd thought eternal."[8]

It was small wonder that comic books such as *Superman* and *Batman* — and their pulp fiction counterparts for adult readers — were achieving high peaks of both dramatic hyperbole and sales. The comics' two-fisted story lines featuring monstrous villains, outrageous criminality, and imminent danger to the public at large bore a disturbing, funhouse-mirror resemblance to events being played out around the world. "We all know," Louise Seaman Bechtel observed, "how closely the tormenting facts of world-wide troubles impinge on the eyes and ears of children. They, too, hear the voices of Churchill and of Hitler, as if they were in the next room. . . . As Mr. Lovell Thompson said in a recent *Atlantic*, surely it is sensible for 'Kid-Brother' to go to sleep with a death-ray gun under his pillow: he is just being prepared, as his father was when he played pioneers and Indians."[9] Even the cheap, throwaway paper the comics were printed on underscored the ephemeral books' weird appropriateness to a perishable, indecorous, and perhaps futureless time.

In 1940 American children purchased an estimated 7.5 million comic books a month — more than ten times the total number of children's books published that year. For the publishers of the comics, this represented an estimated $10 million in monthly gross sales — a staggering sum.[10] For the children's book industry, the statistics cast a pall on an otherwise encouraging trend. In 1920, 410 children's books had been published in the United States. Two decades later, the number published had not only recovered from Depression-era lows but risen to a record total of 852 new titles.[11]

Librarian-critics like Moore reserved their iciest contempt — and an old standby pejorative, "trash" — for any work they associated with the Stratemeyer Syndicate's assembly-line style of publishing. In viewing the comics as series fiction transposed for the picture-book ages, they were substantially right, of course, whatever the merits of their unqualified antipathy. Reaction was intense as the librarians and their colleagues treated the phenomenon as though it were an epidemic requiring emergency countermeasures. In March 1941, on the theory that a milder form of the disease might inoculate young people against the real thing, an organization calling itself the Parents' Institute launched its own *True Comics* as a bimonthly with the avowed goal of offering youngsters a high-minded alternative to the popular ten-cent magazines. The first issue featured an inspiring account of the life of Winston Churchill. Urging readers to keep an eye out for the quixotic venture, *The Horn Book* predicted it was doomed to fail. Turning the logic of the experiment back on itself, the editors ridiculed the notion that Britain's silver-tongued orator could have acquired *his* first knowledge of history and biography "in cheap picture form during his childhood and youth."[12] There could be no substitute for early and regular exposure to literary excellence; in this high-church view of the matter, excellence was bound to triumph sooner or later.

The chances of this happening in the short run, however, appeared to be slim indeed. Taking up the discussion in *The Horn Book* two issues later, Louise Seaman Bechtel appeared unperturbed as she questioned the comics' long-term prospects and argued that as she and her colleagues awaited the genre's demise, the comics might even prove to be a "useful gadfly . . . stinging us all into more concrete action about children and books."[13] Bechtel nonetheless found that she could not escape at least one disturbing conclusion, that "whatever our personal philosophies, we all feel ashamed that in an America which above all cares for education, such a phenomenon as Superman should be so successful."[14]

*   *   *

During the fateful interlude bracketed by the start, during the mid-1930s, of the nation's economic recovery and America's entry into World War II, New York restaked its claim as a world crossroads by becoming the principal refuge for the cream of the Old World's expatriate artists, writers, intellectuals, and scientists. At the same time, the nation as a whole was consolidating its position as the new industrial colossus, poised for stupendous leaps in manufacturing capacity even as Europe once again took up arms.

At some publishing houses, the increasingly favorable economic conditions at home made the time seem right for expansion. In New York a maverick firm founded in the 1920s by Richard Simon and Max Schuster was searching for a distinctive way to make its mark in the juvenile field. The two young founders of Simon & Schuster — Columbia graduates who knew that, as Jews, a publishing career at any of the older houses was barred to them — had come from nowhere in April 1924 to achieve instant notoriety with their very first publication, *The Crossword Puzzle Book*, which Bertha Mahony had written about so approvingly, and which, to industry insiders, had seemed to usher in a new, more irreverent approach to publishing. Before the year was out, the astonished but nimble partners had brought out three sequels, each of which matched the first one in success by reaching the number-one position on the nonfiction bestseller list.[15] In the years that followed, Messrs. Simon and Schuster — in league with the firm's third "S," treasurer Leon Shimkin — proved their house was no nine days' wonder by time and again correctly reading the popular appetite for books as varied as Will Durant's *The Story of Philosophy* and Robert Ripley's *Believe It or Not.*

By the late 1930s, Richard Simon and the thriving company's sales manager, Albert Leventhal, both had young children at home and were eyeing the juvenile trade with growing appreciation, as the economy improved, of its potential for dramatic growth. Recognizing their own lack of expertise in a specialized realm, Simon & Schuster in a bold move hired away production managers Tom and Margaret Bevans from Viking, where the couple had worked on picture books with the great May Massee.[16] Not long after the Bevanses' arrival, the upstart firm had a new coup to celebrate: the acquisition of a picture book by one of the most famous artists in the Viking stable, Ludwig Bemelmans. In a rare lapse in judgment, Massee had declined to publish Bemelmans's *Madeline* on the grounds that its story of a naughty, strong-willed girl was a wee too "sophisticated" for young readers. Having done so, she had, of course, rendered the book fair game for others, including the merry pranksters at Simon & Schuster, who seized upon *Madeline* as an inspired match with a trade list that had been known from the first for its mischievous streak and smart disdain for literary propriety.

The Bevanses soon proved their worth again when an ingenious novelty book for young children by a popular author named Dorothy Kunhardt was offered to the house — a design that called for small bits of real sandpaper, cloth, and other textured materials to be securely fastened to its cardboard pages, and a noise-making "squeaker" embedded in another page (there were other special effects as well), the better for preschoolers to explore the sensory realm for themselves as they followed the adventures of Judy and Paul. Elisabeth Hamilton, Kunhardt's editor at Harcourt, Brace, had expressed initial enthusiasm for Kunhardt's dummy, but as she realized the nightmarish complications that the production of such a book would entail, caution prevailed and Harcourt eventually declined. Then Kunhardt's mockup found its way into the hands of the Bevanses, who blithely rose to the challenge, coordinating the efforts of eleven suppliers and a small army of women assembly-line workers. *Pat the Bunny* — brilliantly launched with a tongue-in-cheek advertising campaign that compared the book favorably to the season's most talked-about literary sensations ("*For Whom the Bell Tolls* is magnificent — but it hasn't any bunny in it") — arrived in bookshops in November 1940, just in time for the Christmas trade, and quickly became the year's bestselling children's book.[17]

In Boston earlier that year, Houghton Mifflin belatedly established a children's trade book department comparable to those set up by the major New York houses (and in Boston by Little, Brown) during the decade following World War I. Houghton Mifflin was hardly a newcomer to the juvenile field, having published in one or another of its earlier incarnations two of nineteenth-century America's legendary children's magazines, *Our Young Folks* and the *Riverside Magazine*, and built up an impressive list of books that included the only authorized U.S. edition of the writings of Hans Christian Andersen and such American classics as Kate Douglas Wiggin's *Rebecca of Sunnybrook Farm* and Lucy Fitch Perkins's *The Dutch Twins*. In recent decades, Houghton's long and profitable tradition of educational publishing had led to the firm's treatment of children's books as an editorial adjunct of that division of the house. By 1940, however, the rationale for doing so had come to seem increasingly out of step with the specialized apparatus of juvenile publishing and library work. That the decision to elevate the status of the children's list within the firm came when it did doubtless owed much to the intense personal interest in the genre taken by the manager of Houghton's general trade department, Lovell Thompson, and to an opportunity Thompson saw just then to hire a woman of proven ability as the founding director of the new department. Grace Allen Hogarth had made her reputation during the previous decade as director of the juvenile department at New York's Oxford University Press before marrying an Englishman and moving to London, where she had continued her career as an editor at Chatto & Windus. By early 1940, with paper rationing having brought children's book publishing in England to a standstill, and with her husband away in the military, Hogarth had decided that the time had come to flee Britain with her children and return home to the United States, where, as Thompson realized, she would need employment.

Hogarth arrived at Houghton with a thorough knowledge of color printing technology, with prior professional experience as an illustrator and book designer as well as in editorial work, and with a host of industry connections. She easily settled into her new job, choosing to make the best of the dingy workspace assigned to her. Houghton Mifflin's clublike offices at 2 Park Street nestled cozily within the most London-like part of town, less than a block from Charles Bulfinch's gold-domed Massachusetts State House and across the way from the graveyard where Elizabeth Goose — by legend *the* Mother Goose of the old children's rhymes — was buried. As no space at 2 Park Street could be spared, the new editor and her secretary were dispatched to a windowless expanse on an open loft floor in the spillover quarters at number 4, where, as if in a recapitulation of the company's history in regard to children's literature, the Education Department was already encamped. "We arrived," Hogarth later recalled,

> with two desks, wastepaper basket, file, and a work table, so arranged
> that they made me think of the houses of overturned chairs and tables
> that were the delight of my childhood. We caused a considerable stir
> and soon discovered that we were to provide a certain amount of colour that had possibly been lacking in the life that went on around us.
> Eleanor Kilgour, who was then my right-hand woman, seemed to de-

light in being on the stage to these unacknowledged onlookers. They, of course, had all the windows so that we worked by electric light and were as visible as though illuminated by footlights.[18]

With a ritual nod to the firm's past, Hogarth was given the small antique desk where, seventy years before, Houghton author and *Atlantic Monthly* editor Thomas Bailey Aldrich had penned his classic novel for young people, *The Story of a Bad Boy.* Now, as she adjusted to the more hectic rhythms and routines of American publishing, Hogarth was astonished at the sheer number of manuscript submissions that piled up on a desk too small to accommodate the volume. Working after hours one evening to keep pace with the mail, she remarked casually to the janitor that a stack of rejected manuscripts she had placed on the floor beside her were "trash." A day or so later, when she could not find the manuscripts and realized that the janitor must have taken her words literally, she and Kilgour just managed to retrieve the missing papers from the basement, where they had already been bagged for transport to a wartime reprocessing plant.[19]

Among the last items of business Hogarth had attended to before sailing for New York had been to contact Hans Augusto Rey, a German Jewish artist whom she had published at Chatto. As Hogarth was aware, Rey and his wife, Margret, who were then living in Paris, intended to leave Europe for the United States sometime soon as well. She won from the Reys the promise of right of first refusal for whatever children's book manuscripts they brought with them to New York.

Bicycling out of Paris on June 14, 1940, the day the German army of occupation entered the city, the Reys reached the United States via Brazil that October. On settling into temporary quarters in an Upper West Side Manhattan hotel, they wrote Hogarth in Boston, who was indeed anxious to call on them. Concerned that some enterprising New York publisher might see Rey's portfolio first, Hogarth arranged to meet the couple in Manhattan a short time later. On November 4, following their cordial reunion, the editor wrote Rey to say that she was "setting the stage to get your books accepted. . . . I shall bend every effort to get the decision through this week." In the meantime, she urged the artist, with whom she had discussed plans for some novelty "lift-the-flap" books aimed at very young children, "if you have the time it would be nice for you and Mrs. Rey to look in on Miss Barksdale, who is in charge of the Children's Books section of the

Doubleday Doran book shop next door to Lord and Taylor's on Fifth Avenue just above 38th Street. She is a good friend of mine and will show you many of the new books which may interest you. Will you ask her to show you especially PAT THE BUNNY which has a mirror in it?"[20]

A tenacious negotiator on behalf of her mild-mannered husband, Margret Rey had demanded, and won, a four-book contract from Houghton Mifflin, an arrangement that would have been highly unusual for the time even had Rey not been a complete unknown to the American market. Two books were planned for the next year, including the one originally called "Fifi," which Hogarth, her boss Lovell Thompson, or one of their colleagues wisely renamed *Curious George*.[21] A third and fourth book were to follow a year later.

In the fall of 1941, *Curious George*, with its jaunty tale of a fearless, devil-may-care monkey hero, arrived on store shelves in time for the holidays and was hailed by critics as just the right kind of funny, action-packed entertainment to give the creators of the comics a run for their money.[22] Rey and his wife, a Bauhaus-trained photographer who wrote, art-directed, and often posed for her husband's picture books, had had no such lofty intention in mind when they cobbled together the first draft and watercolor illustrations for their story in Paris. Be that as it may, initial sales of the book were only respectable, then plummeted briefly as the ill effects of wartime paper rationing took their toll; George's — and the Reys' — fortunes would rise with the birthrate, reaching impressive levels starting in the 1950s.[23]

Appearing on the same Houghton Mifflin list as *Curious George* that fall was an unconventional picture book by the much-admired author-illustrator of *Mike Mulligan and His Steam Shovel*, Virginia Lee Burton. As publication neared, Burton made certain to leave no doubt in the minds of librarians as to her true intent in creating a picture book in comic-book format. *Calico the Wonder Horse; or, The Saga of Stewy Slinker*, she told *The Horn Book*'s readers, represented her determined effort to "compete against" the runaway popularity of the comics. Far from being one more such piece of ephemera, *Calico*, she reported, had grown out of an intensive year of study and experimentation with the comics genre. Burton had in fact plotted out her idea for a "symphony in comics" with Lovell Thompson prior to Hogarth's arrival at the house.[24]

The comic-book craze, as Burton freely acknowledged, had long since invaded her own home, impelling her to consider what it was about the "lurid tales" that "enthralled" children like her own nine-year-old son. With the detachment of an ethnographer chronicling the curious practices of a remote tribal society, she recalled having discovered that

> comic books were like currency. They could be traded for toys. They were collected like treasures. There must be a reason for it.
>
> I soon found out that these books and [radio] programs satisfied a natural craving for excitement . . . action . . . drama; gave the children a hero to worship and an escape to thrilling adventure that is wanted by any normal child.[25]

Burton's breezy commentary masked a chronic insecurity unlike any that Hogarth had previously encountered in an author. As Hogarth later recalled, as Burton's own sons grew beyond the picture-book age, the artist grew less and less sure of her ability to communicate with young children. The editor herself had reason to fear the reaction to *Calico*. While still at Oxford, Hogarth had published a picture book by Georges Duplaix called *Gaston and Josephine in America*, which Anne Carroll Moore had condemned as "a comic strip . . . unworthy of you [the editor]."[26] Burton had originally intended to call the comic villain of *Calico* Stewy "Stinker" rather than "Slinker," but Hogarth had strongly advised against the naughty version of the name, and the editor had prevailed.[27] When it was published that fall, Burton's experiment was well received as the gallant though futile gesture that it was. Her next picture book, *The Little House*, laid out in a conventional picture-book design and format, was awarded the Caldecott Medal for 1943.

Far and away the most notable defender of the comics that spring, however, was the current year's Caldecott Medal winner, Robert Lawson. In comments that must have sent shudders through his admiring award ceremony audience, Lawson used his Caldecott acceptance speech at the American Library Association convention that June in part as an opportunity to make a reasoned defense of the comic-book genre's still-flourishing precursor — the "much misunderstood and maligned" comic strip. "Not that they [the strips and the artists who created them] need it, Heaven knows," as Lawson pointed out. "They are doing very well for themselves. . . . But at the risk of revealing myself as a moronic lowbrow I must confess that I have found a great deal to admire and a great deal to envy."[28]

Lawson praised the deft draftsmanship and compelling storytelling of a number of the strips, especially his own personal favorite, *Joe Palooka*. "They have *real* interest and suspense," he said. "Their characters have *real* and recognizable personality. They are highly moral." Lawson admonished his audience not to

> look down our noses at the newspaper strips. I am sure we cannot afford to just sit back and bemoan the fact that thousands and thousands of children have the bad taste to prefer them to our nice children's books. But we can, by a thorough and open-minded study of them, learn a great deal, a great deal that would help make our books more vital.

In his folksy and eminently reasonable way, Lawson proceeded to salt the wound by arguing that some of the most beautiful picture books then being published — including presumably some destined for Caldecott Medal consideration — were in fact pretentious, overblown examples of the bookmaker's art. Such books might garner prizes from connoisseurs, but they meant little to children. Lawson knew better, of course, than to cite specific examples of this offense. (One has to wonder what Lawson's own editor, May Massee, whom he had taken care to praise at the start of his address, must have been thinking as the attack continued.)

When at last Lawson seemed ready to move on to other matters, he did so by redirecting his fire at another, albeit (for librarians) less controversial target. The "greatest menace to children's books today," Lawson declared, lay neither in the crassness of the comics nor in the excesses of aesthetic refinement. The real threat came from those "few people scattered around in the fringes of things, those natural uplifters and arrangers, who feel the call to plan and regulate everything in sight . . . [to] decide what subjects are suitable for children, what phrases children can understand, what words are to be allowed or forbidden to children of certain ages. They would like to decide, for the children, what type of illustration they like best, what colors and techniques are most suitable." Lawson once again left unnamed the objects of his criticism. Had he been more direct about it, however, there can be little doubt that Lucy Sprague Mitchell and her Bank Street colleagues would have made, if not actually topped, the list. For Lawson, apparently, the efforts of such educators to create age-graded books based on developmental research led to a narrowing rather than an expansion of the range of a child's imaginative thinking. All such efforts to systematize children's literature were doomed to failure for the simple reason that neither "creative genius" nor a child's mind worked that way.[29] "No one," Lawson suggested, "can possibly tell what tiny detail of a drawing or what seemingly trivial phrase in a story will be the spark that sets off a great flash in the mind of some child, a flash that will leave a glow there until the day he dies."[30] Few could deny the eloquence or wisdom of this last remark. Lawson, who had begun his address by casting himself as an outsider who did not consider himself "strictly as a 'children's illustrator,'" a term, he said, that he had always found "slightly condescending to children," had given the insiders much to contemplate.

But it was another of the Massee men, Robert McCloskey, who spoke for the majority of his colleagues about the comics. McCloskey did so, slyly enough, in a children's book, a storybook called *Homer Price*, in which he included a chapter that made pointed fun of the comics by ridiculing the superficiality of their characteristic notion of heroism. McCloskey set the scene for "The Case of the Cosmic Comic" in an interior illustration of the local lunchroom in the typical American small town of Centerburg. Homer's companions appear absorbed in browsing through comic books, an assortment of which is displayed on a magazine rack in the shop. Homer, however, wearing a look of wise indifference, has turned away from the rack.

As the story unfolds, the friends decide to catch the Saturday movie matinee at the local theater. Topping the bill that week is a feature called "The SUPER-DUPER and the ELECTRIC RAY," and, as a special treat, the hero of the film, the Super-Duper himself, is due in Centerburg that day for a personal appearance. Caped and impressively musclebound as he pulls up in his big open car, McCloskey's Super-Duper is, of course, a thinly veiled parody of the greatest comic-book superhero of them all. The boys shake hands with Super-Duper as they pass through the lobby on their way into the show. Later, when the movie lets out, Homer's two companions, who are either young or innocent enough to believe they have met not an actor but the real hero, depart the theater awestruck, while Homer remains as unimpressed as ever. McCloskey might well have ended the story there. But instead he sends the boys on their way, heading home in a borrowed horse cart. Suddenly, as Homer and his friends are bouncing along in their rig, a powerful car rushes past them, disappearing around a curve. It is the Super-Duper! The very next thing they hear is a crashing sound — the Super-Duper driving off the road into a ditch. How embarrassing for the superhero — and revelatory for Homer's friends when they come around the bend and, with the help of their horse and old-fashioned rig, just manage to save the day for the bewildered actor by hauling his car out of the ditch. For anyone caught up in the frenzied comics debate of the 1940s, the meaning of the tale was unmistakable.

The Centerburg of McCloskey's *Homer Price* stories was vintage Americana, as archetypical a representation of an American small town as Henry Ford's reconstituted Greenfield Village or the Arlington, Vermont, of Norman Rockwell's paintings for the *Saturday Evening Post*. It was a benign universe ruled by common sense, hard work, and (except for the comically inept petty crooks who blow into town in one of McCloskey's tales) goodwill toward all. Homer grown up might be Frank Capra's Mr. Smith or a Rockwell family physician. To critics of the time, the stories about Homer seemed above criticism and were read as statements of national first principles. As the *Saturday Review* rhapsodized: "No country on earth but the United States could have produced Homer Price and his fellow citizens."[31] The problem of the comics, McCloskey seemed to say, was bound to take care of itself. American children would see through the sham of the comics' flimflammery because seeing through shams was what Americans tended to do.

In what must be counted as the era's most novel defense of the comics, Josette Frank, staff adviser to the Children's Book and Radio Committee of the Child Study Association, a New York–based research and service group with ties to the progressive education movement, argued that one reason young people read the comics so avidly was to fill the void left by the sheer unreality of the vast majority of children's books they read at the library and at school. The comics, Frank was convinced, were in some ways more true to life than the quaint, taboo-riddled storybooks that publishers created to suit the tastes of librarians.

Asked to comment on the quality of books for young readers that addressed contemporary social concerns, Frank asserted that most publishers seemed "afraid of contemporary material." "For so many years," she argued, we thought we could teach peace and international good will through nice little stories about gay and picturesque little children of other lands. Some still seem to think this is the way. But how do they dare? It is inexcusable to give these books to children today. They present a false picture. Even in a golden age, things go wrong. Even in an age like this some things are right . . .[32]

In a stunning inversion of the more conventional view of the question, Frank went on:

It is true [the comics] are filled with hijackers, bank robberies, kidnappings, and violent doings of every description, but they do respond to the public temper. A typical immediate response is the recent comic villain. He has become German. Our books do not respond so swiftly. . . . I do not want it to be interpreted that I think the comics are therefore ideal, or paint an ideal picture, but I do mean to say that the reason they succeed is that they do keep abreast of contemporary life. . . . True, a superman does come along and expedite matters, but that's where the wishful thinking comes in. Don't we all wish for such a superman to straighten out this upside down world for us?[33]

A pragmatist in the progressive reformist mold, Frank found what she considered the perfect forum in which to tell young readers directly about the latest children's books that she believed would engage them. As a consultant for Fawcett, publisher of *Captain Marvel,* Frank wrote book reviews for publication as a feature in the comics themselves. With print runs of the magazines running well into the millions, a friend pointed out to her, Frank might well have become the world's most widely read woman critic.[34]

Contemplating her imminent retirement from the New York Public Library, which was due to take effect on October 1, 1941, Anne Carroll Moore wrote her niece: "I believe I have had a good time and have felt as free to act on my own initiative as anyone in the U.S.A. I feel no sense of possession and no reluctance to give over." Moore could not resist making a catty comparison between herself and one of her few colleagues with greater seniority in her field. "Unlike Miss [Caroline] Hewins [the founding children's librarian of the Hartford Public Library who had remained at her post until just a few days before her death in 1926 at the age of eighty] I did not marry a library neither that of Pratt Institute nor the N.Y.P.L."[35]

Moore chose as her successor a librarian and author who had once worked on her staff, Frances Clarke Sayers. Writing years later as Moore's biographer, Sayers would recall: "Anne was convinced of her ability to retire. The letters in which she spoke of her plans for the future exuded from their pages the accustomed exhilaration with which she gave account of events of her life. Whatever happened or was to happen was recorded with an edge of triumphant expectation."[36]

In the meantime, honors gilded the momentous passage in Moore's professional life. The previous spring, the University of Maine had conferred upon her an honorary doctor of letters. Also in 1940, the Women's National Book Association chose Moore as the first recipient of its highest form of recognition, the Constance Lindsay Skinner Medal for service to literature.

Having been feted a decade earlier on the occasion of her twenty-fifth anniversary at the library, Moore insisted as the fall approached that her colleagues not give her an elaborate retirement party. Dutiful (or fearful) to the last, they deferred to her wishes, arranging instead to gather one evening in the Central Children's Room for an informal farewell at which the guest of honor would be presented with a handsome set of luggage. A crucial component of the gift was a specially made, extra-small leather carrying case bearing the monogram "N.K.," for the sole "use" of Moore's celebrated wooden Dutch doll and alter ego, Nicholas Knickerbocker. For the last twenty years, this articulated wooden figure had served not so much as a plaything as a presence at library events and dinner parties attended by Moore, as a character about whom the librarian had written for children on two occasions, and as a sort of acid test by which she judged the capacity for make-believe of the people she met. Moore herself would soon have need of luggage, as she was due to travel west for a stint as guest lecturer during the spring 1942 semester at the Graduate School in Librarianship of the University of California at Berkeley.

Making a victory lap of her train journey west, Moore chose a circuitous route that allowed her to visit old friends and colleagues in St. Louis, Cincinnati, New Orleans, Houston, and elsewhere. Once settled in at Berkeley, she climbed the campus bell tower and basked in the glow of her newfound celebrity among the university's faculty and students. In class, Moore lectured expansively about the artists and writers she had known and influenced over the past thirty-odd years, reveling as always in the

chance to hold forth about people and books she cared about. It soon became evident to her, however, that she missed New York, and after stop-
overs in Seattle, Minneapolis–St. Paul, and Buffalo to see still more of her
far-flung colleagues, she returned to the city she loved, now eerily dimmed
at night under wartime blackout regulations, and took up residence at the
Grosvenor Hotel at the corner of Fifth Avenue and Tenth Street, where
from her twelfth-floor aerie she and the Three Owls might hope to keep a
close watch over that portion of the book world in whose creation they had
played so signal a role.

As Moore struggled — with far greater difficulty than she had anticipated — to adjust to her newly diminished status, she searched for new
tasks to perform, or at the very least new ways to perform the old ones. She
began making impromptu visits to room 105, where, to the chagrin of
Frances Clarke Sayers and her staff, Moore made it painfully clear that she
expected everything down to the brass candlestick on the catalog case to remain just as she had left it.[37] A better use of her time soon presented itself
when Bertha Mahony Miller, who had begun to feel her age, took to calling
upon Moore on a regular basis for advice on *Horn Book* editorial matters.
Moore was happy to oblige by going up to Boston for occasional meetings
and between times dispatching a steady stream of bluntly worded, handwritten letters offering critiques of every aspect of the magazine's operation.

Miller was a natural consensus builder whose open mind and steady,
even manner had generally come to her aid over the years whenever she
had been forced to cope with the clashing agendas of colleagues. A genuinely modest person, she had remained a devoted student of the elders of
the tribe — Moore, Massee, Boston librarian Alice Jordan, and a handful of
others — long after she herself had achieved full membership in their circle. Miller, moreover, had allowed herself to become the lightning rod of
her profession, even to the point of selfless disregard for her health as time
and again, for the sake of the greater good, she stoically bore the brunt of
the inflexible arguments of others. Lightning struck once again in the
summer of 1943 when, in anticipation of the fall publication of Robert
McCloskey's *Homer Price*, May Massee went to work to ensure that the artist's first chapter book received the glowing critical reception that she felt it
deserved. It had already been decided that the magazine would depart from
custom by giving the new book a much longer than usual, essay-length ap-

preciation rather than the standard paragraph-long critique of fifty to one hundred words. Keenly aware of *The Horn Book*'s editorial cycles, Massee wrote Miller in early July to raise the delicate (one would have thought inappropriate) question of who should write the *Horn Book* essay. In a proprietary show of force, Massee casually swept Miller's own first choice off the table and then named an acceptable alternative:

July 2, 1943

Dear Bertha:

I am sorry but I would rather not have Walter Brooks review Bob McCloskey's new book. I like Walter Brooks and I like his books, but the older I get the more I realize authors just simply can't review each other's books, especially when they are in the same genre. I never will forget Rachel [Field]'s review of Ethel Parton's and I am afraid the same kind of thing might happen with Walter Brooks.

I think I know the person if he will do it. He is Eric Gugler. He is the man who did my office and he was on the committee that gave Bob the Prix de Rome. He likes Bob and he is a terribly interesting person himself. I could give him advance sheets and I think get the review out of him in time if you would like to have me ask him.[38]

Responding by letter on July 13, Miller gave her assent. "Your idea of Mr. Gugler for the review of Robert McCloskey," she wrote the publisher of *Homer Price*, "seems fine with me." Miller left it to Massee to offer the review assignment to Gugler on *The Horn Book*'s behalf and even to settle on a deadline with him.[39]

As the first post–World War I generation of editors and librarians grew older and prepared to retire, the younger people who would soon fill their positions were starting to arrive on the scene. The most notable new editor of the early 1940s had a colorful personal history as the only child of famous vaudeville comedians. Born in Manhattan in 1910 to the aging heart-throb Harry Dixie and the glamorous young Marie Nordstrom, Ursula Nordstrom by the age of seven had also become a child of divorce and an unhappy boarding-school castaway like the girl she would later describe in her only published novel for children, *The Secret Language*. In 1940, as the newly appointed third director of Harper & Brothers' Department of Books for Boys and Girls, Nordstrom brought to the job both her parents' high sense of drama and her own acute awareness of the bad breaks that can befall a child. Having been rebuffed by her stepfather in her desire for a college education (she would later boast to colleagues that the college she had *not* attended was Bryn Mawr), Nordstrom had instead enrolled in the standard secretarial course that served many young women of her generation as a passport to interim employment prior to marriage. Unable to find the kind of social service work with troubled children that she envisioned for herself, Nordstrom, in 1936, took a clerical job in the College Department at Harper & Brothers. As a schoolgirl, Nordstrom had dreamed of becoming a writer. Whether or not she still harbored any such ambitions, she could as a Harper employee at least claim a modest affiliation with one of the nation's most respected publishers.

At the office, the young woman came to know Louise Raymond, the director of the three-person Department of Books for Boys and Girls, and when Raymond's assistant left, she asked Nordstrom to take the position. For Nordstrom, Raymond's offer represented not only a promotion but also a chance to do socially useful work on behalf of children, and she readily agreed. The work proved interesting indeed, in part because it entailed occasional correspondence with the luminaries of the Harper list, including novelist Laura Ingalls Wilder and picture-book artist Clare Turlay Newberry. Nordstrom, who typed rapidly and read at lightning speed, had also to juggle a heavy load of over-the-transom reading and the usual clerical chores. She tolerated the burdensome parts, but then, as she recalled years later, "the letters started coming in from children who'd read books that I'd had a little bit to do with and that was a terrific thrill."[40]

In 1940 Raymond adopted a baby girl and announced her retirement. Harper's president responded casually to the news by asking: "Well, do you think your assistant could take over?" Nordstrom later recalled the exchange as emblematic of the low regard in which Harper's managers of the time held the "tiny department" that she inherited. "Louise said she was sure I could handle it, and I said to them: 'I will take the job and be very happy about it, but give me enough rope. If I hang myself, I hang myself.'"[41]

Not long afterward, Nordstrom headed for a newsstand to purchase copies of *Dick Tracy* and *Little Orphan Annie*. "I thought, 'I'd better get some comic books and find out what the children like so much in them.'" It did not take the inquiring editor, whose after-hours reading ran the gamut from Shakespeare to *Confidential*, very long to realize the comics' appeal.

"I got hooked myself," she recalled years later. "They have strong characters, funny names and a lot of action. Some of the comic strips are very well drawn."[42]

In the years to come, Nordstrom's unorthodox outlook — she once summed up her publishing philosophy in the motto "good books for bad children" — would often serve to set her apart from her less venturesome colleagues in both the library and publishing communities. Among the first artists and authors she signed up were Clement Hurd, a Fauvist painter and friend of Margaret Wise Brown; Ruth Krauss, a polymath bohemian with a smattering of Bank Street Writers Laboratory training; and Krauss's husband, Crockett Johnson, who, until then, had been best known as the creator of the highbrow comic strip *Barnaby*. Her lack of either library experience or a Seven Sisters pedigree only underscored her maverick status. Asked pointedly by Anne Carroll Moore what qualified her — a nonlibrarian, nonteacher, and nonparent — to publish books for boys and girls, Nordstrom, who had a magnificent way of standing her ground, replied: "I am a former child, and I haven't forgotten a thing." It would be Nordstrom, more than anyone, who redefined first the picture book and then the realistic novel for young people for the post-Romantic, post-Freudian modern age.[43]

To those who worked in the children's book industry of the early 1940s, New York could seem as small as a fairy-tale village. Greenwich Village in particular, long a mecca for artists, writers, and political radicals, had by the 1930s become a sort of picture-book bohemia as well. Living as neighbors in 1942 were Nordstrom, Margaret Wise Brown, Hans and Margret Rey, Leonard Weisgard, Charlotte Zolotow, Robert McCloskey, Marc Simont, Munro Leaf, Marjorie Flack, Kurt Wiese, Esther Averill, May Massee, William R. Scott, Vernon A. Ives, Anne Carroll Moore, and Lucy Sprague Mitchell. Margaret Wise Brown, who had made her picture-book debut on the Harper list a few years earlier under Raymond, was Nordstrom's exact contemporary and shared both her irreverent view of the field and her profound contempt for its more precious tendencies. When the prolific writer had a new manuscript for Harper's editor, she would simply meet Nordstrom for breakfast at Schrafft's, an informal restaurant at the corner of Fifth Avenue and Thirteenth Street, where in warm weather the two women could sit outdoors and observe the comings and goings at rival Macmillan's offices a block away. In the days before authors typically relied on agents to negotiate their contracts, Brown often arrived at these break-fast meetings with Smoke, her snappish Kerry Blue terrier. When Margret Rey, who had arranged for Harper to be the Reys' second publisher, decided that Ursula Nordstrom, who lived alone, was lonely and in need of com-panionship, she turned up one day at the editor's door with the fox terrier that she had selected for the purpose.

Brown would invite her friends and collaborators Leonard Weisgard and Clement Hurd to join her for the lively workshop sessions of Lucy Mitchell's Bank Street Writers Laboratory, or (more terrifyingly) to present their work in progress for criticism to the children in the Bank Street nurs-ery school. Marc Simont, who shared a West Twelfth Street studio with Robert McCloskey, helped the latter artist cope with the flock of live mal-lards that for months McCloskey kept on hand as models for *Make Way for Ducklings*.[44]

Publishers' contracts were no lengthier or more complicated than a foldout travel brochure. With rare exceptions, the money that changed hands was measured in hundreds, not thousands, of dollars. To the extent that the professional world of the publishers of children's books and their authors and artists could be described as quaintly old-fashioned, it stood in sharp contrast to the growing power and glamour of the national news and picture magazines, the new communications and entertainment medium of radio, and the public relations industry of which New York was also the center. Publishers scrambled to understand the new machinery of mass communication at least well enough to make it work for a few of their more promising books. In the fall of 1942, to herald the publication of *The Tall Book of Mother Goose* with its slim vertical novelty format, robust art by the Russian émigré Feodor Rojankovsky, and lower-than-average retail price, Harper made one such foray into the brave new world of publicity when it threw a lavish midtown publication party for the book complete with a live goose rented for the occasion as a sort of guest of honor and with a photographer hired to record the stunt. Plans for this rare bit of "tot" department ballyhoo — which proved splashy enough to garner a notice in *Variety*— had been laid by Frank S. MacGregor, a Harper vice-president who had shown little interest in the department's affairs in the past but who anticipated exceptionally strong sales for the Rojankovsky book, which for Harper represented an experiment in mass-market pub-lishing. Punch-drunk with the thrill of having captured the attention of the "boys on the sixth floor," the ebullient Nordstrom, in the run-up to the launch party, wrote her author and publishing colleague Georges Duplaix that she was considering asking Harper's august head of production and design, Arthur W. Rushmore, to attend dressed as Little Boy Blue and chairman of the board Henry Hoyns to come as Jack Sprat. As for herself, Nordstrom, whose letters were masterpieces of manic assertiveness tempered by self-deprecating caricature, hinted that she might show up as "the cow with the crumpled horn."[45]

The Tall Book of Mother Goose had not reached the Harper list in the usual way — as a manuscript submitted by an author, assigned to an illustrator, and then shaped into final form in consultation with the editors of the house. The project was rather among those packaged for Harper by the Artists and Writers Guild, of which Georges Duplaix was the director.

The Guild, whose parent company was the ever-expanding Western Printing and Lithographing Company, headquartered in Racine, Wisconsin, had its own modest offices south of fashionable midtown Manhattan in a no-frills commercial building occupied primarily by toy manufacturers' showrooms. Few would have suspected at the time that the work being done there represented, in several respects, the wave of the future. Founded in 1907, Western had started out as a small, bootstrap job printing operation. Then one day in 1916, when the shop's only publisher-client, the Hamming-Whitman Publishing Company of Chicago, defaulted on payment, "the boys" at Western suddenly found themselves in possession of a substantial inventory of juvenile books. After managing to sell the books more easily than expected, the partners realized that owning a publishing company would assure them of always having something to print. With this thought in mind, they acquired their bankrupt client outright and moved the company to Racine, renaming it Whitman Publishing.[46]

Whitman published a wide range of inexpensive novelty books, picture books, and storybooks, some of which sold for as little as a dime — and none of which the library world thought worthy of attention. The company's major innovations at this time were, in any case, mainly in the realm of sales and marketing. In 1918 a resourceful salesman on the staff, Samuel E. Lowe, made his first sale of Whitman ten-cent books to a national five-and-dime store chain, S. S. Kresge, which previously had not stocked any children's books. Lowe's initiative opened a lucrative new channel for the distribution of lower-priced juveniles, setting a precedent with far-reaching consequences for Western. During the Great Depression years, Lowe added further to the Whitman brand's fame by devising a hugely popular ten-cent series, the stubby, pocket-sized "Big Little Books," which featured the adventures of such comic-book heroes as Dick Tracy, Orphan Annie, and Mickey Mouse. Although printed on pulp paper with garish, attention-grabbing cover art, the Big Littles earned Whitman a certain grudging industry respect for the marketing savvy and pioneering inroads in the character-licensing realm that had culminated in an exclusive book publishing agreement with Disney and in book sales that regularly climbed well past the half-million mark.[47]

For reasons of cost and efficiency, Western's giant color web presses had to be kept running continuously. With Whitman's proven success as encouragement, Western began to look for new ways to marry its printing business to publishing. In 1934 the company acquired a printing plant in Poughkeepsie, New York, in an effort to attract more business from New York City's major publishing firms. The following year the Artists and Writers Guild opened a Manhattan office, with Samuel E. Lowe in charge.[48] The first new printing client that Western signed as a result of the new strategy was Dell, publisher of Hollywood glamour magazines, pulp fiction, and *Dick Tracy* and *Lone Ranger* comics.[49]

For a project like *The Tall Book of Mother Goose*, the Artists and Writers Guild edited the text, chose and art-directed the illustrator, and created a finished design ready for printing by Western. The enviable economies of scale of Western's printing operation made it possible for Harper to offer the colorful book for just one dollar. Older Harper staff members could not have helped but note striking similarities between the dynamic Midwest-based company's current mode of doing business and Harper's own beginnings, more than a century earlier, as an aggressively striving young printer-publisher.

By 1940 the Guild's principals, Georges Duplaix (the raffish, multi-talented French émigré who had replaced Lowe that year as director) and his editor in chief, Lucille Ogle, felt ready to raise the stakes by seeking out a long-term partnership with a major trade publisher, with the goal of realizing one of the most beguiling dreams of the children's book world: the creation of a list of high-quality picture books that every parent could afford.

Trade publishers had long regarded the retail price of twenty-five cents as an industry brass ring that, if ever attained, would vastly expand the retail market for children's picture books. (The ten-cent Whitman picture books that sold so steadily at Kresge, Woolworth, and other chain stores seemed to industry observers to highlight a dilemma embedded within that goal: parents would indeed buy inexpensive children's books in great quantities, but books that could be sold so cheaply were not likely ever to meet the librarians' high aesthetic and literary standards.) In 1940 picture books typically sold for between $1.50 and $2.00 and were printed in editions of a few thousand copies. During the late 1920s, Macmillan had been able to bring the price down to fifty cents for its Happy Hour picture-book series. A subsequent series published by Grosset & Dunlap had duplicated the feat.[50] Georges Duplaix was convinced that the price of such books could be halved again. Simon & Schuster, a Guild client that had first waded into juvenile publishing only a few years earlier (albeit with a great splash), once again lived up to its reputation for daring when after a round of exploratory meetings at Duplaix's home, at which Simon & Schuster was represented by its brilliant sales manager Albert Leventhal, Lucille Ogle was assigned the task of producing prototypes for a projected line of high-quality, twenty-five-cent picture books — Little Golden Books.[51]

Nearly everything went as planned. Although many of the more high-brow booksellers chose not to stock the books, which first went on sale in October 1942, department store buyers were willing to take a chance. It soon became clear that, at twenty-five cents, millions of parents would take a chance too — by purchasing Little Golden Books not just one at a time but by the handful. Price was not the only factor that accounted for the series' instant and broadly based acceptance. Little Golden Books had sturdy board covers (the first several titles came in traditional dust jackets printed in color), an attractive uniform design, and a substantial number of illustrations printed in color. The place of purchase was also a factor. Less-educated parents found it less intimidating to select books from racks in stores where they already did their shopping than to venture into the forbidding bluestocking domain of the traditional bookshop or department store book department, assuming they lived in a city large enough to offer either of the latter options. To close the sale with parents who needed the reassurance that purchasing a Little Golden Book was a responsible choice, Lucille Ogle had arranged for the copyright page of every book to bear the endorsement of "Mary Reed, Ph.D., Assistant Professor of Education, Teachers College, Columbia University."

Anxious parents might well draw comfort from a progressive educator's imprimatur. But librarians cast as cold an eye on Little Golden Books as they did on the comics and Stratemeyer-style series publishing. Far from impressing the librarians, the endorsement of an authority from Teachers College was taken as inflammatory: as yet another invasion (in a class with the one launched in the 1920s by Lucy Sprague Mitchell) by the pseudo-scientists into the timeless realm of story. The debut appearance in 1946 of Mitchell herself on the Little Golden Books list and of Mitchell's protégée Margaret Wise Brown a year later only confirmed the librarians' deepest suspicions about the nature of the enterprise.[52]

Up until then, almost any new children's book that failed to earn the major librarians' approval tended quickly to drop from view. If *The Horn Book* chose not to notice a book — silence being synonymous with disfavor — how would librarians, a great many of whom could not attend the American Library Association's annual conventions, even know it had been published? If the New York Public Library chose not to feature a book on its annual holiday list, how many bookshops would carry the shunned title and how many librarians and teachers would order copies?

By applying the Pocket Books model of distribution to juvenile publishing, however, Little Golden Books bypassed the old review system altogether. Parents, often with restless young children in tow, encountered the books while shopping for Band-Aids or needles and thread and simply decided on the spot whether or not to purchase a twenty-five-cent book too. Further enhancing the books' appeal for parents was the fact that the first twelve titles were "mostly tried-and-true standbys" — colorful repackagings of traditional stories and rhymes that most people could be counted on to know: *Three Little Kittens, Mother Goose, The Little Red Hen,* and *The Golden Book of Fairy Tales.*[53] Authors' and illustrators' names, most of which would have been unfamiliar to the public, were left off the front covers altogether in order to keep the spotlight entirely on the line itself. In less than a year, notwithstanding wartime shortages, Simon & Schuster shipped a phenomenal 2.7 million Little Golden Books to stores and accumulated back orders for another 2 million volumes. If the principals in the venture were at all surprised, it was by the sheer magnitude of their triumph and by the curious fact that the most popular title of the first dozen proved not to be one of the list's generic "classics" but rather a little-known Texas author's gently mischievous original tale called *The Poky Little Puppy.*

In 1944 the two partners in the venture restructured their joint operation. Parallel to Western's Artists and Writers Guild, Simon & Schuster now established its own special office, Sandpiper Press, to carry out some of the editorial work needed for the rapidly expanding Golden Books list. Georges Duplaix crossed over from the Guild to head Sandpiper, whose precise relationship to the Guild had been left purposefully vague to promote a spirit of competitive enterprise.

Duplaix, who preferred painting pictures to running an office, had a keen eye for illustration talent and wide-ranging European connections that stood the new venture in good stead. The creation of a strong stable of artists was another important element in his plan to keep the Western presses rolling profitably. It was Duplaix who, just as the Atlantic commercial sea lanes were about to close for the duration of the war, secured the eleventh-hour passage to New York of Russian émigré artist Feodor Rojankovsky in return for an exclusive contract with the Guild. A year earlier he had signed Tibor Gergely, the prolific, Hungarian-born Jewish émigré artist, to a similar agreement.

Gradually, Duplaix delegated most of his major day-to-day responsibilities to his capable assistant, Dorothy A. Bennett, who had come to Sandpiper Press with a background in academic publishing and museum education. Bennett's idealism was reflected in an early Little Golden Books sales slogan — "Books and Bread" — that underscored the venture's populist inflection. If there was an echo in the earnest catch phrase of American labor movement sloganeering (or Soviet-style propaganda), those responsible for the books took care not to lose sight of the profit motive. As Bennett later recalled, rather cattily, her Artists and Writers Guild counterpart, Lucille Ogle, never accepted a book for publication before first seeing whether the doorman at Western's offices found it amusing.[54]

Ogle, a brisk, big-voiced midwesterner with degrees in education and marketing, took a no-nonsense approach in budgetary matters. In disputes between them, Bennett, a contrastingly small and wiry but equally intense woman, usually took the side of art for art's sake as against Ogle's more pragmatic approach. Neither woman yielded ground readily, and the creative sparks their clashes generated had much to do with the lasting value of so many of the books they published together.

With print runs, sales, and revenues that dwarfed those of the traditional houses, and with the editors' strong commitment to making good on their claim to quality bookmaking, Golden Books aggressively pursued the best writers and illustrators in the field. In a foretaste of later industrywide practices, old-fashioned author-to-publisher loyalties fell by the wayside as potentially lucrative contracts were proffered against a backdrop of proven sales in the hundreds of thousands and even millions of copies per title. While most Golden artists and writers received one-time payment on a "flat fee" basis, the increasingly sought-after marquee figures were offered the greater lure of royalties. With Golden's phenomenal sales results a given, the royalty percentages being offered, though far lower than the industry standard, seemed more than likely to pay off in the end. Other publishers trembled at the thought. Margaret Wise Brown, who as a prolific writer necessarily worked with more than one publisher anyway, took full advantage in her negotiations with Ursula Nordstrom and others of this widespread fear of the young behemoth in their midst. Brown met Garth Williams at Simon & Schuster's office not long after Nordstrom hired Williams to illustrate Brown's *Little Fur Family*, an extravagant fur-bound picture-book novelty, the costly details of which Nordstrom had most likely agreed to only out of fear of losing her star author altogether to the publisher responsible for *Pat the Bunny*.[55] Led by Gustaf Tenggren, several of the Disney Studio's leading animation artists abandoned their famously autocratic employer to become Golden Books author-illustrators, having decided that the picture book offered a greater chance for artistic freedom than work for Disney ever had, and that the Artists and Writers Guild, with its Disney film tie-in experience and large scale of operation, was a publisher likely to appreciate their worth.[56]

The initial triumph of Little Golden Books was the more remarkable for its timing. The first set of twelve books went on sale less than a year after the bombing of Pearl Harbor, during the first fall holiday season after the United States entered World War II. For those left on the home front, it was a time for caution, for making do with less, and for all sorts of government restrictions. For printers and publishers, paper rationing went into effect in 1943. Simon & Schuster and Western's ability to sustain their Golden partnership may have owed something to the latter company's wartime role as a major government contractor: Western held key military contracts for the printing of maps, playing cards, and other printed materials required for the war effort.[57]

In any case, as other basic materials such as metal and rubber became even scarcer than paper, American toy production dropped off significantly, and books often took the place of such playthings as gifts of choice for children. Little Golden Books, low-priced options available for purchase at tens of thousands of retail outlets, benefited greatly from the trend.

Demand for the books was also fueled by changes in the nation's demographics. Although the baby boom is generally regarded as a postwar phenomenon, the national birthrate in fact began its dramatic rise in 1942 — the first full year of wartime. In 1940 the population of the United States stood at 132 million, an increase of 7.3 percent over the previous decade — the smallest increase in the nation's history.[58] By the start of the new decade, however, a great many couples who had postponed parenthood owing to the financial burdens imposed by the Depression realized they were running out of time. The war doubtless inspired a fatalistic attitude in others: it was now or never, and who knew what the future might bring. In August 1943, *Publishers' Weekly* reported that at the nursery schools that had been established at every "war industry center" throughout the country, "parents . . . are being taught the importance of having books for their children from the nursery Mother Goose age on up." According to one Seattle bookseller, "The fact that many of these parents are industrial workers who never before have had the money or, in many cases, the interest in buying books for their children is one of the most stimulating and constructive features of the boom in children's books."[59] It was as if Little Golden Books had been made for these new book buyers.

World War II was the first radio-age war. In millions of American households, an ornate, wood-encased "receiver" — as much icon as machine — occupied an altarlike place of honor in the family parlor. The war-related messages it broadcast for all at home to hear — whether in the form of news bulletins or evening newscasts or President Roosevelt's "Fireside Chats" — dissolved the age barrier that in other areas of everyday life had been designed to hold children at a safe remove from adult concerns. There were other ways as well for American children — even those without fathers sending letters home from the front — to learn about the war. There were the war-front photographs published weekly in *Life* and the newsreels shown at the start of Saturday movie matinees, all of which gave millions of boys and girls a sense of eyewitness involvement that could be thrilling or terrifying or more likely both. Youngsters received their own ration books, participated in drives to collect tin cans, old keys, and other scrap metal for recycling as armaments, and posted enemy aircraft charts in their rooms. At school they practiced emergency procedures in the event of an air raid. At every turn they were reminded by authorities from Eleanor Roosevelt on down that in wartime good table manners, cooperative behavior at bedtime, the drinking of milk, and the brushing of teeth after meals all counted as patriotic acts.[60] As Louise Bechtel, writing in *The Horn Book* for March 1942, observed with characteristic good sense and from a deep knowledge of psychological theory, there was a sound case to be made for offering children a solid sense of participation: "Children of six to twelve have so much physical energy to spare, and should not be asked to 'run away and play.' They know and hear all about the war, they make model planes, battleships, tanks, and long to have a dramatic part in national defense. To plan intelligently for them should not be too far a stretch of our imagination."[61]

Like Bechtel, publishers assumed that grade school children were well aware of the war and saw no point in pretending otherwise. They also assumed that children received a substantial portion of their war news from sources other than books and that a useful role publishers might therefore play would be simply to continue to publish a wide variety of books, both fiction and nonfiction, thereby affirming for young readers that life did indeed go on. As Houghton Mifflin's Grace Allen Hogarth wrote: "Children emerging from rattles to picture books, children who are today living in an upside-down world, need books to make them laugh, to make them feel secure, and above all, to make them believe in the permanence of good and beautiful things."[62] Even so, nearly every list included at least one title that made specific reference to the war. In 1941, months before the United States entered the conflict, Harper published Creighton Peet's *Defending America,* illustrated by Fritz Kredel, a nonfiction stock-taking of the nation's military arsenal. The following year Frederick A. Stokes featured Munro Leaf's *A War-Time Handbook for Young Americans,* with the author's own loopy, stick figure–style drawings of happy young Americans tending a victory garden and performing other helpful tasks.[63] Houses historically associated with series fiction, notably Grosset & Dunlap and Whitman, swiftly retooled their operations to produce scores of novels like *Dave Dawson at Dunkirk* and *Skeezix Goes to War.*[64] Comic-book publishers likewise adapted the bombast and derring-do of their crime-busting superheroes to wartime scenarios, a realignment that did little to enhance their critical standing with the library world but nonetheless further fueled sales.[65]

As popular as the genre had long been anyway, historical fiction and in particular Americana attracted heightened interest during the war years. The Newbery Medal for 1942 went to Walter Edmonds for *The Matchlock Gun*, a story of frontier bravery set in the days of the French and Indian Wars. Two years later, Esther Forbes won the Newbery for her Revolutionary War novel *Johnny Tremain*. The manuscript of the latter book had come unexpectedly to Grace Allen Hogarth from the senior editor in the adult trade department at Houghton Mifflin, who had worked with Forbes on her 1942 Pulitzer Prize–winning biography, *Paul Revere and the World He Lived In*. Forbes, who had never before published a children's book, was leery of entrusting her serious work to the editor of *Curious George*, and she made it known that Hogarth could have the book for her list only if she agreed, in advance, to publish it "exactly as . . . written."

"I gulped and thought furiously," Hogarth later recalled. "In those days, the risk of financial loss on an unsuccessful book was far less than today. I knew we could print only a few thousand copies if necessary. If we failed to sell them all, we were unlikely to be in the least crippled."[66] So went the cautious wartime mental calculations that prepared the way for one of Hogarth's most notable successes.

Wartime rationing affected every aspect of book production and design. Children old enough to have a basis of comparison were reminded of the impact of the war every time they held a new book in hand. Two years into the conflict, Eunice Blake, now the children's editor at New York's Oxford University Press, reported a long list of adjustments in bookmaking standards and strategies. Cheaper, lighter-weight paper — 60-pound rather than 80- or 100-pound — had become the norm. Half-title pages, blank pages backing up full-page illustrations, decorative stamping on front covers (which was done with brass dies), and other amenities associated with superior book design were being dispensed with. Margins were becoming narrower. A new chapter no longer necessarily started on a new page. Books for younger children were apt to have fewer color illustrations; those for older children were less likely to have any. The departure for military service of skilled production personnel had resulted in a decline in the overall quality of color printing and bookbinding. Owing to materials shortages, different copies of the same book might sometimes be bound in different-colored cloth. If there was a bright side to all this accommodation to circumstance, Blake suggested, it lay in the publishers' newfound determination to concentrate all their limited resources on only the most compelling projects that came their way and on producing them well against the odds. "Children's book departments have always been in the forefront of experimentation in printing processes and formats. The war situation gives them a new opportunity to use their ingenuity in finding out how to do the impossible."[67]

As part of its wartime coverage, *The Horn Book* introduced a page called "The Watchtower," which recommended war-related adult titles of potential interest to teens. As eighteen-year-olds were going off by the shipload to fight and die overseas, it made less sense than before to suppose that home-front readers who were nearly that old needed specially tailored versions of events. An informal survey conducted by *Publishers' Weekly* found that older boys were above all eager for "factual books about planes, jeeps, and all phases of the war. The same thing is true in public libraries where teen-age boys are reading the adult war experience books."[68] Patriotic fervor ran deep among young people, but as the eventual outcome of the war became clearer, at least one of the more disturbing implications of all the patriotic rhetoric and home-front measures was becoming a matter for reflection for some. In January 1945, just ahead of the publication by Houghton Mifflin of *The Moved-Outers*, Florence Crannell Means's novel for young people about the wartime internment of Japanese Americans, adventure novelist Howard Pease wrote movingly, from San Francisco, to condemn the practice of internment and to herald the arrival of a brave and provocative book. "The reception of *The Moved-Outers*," Pease warned, "will be a test of our own intelligence and our own integrity."[69] In New York the Child Study Association gave Means's novel an award later that year, citing it as an example of the kind of children's book that squarely addressed present-day concerns — the honest, hard-hitting kind that book critic Josette Frank, just a few years earlier, had found to be such a rarity. The following year the American Library Association chose *The Moved-Outers* as one of four Newbery runners-up behind Lois Lenski's *Strawberry Girl*.

Some publishers saw the coming end of the war as a time to expand. Rand McNally, the Chicago firm that had made its reputation during the late nineteenth century as a leading publisher of maps (and of an eclectic list of inexpensive paperbacks earmarked for the entertainment of long-distance rail travelers), had a tradition of innovative juvenile publishing as well, primarily of picture books at the lower-priced end of the market.[70] In April 1945, the firm, with a view to burnishing its reputation in the field, hired Dr. Mary Alice Jones, most recently the head of work with children and curriculum work at Chicago's International Council of Religious Education, to direct its juvenile trade department. A sociable Texan and herself the author of several popular Rand McNally juveniles with religious themes, Jones stepped into her new role with the immediate goal of introducing trade fiction to the department's list and, more broadly, of "finding and developing the best books for children, . . . not . . . specifically religious books, but those . . . which aid children to come to full spiritual stature."[71] Jones, who had traveled the world and once remarked that "people" were her hobby, was a guest at a Christmas dinner party when she "first heard of the exciting yearly roundup of ponies on Chincoteague Island, off the Virginia coast. I said, 'That's it!' I got hold of Marguerite Henry and Wesley Dennis. When we went to Chincoteague . . . the story unfolded before our eyes." The book that came out of the adventure, *Misty of Chincoteague*, was both a critical and commercial triumph; its sequel, *King of the Wind*, took the Newbery Medal for 1949.[72]

For some editors with long experience in the field, the end of the wartime emergency became a time for professional stock-taking and transition. At New York's Harcourt, Brace, Elisabeth Hamilton, the vigorous children's book editor who had helped to keep the company running successfully throughout the war, seized the moment to ask for a promotion. During the war years alone, books on Hamilton's list had captured one Caldecott Medal and four Newbery Honors. When the Harcourts and Braces who together owned the firm refused to make her a vice-president, Hamilton resigned; it would not be the last time that a key figure at a small, family-run house learned the hard way that membership in the innermost circle did in fact remain closed to outsiders.

Hamilton's departure from Harcourt in September 1945 created a job opening that proved to be a golden opportunity for a young librarian just back in New York following military service in the U.S. Office of War Information. Margaret K. McElderry, a self-possessed, capable Pittsburgh native with a passion for books, had come to her plum wartime postings in London and Brussels with prior experience as first assistant to none other than Anne Carroll Moore and then her successor, Frances Clarke Sayers. During her time in Europe, visiting executives from Houghton Mifflin and Little, Brown had both courted her on behalf of their firms.[73] McElderry, who had dreamed as a Mount Holyoke undergraduate of making a name for herself in the "glamour industry" of publishing, had been intrigued by these overtures while at the same time feeling the continued pull of library work. "Then one day," as she later recalled, "Mabel Williams, superintendent of school work for the New York Public Library, met Fred Melcher . . . on the street [in front of the Forty-second Street Library in midtown Manhattan]. He said, 'Harcourt, Brace needs a children's book editor. They called me and the only person I could think of is Margaret McElderry, but she's overseas.' And Mabel said, 'No, she just got back yesterday.'"[74] With Melcher, Williams, Sayers, and not least of all Anne Carroll Moore to recommend her, McElderry easily got the job.

McElderry soon discovered to her horror that Hamilton had persuaded most of Harcourt's authors to postpone signing new contracts with the house until her own situation had righted itself elsewhere. As a result, as McElderry set out to plan her first season, she found herself with far fewer authors and artists to rely upon than she had had reason to expect.[75] In the end it was the editor's impeccable New York Public Library connections, combined with her own resourcefulness, that came to her rescue. The immediate postwar years revealed McElderry to be a publisher of keen business instincts, refined taste, and an editorial boldness of vision that put her at the forefront of her colleagues as a champion of the international style of design and illustration, of contemporary British fantasy, and of literature in translation. Before the decade was out, McElderry would issue the first children's book by a Japanese American writer, Yoshiko Uchida's *The Dancing Kettle*. A few years later she would publish in translation the first contemporary novel for young people from postwar Germany, Margot Benary-Isbert's *The Ark*. McElderry's library credentials and ever-increasing stature assured controversial books such as these an open-minded reception. American children's book publishing had never before been so outward-looking or so urbane.

Hamilton meanwhile had reemerged as the editorial director of William Morrow and Company's newly renamed and reinvigorated Morrow Junior Books imprint. The eponymous founder of the house, who had mastered his trade as second in command at Frederick A. Stokes, had launched Morrow in the fall of 1926 with a list led by a historical novel for children written by his bestselling wife. The success of *On to Oregon!* had extended the streak of Honoré Willsie Morrow's commercial triumphs. But Morrow's juvenile list had remained an eclectic one, even after the house attempted to regularize matters with the creation of Morrow Books for Young Americans on the eve of U.S. entry into the war.[76] Recognizing the postwar era as a promising time for growth in the field, Morrow had hired Hamilton with the goal of building up the firm's reputation as a publisher of books of special appeal for school libraries.[77]

School systems around the nation were indeed laying plans for rapid expansion to meet the educational needs of young baby boomers. Hamilton's early professional experience as supervisor of public school libraries in New Brunswick, New Jersey, made her the ideal candidate. A tall, formal woman of gallant Huguenot bearing, she had a wide-ranging intellect and special affinity for publishing nonfiction — the meat and potatoes of school reports. She also favored the sort of realistic fiction that examined home and school life from a child's point of view. It was Hamilton who first published the humorous and perennially popular chapter book novels of Carolyn Haywood and the sports novels for boys of John R. Tunis, and who later discovered Beverly Cleary.

Tunis's books were never only about sports. The author's determination to offer his readers basic lessons about good citizenship and fair play, and a chance to reflect on such rarely discussed social issues as racial equality and anti-Semitism, reflected Hamilton's own concerns as much as the author's. Hamilton's father, Louis Bevier, had been dean of Rutgers University when Paul Robeson was admitted there as an undergraduate. When the university refused to provide housing for the gifted African American student, Bevier took Robeson in to live with his own family. The experience left a lasting impression on his daughter. Her professional coming of age coincided with Robeson's own emergence as both a performer of international stature and an eloquent spokesperson for people of color. Long before it was fashionable to do so, Hamilton would lead her colleagues in publishing books that challenged prevailing racial and ethnic stereotypes.[78] Among the books on Hamilton's early Morrow lists were *North Star Shining: A Pictorial History of the American Negro* by Hildegarde Hoyt Swift, illustrated by Lynd Ward; and Dorothy Baruch's *Glass House of Prejudice*, a searing case history–style narrative probing the causes and consequences of discrimination against Mexican, Asian, and African Americans. If Hamilton did not publish a great many more such books, it was only because the market for them remained so limited as to render the effort unsustainable.

Hamilton had not been altogether alone in her efforts to publish respectful children's books for and about the "American Negro." By the late 1930s, as at least some librarians and publishers began to recognize the dearth of such books as a significant gap in the literature, lists of acceptable available titles, all of them highlighting the work of Arna Bontemps, Hildegarde Hoyt Swift, and a handful of others, found their way into print, typically at the conclusion of a soul-searching article in one of the professional journals in which good intentions were apt to mingle cheek by jowl with received racial stereotypes. "A Negro child," asserted school librarian Marjorie Hill Allee, "will not be fooled by shoddiness of characterization, nor will he be tolerant of muddled action, any more than the white child; perhaps less, for his mind seems to work with a more direct simplicity."[79] Throughout the 1940s, one of the key questions for debate was that of the appropriateness of Negro dialect in juveniles, with some writers on the subject taking the view that dialect represented faithfulness to the Negro experience while others argued that its use was merely another form of racist caricature.[80] Modest efforts were meanwhile also being made to draw the voices of Negro writers into the field. At the Bank Street School, Lucy Sprague Mitchell recruited a young Harlem journalist named Ellen Tarry for the Writers Laboratory in the hope of encouraging her to create *Here and Now*–inspired children's books expressive of American Negro life. The first picture book written by Tarry as a member of the Writers Lab, *Janie Belle*, received a favorable reading at Doubleday, followed by the offer of a contract. Then, however, someone at the house demurred, fearing that Doubleday's southern customers might take offense at the story of a white nurse's decision to adopt an abandoned black baby. It appeared for a time that Doubleday's offer of publication would simply be withdrawn. In the end, *Janie Belle* was consigned to publication by the firm's less prestigious "Garden City" imprint.[81] By the mid-1940s, Tarry had met May Massee, who, of course, had Doubleday war stories of her own. Tarry eventually was far more happily published by Massee at Viking, though as a Negro writer for children she would continue to have few peers in the field for decades to come.[82]

In October 1945, as the baby boom reshaped the nation's demographics, Harper published a fantasy for children that seemed slyly to comment on the phenomenon. *New Yorker* writer E. B. White's first children's book, *Stuart Little*, told a droll tale about a mouse-child born to a red-blooded American couple living in Manhattan. An amusing departure for the author who had firmed up his reputation with adult readers as the coauthor (with James Thurber) of the satiric *Is Sex Necessary?*, *Stuart Little* calmly took aim at two of the more widely shared preoccupations of postwar Americans: the wish for "perfect" babies and the fear of being judged "abnormal." Whatever its appeal for children, White's book was well timed to offer much-needed comic relief to anxious, war-weary parents, and *Stuart Little* instantly became one of those rare crossover works that adults purchased as much for their own enjoyment as for their children's. The illustrator of the book, Garth Williams, who had trained as a sculptor in England before fleeing to the United States after the London Blitz, was so gratified to catch glimpses of adults reading the book on Manhattan buses all around town that he decided children's book illustration was the career for him.[83]

The warm public reception of *Stuart Little* had come about despite, rather than with help from, the critic who six years earlier had done the most to encourage White to attempt writing a children's book in the first place. As White's book was being readied for publication, Harper sent a set of page proofs to Anne Carroll Moore as a courtesy as well as in the hope, of course, of receiving the Owls' blessing. Neither White nor Harper was prepared for Moore's reaction, which she set down in a fourteen-page handwritten letter addressed, as one critic to another, to the author's wife. Moore's letter, White recalled with rising sarcasm in a *New York Times Book Review* piece marking *Stuart Little*'s twentieth anniversary, had been

long, friendly, urgent, and thoroughly surprising. . . . She said she had read proofs of my forthcoming book . . . and she strongly advised me to withdraw it. She said . . . that the book was non-affirmative, inconclusive, unfit for children, and would harm its author if published. These were strong words, and I was grateful to Miss Moore for having taken the trouble to write them. I thought the matter over, however, and decided that as long as the book satisfied me, I wasn't going to let an expert talk me out of it. It's unnerving to be told you're bad for children; but I detected in Miss Moore's letter an assumption that there are rules governing the writing of juvenile literature — rules as inflexible as the rules for lawn tennis. And this I was unsure of. . . . I was shook up by the letter but was not deflected.[84]

Moore's successor at the New York Public Library, Frances Clarke Sayers, evidently agreed with her mentor about the book, and soon a well-known New York gossip columnist, the *Post*'s Leonard Lyons, was predicting a "to-do" over the library's "reluctance" to put *Stuart Little* on its shelves.[85] After taking a day to regain her composure, Katharine White responded to Moore by thanking her for a letter that she realized "must have been very hard" to write. Reaffirming her own and her husband's faith in the book, White let her exasperation show through only once, when she demanded rhetorically, "Didn't you think it even *funny?*"[86] *The New Yorker* editor and critic and her closest friend in the children's book world, Louise Seaman Bechtel, would laugh ruefully over this episode for decades to come.[87]

In postwar America, where the mass media and public relations increasingly colored the personal tastes and opinions of millions of ordinary people, one of the ultimate accolades was to be deemed worthy of notice in the glossy pages of *Life* magazine. As the prolific author of quintessential bedtime books for America's new generation of babies and toddlers, Margaret Wise Brown had become just the kind of behind-the-scenes personage whom *Life*'s editors prided themselves on bringing to the public's attention. The droll celebrity profile of Brown that ran in the December 2, 1946, issue was the handiwork of Bruce Bliven Jr., a veteran journalist and old friend of the subject. It doubtless helped that Brown bore a striking resemblance to Ingrid Bergman. (The *real* Ingrid Bergman, as it happened, appeared on the issue's cover dressed in medieval armor for her star turn in the Hollywood film epic *Joan of Arc*.) Librarians were appalled by the defiantly alluring portrait of the author that emerged from Bliven's narrative, Brown's own flip remarks, and the glamour shots by photographer Philippe Halsman of Brown, her dog, and her Manhattan Wonderland cottage. For the opening spread, Brown had even posed for Halsman in bed, holding a blue heron feather pen as though equally prepared for romance or inspiration to strike. The article made good sport of a favorite pastime of the author of *The Runaway Bunny* — rabbit hunting — and quoted Brown as claiming not to like children especially, at least not "as a group."

Brown for her part was pleased to have rattled her spinsterly detractors. But even Louise Seaman Bechtel, who as a critic had done more than anyone to champion Brown's unorthodox books, had been a bit put off by the piece in *Life* — a magazine, she hastened to assure Bertha Mahony Miller, that she did not ordinarily read. Bechtel had recently persuaded Miller to allow her to write an appreciation of the author for *The Horn Book*. Having read the *Life* article, however, which she supposed that "everyone" had seen, Bechtel ruefully wrote to Miller that there was "no need to finish mine now."[88]

Two years later, in December 1948, "as a Christmas present to younger readers," *Life* reprinted in conflated form Robert McCloskey's newly published picture book, *Blueberries for Sal*.[89] McCloskey by then was a Caldecott medalist for *Make Way for Ducklings* and had had a second major success with *Homer Price*. As May Massee's protégé and the son-in-law of Newbery Medal winner Ruth Sawyer, McCloskey, his genuinely modest midwestern manner notwithstanding, was as close to being picture-book royalty as it was possible to come.

Authors of children's books more often had to settle for far more modest forms of attention. At a time when most children's book departments were fortunate to have even one full-time staff member assigned to the promotion of the juvenile list, efforts in this regard were generally limited to the personal diplomacy of discreet face-to-face encounters at book conventions, highly focused letter-writing campaigns, and the occasional well-placed advertisement. With out-of-town appearances and book tours by authors still a rarity, the publishing world took note when, in the fall of 1948, Bill Martin Jr. and his brother Bernard masterminded a nationwide road show to promote the picture books they wrote, illustrated, and self-published through their Kansas City–based Tell-Well Press. The brothers Martin did impeccable advance work, furnishing book and department stores with ready-made press releases, model ads, suggestions for posters and window displays, and the like. The planning paid off. At Milwaukee's The Boston Store, Bill Martin signed 1,500 books in a single day.[90]

In late 1943, as the war moved into a new phase, and with victory not yet in sight but appearing ever more likely, children's book publishers had begun not only to plan for their own postwar futures but also to look for new ways to collectively lift the status of the field as a whole. Writing that fall in *Publishers' Weekly*, Frederic Melcher noted with pride that, during the thirty years of his career, children's book publishing had grown from exceedingly modest beginnings to become "almost a separate industry."[91] Fifty publishers, he reported, maintained full-fledged juvenile departments, and twice that number published children's books at least occasionally. In 1944 representatives of thirty publishers met to establish the Association of Children's Book Editors. The following year, the Association, in turn, created the Children's Book Council to administer Children's Book Week and to serve as an industry public relations office and clearing-house for information. As the Council's first director, Laura Harris, pointed out, having this new resource at their disposal would mean "that all groups and organizations, as well as libraries, schools and bookstores, will have access to current news of what others in allied fields are doing to promote increased reading and 'more books for more children.'"[92]

It was striking that leadership of the Council had been entrusted to the former Grosset & Dunlap editor most closely associated with the runaway mass-market success of Nancy Drew. Harris clearly was someone who understood how best to reach a large audience. Before the decade was out, there were definite signs that the Council's efforts, in confluence with the market realities that had warranted its creation, were already bringing about a changed appreciation of the field. In the fall of 1947, the *New York Times* and the Council cosponsored a well-attended children's book fair at the American Museum of Natural History, where, by one account, hordes of children admonished their parents, "But I don't want to wait 'til Christmas. I want it now."[93] In June 1948, at its annual convention in Chicago, the American Booksellers Association held its first general session devoted entirely to a discussion of books for children. Aware that she faced a skeptical audience, Harcourt's Margaret K. McElderry, who presided at the event, began by citing the latest birth statistics — 333,000 babies, she reported, would be born in the United States each month that year — and declared that she had come not to wax eloquent about her high-minded convictions but rather "to talk about children's books as profitable merchandise for the bookseller."[94] Booksellers who ventured to stock juveniles that year had a record one thousand new titles from which to choose.[95]

The postwar period was a time of international as well as national association building. As early as 1944, the Association of Children's Book Editors had made contact with colleagues in England, Australia, the Soviet Union, South Africa, and elsewhere and arranged for their participation in what they hoped would become an annual worldwide celebration of Children's Book Week. In Europe after the war, a German-born Jewish philanthropist named Jella Lepman led the effort to found two world organizations dedicated to children and books: the International Youth Library, which opened in Munich in 1949 as an inspection library where children's literature from every part of the world could be viewed and read; and four years later, the Zurich-based International Board of Books for Youth as a world counterpart to the new American CBC. Lepman envisioned these companion institutions as tools for world understanding.[96] McElderry quickly emerged as the unofficial chief U.S. emissary in this arena as well.

In October 1949, at a forum organized by the Authors Guild of America and attended by three hundred writers, editors, booksellers, and other professionals at New York's Hotel Astor, the president of Random House, Bennett Cerf, made a remarkable public admission: "The tail is now wagging the dog," he said. "*Golden Books* are now the biggest part of Simon and Schuster and Walter Farley's horse books are among the biggest money-makers at Random House."[97] Publishers who once looked down their noses at juvenile publishing now, it seemed, were beginning to see that they could ill afford to do so.

Other speakers, detecting what they took to be the broadly based postwar mood of the nation's younger generation, reported that children at every age level wanted realism and hard fact in their books. In the season that saw the publication of Ruth Krauss and Marc Simont's *The Happy Day*, Marcia Brown's *Henry Fisherman*, and *Bartholomew and the Oobleck* by Dr. Seuss, by far the most popular new picture book at Brentano's bookshop on Fifth Avenue was Margaret Williamson's *The First Book of Bugs*. A representative of the New York City Board of Education stated that high school students craved books about "real people."[98]

Taking the rapid expansion of the juvenile field as a sign of the industry's overall good health, Vernon Ives, founder and president of Holiday House, told conference attendees that mass-market imprints like Golden Books had not overwhelmed the market for children's picture books, as was sometimes claimed, but rather had carved out a new market for themselves that coexisted with the traditional market.[99] On this generally upbeat occasion, only Martha King, reviewer of young books for the *Chicago Sun-Times*, sounded a cautionary note for the days to come. King feared a future in which children commonly believed Walt Disney to be the author of

Snow White, Pinocchio, and *Bambi:* "Books," she said, with a nod to the rapidly changing world of children's popular culture, "should be made more vital and more fun than movies and television."[100]

In 1946 approximately 11,000 American households had at least one television set; within six years' time the number of television-owning households had jumped to 14 million.[101] It would be years before publishers devoted much concentrated attention to the point made so offhandedly by King that day at the Hotel Astor about the necessity of coming to grips with the new and still quite unfamiliar medium of television. Critics and educators were beginning to consider the question, and at the forefront of the discussion (as usual) was Louise Seaman Bechtel, who, in a pair of anniversary lectures delivered at the end of the decade, paused to reflect on some of the major changes in the field that had occurred during her long professional lifetime.

In an address given on September 25, 1949, to mark the twenty-fifth anniversary of the *New York Herald-Tribune Weekly Book Review,* Bechtel remarked that the "most obvious change" she had witnessed was

> the change in atmosphere created by comic books, radio, movies, picture magazines, and now by television. As every storyteller knows, they have changed the child's span of attention. Picture-mindedness would naturally have an effect on reading. It discourages a lazy child's interest in the act itself; also it offers him in his movies, etc., much more adult material than do most of his children's books, or than his word-reading power can cope with. So of course he likes the non-book mediums better. Also, the tone of the majority of comics and movies has been tough, even though the ending is morally right. This has built upon children's natural love of excitement . . . and has quickened it at an earlier age.

As a consequence of this shift, the longer classics were no longer widely read for enjoyment; writers had simplified their style, sometimes to the point of evisceration; and many categories of books had simply lost their former appeal.[102]

All in all, it was a not very encouraging report. But the following year, in an address to the American Library Association in honor of that organization's golden anniversary, Bechtel had a somewhat more hopeful message for her listeners. She was gratified to observe that the librarians' approach to evaluating children's books had grown less rigid, and thus more mature, with the passing of years. It was a development that suited not only the profession, she said, but the times. "What do we all agree upon as great literature?" Bechtel asked. "Fifty years ago, an agreement was more taken for granted. Today, people are much franker about what bores them, and more disinclined to agree that anything is great. May Lamberton Becker has said: 'There is no such thing as a best book; there are books that are best for you.'"[103] The newfound flexibility Bechtel detected was sure, she said, to serve librarians and children alike as they entered a complex future governed by once-unimaginable new technologies and by forces and events played out with breathtaking consequences on the national and global scale. "The new emphasis," she said, "should be on all children reading, and the old classics should be reevaluated for the child of today." The television age would not be a time for standing on ceremony or for clinging to well-intentioned but shopworn pieties. Children were not alone in wanting more realism. "We are now at a thrilling turning point. Publishers, authors, artists are well aware of it. New leaders are arising in the library world, with vision, sense, and imagination. . . . In the words of *The Hunting of the Snark*," Bechtel wryly concluded, "'forks will be added to hope.'"[104]

6

FUN AND FEAR: The 1950s

At this moment the first man-made moon [*Sputnik I*] is circling the globe.

— New York Times, October 6, 1957

See Spot run. Oh, oh! This is fun.[1]

— Fun with Dick and Jane

"THEY'RE NICE AND ALL — I'm not saying that — but they're also touchy as hell."[2] Grasping for the honest truth about his well-bred, well-to-do, and seemingly unknowable parents, Holden Caulfield echoed the bittersweet mood of middle-class Americans everywhere as they struggled to make peace with their perplexing postwar legacy. There was all the new wealth that had begun to come their way: the new homes and cars they could point to with pride and the myriad labor-saving appliances and recreational devices and opportunities at their disposal, not least of all the technological miracle of television. And yet Americans could not understand how it was that, in the midst of seeming ease and prosperity and only a few short years after achieving an overwhelming moral and military victory in World War II, their nation now found itself in a position of potentially catastrophic vulnerability. With the Soviet Union's emergence as a hostile power armed with atomic weapons, the news of the day read as a starkly lit, high-stakes melodrama governed — if "governed" was the word — not so much by Washington's battle-hardened, dark-suited men as by the law of unintended consequences. As E. B. White wrote in "Here Is New York," an essay on the protean nature of midcentury America's most robust and forward-reaching city:

The subtlest change in New York is something people don't speak much about but that is in everyone's mind. The city, for the first time in its long history, is destructible. A single flight of planes no bigger than a wedge of geese can quickly end this island fantasy, burn the towers, crumble the bridges, turn the underground passages into lethal chambers, cremate the millions. The intimation of mortality is part of New York now: in the sound of jets overhead, in the black headlines of the latest edition.[3]

For all the sunny, placid surfaces of its glass-box skyscrapers and suburban tract homes, the 1950s would unfold as a time of acrid political and social contradictions and short-fused fears, the decade both of "Dick and Jane" and *Brown v. Board of Education*, of Senator McCarthy and Dr. Seuss. The experts who got the bomb right had left the "average American" believer in technological progress and national destiny with a great deal either to deny or to question. Mothers reassured and strengthened by the famous opening words of Dr. Benjamin Spock's bestselling *The Common Sense Book of Baby and Child Care* — "Trust yourself. You know more than you think you do" — proceeded to wear their copies ragged with concern. First published in 1946, Spock's compendium of straightforward reassurance would go on to become the second-best-selling title in history, after the Bible. Tellingly, in the first revised edition, published in 1957, "Common Sense" was dropped from the title in a nod to the author's deepening reluctance to presume that anyone — parent or doctor — had all the answers.[4]

Marching to the mantra of "fun" as they moved to the suburbs in search of peace and perspective, 1950s Americans proceeded to worry that they themselves, and more especially their children, might not be having enough fun, or not the right kind of it. As a leading cultural anthropologist of the period, Martha Wolfenstein, observed: "Play, amusement, fun have become increasingly divested of puritanical associations of wickedness. Where formerly there was felt to be the danger that in seeking fun, one might be carried away into the depths of wickedness, today there is a recognizable fear that one may not be able to let go sufficiently. . . . From having dreaded impulses and being worried about whether conscience was adequate to cope with them, we have come round to finding conscience a nuisance and worrying about the adequacy of our impulses."[5] Aptly, "Reading Is Fun" was chosen as the Children's Book Week slogan in 1952 and, as though to drive home the point, in 1953 as well. Theodor Geisel, as Dr. Seuss, would sum up the new dilemma in which Americans young and old found themselves in the pages of the decade's quintessential children's book: "It is fun to have fun/But you have to know how."[6] But what if you did *not* know?

In its review published in July 1951 of J. D. Salinger's *The Catcher in the Rye*, the *New York Herald-Tribune Sunday Books* supplement bitterly complained that "recent war novels have accustomed us all to ugly words and images, but from the mouths of the very young and protected they sound peculiarly offensive."[7] The book-buying public either disagreed or did not care, however, as Salinger's book became a bestseller. Had not the experience of the war and the collective impact on their younger brothers and sisters of the changed lives of millions of returning veterans altered the terms by which questions of propriety like those raised in the *Herald-Tribune* review had to be judged? For the generation reaching majority at the start of the first postwar decade, Salinger's fractured, rueful monologue seemed to encapsulate the sadness they felt not only over their own lost youth but also over the lack of a noble purpose that might have given the loss meaning. *The Catcher in the Rye*, after being declined for serialization by *The New Yorker*, was published in 1951 by Little, Brown as a work of adult fiction. By the mid-1950s, however, it had achieved an anthemlike status among America's teens. In a minor demonstration of the unpredictable nature of experience, Salinger's novel would prove to be one of the decade's most consequential books not only for young people but also for the publishers concerned with young people as a market — the foundation work of the new genre of teenage reading that came to be called "young adult" literature.[8]

In 1950 a "visitor from Mars" — the conceit was a favorite rhetorical flourish of the early Cold War years, when on more than one occasion rumors of actual Martian invasions swept the jittery nation — would have had no choice but to conclude that postwar middle-class Americans were obsessed with providing the utmost in material well-being for their children. Statistics bore out the impression. For suburban boys and girls, ownership of a bicycle, a swing set, and a chest — or "play room" — full of toys had become a sort of unwritten birthright. During and immediately following the war, shortages of metal, rubber, and other basic materials had drastically curtailed the manufacture of children's playthings. Between 1950 and 1960, as the peacetime economy roared back, bicycle production increased from 2 million to 3.8 million annually. As excited schoolyard and dinner-table talk of the latest "fads" became a staple of Americans' conversation, parents discovered the power of television both to generate and to spur word of mouth in the creation of instant child-centered consumer demand, whether for faux-coonskin caps and other frontier-style paraphernalia inspired by the 1954 televised Disney serial about the adventures of Davy Crockett, or for Hula-Hoops, the rings of lightweight plastic tubing that became indispensable household equipment four years later. The Crockett craze, which lasted a year, proved to be good for $100 million in merchandise sales; in half that time, 30 million Hula-Hoops were sold, presumably to parents unwilling to allow their children to fall behind their peers in the quest for fun.[9]

Few books stirred children's longings or prompted their parents' acquiescence at the point of sale with anything like the same level of intensity — except, of course, for the books published expressly to capitalize on these same fads. The publishers of Golden Books, with their exclusive book-licensing contract with Disney still in force, often found themselves in a unique position to take advantage of the growing number of such opportunities. During the early and mid-1950s, the partnership between Western and Simon & Schuster proved golden indeed as the variety of books and formats published on the list continued to expand and as perennially strong sellers proved their worth year after year. As of 1950 over 300 million copies of the more than two hundred Little Golden Books then in print had already found their way into American homes. Notwithstanding the library world's continued disapproval, the Golden list appeared almost alone in having carved out a significant foothold for itself in the brave new world of American commercial child culture.[10]

Other publishers, seeing big money in children's books, reassessed their plans in light of the swelling demand. Bennett Cerf, cofounder of Random House, had been vacationing with his family on Cape Cod during the summer of 1948 when one such opportunity unexpectedly revealed itself to him. On the beach one day, Cerf had asked his older son, Christopher, if he realized they were standing within view of the very spot where the Pilgrims had landed more than three hundred years earlier. When the boy replied: "You're wrong, Dad. They landed at Plymouth Rock," Cerf suggested that they head over to the local bookstore to settle the question.

The publisher had been right about the *Mayflower*'s first North American landfall, but what he learned at the bookstore greatly surprised him:

that not one first-rate children's book about the Pilgrims was currently available from any American publisher. "I began thinking about it," Cerf recalled years later, "and suddenly it struck me that there should be a series of books, each one on some great episode in American history. By the time we left Provincetown, I had made a list of the first ten titles and had a name for the series: Landmark Books."[11]

At the time that Cerf had these thoughts, he was already the proud publisher and good friend of Theodor Geisel (one of the two geniuses, he boasted, on the Random House list, the other being James Joyce); an admirer of the late French artist Jean de Brunhoff, whose elegant picture books about Babar the Elephant had been published by Random House in the United States since 1934; and the happy beneficiary of the immense popularity of Walter Farley's "Black Stallion" series. Cerf had never taken much personal interest in children's books as a genre, however, and had been known at times to heap scorn on "baby books."[12]

In the beginning, Cerf had left it to his wife Phyllis to attend to whatever juvenile projects came the firm's way. But in 1936, when he and his partner merged their firm with Smith & Haas, another small but distinguished publishing company with William Faulkner and Robert Graves on their list, Cerf had decided to take on a full-time juvenile editor at Random House. His choice for the job, Louise Bonino, had been a director of Smith & Haas and was a practiced publishing hand. She had come to work with children's books by chance after being shown — and falling in love with — the original *L'Histoire de Babar* at a party.[13]

As plans for a Random House juvenile history series began to unfold, Bonino, with a long backlog of successes in the field to her credit, including popular titles by de Brunhoff, Farley, Esther Averill, Noel Streatfeild, and others, stood ready to help.[14] Rounding out his reminiscence of this time with a cavalier flourish, Cerf recalled for posterity: "I also decided not to get authors of children's books [for the new series], but the most important authors in the country."[15]

Writing nearly thirty years after the fact, Cerf had given a broad-brush account of events that swept over the vital contributions of Bonino and others. The true story of Landmark Books' beginnings was, if anything, more remarkable. While Cerf may have worked out an overall outline of the history series on Cape Cod, the first in-house discussions of the plan had not taken place for another six months after his return to New York —

a mere eighteen months before the series' full-throttle nationwide launch in stores. Cerf later claimed that Bonino had been dismissive of his idea: "In the first place," he quoted her as saying, "you won't be able to get such people [America's leading journalists and historians] to write books for children. Second, I don't know whether there'll be enough demand for a whole book about the Pilgrims or, say, a whole book about the first transcontinental railroad."[16] Cerf shelved the scheme (perhaps after this exchange) until the following spring, when Bonino came to him to relate a conversation she had just had at the Association for Childhood Education's annual convention. Unbidden, an educator had asked her: "Why don't you publish a series of biographies aimed at fifth and sixth graders?" Perhaps, Bonino now thought, Cerf *had* been on to a timely idea. Cerf, with Cape Cod memories fresh in his mind, had been quick to reply: "No. I want to do a series of books on important and significant episodes in American history. Maybe some biographies, but episodes and events primarily."[17] There followed a period of intensive research conducted by Cerf's partner and detail man Donald S. Klopfer, with the aim of determining the most marketable format and retail price for such a series. In October 1949, with sample layouts and a list of potential titles in hand, Bonino toured the Midwest to test the material on librarians and "key people in bookstores, department stores, and the schools."[18] Only then did Cerf feel ready to embark on the pivotal quest for marquee authors. As on so many other occasions, the publisher's gregarious nature and endless dance card of literary and social connections served the house supremely well. "The keystone of the whole thing," Cerf recalled, "was Dorothy Canfield Fisher, who, in addition to being a distinguished novelist, was a noted authority on children and a judge of the Book-of-the-Month Club. . . . I wanted a book by Mrs. Fisher desperately." Ignoring the advice of a Random House colleague who was sure the author was far too busy to consider such an offer, Cerf summoned Fisher to lunch. "I told her my idea, and then I said, 'My dream is, Dorothy, that you would do one of these books for us.'" Fisher replied: "'Do *one* of these books? You've shown me your list of the first ten, and I want to do *two* of them!'"[19] With Fisher now on board, and with the priceless endorsement of the venture that her involvement implied, the roster of Landmark authors rapidly filled itself out. By September 1950, just a year and a half after Bonino and Cerf had begun hashing out the details of the series, all ten inaugural titles had been commissioned, written, edited, illustrated, and designed and had rolled off the press, each in a huge initial printing of 100,000 copies. Stories about the lightning speed with which Random House had managed to realize the complex project fueled industry anticipation of the risky venture, which Cerf believed had the potential, in terms of its scope and profitability, to become the field's next Golden Books. Bonino later recalled a bleary-eyed, end-of-the-day encounter with Cerf in the weeks just before the official series launch date. Booksellers had responded enthusiastically to the series, and the first warehouse load of Landmark Books had already shipped to stores. Having come through the whirlwind of the last eighteen months together, both publishing veterans were feeling guardedly optimistic: "Well," Cerf said, cracking his familiar grin, "we'll soon know whether our gamble paid off."[20]

Pay off it did, so rapidly and on a scale so extravagant that Bonino later likened the outcome to a "fairy tale."[21] Bookstores reported that many of their customers were purchasing complete sets of the first ten Landmarks rather than selecting individual titles. The publishers of Little Golden Books had had this same happy surprise when their first twelve books arrived in stores nearly two decades earlier.

Cerf later credited his son Christopher with having suggested numbering the individual volumes as an aid to book buyers interested in owning a complete set (though numbering was by then a well-established practice of series publishing, in use with the Hardy Boys, Nancy Drew, and Little Golden Books, among others). Newspapers around the country, like book buyers, tended to treat the Landmarks as an entity, heaping lavish praise on the series and thus helping to establish Landmark Books as a brand. Filmstrip adaptations and dramatic recordings as well as special school, book club, British, and foreign language editions all followed in rapid succession.

The ebullient Random House chairman, who gamely juggled thriving after-hours careers as a joke-book author, banquet speaker, and television "personality," took full advantage of his whirlwind cross-country travels to call upon store managers who sold — or might be persuaded to sell — Landmark Books and other Random House titles. It was at least in good part due to his persistent efforts that in cities and towns too small to support even a single bookshop, it became common for the local stationery store to set aside a shelf for Landmarks, where parents, who had come to consider the books ideal birthday presents for grade school children (especially boys) could find them. By 1952 the scope of the series had expanded to encompass seminal episodes from all of world history. Preliminary steps were even taken to launch a television series based on the books.[22]

Other publishers, notably Grosset & Dunlap with its Signature series of biographies of historical personages begun in 1952, did their belated best to compete. At Harper, Ursula Nordstrom, whose editorial policies and judgments were rarely questioned, came under intense scrutiny by the firm's top executives, who wanted to know why she had not had the brilliant idea for Landmark Books herself. The pressure was such that Nordstrom finally engaged historian Walter Lord to oversee an ambitious project whose working title, the Breakthrough Series, came back to haunt her when the long-delayed first volumes finally rolled off the press in 1962 and then failed to break through to their potential audience.[23]

Although older houses like Dutton, Scribner, and Harper never conceded the retail side of the business to the publishers of Golden Books and their imitators, they continued to concentrate their efforts primarily on their profitable relationships with their old friends in the library and education worlds. Postwar prosperity strengthened and expanded those ties even as most booksellers continued to ignore a specialty they considered bother-some. As the 1952 Book Week poster implied with its image of an older boy perched atop a stepladder before an imposing floor-to-ceiling wall of books, if children wished to experience the "fun" of reading, they might consider visiting the local library.

Responding to the postwar needs of their customers, department stores around the country were, however, giving children's books greater promi-nence, thereby making it easier than ever for parents to purchase a wide selection of the best trade books. The efforts of one such store, Carson Pirie Scott, even attracted national attention when, in March 1949, Lucile Pannell, manager of the venerable Chicago emporium's Hobby Horse Book Shop, became the first bookseller to win the Women's National Book Asso-ciation's prestigious Constance Lindsay Skinner Award.[24]

With the Children's Book Council to back them up and with rising profits to show for their efforts, editors felt confident as never before. Decked out in their proper white gloves and smart little hats, May Massee, Ursula Nordstrom, Louise Bonino, Alice Dalgliesh, Margaret K. McElderry, Elisabeth Hamilton, and their fellow department heads gathered monthly in New York at Council-sponsored luncheons to discuss matters of common concern. Every summer they represented their respective houses at the festive American Library Association conventions that rotated from city to city across the country. Each November they gathered again as the Council inaugurated Children's Book Week with a gala banquet, attended by hundreds of industry professionals, in the grand ballroom of New York's Hotel Astor. Some editors now even occasionally accompanied their star authors as they made the rounds of the expanding circuit of pre-Christmas children's book fairs that dotted the eastern third of the country, each sponsored by a local newspaper in association with the Children's Book Council and hosted by a local museum. In 1953 such fairs, which served either as the lead-in to Book Week or as the centerpiece of the celebration, took place in New York, Washington, D.C., Cleveland, Detroit, Little Rock, and Chicago, and all were heavily attended. In Chicago alone that fall, forty-eight thousand people filed into the Museum of Science and Industry to view the book displays and meet such notable authors and artists as Lynd Ward, Don Freeman, and the d'Aulaires. Parents who did not purchase books for their children then and there were observed dutifully jotting down titles for ordering later at local bookshops or department stores. Publishers could not have been more pleased to have this new way to call attention to the holiday books they most counted on to succeed.[25]

That same year the still-new medium of television, which was soon to become the most controversial factor in the equation for everyone dedicated to bringing books and children together, was briefly harnessed to the service of literacy when the Ford Foundation–sponsored program *Excursion* devoted a half-hour to Book Week readings and commentary by stage and screen stars Burgess Meredith, Helen Hayes, and Raymond Massey. For one week children's books also commanded attention on the popular *Howdy Doody Show* and on Dave Garroway's *Today Show*. In past years mayors and governors had issued proclamations commending Book Week's worthy goals. In 1953, for the first time, the president of the United States lent his support to the effort. In a carefully crafted letter addressed to the chairperson of the Children's Book Week Committee, Helen Hoke Watts, President Eisenhower took up the mainstream view in the continuing debate over the impact of comic books on America's youth: "At a time," the president noted, "when the reading matter available to both young and old covers such a great number of subjects and such varying degrees of interest and value, guidance is particularly necessary. A child who learns at an early age that the books which his elders consider worthwhile can give him greater enjoyment than can more frivolous reading will have taken a great leap toward maturity."[26] Librarians and publishers familiar with the former general's own reading preferences, which were reported to center on whodunits and highly colored tales of the Old West, must have chuckled over the discrepancy between presidential theory and practice. Writing to Harper author Janette Sebring Lowrey, Ursula Nordstrom could not resist repeating the joke that the man in the White House suffered from "delusions of adequacy."[27] But few professionals concerned with children's reading would have disputed the main thrust of the president's argument or dismissed the symbolic value of so prestigious an endorsement of their work.

Armed also with a renewed sense of purpose and an underlying confidence in their hard-won ability to adapt to circumstance, the close-knit children's book community of the 1950s functioned with impressive efficiency and ease. In the early spring of 1950, veteran bookseller Frances Chrystie of the famed mid-Manhattan toy store F. A. O. Schwarz took it upon herself as a matter of course to arrange an informal encounter between her good friend, Harper's Ursula Nordstrom, and a gawky but gifted member of the store's display staff, a twenty-two-year-old artist from Brooklyn named Maurice Sendak. Chrystie had admired the young man's sketchbooks filled with animated drawings of city street kids at play and decided that Nordstrom, who was always on the lookout for newcomers to champion, should see the sketchbooks. The editor was indeed impressed, and she promptly offered young "Mr. Sendak" his first Harper contract.

Nordstrom by then was already legendary for her ability to recognize nascent talent and nurture it to great effect. But every editor had some such story of a career-shaping professional contact made casually through friends. Staff members at the New York Public Library often played matchmaker on behalf of young artists and writers who had first become known to them as patrons of the library's fabled collections. It was thanks to Karl Kup, the library's curator of prints and drawings and a friend of Margaret McElderry's, that the Harcourt editor first met printmaker Antonio Frasconi. From out of their conversations came some of the most innovative American picture books of the 1950s.[28] Another Harcourt picture-book author, Will Lipkind, was married to Maria Cimino, the chief of the Central Children's Room. Scribner's Alice Dalgliesh met picture-book artist Marcia Brown (later the first artist to win the Caldecott Medal an astounding three times) while the latter was herself still a member of the Central Children's Room staff.

But if it was a small world, it was a big and sometimes fraught world as well. In the fall of 1950, Schwarz, which boasted one of the city's best selections of children's books, decided to feature in its Fifth Avenue display windows a graphically bold new picture book on which Harcourt's McElderry had taken a chance. No sooner had an impressive arrangement of copies of the book been massed in the windows, however, than an order came down to Frances Chrystie from the store president to remove the books at once. "What do you think you are doing," he demanded, "putting a book called *The Two Reds* in our window?" Making matters worse, the illustrator, Nicolas Mordvinoff, had a name that sounded unmistakably Russian. To a merchant fearful that even a mistaken impression of pro-Communist sympathies could damage his store's reputation, it mattered not at all that Mordvinoff was a White Russian, nor that his collaborator, Will Lipkind, had written an innocuous tale about a redheaded boy and his ginger-colored cat.

Earlier that year, Senator Joseph R. McCarthy, Republican of Wisconsin, had demonstrated his growing power by administering a tongue lashing to the sitting secretary of state, Dean Acheson, tarring his victim with the pariah epithet "the Red Dean." McCarthy had then gone on to accuse the U.S. ambassador to the United Nations, Philip Jessup, of "preaching the Communist Party line" — a shameless act of demagoguery for which no one had dared to call the senator to task.[29] To those enraged or terrified by the scare tactics of McCarthy, the House Un-American Activities Committee, and others, no outrage now seemed beyond imagining. As the artist Fritz Eichenberg, risking his own reputation to do so, observed at the time: "It takes great courage, for reasons too numerous and obvious to mention, to name a children's book *The Two Reds*" — or, as he might also have said, to publish one.[30]

In the face of the appalling spectacle in Washington, the village elders of the children's book world closed ranks around a book they considered praiseworthy. In her weekly *New York Herald-Tribune* column, Louise Seaman Bechtel wrote of *The Two Reds*: "The publication of this book restores one's faith in the experimental daring of American publishers."[31] Months later the Newbery-Caldecott Committee honored the book as one of six Caldecott runners-up for 1951. As though not to let the matter drop, and all the more remarkably considering the steady rise in the temperature of official Washington, the next year's committee awarded Mordvinoff the Caldecott Medal for his second collaboration with Lipkind, *Finders Keepers*. Winning the great prize did not completely inoculate the latter book against attacks from at least a small minority of frightened readers. The endpapers depicted the story's two canine protagonists and the bone they had fought over. Margaret McElderry recalled: "I had a long, tortured letter from a children's librarian saying that this was obviously a Communist book. Why? Because on the endpapers she had traced maps of Russia."[32]

As a group, however, the authors and illustrators of children's trade books suffered far less for their affiliations (real or merely suspected) with leftist political organizations, including even the Communist Party, than did Hollywood screenwriters, novelists, and playwrights for adults, radio and television entertainers and backstage personnel, and other arts professionals. Public school teachers and librarians likewise lost their jobs by the thousands on the basis of their political views and affiliations, and the authors of textbooks came under severe government scrutiny. But the people responsible for creating the children's books that librarians purchased with public funds and that parents and grandparents gave as gifts to the children they loved were viewed by the new government overlords of ideological purity as of too little consequence to be worthy even of investigation. It was fortunate, of course, for those authors and artists for children who might otherwise have run afoul of the authorities that McCarthy and the others had chosen not to bother with them. Still, to those who cared deeply about children, their books, and the future of literacy, the politicians' very indifference amounted to a bitter commentary on the status of the enterprise.[33]

Mordvinoff's victory in the medal sweepstakes helped cinch an even greater professional triumph for Harcourt's McElderry, who in 1952 became the first editor to publish both the Newbery and Caldecott Medal winners in the same year. On the morning when the confidential first word of the awards was anticipated, the avuncular Frederic Melcher, donor of the medals, had swept briskly into the waiting room of Harcourt's offices and, asking to "see Miss McElderry," had delivered the extraordinary news to his longtime friend in person. For McElderry, who was well aware that a visit from Melcher on that particular morning could only mean that *some* good news was in the offing, it was a meeting to remember: "He said that we'd won the Newbery with [Eleanor Estes's] *Ginger Pye*. I practically collapsed," McElderry often said afterwards, as if daring her audience of the moment to imagine such an out-of-character spectacle. "Then he said, 'And that's not all. . . .'"[34] Melcher then reported on the Caldecott balloting that had rendered Mordvinoff the other big winner. Sworn to secrecy for the weeks preceding the formal public announcement of the winners in Melcher's own office, McElderry kept a midday appointment and attended the monthly Children's Book Council luncheon, where she knew it would take every ounce of the regal self-discipline that was her hallmark to maintain her poker face in a roomful of intensely curious (and secretly disappointed) colleagues.

As in a scene from an Agatha Christie mystery, McElderry gamely chose as her lunch companion her voluble old friend and rival, Harper's Ursula Nordstrom, who was predictably beside herself. As of that year, no Harper author or artist had yet won either of the two coveted medals. The latest cold comfort had come that very morning with the news that a Harper picture book, *All Falling Down* by Gene Zion, illustrated by Margaret Bloy Graham, had been chosen a 1952 Caldecott runner-up. If there was any solace to be found that day as Nordstrom struggled to make small talk, it lay in the secret knowledge that a book then working its way through her office for publication the following fall stood perhaps the best chance of any she had published of capturing the Newbery. "Thanks for your letter telling me that you've recently finished another children's book," Nordstrom had written the author, E. B. White, months before, just ahead of receiving the manuscript of *Charlotte's Web*. "That's the best news I've had in a long time."[35] As it turned out, White's second children's book would add yet another Newbery runner-up distinction to Harper's long list, an outcome that was all but foreordained by the somber response from Anne Carroll Moore, who wrote — first privately to the Whites and then in *The Horn Book* — that while she had found *Charlotte's Web* "entrancing," she believed that the author had failed adequately to develop the character of Fern and that he had produced a mongrel work, part realism and part fantasy, that was destined to leave young readers in a state of confusion. Nordstrom tried to shrug off the attack, noting in a letter to White that

Moore's "reservations about *Stuart Little* preceded a wonderful success for that book." Referring to the rave review of *Charlotte's Web* published in the *New York Times Book Review*, Nordstrom went on: "Well, Eudora Welty said the book was perfect for anyone over eight and under eighty, and that leaves Miss Moore out as she is a girl of eighty-two."[36] But Nordstrom knew the damage had been done.

The much vaunted veil of secrecy surrounding the award committees' deliberations made it impossible to be sure just why, in any given year, Harper books, including work by Laura Ingalls Wilder, Meindert DeJong, and Garth Williams, had been passed over. Tongues wagged anyway, of course, with the speculation centering on the Harper editor's famously chilly relationship with Moore, who, in retirement from the New York Public Library since 1941, remained a powerful critic. Compounding the dilemma, the Harper editor was having no better luck with Moore's successor at the library, Frances Clarke Sayers. Nordstrom had done her best over the years to dilute the impact of the New York Public Library's animus by cultivating friendships with powerful librarians in Boston, Chicago, Kansas City, Los Angeles, and elsewhere — as well as with key reviewers like the *Herald-Tribune*'s Louise Seaman Bechtel and the *New York Times*' Ellen Lewis Buell, whose opinions presumably got factored into the awards calculus to some extent. But for all her efforts, Nordstrom remained something of an outsider to the librarians' world, the village eccentric known (and in some quarters no doubt privately admired) for having stood her ground against the imperious Moore over the latter's objections to *Stuart Little*; for having championed the work of quirky, iconoclastic writers like Margaret Wise Brown and Ruth Krauss; and, in 1953, for having published a splendid uniform edition, newly reillustrated by Garth Williams, of Laura Ingalls Wilder's chronicle of life on the American frontier.

The Wilder books, for all their admirable writing and the mainstream appeal of their saga of the hardscrabble lives of Laura and her family, had presented a particularly nettlesome dilemma for Newbery-Caldecott Committee members who, year after year, had found themselves unwilling to confer their ultimate accolade on a work of series fiction. Wilder had won Newbery runners-up in 1938 for *On the Banks of Plum Creek*, in 1940 for *By the Shores of Silver Lake*, in 1942 for *Little Town on the Prairie*, and in 1944 for *These Happy Golden Years*. But the sum of it all, in the minds of many, was faint praise indeed, and by the mid-1950s enough librarians were chagrined over Wilder's exclusion for the matter to be made an issue at the American Library Association's midwinter convention in February 1954 in Chicago. Ursula Nordstrom was among those whose voice was heard, and no one left the meeting more pleased by the outcome, the librarians having decided to add to the Caldecott and Newbery Medals a third major award, this one honoring lifetime achievement by a writer or artist for children. The new prize would be known as the Laura Ingalls Wilder Medal, and Wilder herself was to be its first recipient.

Wilder had published her first book at the age of sixty-five in the Depression year of 1932. The librarians' belated recognition of her achievement came just in time to justify Nordstrom's costly investment in the new eight-volume edition. Librarians across the country would now feel compelled to purchase the series for their collections. In part in recognition of this important victory, Nordstrom in early 1954 became the first woman to be elected a member of Harper & Brothers' board of directors.

The first major honor to be bestowed on Nordstrom herself filled the tough-minded but self-mocking forty-four-year-old with mixed emotions of amusement and awe. For a woman of her generation, major success in publishing all but inevitably came at a price, and even a place in the Harper boardroom did not immunize her from the occasional potshots of her colleagues, as when at the start of one of the first weekly meetings she attended one of the men asked her whether she would not be kind enough to make the coffee. The director of the Department of Books for Boys and Girls easily parried the assault with a tart profession of ignorance: "I'm sorry but I don't know how." The gentlemen's club of an old-line house like Harper was not about to reform itself without a struggle.

Meanwhile, awards and other forms of professional recognition were now landing, with ever-increasing regularity, on her doorstep. In 1954 Nordstrom won election to a one-year term as Children's Book Council president. The next year Meindert DeJong, a midwestern fiction writer — and church janitor — whom she had encouraged over the course of a correspondence of epic proportions carried on since before the war, won the Newbery Medal for *The Wheel on the School.* Then in 1957 Harper finally got its first Caldecott Medal winner with the selection of Marc Simont for his illustrations for Janice Udry's *A Tree Is Nice.*

If Nordstrom had had to endure years of skepticism, if not outright disdain, from librarians and critics before finally gaining the general respect of her book-purchasing colleagues, Margaret K. McElderry had had no such difficulties. Having entered publishing with the finest imaginable library pedigree, she had seemed from the first less like a newcomer than a consummate insider: a polished, incisive, quietly competitive publishing leader in the May Massee mold. McElderry was an enthusiastic Anglophile and world traveler and became the first American editor to see an important opportunity in the postwar resurgence of British fantasy writing for children. At a time when beleaguered London firms especially welcomed the business, she was quick to acquire North American rights to much of the best new work. (Ursula Nordstrom, who detested both overseas travel and the fantasy genre, gladly ceded this territory to her and remained keenly focused on acquiring the kind of emotionally bracing, irreverent realistic fiction that Salinger had done so much to inspire.)

McElderry dealt as decisively with her authors from abroad as she did with those who were closer at hand. On signing the 1952 Carnegie Medal winner Mary Norton's *The Borrowers* for publication by Harcourt the following year, McElderry proceeded to re-edit the book with a firm hand for the American market. Of necessity, communication with Norton was at first entirely by letter. With stunning self-assurance, Harcourt's editor urged Norton to delete, as unnecessary, the opening paragraph of the opening chapter of her prize-winning book. The latter acceded to this request (just how readily is not known, although she did eventually think better of the change and restore the paragraph in a later edition). McElderry also commissioned a frothier set of new illustrations by Beth and Joe Krush that better suited the upbeat postwar American mood than the brooding English edition originals by Diana Stanley.[37]

Another British fantasy writer signed by McElderry, Lucy Boston, left a memorable portrait of the American editor who grew to become one of her closest friends:

> She is like a figurehead riding the great waves, if one could imagine a figurehead that constantly dissolved into jokes and always imagined itself to be at the stern. She is a driving force as sensitive as a gramophone needle and by nature self-effacing and shy. . . . She has an iron will and must be formidable at her desk. I have . . . seen her winding up a week's business trip in Brown's Hotel, expertly and precisely packing her many cases while the telephone rang continuously and people

pleaded for last-minute interviews. When she actually left, the management and all the staff formed two rows to bow her out and she sailed
forth, leaving me feeling like waste paper after royalty had passed.[38]

Although children's editorial departments remained small during the
1950s, those at the larger houses underwent a series of subtle, maturing
transformations. By the end of the decade, nearly every department head
had, at a minimum, acquired a trusted second in command. Such arrangements were not entirely new in the 1950s; it was the underlying attitude inside the departments that had changed: the pioneer mentality of the prewar
years had gradually given place to a less tenuous, more firmly planted
homesteader culture. With the permanence of their enterprise now seemingly assured, the more senior editors could afford to devote more thought
to questions of expansion and succession, as emotionally complicated as
this often proved to be for the pioneers.

At Viking, May Massee hired Annis Duff, a Canadian-born author,
former librarian, and bookseller who, it appeared, was being groomed
to take over for her — though it was never made clear when. Massee did
little to make life easy for her protégée. On the contrary, she went to
great lengths to limit and even undermine the younger woman's authority,
watching over her actions with a controlling eye and insisting that authors
come to see her privately, at her Greenwich Village apartment, before discussing any matter of substance in the office with Duff.

At Scribner, Alice Dalgliesh had an easier time of entrusting her assistant, a literature major from California named Frances Starbuck (later Foster), with substantial responsibility, allowing her to work directly with
certain authors on their manuscripts and to be privy to more or less everything that she herself was engaged in doing.[39] At Doubleday, Massee's successor at that house, a former journalist named Margaret Lesser, had likewise committed herself to honing the publishing skills of a young southern
woman named Morell Gipson, whom she had hired in part with an eye to
her own retirement.

By the mid-1950s, Ursula Nordstrom presided over a growing staff at
Harper with the help of a coolly confident, intellectually brilliant senior
editor named Susan Carr, who for the next decade would act as the tem-
pestuous publisher's ideal alter ego. Following graduation from Wellesley,
Carr had served her apprenticeship at two vastly different houses: at pres-

tigious Knopf and at the office that, although usually pegged as the bottom rung of the status ladder, she afterwards considered the best possible place for her to have trained — Simon & Schuster's Sandpiper Press, of Golden Books fame.[40] Another Harper editor, Mary Russell, made a specialty of nonfiction, leaving Nordstrom free to direct her own protean energies elsewhere.

For the first time, juvenile departments were also likely to have a staff member responsible for "promotion," a job that, depending on the house, might entail writing flap copy, dispatching sales letters about upcoming highlights to important librarians and other top accounts, preparing copy for the department's seasonal catalogs, making certain that reviewers had the advance materials they needed, making arrangements for an occasional bit of low-key entertaining, and perhaps cultivating national media contacts of one kind and another, including in television. Every house had its own way of parceling out these responsibilities, all of which, in the past, would have been considered part of the editor's job. It was notable in a field still overwhelmingly staffed by women that the people chosen for the new promotion managers' jobs were as likely as not to be men. In 1950, for example, Viking Junior Books hired a clever pitchman named Arthur Bell to tout its much-bemedaled list.[41] In the male-dominated business and professional arenas of the 1950s, commercial television, with its unprecedented demographic reach and culture of big money, was widely perceived as an extension of the male domain, best approached by other males. By the end of the decade, even the most insulated of publishers for children had not failed to notice television's impact on the young or to ask how best to adapt their efforts to the new reality.

Many in the literary world did their best, at first, simply to dismiss television as a "lowbrow" phenomenon. Journalist Dan Wakefield, whose writer friends in the New York of the 1950s included Norman Mailer, Allen Ginsberg, William F. Buckley, and Calvin Trillin, later recalled that for himself and his contemporaries, television "was still an oddity, of little interest except for a few distinguished live drama series like 'Playhouse Ninety' and the local interview program 'Night Beat,' hosted by a tough-minded interrogator we admired, Mike Wallace. We would sometimes seek out one of the few TV owners we knew or go to a bar with television to watch Wallace, but owning your own set was considered gauche for writers and intellectuals, a sign of decadence and mental sloth."[42] Not surprisingly, Ursula Nordstrom, who had already shocked some of her colleagues by flaunting her admiration for the comics and confessing her weakness for *Confidential*, was among the first children's book editors to buck the trend, freely admitting to Harper children's novelist Janette Sebring Lowrey that she owned a television "receiver" and had found some shows that she considered worth watching.[43] While making good sport of the absurd claims and faulty grammar that were among the hallmarks of the new medium's commercials, she recommended Edward R. Murrow's news documentary program *See It Now* and wrote of being riveted by the live coverage of the McCarthy-Army Senate hearings, which ran from April to June 1954. It was through the impact of those broadcasts that the unprecedented power of television to refocus public attention on a single topic first became apparent to a great many Americans.[44]

No publishing figure of the time, however, rivaled Bennett Cerf in his enthusiasm for television or his sanguine assessment of its long-term impact on literary culture. Cerf was quick to recognize television's potential as a marketing tool. In the tradition of Robert Benchley and Clifton Fadiman, literary men who, a generation earlier, had seized the chance to reach a national audience via radio, he eagerly grabbed every opportunity that came his way to appear "on the air." Starting in 1951, Cerf in his weekly role as a panelist on the hit Sunday evening television game show *What's My Line* helped to fix the image of the publishing executive for millions of Americans as a glamorous, tuxedo-clad man about town with a disarming jack-o'-lantern grin and fondness for corny wordplay. Hardly a week passed when Cerf failed to "plug" at least one new Random title as he traded debonair remarks with his fellow panelists and honed in on the occupations of the show's parade of guests. Cerf also reaped untold behind-the-scenes benefits for Random House through his association with the program's producers, Mark Goodson and Bill Todman. In 1958, for example, the year he sent the author of *The Cat in the Hat Comes Back* on his first national publicity tour, Cerf landed Theodor Geisel — or Dr. Seuss — a coveted spot as a "mystery guest" on Goodson-Todman's game show *To Tell the Truth*.[45]

Apart from Cerf, only his colleagues at Golden Books and their competitors at Rand McNally and elsewhere in the mass-market domain seemed to have the freedom from traditional editorial constraints to explore the new medium's potential, whether as a marketing tool or a source of content. Taking their own licensing agreement with Disney as a model, the publishers of Golden Books negotiated similar contracts that made it possible for them to publish Little Golden titles featuring a long roster of popular television stars, including Gene Autry, Roy Rogers and Dale Evans, Captain Kangaroo, and Howdy Doody. In 1950 Simon & Schuster joined forces with the health care products giant Johnson & Johnson to promote a Little Golden Book called *Doctor Dan the Bandage Man* (by Helen Gaspard, illustrated by Corinne Malvern), for which a record first printing of one and a half million copies was ordered. Each copy of the trim twenty-five-cent book came with six actual Band-Aids affixed to the inside cover as a promotional bonus, and a special counter display was devised for selling Band-Aids and books side by side in drugstores. There was nothing new in the idea of a "free" trifle as an inducement to purchase a children's book — the practice dated all the way back to the bouncing ball and pincushion days of John Newbery. The real novelty lay in Johnson & Johnson's decision to bankroll an unprecedented advertising campaign for *Doctor Dan* on national television.[46]

The *Doctor Dan* campaign was a rarity, but by the early 1950s the television networks had already begun to turn their attention to children's programming and were starting, at least in a small way, to consider how children's books might serve their medium's need for material. During the fall of 1952, a half-hour-long morning show broadcast locally by Chicago's WBNQ called *Ding Dong School* proved so popular that, six weeks after its premiere, NBC picked it up for airing nationally. Featuring a variety of craft and educational activities for preschoolers, the program was hosted by a kindly "teacher" named "Miss Frances," who summoned viewers at the start of the show by ringing an old-fashioned school bell. She would then look directly into the camera and ask, "How are you today?" Many children at home believed that Miss Frances was speaking to them alone. In less than a year's time, *Ding Dong School* had a devoted audience of 2 million viewers; at its peak three years later, it had 3 million.[47]

The fact was never stressed on air, but the program's benevolent host, Frances R. Horwich, held a doctorate in education from Northwestern University and was on leave as chairman of the Department of Education at Chicago's Roosevelt College when she ventured onto the airwaves. The welcoming tone and well-conceived, age-appropriate sets of activities offered each morning on *Ding Dong School* were the result of thoughtful, theory-based lesson planning and an impressive background of actual classroom experience. Five minutes before the end of each program, Horwich asked viewers to "Go get Mommy," and would then review the day's activities, explaining why each project was beneficial and what everyday materials were needed to try each one of them at home. In the case of a picture-book story read aloud, Horwich repeated the title and author's name. Starting in Chicago, booksellers in cities where *Ding Dong School* was broadcast learned to expect a sizable jump in sales for any children's book featured on the program.

Publishers were not all equally impressed by the anecdotal evidence. Whether out of wariness or disdain, some publishers refused to grant NBC permission to have their books read on the air. Others, however, most notably the comparatively small William R. Scott and Company, whose Bank Street–inspired picture books were aimed primarily at preschoolers, were only too happy to cooperate. For Scott, after years of seeing his books ignored by the library world, the chance to have them recommended directly to millions of parents was an opportunity not to be missed. By 1955 a rival morning program on CBS, *Captain Kangaroo*, hosted by the avuncular Bob Keeshan, had established itself as a second television showcase for picture books.[48]

The more receptive publishers might hope and pray for such chances for publicity to come their way. Meanwhile, a young filmmaker living in rustic splendor in the Connecticut woods named Morton Schindel was busy with plans to forge a more permanent bridge between the worlds of children's publishing and television. Schindel had devised an ingenious, labor-intensive, but relatively low-cost shooting style for use in adapting picture books to film. This scheme, which he named the "iconographic method," entailed mounting the illustrations of a book on an easel one at a time and slowly moving each in turn in front of a fixed camera in order to simulate a reader's exploratory gaze. A young father with a Wharton business degree but no library, teaching, or publishing experience, Schindel had wisely sought the advice and blessing of Viking's May Massee and other experts in the field before choosing the picture books to adapt by this innovative method. It was a sign of changing times that once Massee and the others (including the New York Public Library Central Children's Room's Maria Cimino) became convinced of Schindel's skill and commitment to preserving the spirit of the books, they lent their wholehearted support to his efforts.

Schindel had undertaken the venture with little besides a bankroll of family money and the quixotic hope of finding a place for his work on television. For a time, the gamble seemed ripe for a major payoff. But when the producers of the *Captain Kangaroo* show, which premiered on CBS in the fall of 1955, backed away from an initial expression of interest — opting instead to feature the more obviously entertaining *Tom Terrific* cartoon shorts on their morning program — Schindel felt obliged to reconsider his plan; in the end he concluded that the nation's schools and public libraries represented the likeliest market for his impeccable work.

To test-market this new idea Schindel mailed copies of his first nine films to forty libraries around the country with circulating film collections (though none collected children's material). He recalled years later:

> I said that if they didn't want the films, to send them back. We had a rural mailbox and I'd look in it every morning for films coming back. And there wouldn't be any. So one day I went to the post office and said, "Look, you've got a whole bunch of packages here for me, don't you know where I live?" They looked around and said, "We don't have any." So I phoned the libraries and they said they were keeping them, that they needed films for children and these fit with their collections. Seldom were any sent back.[49]

Schindel next arranged for a screening of his short films at the Museum of Modern Art in New York, to which he invited five hundred educators, librarians, publishers, and others. To his delight, three hundred people showed up, and the Museum afterwards chose three of the films for its permanent collection.[50] On what amounted to his second try, Schindel had identified an untapped market that in the years to come his Weston Woods Studios would dominate. His disappointing initial encounter with the movers and shakers of commercial television would prove paradigmatic: apart from readings from picture books on programs like *Ding Dong School* and *Captain Kangaroo*, television executives would have little to offer children's book publishers or the people who used their books (apart from licensed character spinoffs) anytime soon.[51]

Walt Disney meanwhile was moving confidently into the television arena with the launch in December 1954 of his weekly *Disneyland* program on ABC, a show shrewdly conceived as a nonstop commercial both for the entertainment company's soon-to-open southern California theme park and for whatever upcoming feature film the Disney Studio might have in the offing. It was hard not to be impressed by the well-oiled workings and all-encompassing nature of the Disney empire, which earned substantial revenues each year from its myriad product licensing agreements, including the one first negotiated in the early 1930s that granted the Western Printing and Lithographing Company the exclusive right to publish children's books about the Disney Studio's iconic characters. Out of public view, Walt Disney and his business partners found other ways to advance their mutual interest. Both ABC and Western lent Disney substantial portions of the money needed to build the Anaheim park, whose shops and rides picked up on themes and characters also featured in Golden Books and on the network's programs.[52] When the Davy Crockett craze took off following the airing of a three-part *Disneyland* dramatic series about America's "King of the Wild Frontier," Golden commissioned suitable books for its list in time to capitalize on the merchandising bonanza.[53] As a new generation of children's librarians — heirs to the legacy of Anne Carroll Moore, Alice M. Jordan, and Clara Whitehill Hunt — monitored Disney's steady rise in influence over all aspects of children's culture, what they saw happening was the realization of their mentors' worst nightmares.

Another, perhaps less ominous encroachment on the librarians' authority came in the form of a wave of new advice columns addressed to baby boom mothers. The most popular of these was the work of Frances L. Ilg and Louise Bates Ames, two protégées of the noted child development researcher Arnold Gesell. In their nationally syndicated newspaper column, "Child Behavior," which appeared as often as five times weekly, as well as for a time on a weekly television program, Ilg and Ames dispensed a sprinkling of book recommendations along with strategies for coping with crankiness, resistance at bedtime, and myriad other matters of concern to parents. A favorite bedtime book of theirs was *Goodnight Moon*, about which they wrote in their column for March 30, 1953: "This is really one of the most delightful books that we know of from an adult's point of view. And it captures the 2-year-old so completely that it seems almost unlawful that you can hypnotize a child off to sleep as easily as you can by reading this small classic." They had, they pointed out, "mentioned [*Goodnight Moon*] before but cannot mention [it] too often." With each fresh endorsement from Ilg and Ames, sales of *Goodnight Moon* climbed further, reversing the decline that might otherwise have doomed it four or five years after publication. The book's illustrator, Clement Hurd, later credited their column, plausibly, with having started the book on its way to the phenomenal success it enjoyed in the decades to come.[54]

If *Goodnight Moon* exemplified the rare case of a "sleeper" slowly roused, another publishing phenomenon of the postwar years, Dr. Seuss's *The Cat in the Hat,* proved that a children's book did not have to sell for twenty-five cents in order rapidly to make its way into hundreds of thousands of American homes. All a children's book had to do was to come along at precisely the right time and to appear to hold the perfect solution to a great and deeply troubling national dilemma.[55]

Set against a bright blue background, the red-and-white-striped stovepipe hat and jaunty red bow tie sported by the lanky, loose-limbed Cat aptly suggested an Uncle Sam–like father figure, though one who had somehow gone agreeably haywire. The quintessential 1950s paean to "fun," *The Cat in the Hat* gaily concealed the quantum of public concern and educational theory that had teased it into existence. Writing in *Life* in the spring of 1954, novelist John Hersey had asked why children "bog[ged] down on [the] first R" and answered the question with a searing critique of the school primers — most notably the "Dick and Jane" readers published since 1930 by Scott, Foresman and Company — then currently in use in most American schools. "Why," wrote Hersey, "should [children] not have pictures that widen rather than narrow the associative richness the children give to the words they illustrate — drawings like those of the wonderfully imaginative geniuses among children's illustrators, Tenniel, Howard Pyle, 'Dr. Seuss,' Walt Disney?"[56] But according to Hersey, the problem with such books went beyond the quality of the art. The doggedly repetitive texts, with their pedestrian tales of "abnormally courteous, unnaturally clean boys and girls," offered at best a "pallid" foretaste of literature. It was no wonder, Hersey argued, that children failed to respond in the desired way. Rudolf Flesch's bestselling jeremiad on the subject, *Why Johnny Can't Read,* published the following year, only served to intensify the debate.

It was against this backdrop of national jitters about the state of American literacy that William Spaulding, a wartime army comrade of Geisel's and now director of Houghton Mifflin's Education Department, had summoned the author to Boston in the fall of 1955 to talk over a project he had in mind. Spaulding invited his old friend to take home a copy of the list of 225 words that Houghton's literacy experts had determined were the ones most easily recognized by six-year-olds. He challenged Geisel to create a children's book, or "supplementary reader," composed entirely from the words on the list, to extract from the crude ore of the reading specialists' "controlled vocabulary" a blithe bit of Seussian gold. "Write me a story," Spaulding exhorted him, "that first-graders can't put down!"[57] Geisel by then was well ensconced as a Random House author. He left it to Spaulding to secure Bennett Cerf's approval before pursuing the matter further. To Geisel's surprise (and, it would seem, initial disappointment), Cerf agreed to let Houghton publish the school edition of whatever the author came up with, provided that Random House retained the exclusive right to publish the book for the retail trade.

When Random House announced *The Cat in the Hat* on its spring 1957 list, Ursula Nordstrom fell into a dark mood. Serendipitously for the past year, she had had a similar project of her own under development. *Little Bear* by Else Holmelund Minarik, with illustrations by Maurice Sendak, was to be the first title in the Harper "I Can Read" series and was due to be published in the fall — one season *after* the Seuss reader. The latter book was sure to steal some of *Little Bear*'s thunder. The sting to Nordstrom's competitive pride notwithstanding, the news that another publisher had also been stirred to action by Hersey's widely discussed article and Flesch's book could not have been altogether surprising to her. In Nordstrom's case, another prompt to action had been a conversation with the Boston Public Library's Virginia Haviland, who had recounted for her the story of a young child who burst into the children's reading room one day and announced to Haviland: "I can read! I can read!" The child had then asked her where in the room he would find the books that were just right for a brand-new reader like himself. Haviland had had to admit that there were no such books in the library's collection.

Haviland's story had fascinated Nordstrom, but she had not known how to go about filling the gap in the literature that her friend had identified for her until a Danish-born former first-grade teacher named Else Minarik turned up unbidden in her office one September day in 1956 with the manuscript for what was to become the opening chapter of *Little Bear*. Minarik had come armed with a rather amateurish-looking dummy meant to persuade the editor that her story would make a suitable picture book. Nordstrom quickly saw past the crudeness of the graphics to the little narrative's potential as part of a larger work and asked the author if she might be willing to write a few more stories about her bears. Minarik agreed to do so, and within a few weeks' time she had provided the additional text, all of which hewed rigorously to the author's high standard of age-appropriate simplicity, and without resort to a controlled vocabulary list (as those promoting the book would later note with pride). Nordstrom then called upon her young star illustrator, Maurice Sendak, to illustrate the book. The resulting work, as was widely recognized from the first, ranked at a minimum as some sort of minor masterpiece.[58] *Little Bear* served as the template for the "I Can Read" series as a whole, the second volume of which, Syd Hoff's *Danny and the Dinosaur*, followed a year later, once the final text had been carved out of a much longer manuscript that Nordstrom had kept on the "undecided" table in her office for months on end, until *Little Bear* had come along to point the way.[59]

Meanwhile, although nearly each and every one of Theodor Geisel's "Dr. Seuss" books going back to *And to Think I Saw It on Mulberry Street* had enjoyed enviable sales, it was *The Cat in the Hat* that now made Seuss a household word and its creator a celebrity.[60] So strong was the response in bookstores that the publisher's wife (and sometime editor of children's books) Phyllis Cerf proposed to Geisel that the two of them join forces as partners in a new publishing venture, to be called Beginner Books, for the purpose of producing an ongoing series of readers by Geisel and others in the same format. Random House would distribute the books, and the principals would all make heaps of money. Over lunch at chic Quo Vadis in midtown Manhattan, Geisel, who preferred the artist's unbuttoned life to that of the profit-minded entrepreneur, reluctantly agreed to the plan, with the condition that ownership of Beginner Books be shared equally with a third partner, his wife, Helen Palmer. Geisel considered Palmer, who was an author of children's books in her own right, his own best editor.[61] Because Palmer was in declining health, it was decided that she would work from the couple's home in La Jolla, California, while Geisel (shuttling between coasts) and Phyllis Cerf oversaw the day-to-day details of the operation from New York. An attic office under the eaves of the old Villard Mansion on Madison Avenue, where Random House was headquartered, was set aside for them. By way of shrugging off the stuffier implications of his new executive status, Geisel decorated the approach to the new inner sanctum with a series of prankish, hand-painted signs: THIS WAY TO DR. SCHMERECASE, and the like.[62]

Would-be authors and artists soon learned, however, that editor Geisel was all business, a cool, appraising taskmaster with a robust appetite for revision. Stan and Jan Berenstain — already well known as magazine and greeting card illustrators but as yet untried in juveniles — left their first meeting at Beginner Books impressed by Geisel's single-minded dedication but also a bit rattled by the sheer ferocity of the exchange. "Now let's talk about your rhymed verse," Geisel had proposed after first guiding the couple through a more finely nuanced character analysis of the family of affable bears they had written about than the couple had thought possible. Until then, the Berenstains had held a very modest view of their latest undertaking, believing that all they had aimed, or needed, to do was to produce a light, straightforward entertainment for children. As the dissection continued, however, it struck them both that to work for the author of *The Cat in the Hat* was to pledge one's fealty to a high and exacting calling. "Your scansion is pretty good," Geisel had conceded. "But again, it's too complicated. And your line lengths are all over the place. They won't look good on the page. Try to even them up. Also, you've got a few interior rhymes. Let's leave interior rhymes to Cole Porter and Ogden Nash. And I've counted at least 10 convenience rhymes," by which he meant rhymes that added nothing to the narrative. Some befuddlement on the visitors' part was certainly in order when, at the conclusion of this editorial tongue-lashing, Geisel cheerfully showed the couple to the door and, taking them in hand, declared: "Berenstains, I can't tell you how happy I am to be working with you. I just know we're going to get a wonderful book."[63]

Heading Beginner Books' fall 1958 inaugural list of four titles was a sequel to the one that had inspired and bankrolled the new company. *The Cat in the Hat Comes Back* had all the makings of another bestseller, and as the holiday gift-buying season approached its peak, Random House sent Geisel out on the road for a triumphal tour that, over the course of ten heavily scheduled days, took him to cities all around the Northeast and Midwest. While the annual fall children's book fairs in New York, Cleveland, Chicago, and elsewhere now gave many thousands of urban youngsters the chance to "touch and smell" an author, as Robert McCloskey once characterized the experience, the barnstorming national author tour was still a newsworthy novelty in the 1950s. The Seuss road show, orchestrated by Random's star publicist (and future president) Robert Bernstein, featured stops at major department stores in Chicago, Dayton, Minneapolis, Detroit, Rochester, Newark, Boston, Philadelphia, Washington, Pittsburgh, and Cleveland. Along the way, Geisel participated in press luncheons, a network television program, an award ceremony attended by educators, and a well-publicized visit with the director of the Washington Zoo. At every event, children received free "Cat in the Hat" buttons. At Marshall Field's downtown Chicago store alone, one thousand books were sold in an hour and a half. The J. L. Hudson Company of Detroit hired a helicopter to fly the author from its downtown flagship store to signings at two of its outlying branches. In each instance, Geisel, on alighting from his special chopper, had been surrounded by a sea of young fans. "It was," he later told a reporter, "as if I were Santa Claus."[64]

By the fall of 1958, Americans' concerns about their children's reading skills had been subsumed by a larger, still more alarming national worry. The previous October the Soviet Union's surprise launch of the *Sputnik I* satellite had precipitated the crisis, as Americans already living in dread of the heavily armed Communist nation's expansionist ambitions suddenly learned that they had new reason to fear the worst. Then, only a month later, in November 1957, had come the yet more terrifying news of the launch of *Sputnik II*, which for the first time had successfully sent an animal into space — a dog named Laika. Cold War fear of the "Russian menace" now crystallized around public concern that Americans lagged behind the Soviets not only in technological know-how but also in science education from the grade school level on up. Early deficiencies in reading skills now came to be seen as an underlying cause of greater educational failings with potential life-and-death consequences. *Time* magazine quoted Dr. Edward Teller's terrifying suggestion that "the Russians [could] conquer [the United States] without fighting, through a growing scientific and technological preponderance."[65]

Time proposed a two-part prescription for averting this disastrous outcome: "1) more basic research, and 2) more and better science education in the high schools."[66] Yet if there was any truth to Jack Kerouac's storm-tossed autobiographical novel *On the Road*, published that September, with its searing appraisal of postwar America's youth as a generation of the rootless, the footloose, and the spiritually "beat," it was hard to see how either of these national imperatives could be conveniently satisfied. In December 1957, further doubt had been cast on America's competitiveness when a satellite-mounted Vanguard rocket — intended as the nation's response to the Russians' show of technological wizardry — exploded on liftoff.

The following March a soul-searching photo essay in *Life* focused on the human dimension of the crisis by contrasting the educational experiences and daily lives of two typical teenage boys, one American, the other Soviet. The unmistakable impression left by the piece was that not only did the latter young man possess greater personal discipline than his American counterpart, but that he also ranked two full grade levels higher in his studies. In the face of these findings, *Life*'s readers could but wonder whether with television, the movies, rock 'n' roll, and countless other modern distractions all competing for their time and attention, America's youth had not embraced the new "fun morality" too zealously for their own or the nation's good.

In an effort to redress the worrisome imbalance, Congress in the late summer of 1958 passed the National Defense Education Act (NDEA), wide-ranging legislation that, while primarily aimed at bolstering training and research in the realm of higher education, also allocated substantial sums for the purchase by public schools of non-textbooks on all aspects of science and mathematics. Another, less widely publicized objective of the NDEA was to foster foreign-language study by the nation's public school children.

As latecomer publishing houses scrambled to stake their claim as producers of science books worthy of purchase with federal dollars, those with a long-standing commitment to science publishing for children, including William Morrow, T. Y. Crowell, Franklin Watts, and Golden Press, profited from their foresight and the government's newfound largesse. Morrow's mighty arsenal of such books featured dozens of backlist titles by respected authors (and former schoolteachers) Herbert S. Zim and Millicent E. Selsam. Under the bold departmental leadership of Elizabeth Riley, Crowell had published its first children's book about space exploration, *Lodestar: Rocket Ship to Mars* by Franklyn M. Branley, in 1951.[67] In 1955 Riley had brought out the decade's most original anthology, Helen Plotz's *Imagination's Other Place: Poems of Science and Mathematics*. The pride of the Watts list was the firm's ever-expanding series of "Firsts" — *The First Book of Flying*, *The First Book of Stones*, and scores of others — a series begun in 1943 to satisfy young children's curiosity on a wide range of topics including but not limited to science. By the mid-1950s, Scribner had an established tradition of publishing juveniles both of science fact and science fiction. Young readers of Ruthven Todd's *Space Cat Visits Venus*, published by Scribner in 1955, were perhaps better prepared than their parents for the news of *Sputnik II.*

The Hayden Planetarium at New York's American Museum of Natural History was among the leading cultural institutions around the country to expand its science-based education programs in response to the outcry over *Sputnik.* By the end of the decade, Franklyn M. Branley, now also the Planetarium's education director, had undertaken the authorship of an ambitious series of early-grade-school-level "Let's-Read-and-Find-Out" books for Crowell. Intended for children not much above the skill level of Random House's "Beginner Reader" and Harper's "I Can Read" series, the Crowell books — "dynamic, . . . attractively illustrated [treatments of] single, narrow subjects . . . written with an understanding of how children think" — were perfectly matched to the needs of the market and the moment. With enthusiastic support from Crowell's Elizabeth Riley, the "Let's-Read-and-Find-Out" series proved a stunning commercial as well as critical success even by the elevated standards of a decade that was largely defined by highly profitable, groundbreaking series.[68]

It went without saying that the Watts "First Books," with their formulaic titles, uniform page size, four variations in length, and other standardized features, had no chance of garnering Newbery or Caldecott laurels. For some critics, the books of that series (more so, it would seem, than those of the more distinctively illustrated Crowell books) even raised the specter of a latter-day Stratemeyer at large in the ranges of nonfiction. In response to a comment by the New York Public Library's Frances Lander Spain, who had complained that series like the "First Books" encouraged authors to produce merely "pedestrian" writing, Franklin Watts himself rose to the defense of the enterprise, arguing that the very opposite was the case because "each new title carries the reputation of the entire group, [every] . . . title . . . must be worked over until it is right."[69] The savings accrued from the somewhat simplified design and marketing stages in the publication of new titles in an "established group of books," Watts noted, even gave him the leeway to take an occasional chance on an unusual book that might not otherwise have found its way into print at all. The example he offered to illustrate the point was the *First Book of Rhythms* by Langston Hughes, the Harlem Renaissance literary figure and columnist whose first published poems had appeared in a children's magazine, *The Brownies' Book,* thirty years earlier. Hughes's relationship with Franklin Watts (and his wife and partner, Helen Hoke Watts) was rather more complex than Watts let on. The couple had commissioned an earlier book in the "First Books" series from Hughes, *The First Book of Negroes*, in response to the urgings of authors Franklin Folsom and Mary Elting Folsom to open the series to African American authors and subject matter. But the Wattses had made a point of obtaining, on that earlier occasion, a public denial from the writer of "past or present membership in the Communist Party." Despite the raw feelings laid bare by an episode that touched directly on questions of race and radical politics, the Wattses and Hughes had apparently felt comfortable enough with each other, and sufficiently satisfied with sales of the latter's initial pair of "First Books," for Hughes to contribute a third volume to the series, *The First Book of Jazz*, in 1955, followed by several more titles on into the next decade.[70]

If 1950s librarian critics tended, in line with their predecessors, to regard series publishing as the dubious triumph of mass-production standards over individualized sensibility and taste, the new postwar generation of social scientist commentators seemed prepared to confirm their suspicions. Originally published in 1950 in a scant university press printing of three thousand copies, sociologist David Riesman's analysis of the "changing American character," *The Lonely Crowd*, quickly emerged as one of the year's surprise bestsellers. Riesman and his coauthors Nathan Glazer and Reuel Denney claimed to have detected a tectonic shift in the way Americans related as individuals to their colleagues, to their neighbors, and to other groups to which they belonged, and they stated their case with a degree of authority that Americans hungry for expert guidance found revelatory if not quite reassuring. As the *New York Times* later noted, *The Lonely Crowd* "was among the first of the postwar classics written by academics who gained unanticipated fame and fortune because an anxious public believed that their works had uncovered some deteriorating and alarming condition in American society."[71]

For children's librarians, the key passage in Riesman's book came in the chapter on "Agents of Character Formation," in which consideration was given to the impact of the "mass media" and an example was made of the character-modeling message conveyed by one of the most popular American picture books of the 1940s, a Little Golden Book written by Gertrude Crampton and illustrated by Tibor Gergely called *Tootle the Engine*.

In *Tootle*, Riesman and the others believed they had found evidence of the emergence of a new American culture of mass conformity. In this simple-seeming story, a young locomotive (the child-surrogate figure) wandered off the track to play in the flowers, doing so with much the same careless abandon that had landed a memorable child character of an earlier age, Little Red Riding Hood, in mortal danger. According to the authors, the salient difference between the two tales lay in the extent to which their respective morals could be deemed realistic. "The story [of Red Riding Hood], though it may be read as a cautionary tale, deals with real human passions, sexual and aggressive; it certainly does not present the rewards of virtue in any unambiguous form or show the adult world in any wholly be-nevolent light." *Tootle*, in contrast, seemed calculated to mislead children into a false faith in the benevolence of their elders' — and society's — mo-tives. "There is something overvarnished in this tale," the authors found. "The adult world (the teachers) is *not* that benevolent, the citizenry (the peer-group) *not* that participative and cooperative, the signals are *not* that clear. . . . At the end Tootle has forgotten that he ever did like flowers any-way — how childish they are in comparison with the great big grown-up world of engines, signals, tracks, and meetings!"[72] In Engineville, even the community's respected elders were prepared to lie in order to ensure a basic level of conformity from the young. To librarians already ill disposed to-ward Golden Books, *The Lonely Crowd*'s commentary came as bittersweet confirmation of the books' suspected lack of integrity.

While social critics like Riesman noted the trend in white, middle-class America toward "other directedness," or increased conformity in so-cial behavior, some members of the African American community had be-gun to challenge publicly the societal norms under which they lived. Ap-plying a variety of methods, from civil litigation to civil disobedience, what came to be called the civil rights movement aimed at securing greater eq-uity under the law for people of color. Rosa Parks's Montgomery, Alabama, bus protest of December 1955 and the court-ordered desegregation eight-een months later of Central High School in Little Rock, Arkansas, were milestone events that captured the nation's attention — albeit not to the extent of prompting anything like a concerted response on the part of the publishers of children's books. The "First Books" written by Langston Hughes, the occasional children's novels written by Jesse Jackson, a former postal worker and reporter published by Ursula Nordstrom at Harper, and

the books for young readers by Harlem writer Ellen Tarry were still anoma-
lies in the late 1950s.

A children's book that commented or even appeared to comment on
the issue of racial integration had the potential for becoming a flashpoint
of public controversy. In 1958 Harper published just such a picture book.
Garth Williams's *The Rabbits' Wedding* describes the moonlit wedding of
two small, lop-eared animals, one covered in white fur, the other one covered in black. Not since *The Story of Ferdinand* had been attacked in the late
1930s as a sub-rosa commentary on the Spanish Civil War had a book for
young children created a comparable furor. *The Montgomery Home News*, a
publication of the Montgomery, Alabama, chapter of the segregationist
White Citizens Council, condemned Williams's story for its seeming endorsement of the practice of interracial marriage. Alabama politicians, led
by state senator E. O. Eddins of Marengo County, railed against the book,
its author, and before long also against the director of the Alabama Public
Library Service Division (the state's central library), a white woman named
Emily W. Reed, who in response to the Council's criticism ordered copies
of *The Rabbits' Wedding* for the central collection's reserve shelves. Under
this arrangement, Alabama public librarians could borrow copies of the
book for their local libraries but only by going to the central library in
Montgomery and specifically requesting to do so. Reed's attempt at a com-
promise failed to appease Senator Eddins, who proceeded to question her
about her views of racial integration. When he did so, Reed refused to answer directly, stating that her views on the question were irrelevant to her
ability to do her job. The state legislature then attempted to force Reed
from her post. In 1960 the North Carolina native left Alabama to become
the coordinator of adult services for the Washington, D.C., public library.[73]

After the war, Robert McCloskey, whose meticulously crafted picture books
epitomized the antithesis of the mass-market approach to bookmaking,
turned for subject matter to his own family's rustic day-to-day life on and
around Little Deer Island, off the coast of Maine in Penobscot Bay. If the
old-fashioned New England virtues of hard work, thrift, patience, and for-
titude still meant anything, here they all were — played out in a blueberry
patch, before the hearth of a modest clapboard cottage, and at the water's
edge. In 1958 McCloskey became the first artist to win the Caldecott Medal
a second time, a feat that elevated him, more or less against his will, to the

status of an elder statesman. In his second Caldecott acceptance speech, delivered in San Francisco on July 15 of that year, he dutifully rose to the occasion to deliver a contrarian's response to the prevailing outcry for more science books and science education for America's children.

Announcing his intention to "say something that needs saying right now," he began by taking a gentle swipe at authorities in general: "'What this country needs,'" he said, "is a phrase that keeps popping up. What this country needs is more exercise, or more religion, or a good five cent cigar, or, as of the moment, better education and more scientists."[74] McCloskey then explained why he doubted that this was the area of education that should really matter most to Americans.

"With everyone clamoring for more scientists, I should like," he said, "to clamor for more artists and designers. I should like to clamor for the teaching of drawing and design to every child, right along with reading and writing. I think it is most important for everyone really to see and evaluate pictures and really to see and evaluate his surroundings." Citing examples of deliberately misleading print advertising and television images and of the kind of runaway land development that was blighting larger and larger swaths of the American landscape, McCloskey argued that at a time when such excesses were commonplace it was essential for people to know how critically to evaluate every aspect of their visual environment. There was no better way, he concluded, to accomplish this vital goal than by teaching people how to draw from an early age.

It was a noble thought, and the audience cheered. McCloskey's urgings did little, however, to stem the fever tide of science publishing or to inspire a countertrend of interest in books designed to develop children's visual literacy and art-making skills. By the end of the decade, it could at least be said that American children were being exposed to more children's books (nearly all of them illustrated) than ever before, as total annual sales in the category nearly tripled from what they had been in 1950, reaching a record high in 1960 of $88 million.[75] It may have seemed the right moment for McCloskey's own mentor, May Massee, finally to step down, and in 1960 Massee agreed to relinquish the directorship of her department in favor of her longtime assistant, Annis Duff, and to stay on for a time in an advisory role. Out of deference to her predecessor, Duff postponed moving into Massee's wood-paneled office for nearly a year.

The previous summer the American Institute of Graphic Arts had presented its annual medal to Massee. Her selection marked the first time that a member of the children's book community had been so honored.[76] If receipt of a medal of her own — the inscription read: HER GUIDANCE AWAKENS INSPIRATION — made a fitting cap to a career characterized by continuous innovation, Massee did not take to semiretirement any more gracefully than had a number of her peers. She returned to Viking's offices far more often than had been anticipated under the new arrangement, and it was only when, her eyesight failing, she was nearly struck by a passing car on her way there that Viking's president, Thomas H. Guinzburg (the son of the man who had hired her nearly thirty years earlier), finally told her not to come in unaccompanied anymore. She lived on for another six years, dying peacefully at home on Christmas Eve 1966. However fortuitously, the impresario of the book beautiful and of the well-told tale had breathed her last in what those who revered her could not but have felt was the perfect storybook ending.

It was the timing of Anne Carroll Moore's death, however, nearly six years before, that colleagues still talked about decades later. Moore died on January 20, 1961, the morning of John F. Kennedy's inauguration as president of the United States. At the New York Public Library's Central Children's Room, the librarians were caught up both in the excitement of the events in Washington and in the sadness of the news about their great mentor and leader and were going about their business when the telephone rang. The youngest staff member, having answered the call, turned to a more senior librarian to say that a reporter from the Associated Press was on the line requesting information. The new president, in his inaugural address, had just said, "In the past, those who foolishly sought power by riding the back of the tiger ended up inside." The reporter wished to have the complete text of the source of the passage, which he had been told was a limerick by Edward Lear. The more senior librarian informed him that he was mistaken, that the author of the limerick alluded to by the president was Cosmo Monkhouse. She then proceeded to read him the five-line ditty. "You see," said the older librarian to the younger one after putting down the receiver, "this is just what Miss Moore worked for all her life" — to raise children's librarianship to the level of honor and respect that would prompt a national reporter on the day of a presidential inauguration to turn to the children's room as a valued repository of literature and knowledge.[77] The Owls, it seemed, had trained the next generation well.

7

SHAKEN AND STIRRED
The 1960s

Why are they always *white* children?[1]

— A five-year-old African American girl as she browsed
in a picture book at her nursery school, c. 1965

"WORLD EVENTS HAVE convinced many that man is not inherently good, that life on earth is threatened by automobiles and hydrogen bombs and missiles, that those who love God suffer along with those who do not, and that there is no assurance that the world is getting better. Since security cannot be found in the brave new world, there is a desire to return to the assurances of the Bible."[2]

This somber assessment of the nation's mood came in the report of the Kansas delegation to the Golden Anniversary White House Conference on Children and Youth, held in Washington, D.C., from March 27 to April 2, 1960. Not all Americans, of course, shared the Kansas delegates' response to the problem of coming to terms with the new age of anxiety. But as the *New York Times* suggested, if the informed citizens of a state far removed from the coastal areas most likely to be targeted for nuclear annihilation now sought spiritual cover in "a new theology called neo-orthodoxy, or the New Reformation," how might New Yorkers and other easterners living in the very shadow of Armageddon feel impelled to react? As they debated the future and crafted some 1,600 specific recommendations for the improvement of the lives of America's youth, it was all that the 7,500 conference delegates could do to put a good face on a bad situation.

Approximately 1,500 high school and college students had come to Washington as fully accredited conference delegates. The more than token representation of young people — the 1960 conference was the first in which any had participated — was doubtless intended to counter the post-*Sputnik* impression of American teenagers as a spoiled and irresponsible cohort of beatniks, rock 'n' rollers, and James Dean rebels. But as the national press reported each day, in session after session experts rose to document and voice their concern about the growing problem of "juvenile delinquency." One authority, Milton G. Rector, issued the dire prediction that "in some cities 20 to 25 per cent of the boys would be arrested before they reached the age of 17." Rector, who was director of the National Probation and Parole Association, went on to note that his estimate "does not include those who will become emotionally disturbed without committing delinquent acts."[3]

To be sure, President Eisenhower in his remarks at the conference's opening session had sounded a determinedly upbeat note, reaffirming his faith in the vast majority of the nation's young people. But at a press conference a few days later, the president dodged a reporter's question when asked whether he believed that American children were "less rugged . . . morally than those of a few generations ago." Conceding that American youngsters were undoubtedly less *physically* fit than in the past, the president suggested that this was an inevitable byproduct of the nation's unprecedented affluence, and that while it warranted concern, it was not necessarily any cause for alarm. "It's just [that] our mode of life has brought up something we have to overcome. That's all," he said in his brisk, matter-of-fact way, brushing aside all consideration of cultural or character-based explanations. "And we have to do it very earnestly." Unconvinced by the president's assurances, the *Times* reported his remarks under the headline: "Eisenhower Fears Softness in Youth."[4]

Ruth Hill Viguers, representing *The Horn Book* at the gathering, reported afterwards that of the 1,600 resolutions offered by delegates, half "were in the field of human rights; many were related to creative learning as opposed to the assimilation of facts; many to the impact of television and its possible control." Of her own participation, Viguers wrote obliquely: "Resolutions presented to the Forum from the Workgroups on Books, Magazines and Newspapers showed an awareness of the important role books can play in young people's lives and the need to make adequate library service available to everyone."[5]

Perhaps the most talked about topic at the conference, apart from juvenile delinquency, was that of the "sit-ins" then being carried out by black students at lunch counters throughout the segregated South. Speaking at an assembly of all 7,500 delegates, Lester B. Granger, executive director of the National Urban League, put the issue in terms that would reverberate throughout the decade and beyond:

Has the time not come when the American people of all regions and types of political and social outlook can look coolly at this divisive factor of race . . . so as to understand the irreparable damage inflicted by racial segregation not only upon the personalities of colored young people who are deprived of the free man's opportunity in an otherwise free society, but also upon the children of those very ones who have established the aggressive pattern, who fight to retain racial discrimination?[6]

By 1960 Americans had largely refocused their fear of communism on the Soviet government and whatever designs its leaders might have on worldwide domination. That May, the downing of an American U-2 spy plane over the Soviet Union provoked the latest in a series of hair-trigger confrontations between the two nuclear superpowers. In the presidential campaign of that year, dire talk of a "missile gap" and the threat of Soviet expansionism favored the candidate of "vigor" and youthful promise as a spiritually spent and profoundly wary electorate grasped for any straw that might make them feel a bit less vulnerable.

Declaring in his stirring presidential inaugural address of the following January that the "torch" had been "passed to a new generation," John F. Kennedy had not, of course, been speaking of the nation's children, but rather of the men and women who, like himself, were young enough to have been the sons and daughters of President Eisenhower or Truman. Even so, it was not by chance that the premium placed by the president on youth and new beginnings made a deep impression on the nation's youngsters. For the first time in more than a generation, young children inhabited the White House. And as the president urged America's schoolchildren to vie for success as participants in the President's Youth Physical Fitness Test, Kennedy himself, a naval war hero celebrated for his valiant rescue at sea of crew members under his command in the Pacific, made a point of showing the world that at the age of forty-three he still took boyish pleasure in an impromptu ocean swim or spirited game of touch football. The media-savvy Kennedys further burnished their public image as a well-rounded, youthful family and set an example for the nation through the release of a series of photographs in which the First Lady was pictured reading to her preschooler, Caroline. (Featured in the photographs were Ludwig Bemelmans's *Madeline* and Ruth Krauss and Mary Blair's Little Golden Book

I Can Fly.) The president-elect (or his staff) had even taken the time to prepare a specially abridged "Young Readers' Edition" of Kennedy's Pulitzer Prize–winning study of political grace under pressure, *Profiles in Courage.*[7] Harper timed the release of the new edition to coincide with the start of the new administration.[8]

If the Kennedys made an exhilarating public display of their high regard for books and culture, parents who wished to follow their example still had to contend with the stubborn fact that few bookstores around the country thought it worth their while to stock books for boys and girls. As *Publishers' Weekly* complained in an editorial: "Too few booksellers . . . employ any help who know Peter Rabbit from Stuart Little. Booksellers will tell you that they cannot be expected to sell books that are slight in story and overpriced, or that deal in detail with the life cycle of the salmon."[9] Publishers for their part — with the notable exception of the Golden Press and its growing number of mass-market rivals — seemed to have settled for the modest success that flowed so predictably from established routines and relationships with like-minded librarians and educators. It was more pleasant after all to concentrate one's efforts within the circle of one's friends, and the friends of one's friends. Before the end of the decade, however, the white gloves would at last come off.

The generational transfer of power signaled by the arrival of the Kennedy administration had its parallel in numerous changes of the guard within the publishing establishment. At Viking, where cofounder Ben Huebsch had retired in 1956, Harold K. Guinzburg delegated ever-greater authority to his son and chosen successor, Tom. In the firm's Junior Books Department, May Massee, in a grudging bow to her failing health, had finally accepted a diminished role as advisory editor as of January 1961.[10]

On May 1, 1962, Harper & Brothers merged with Row, Peterson & Company, a publisher of music books and textbooks based in Evanston, Illinois, to become Harper & Row, Inc. ("Poor Mr. Peterson," a longtime member of Ursula Nordstrom's staff, William C. Morris, would wonder aloud years later. "I don't know what happened to him!")[11] The merger gave the newly constituted firm an important foothold in the highly profitable "el-hi" school market. It also prepared the ground for a historic change in the company's management culture. Five years later, when Cass Canfield Sr. stepped down from the chairmanship of Harper's executive committee, power passed to Row, Peterson's Gordon Jones. A rapid sequence of additional reshufflings confirmed that, as publishing historian John Tebbel later wrote: "the house was now in the hands of business-oriented people, while those who combined business with editorial creativity were out of control."[12] Ursula Nordstrom remained director of the Department of Books for Boys and Girls (renamed Harper Junior Books in 1968) and published many of the most memorable books of her career during that decade — *Where the Wild Things Are, Harriet the Spy,* and *Bread and Jam for Frances,* among others. But as Harper took on more and more of the trappings of a modern-day corporation, Nordstrom felt increasingly ill at ease in her role there. As her department prospered and expanded, she increasingly withdrew into a small, protective inner circle of loyal staffers as she gave over more of her time to administrative chores and parried the demands of the new balance sheet–minded managers.

At Dutton, dashing young Jack Macrae succeeded his once-dashing uncle John as head of the firm. At Random House, Bennett Cerf and Donald Klopfer — not long after gaining possession of one of publishing's crown jewels with the acquisition of Knopf — sold Random to RCA. As a condition of the sale, the longtime partners had won guarantees from the broadcast giant that the house they had founded would maintain its operational independence, with their handpicked successor, Robert Bernstein, in charge.

Generational transitions within an owner family were business as usual at the more traditional firms. More newsworthy by far was the rare case of what passed in publishing circles for youthful rebellion. In 1959 editor and heir apparent Alfred A. Knopf Jr. had turned heads by announcing his intention to leave his father's eponymous firm in order to found a house of his own, Atheneum, in partnership with editor Simon Michael Bessie of Harper & Brothers and Hiram Haydn, Random House's editor in chief. "Pat" Knopf's decision to renounce his family legacy may well have been what finally convinced his proud parents to sell.[13]

The *New York Times* likened the newly formed partnership at Atheneum to an improbable alliance between the heads of Ford, Chrysler, and General Motors, and predictions that the threesome would not stay together for long were soon borne out. The firm they cofounded set down strong roots, however, as a literary house that counted Wright Morris, Loren Eiseley, and William Goldman among its authors. By 1961 Atheneum also had a major bestseller, Theodore H. White's *The Making of the Presi-*

dent. That same year the firm announced the creation of Atheneum Books for Children.

Featured in the imprint's inaugural spring 1962 catalog of seven titles were books by Ellen Raskin, Ruth Krauss, and Tomi Ungerer. The latter two authors were both veterans of the Harper list, and their involvement did much to establish the credentials of the editor in charge, Jean Karl, as an innovator and risk-taker. Karl would later be remembered for her response to an Atheneum executive who had smugly referred to her as the "juvenile editor." Addressing him in return as the "senile editor," she scolded: "Good children's books are never juvenile."[14] Whatever the partners' initial ambivalence, they soon had reason to thank themselves for having reserved $250,000 of their original capital to start the department and for having hired Karl to run it. Bessie, who left the house in 1975, later recalled that Atheneum Books for Children "turned out to be perhaps the most successful operation we had." He had hoped to lure Margaret K. McElderry, whom he had met during the war in the Office of Wartime Intelligence and who was now his neighbor both in New York and on Nantucket, to head the department. Clearly tempted, McElderry had left the door open for the better part of a year before finally saying no out of loyalty to the many authors she published at Harcourt, Brace. It was McElderry who had then proposed Jean Karl as a suitable alternative.[15]

A soft-spoken but tenacious woman of conviction, Karl had an unlikely background for a publishing rebel. Born and raised in Chicago, she attended Mount Union College in Alliance, Ohio, where she majored in English and earned accreditation as a high school teacher. Having decided to try for a career in publishing, she then returned to Chicago and found a job with the educational publisher Scott, Foresman, where she worked on, of all things, the "Dick and Jane" readers. In 1956 Karl moved to New York to become the children's book editor of the Abingdon Press, the general trade division of the United Methodist Publishing House, which was headquartered in Nashville. While the Nashville office saw to the needs of Sunday schoolers, Karl, herself a devout Methodist, had a mandate to publish children's books that, while broadly reflecting Methodist ideals, would also have general appeal.[16] During semiannual trips to Nashville to present her lists, Karl would be obliged to field the objections of her more parochial colleagues, patiently explaining to them the need, for example, in a book that described a Passover Seder for a reference to wine.[17]

In the introduction to her first Atheneum catalog, Karl summed up her high-minded, intellectually rigorous publishing philosophy: "Children," she declared, "need the unfettered product of a searching mind and a disciplined imagination to take them out of themselves, or into themselves, beyond familiar thought patterns to that place where exciting new insights occur."[18] A press release announcing the launch made it clear what the new department would and would not do to capture its fair share of the lucrative institutional market. "Special attention has been given to designing a reinforced library edition (to be sold at a net price) as well as a trade edition, for all picture books. . . . Books for older children appear in only one edition, but it is sturdily bound and also features a washable cloth."[19] What Atheneum would *not* do was publish series. On the contrary, each book, Karl announced, would be "treated as an individual unit and . . . produced in the format most suited to its nature." The message to the library world was unmistakable; this was Anne Carroll Moore chapter and verse. Thus, by the time "individual units" with challenging, strange titles and story lines debuted on the Atheneum list, books such as E. L. Konigsburg's *From the Mixed-Up Files of Mrs. Basil E. Frankweiler* and, a few years later, Judith Viorst's *Alexander and the Terrible, Horrible, No Good, Very Bad Day*, librarian critics were primed to give them the benefit of their most open-minded attention.

In 1961 Augusta Baker became the New York Public Library's — and the nation's — first African American citywide coordinator of children's services. Baker was not the first black children's librarian to rise to a position of authority, but she was only the second. Chicago librarian Charlemae Rollins had come to prominence in 1932 as the first head of children's services at a Chicago branch library devoted to African American literature and culture; as the author, in 1941, of *We Build Together: A Guide to Negro Life and Literature for Elementary and High School Use*; and, in 1957–58, as chair of the Newbery-Caldecott Committee. Overall, however, librarians of color had tended to rise only so far up the professional ladder of the systems in which they worked.[20] Baker's appointment to the position first filled by Anne Carroll Moore represented a stunning advance.

Born in Baltimore in 1911, Baker had joined the library staff in 1937 as an assistant children's librarian for the system's 135th Street branch in Harlem (later renamed the Countee Cullen Regional Branch Library). From the Harlem post, she had been promoted in 1955 to head of the storytelling program for the entire library system, thus becoming the first African American to hold an executive position at New York Public. "I was summoned by Anne Carroll Moore," Baker afterward said with pride.[21] Baker's daily contacts with Harlem children during the 1930s and 1940s had left her distressed about the children's lack of knowledge about and pride in their cultural heritage. "I could not bear it," she later recalled, "when classes of children — black children — came to the library unaware of the great people and events in their background, and we had practically no books on the subjects."[22] Baker resolved to dedicate her life to remedying the situation. Her efforts, along with those of Chicago's Charlemae Rollins and later Hellen Mullen of the Philadelphia Free Library, would have far-reaching consequences for librarianship and publishing.

As first steps, Baker in 1939 established the James Weldon Johnson Memorial Collection of books for children at the 135th Street branch and in 1946 compiled and published an annotated bibliography in pamphlet form, "Books About Negro Life for Children," with one hundred recommended titles. In her introduction to the list, Baker discussed her criteria for selection, which included language, theme, and illustration. Books containing condescending dialect had been omitted, as had those preserving offensive stereotypes in word or image. The selection of Helen Bannerman's controversial *The Story of Little Black Sambo* warranted a paragraph-long defense that served indirectly to cinch Baker's larger argument for the need for more books of black interest. Bannerman's book, she suggested, had made it onto the list in part by default, "because there is a lack of material for the pre-school and primary age groups."[23] Baker periodically revised the bibliography. In her introduction to the 1963 edition, she noted that measured progress was being made in at least one regard: "Within the past few years some authors have written books with Negro characters in minor roles that are not stereotypes. This is to be commended, for the ideal portrayal of the Negro is as an integral part of society."[24] (*The Story of Little Black Sambo* had been dropped from the list more than ten years earlier.) Among illustrators, she praised two well-known white artists, the veteran Elizabeth Orton Jones and Paul Galdone, for "hav[ing] included Negroes in their pictures of everyday scenes as a matter of course when they have illustrated stories not especially about the Negro."[25]

In 1963 Baker's and Rollins's continuing efforts to champion books that furthered the goal of racial equality in American life received a resounding endorsement in the selection that year of Ezra Jack Keats as the winner of the Caldecott Medal for *The Snowy Day*. The simple picture-book text about an urban preschooler's sidewalk idyll during a blizzard made no reference to the child's racial identity. But the illustrations — festive cut-paper collages with playful modernist touches — showed that Peter was an African American. Many readers at the time assumed that the artist, too, must be black, but Keats (born Jacob Ezra Katz on March 11, 1916) was in fact the first-generation American son of eastern European Jewish immigrants who had settled in Brooklyn during the late 1800s. Raised in tenement poverty and precocious about art, young Jacob Katz had drawn inspiration from the example of Honoré Daumier, whose work honored the dignity of society's underdogs, and from the paintings of the American visionary painter Albert Pinkham Ryder, whose enigmatic, moonlit canvases implied the possibility of liberation from earthly suffering. In *The Snowy Day*, Keats had effortlessly combined a Daumier-like respect for the "little guy" with a Ryder-esque sense of earthly transcendence. To the extent that *The Snowy Day* was a book about race, it addressed the issue with a degree of subtlety that perhaps stood the best chance of gaining acceptance among white readers who were comfortable with the nonviolent protest strategies pursued by Dr. Martin Luther King Jr. — and terrified by the militant rhetoric of King's chief rival for leadership of the civil rights movement, Malcolm X.

Sharing the limelight with Keats at the awards ceremony in Chicago that July was the year's Newbery Medal winner, Madeleine L'Engle. The novelist and former actress had won the literature prize for a work of fiction very unlike the realistic family stories for which she had been known until then. Twenty-six publishers had in fact been baffled or surprised enough by *A Wrinkle in Time*, a science-fiction fantasy with religious overtones, to have rejected it before Farrar, Straus and Giroux finally took a chance on the experiment.

The American Tolkien craze, which would serve to legitimize fantasy literature at every level, still lay a few years out on the horizon. Most American children's book editors and librarians still looked askance at fantasy fiction as a form of fringy, escapist reading, little better than the comics — except perhaps when the fantasy came with a British pedigree.[26] Just what had impelled the Newbery-Caldecott Committee to select not one but two genre-stretching, potentially controversial books for their highest accolades in preference, say, to *Mr. Rabbit and the Lovely Present* (a picture book by Charlotte Zolotow, illustrated by Maurice Sendak) and *Men of Athens* (by Olivia Coolidge, illustrated by Milton Johnson), each of which had instead received a runner-up award in its category, would, of course, forever remain a mystery. But clearly the committee had been in a maverick mood. In any case, the wild-eyed (and privately terrified) hipster artist Keats and toweringly glamorous L'Engle made a fascinating pair as they rose in turn to accept their medals. Keats later set down notes about the experience:

> Seated at the dais I stared, frightened, at a sea of people. Food was served, but I had no appetite and barely touched it. The huge dining room buzzed with conversation and laughter. The lights dimmed, a bright spotlight focused on a door in the rear. Two waiters emerged, carrying long poles on top of which were immense gold-plated replicas of the Caldecott and Newbery Medals. They twirled the poles as they wove through the tables, spotlights following them, greeted by stormy applause. I popped half a Valium in my mouth and swallowed hard. I was introduced and suddenly was up there speaking.[27]

Absent that year for the first time from the presentation ceremony was Frederic G. Melcher, the patron of the awards, who had died on March 9, at the age of eighty-three, just one week before his scheduled public announcement of the winners. A beloved industry figure, Melcher throughout his career had remained an ardent advocate for excellence in children's literature as one of the necessary underpinnings of a literate, well-informed democratic society. Yet his sheer persistence on the point had at times been regarded by colleagues on the adult trade side of the business as something of an eccentricity — even as a growing number of the heads of houses, if pressed, would have had to acknowledge that children's books were becoming big business, often accounting for as much as one-third to one-half of their company's total revenue.[28]

One development that must have gratified Melcher greatly came just days before his death. On March 3, 1963, the Library of Congress inaugurated its long-awaited Children's Literature Center. Under the direction of Virginia Haviland, formerly of the Boston Public Library, the Center, with modest quarters in the Jefferson Building, represented the culmination of efforts begun more than a decade earlier by Frances Clarke Sayers, who had cheerfully taken on the task of devising a master plan for the reorganization of the library's sprawling juvenile holdings. In her final report, Sayers had noted:

> Children's books, and publications and information concerning them, are already part of the existing collections in the Library of Congress. They have infiltrated almost every department of the library. As a subject area in their own right, they need to be reconsidered in relation to the increased and increasing demand for their use.[29]

Perhaps the Center's second most ardent backer after Sayers had been a longtime Washington, D.C., resident and official of the National Food and Drug Administration, Dr. Irvin Kerlan. During the 1940s, Kerlan had begun collecting original art from contemporary children's books as well as autographed first editions of Newbery and Caldecott Medal books. In pursuit of his hobby, he had undertaken a vast correspondence and, as his relationships with the artists deepened, he had made annual trips to visit with a great many of them in their studios. In taking a serious interest in the art created for children's books, Kerlan had found his way into a largely unexplored, and undervalued, area of the art world. So little valued were the paintings and drawings that had become his passion that the illustrators he assiduously courted routinely gave him examples of their work simply because he so clearly appreciated what they had done. In 1950 Kerlan arranged for a permanent home for his collection at the library of his alma mater, the University of Minnesota. By then, the Kerlan Collection had also come to include original manuscripts, preliminary drawings and dummies, and examples of prize-winning children's books from around the world.[30] Now, little more than a decade later, the Library of Congress, with its central place in the nation's literary life, had conferred a sort of diplomatic recognition on the area of literature that gave rise to the art. Not only had Dr. Kerlan urged the library to take this symbolically important step, but for the past three years he had served as an unpaid consultant at the library. Now his enthusiasm for "a field in which there will be rewards for those who have imagination in collecting and willingness to adventure in uncharted fields" had at last proven contagious.[31]

That February, from the battle station of her clamorous manual typewriter, Ursula Nordstrom pounded out the sort of gingerly note she reserved for

Harper authors she secretly feared might be about to desert her. Nordstrom had noticed that the prolific, self-starting Maurice Sendak had of late been accepting more than the usual number of projects from other houses in addition to the steady stream of work that Harper offered him. Greatly complicating their relations was the editor's recent decision to engage another artist, Hilary Knight of *Eloise* fame, to produce a companion work to Sendak's commercially successful "Nutshell Library" after Sendak himself had declined to follow up with a sequel of his own.[32] For pragmatic as well as creative reasons, Nordstrom wanted nothing more than to concentrate Sendak's efforts on an all-consuming project that would help to repair, and further cement, her relationship with him and with Harper as his creative "home."

"I was glad to hear the other day, when you were in the office," Nordstrom began her February 19 note, affecting her breeziest manner, "that you're hoping to write and illustrate your own beautiful picture book next — instead of doing a lot of illustrating for other people. That will be wonderful. You can do something beautiful and I hope you will soon."[33]

Such was the importance that Nordstrom placed on her goal that she was prepared to stretch her department's production schedule to the limit in order to accommodate Sendak's myriad commitments. She went on to allude to the bare beginnings of the idea that the artist had described to her for a story that was to be about "something, or someone, or some little animal, getting out of some enclosure." It was not much to go on, but be that as it may, Nordstrom's gentle nudge of encouragement accomplished all that she might have hoped it would. In a few weeks' time, Sendak purchased a spiral notebook and by April had launched himself on an intensive effort to complete a story that he tentatively called "Where the Wild Horses Are," with a new draft appearing every few days in the notebook.[34] The first drawings followed in late May, by which time the manuscript was nearing final form. Fueling the furious pace of creation of a book that traced the trajectory of a small child's rage against his mother was the ongoing, increasingly bitter dispute between Sendak and Nordstrom over the Nutshell Library sequel. Feeling utterly betrayed by his once-trusted mentor, Sendak that summer bogged down over the last remaining bit of text of the story he now called *Where the Wild Things Are*. Still missing were the words needed to ease Max out of the story's wordless "rumpus" interlude, words to explain why that brash little boy, or anyone for that matter, might choose to leave a place as unfettered and pleasure-driven as Wild Things Island. For Max, of course, the motive and answer in the end lay in the primal wish to regain his own mother's warm and loving embrace. As for Sendak himself, Nordstrom succeeded in shoring up her standing as the primary nurturer and leading patron of his ever-expanding career. But in one key respect their relationship became markedly more distant. In business matters, a lawyer, not the artist himself, would now shout "No!" to Nordstrom when necessary.[35]

As the clock ticked on into September, Nordstrom grew increasingly anxious about the chances of fall publication. While assuring the artist that she would, if need be, gladly postpone publication until the following year, she reeled inwardly at the prospect of a delay. On September 23, in an ultimately successful bid to ensure a place on the *New York Times Book Review*'s prestigious Ten Best Illustrated Books of the Year awards list, Nordstrom had a mockup of *Where the Wild Things Are* prepared from galley proofs and dispatched by messenger to the *Times*' offices.[36] But in Harper's major fall display ad in the October issue of *The Horn Book*, which Nordstrom would have had to prepare earlier, *Where the Wild Things Are* was omitted from the roster of forthcoming titles. It must have pained her greatly to approve that ad.[37] Two things by then were clear to the editor: that *Where the Wild Things Are* was going to be a masterpiece, and that it would be a lightning rod for controversy. Consumed with nervous anticipation on both counts, she was eager for the book to make its mark sooner rather than later.

Then there was the ultimate prize: the Caldecott Medal. After five near-misses in the form of Caldecott runners-up, the most recent one having come just the previous year for *Mr. Rabbit and the Lovely Present*, Sendak and Nordstrom once again braced themselves for disappointment.[38] As it happened, both inveterate pessimists were to be robbed that year of the chance to grumble and grouse. Sendak's victory, more than most Caldecott selections, seemed to put into sharp relief the whole of a large and complex body of work. It crystallized his reputation and in one stroke transformed the increasingly self-assured and immensely articulate thirty-five-year-old into a public figure.

At the start of 1964, Ursula Nordstrom, too, ascended to greater glory on becoming only the second editor after Margaret K. McElderry to have published the winning titles of both medals in the same year. Harper's first

Newbery winner, *It's Like This, Cat* by Emily Cheney Neville, was a novel in the J. D. Salinger mold about preteen upper-middle-class alienation, set against the backdrop of New York City. Nordstrom's double success seemed all the more remarkable to her colleagues for the fact that in the turbulent times in which they lived — the Kennedy assassination had occurred within weeks of the publication of *Where the Wild Things Are;* American "advisers" were dying in increasing numbers in Vietnam; and the civil rights movement was stirring up a backlash of often horrific violence — it was far from clear where children's literature was headed. Nordstrom, more than any of her colleagues, seemed to know the answer.

Nordstrom had ample cause for jubilation, but emotions of all sorts were running high at Harper just then. Soon after the Caldecott and Newbery announcement, Nordstrom's staff learned of her abrupt dismissal of managing editor Susan Carr Hirschman — who had so recently written perfect flap copy for *Where the Wild Things Are* and who over the past decade had discovered and nurtured Arnold Lobel, ably run the office in Nordstrom's absence, and contributed to the success of numerous other departmental projects. Even considering her near-total inability to separate her professional self from her private emotions, it was striking that Nordstrom had chosen the moment of her greatest editorial triumph to eliminate the member of her staff who was clearly most capable of replacing her. There would be no hot supper for Hirschman, as there was for Max.

Almost unnoticed at first, more men were now entering the field. At Harper, Nordstrom filled Hirschman's coveted job by promoting a staff editor and author of historical fiction named Ferdinand N. Monjo. At Houghton Mifflin, the department's widely respected art director, Walter Lorraine, was elevated to the top position, department manager. A Yale graduate with a theater background and sparkling manner, Richard Jackson emerged from New York University's Graduate Institute of Book Publishing — a lively craft-oriented program that combined classroom study with on-the-job training — to accept an apprenticeship in Doubleday's manufacturing department. Frances Keene, an instructor at NYU and Knopf's juvenile editor, had first urged Jackson to consider a career in children's books. When he tried to shrug off the suggestion, Keene had persisted: "Well, you should," she told him, pressing home her point, "because you're interested in visual things." Jackson was dyslexic. As a child, reading had seemed beyond him. Now Keene's comment prompted him to wonder whether, through work with children's books, he might somehow "retrieve a patch of childhood I'd hardly had, a time with books."[39]

Still working in Doubleday's manufacturing department, Jackson finally acted on Keene's advice and telephoned the firm's children's book editor, Margaret Lesser, to ask whether she might be willing to help him transfer out of manufacturing and take him on as an intern in her own department. Lesser's first reaction was hardly more sympathetic than Jackson's own had been: "What would I do with you?" she gasped, only half in jest. "You're a man!" Months passed before the reassignment could be managed. On settling in, Jackson soon found that he had indeed stumbled onto interesting work.

Jackson's new mentor, Margaret Lesser, was the former journalist who had succeeded May Massee at Doubleday in 1934, following the latter's firing. Lesser took a stewardlike approach to her job, devoting much of her time to guiding into print the late works of such longtime contributors to the list as Marguerite de Angeli, the 1950 Newbery winner for *The Door in the Wall*, and Ingri and Edgar Parin d'Aulaire. Although Lesser's department generated few of the sparks that one associated with Harper or Viking, Doubleday was still a fine place at which to master the editor's craft.[40] As a first assignment, Jackson prepared the index for (and thereby became intimately acquainted with) the d'Aulaires' glorious *Book of Greek Myths*.

Then, in 1964, Keene telephoned Jackson to say she had just been named director of the children's book department at Macmillan. With this news came an invitation to join her as associate editor. Seizing the chance, Jackson took his place as the department's second male editorial staff member. The first, Michael di Capua, had started at the house two years earlier. (Di Capua would soon leave Macmillan for Pantheon.)

Keene's tenure at Macmillan proved both ill starred and brief, the department she inherited having long since fallen from the heights of its glory days under Louise Seaman Bechtel. With Macmillan management refusing even to pay for proper copyediting of the reprinted "classics" that had become the department's mainstay, Keene could perhaps be forgiven for not seeing how all the pieces might be put back together. The task of doing so, in any case, now passed to Susan Hirschman, who, having been dismissed by Harper in early 1964, had spent several unemployed months in a funk of bittersweet reflection before agreeing to take the director's job at Macmillan.

Despite marked differences of background and temperament, Hirschman and Nordstrom had drawn personally close to one another during the years they worked together. One formative experience they shared was the emotional devastation of having grown up as children of divorce. Hirschman's firing by Nordstrom had come as a blow of nearly comparable magnitude, as something very like a parent's betrayal. Such was the impact of Nordstrom's personality that, for months afterward, the younger woman continued to make all her decisions with her former mentor keenly in mind: if she did not choose the course of action that Nordstrom would surely have chosen, Hirschman deliberately, even defiantly, chose to do the opposite, thereby remaining within the older woman's emotional orbit no matter which way she turned.[41]

Upon her arrival at Macmillan, however, Hirschman found the ideal way to break free of Nordstrom's gravitational pull. She arranged to make a ceremonial pilgrimage to the elegant Mount Kisco, New York, estate of the department's founding director, Louise Seaman Bechtel. Bechtel, the trailblazer not only at Macmillan but also for the profession as a whole, had begun her career in publishing when Ursula Nordstrom was an unhappy nine-year-old. Now arthritic and in her eighties, Bechtel received the self-assured younger woman more warily than Hirschman might have wished, but she could not help but be impressed, and gratified, by the visitor's thorough knowledge of the backlist Bechtel had so lovingly built up, and which Hirschman now vowed to revivify. The two women even shared a satisfied laugh when the conversation turned to *Men at Work*, Lewis W. Hine's photographic essay about modern skyscraper construction, which Bechtel had published as a children's book in 1932 and which had since come to be recognized as a classic work of documentary photojournalism. Anne Carroll Moore, having disapproved of the book (presumably because she associated it with the pernicious influence of Bank Street here-and-now realism), had done her best to ensure its demise. Lying prone in bed until then as she and her visitor chatted, Bechtel suddenly sat bolt upright at the thought of the imperious librarian, her rage over the incident having not completely run its course in thirty years.[42]

The upheaval surrounding Frances Keene's firing left her protégé Richard Jackson untouched. Jackson stayed on at Macmillan under Hirschman, where he continued to learn and thrive as one of a small group of talented young people who had joined the staff and befriended one another. The group included Rosemary Wells and Susan Jeffers, both members of the art department; and Janet Schulman, who as a writer in the advertising department had produced copy by the yard for both adult and children's titles before deciding to specialize in the latter.

A facile phrasemaker with a quick, sardonic sense of humor, Schulman had honed her craft in the advertising department at a time when advertising and journalism were both becoming less stuffy and more youth-oriented and "hip." In the increasingly youth-driven publishing culture of the 1960s, a flair for irreverence when it came to one's passion for books had become what mattered. Two corporate restructurings at Macmillan resulted in Schulman being elevated to a new position whose creation at the house was itself a sign of changing industry times. First, Schulman was reassigned to one of several new division-wide marketing departments. (Hers — trade marketing — generated advertising, publicity, and promotional materials for both adult and children's titles.) Then, in 1966, she was appointed Macmillan's first children's marketing director. The creation of the new position signaled the coming end of the time when "promotion" specialists could be counted on to do all that was required to introduce a house's upcoming list by means of a series of discreet face-to-face encounters with key librarians, booksellers, and school administrators. The market was simply becoming too large and many-faceted for publishers to rely primarily on the strength of their personal contacts.[43]

The change did not occur all at once, of course. As Atheneum's promotion director in the late 1960s, Suzanne Glazer traveled eighteen weeks out of the year — a frantic pace by later standards. To hold down the expenses of her comparatively small house, Glazer arranged to travel with her counterpart at Dutton, Mimi Kayden. The two friends even entertained book purchasers together. Such was the cooperative spirit that prevailed within the industry that no one thought to question the arrangement.

Schulman had kept in touch with an Antioch College friend and aspiring writer named Virginia Hamilton who was now living in New York. Recalling a short story by Hamilton, who was African American, from their student days, Schulman urged her friend to expand it into a novel for young readers. When Hamilton presented her with the completed manuscript of *Zeely*, Schulman took it in to Macmillan to show Richard Jackson, who, thrilled by what he had read, passed it on to Susan Hirschman. Upon accepting *Zeely* for publication, Hirschman wisely handed Hamilton's manuscript back to Jackson to edit — just as Ursula Nordstrom had allowed her to work directly with the authors she had taken the lead in discovering. Notwithstanding his dyslexia, Jackson was becoming known as a gifted editor of serious fiction. Another novelist he first edited while at Macmillan would be Paula Fox.

Acts of horrific violence were increasingly complicating the national drive for civil rights for people of color. On the evening of February 21, 1965, Malcolm X was gunned down while addressing a group of his followers in a Harlem social hall. The following month Dr. Martin Luther King Jr. led a massive nonviolent protest march from Selma to Montgomery, Alabama. Fearful that King would not be able to sustain his peaceful approach to political protest much longer, Congress rushed to enact the Voting Rights Act of 1965, which President Lyndon Johnson signed into law on August 6. Just one week later, a major riot broke out in the Watts section of Los Angeles.

The following month, in response to these and other events, Nancy Larrick, writing in the *Saturday Review*, issued a searing indictment of what she termed the "All-White World of Children's Books."[44] A former president of the International Reading Association, Larrick lambasted her colleagues in the publishing world for having at best engaged in tokenism rather than squarely addressing the urgent need for racial diversity in children's literature. After surveying more than five thousand children's trade books published between 1962 and 1964, Larrick had concluded that while "integration may be the law of the land, . . . most of the books children see are all white." Far from bearing witness to publishers' enlightenment, she argued, the appearance of an occasional book such as Ezra Jack Keats's *The Snowy Day* merely confirmed the children's book world's obliviousness to the scope of its own inaction.

Larrick faulted Keats himself on two counts: for "omitting the word [Negro] in the text" and for portraying the young protagonist's mother as "a huge figure in a gaudy yellow plaid dress, albeit without a red bandana" — that is to say, as the embodiment of an unfortunate racial stereotype. She also cited the example of the 1946 Caldecott Medal–winning book, Maud and Miska Petersham's *The Rooster Crows*, four pages of which had featured demeaning depictions of Negro children with "coal black skin, and bulging eyes" — until, that is, "after eighteen years enough complaints had been received to convince the publisher that the book would be improved by deleting" the offending illustrations. In the new, 1964 edition of the award-winning book, Larrick ruefully reported, "only white children appear." She recalled a widely discussed article of the previous year by Whitney M. Young Jr., executive director of the National Urban League, who, writing in his nationally syndicated column, had chastised America's publishers for children for presenting image after image of contemporary American life in which people of color rarely figured at all, let alone in a positive light.[45] Larrick found at least one bright spot in all the gloom: the recent establishment of the Council on Interracial Books for Children, a watchdog organization dedicated to setting appropriate standards for books about the African American experience and to encouraging the creation of more such books through the awarding of an annual prize that included a guarantee of publication. At the helm of the Council was Franklin Folsom, the writer who had persuaded the Wattses to publish Langston Hughes.[46] Hughes himself, along with Benjamin Spock, Ben Shahn, and Child Study Association director Sidonie M. Gruenberg, were among the new organization's sponsors. Of the group's chances for making a constructive contribution, Larrick pointedly remarked: "Whether the Council gets many books into print or not, it can accomplish a great deal simply by reminding editors and publishers that what is good for the Ku Klux Klan is not necessarily good for America — or the book business."

Larrick's wholesale indictment did not go unchallenged. Writing in *The Horn Book*, Ruth Hill Viguers bristled at the suggestion that literary creation could be made to serve the requirements of any political agenda, however praiseworthy. "Literature," she argued, launching an analogy that seemed hopelessly quaint under the circumstances, "is not put together like a casserole and seasoned with a pinch of this and a dash of that."[47] Stung by Larrick's criticism, Ezra Jack Keats in a letter to the *Saturday Review* responded with a mixture of sarcasm and indignation: "In a book for children three to six years of age, where the color of one's skin makes it clear who is a Negro and who is white," Keats demanded to know, "is it arbitrarily necessary to append race tags? Might I suggest armbands?"[48] The argument did not stop there, with the attacks against Keats growing if anything more bitter before the debate — by far the most contentious exercise in industry soul-searching that anyone could recall — finally died down. In a fictionalized account of the impact of Larrick's article on the young, white, still predominantly female editors of the 1960s generation, Ann Durell of Holt, Rinehart and Winston would write:

"In Bunky's case [Bunky Bannister is the fictional editor]," responding to Larrick's essay

> was one of her first experiences in consciousness raising. She began to try to find Black authors and artists; she also began, painfully, to examine herself and her WASPish-ness. Why were there no Black authors on the Dolphin list? Did good Black writers not exist, or was she not recognizing them because they wrote in an idiom she did not understand and appreciate? Should she publish a book that seemed to her poorly written just because the author was Black? Maybe it was well written by other than middle-class, white standards. And if that were the case, how would she know? How indeed?

The venturesome real-life counterparts of Bunky Bannister who had entered the serene world of children's book publishing of the 1950s had come primed to believe that publishing should and could be "fun." But as the new decade unfolded and a series of disturbing jolts seemed, *Alice*-like, to render their reasonable expectations and prior life experiences equally irrelevant, the promise of fun gave way to something like a crisis atmosphere. What had long been thought settled would now have to be relearned. As Durell wrote of her imaginary heroine (and her own younger self): "For the first time in her working life Bunky found herself feeling deeply insecure about her own ability to judge and select children's books."[49]

Toward the end of 1957, Albert Leventhal, the sales and marketing mastermind behind the historic triumph of Little Golden Books, concluded that the time had come for him to move on — or rather to reshuffle the Golden deck in such a way as to exchange his executive vice-presidency at Simon & Schuster for a still more lucrative position as operating chief of Western's Artists and Writers Press. Changes in the ownership of Simon & Schuster, the physical decline of cofounder Richard Simon, and the death of his closest friend at the house, Jack Goodman, had persuaded Leventhal to pursue a new phase of what had already been an extraordinary career. Then, in late 1964, the Western Publishing Company (the new corporate name, as of 1960, acknowledged the fact that publishing had at last overtaken printing as the company's primary business) became the sole owner of the Golden properties, and Leventhal became the man with complete editorial control over them.

Although the Golden titles that Leventhal and his colleagues now published could still be counted on *not* to win Caldecott and Newbery Medals, a growing number of them were finding their way onto school and public library shelves and garnering praise from the American Institute of Graphic Arts.[50] But if the institutional recognition that came their way remained limited, Leventhal and company still had their usual reason not to care too much about it. Annual sales were climbing and, through a steady series of acquisitions, the company was expanding at a prodigious rate. By the mid-1960s, Western Publishing was well on its way to becoming the largest publisher of children's books in the world.

By mid-decade, the children's book publishing industry as a whole had become a booming enterprise with growth potential to spare. In 1964 total sales of children's books reached $112 million — only slightly less than the figure of $117 million for adult trade hardcover sales. Just under three thousand children's books were then being published annually, a figure equal to about 10 percent of the industry output. If juvenile trade publishers had one major problem to contend with, it was how to meet the accelerating demand for the books on their lists — in particular, the growing demand from schools.[51]

In the wake of the Kennedy assassination, and amid the continuing threat of civil disorder, the Johnson administration introduced a massive battery of federal initiatives, collectively called the Great Society, meant to unite Americans behind the idealistic goal of ridding the nation of poverty and social injustice. Among the architects of the enabling legislation were educators who had successfully made the case for an expanded role for children's trade books in the public school curriculum. The concept was given meaningful expression in Title 2 of the Elementary and Secondary School Act of 1965, which funded the purchase by school libraries of such books on an unprecedented scale. States received lists of approved trade books and substantial budgets for the purchase of multiple copies, always by a certain deadline. Department heads could hardly conceal their astonishment or contain their jubilation. In a letter to author-illustrator Russell Hoban, Ursula Nordstrom reported: "Pennsylvania ALONE has about 4 million bucks to spend on the books on their list."[52] Most publishers rushed to expand (or, as it turned out in some cases, to overexpand) their programs in an effort to make the most of the windfall. With book purchases for use by Head Start preschool programs also covered under the legislation's mandate, Susan Hirschman added many new early picture books, a specialty for which she had a particular affinity, to the Macmillan list, including innovative work by (among others) Harper carryovers Ezra Jack Keats and Arnold Lobel and a recent discovery, photographer Tana Hoban.

With so much federal money on the table, it seemed a better time than most to think about starting a publishing company of one's own, especially one dedicated to juveniles. A former actor and theater-producer-turned-editor from Minnesota named Harlin Quist was having just such thoughts as he manned his modest editorial perch at the burgeoning new children's book department at Dell. In 1967, in the second year of the Title 2 bonanza, Quist bravely entered the fray, setting himself up as an eponymous, boutique-like independent house, with a small but provocative list of illustrated children's books that reflected his enthusiasm for, of all things, avant-garde contemporary European graphic design.

As though to seal the tiny firm's reputation for unorthodox behavior, Quist soon opened a second editorial office in Paris. The books on his cosmopolitan list featured elegant graphics by the Swiss American artist Etienne Delessert, the French expatriate Guy Billout, and others, and texts by the illustrious Romanian-born French absurdist playwright Eugene Ionesco, among others. The books seemed intended as much for collectors as for children — as well as perhaps for the growing number of college students and other adults who talked about cultivating their "inner child." Quist picture books had quirky titles like *Shhh!* and *A Book of A-Maze-Ments*. With the help of the mighty Dial/Delacorte sales force, they were soon being noticed. *The Geranium on the Windowsill Just Died but Teacher You Went Right On*, written and illustrated by Albert Cullum, became an international bestseller. *Story Number 1*, Delessert's first collaboration with Ionesco, was chosen as a *New York Times* Best Illustrated Children's Book for 1968.[53]

As in past eras of expansion, not every new venture took hold. In 1966, with Susan Hirschman firmly ensconced in the director's chair at Macmillan and with a growing reputation of his own for discovering new voices in fiction, Richard Jackson had decided to seek advancement elsewhere. Jackson had jumped at the chance to create a junior books department at the small New York house of David White, a publisher known until then primarily for its cookbooks. Poorly financed and run with what Jackson came to regard as a dispiriting lack of imagination, White, it appeared, had simply decided to join the rush to cash in on the Title 2 phenomenon and was taking Jackson along for the ride. After a frustrating year and a half, the editor quit and once again began pounding the pavement.

A job interview at Prentice-Hall, a New Jersey–based house with a hand in both the educational and trade sides of the book business, would set him on his path for years to come. Although Jackson did not get the job he had come to apply for, he became fast friends with the interviewer, a vice-president for sales named Robert Verrone. In addition to liking each other, the two young men were both fathers with a keen interest in the quality of the books their own children would grow up reading. They talked about ways they might work together, and when Prentice-Hall agreed to finance them, Verrone and Jackson teamed up as publishers of a small, resolutely experimental trade list. In 1968 the partners bought out Prentice-Hall's interest in their start-up venture and went into business for themselves as co-owners of the Bradbury Press.

With modest offices transplanted from New Jersey to second-floor quarters along a shopping street in suburban Scarsdale, New York, the two men set about "doing a little mischief," as Jackson later recalled.[54] To potential backers and anyone else who would listen, they cheerfully declared their intention to publish children's books from a "man's point of view." Adding to the aura of maverick nonconformity, the partners made a point at first of *not* attending the library and booksellers' conventions where most publishers gathered to display their wares. One year they even made an amusing show of returning to work from their summer vacations sporting matching beards. All theatrics aside, however, Jackson, who concentrated on fiction, and Verrone, who edited Bradbury's picture books, were quite serious about rattling the industry's cages. Among the first authors they signed up was an unknown novelist from New Jersey named Judy Blume. As it happened, Bradbury's artfully cultivated antidisestablishmentarian image had little if anything to do with Blume's decision to submit her groundbreaking stories for preteens and teens there. She had done so, Blume later recalled, because Bradbury was not located in New York City, where she felt ill at ease walking the streets alone. With Bradbury for a publisher, Blume would not have to take another bus into Manhattan anytime soon.

Blume arrived on the scene just a few years behind Louise Fitzhugh, whose *Harriet the Spy*, published by Harper in 1964, had been instantly recognized (if not universally praised) as a landmark work for preteens that ventured deep into uncharted emotional waters. Next was S. E. Hinton's *The Outsiders*, a bracing account of teen gang warfare in an outwardly placid American town that caused a comparable stir when in 1967, after much internal debate, Viking Junior Books published it in hardcover. Adding to the drama surrounding the latter book was the fascinating fact that its first-time author was herself still a teenager.

Just as the "new realism" was emerging as the dominant trend in children's and teen fiction, a new realism about the economics of book consumption prompted juvenile trade houses to lower their pride and experiment with a book format, and approach to trade publishing, that they had long considered beneath them. Publishers, librarians, and booksellers alike had traditionally shunned paperbacks for reasons of both durability and prestige — the latter because of paperback publishing's tawdry associations with comic books, pulp fiction, and other "cheap" series sold at newsstands. Booksellers, of course, disliked any low-priced book for the small profit it yielded them relative to the shelf space required to stock it. George M. Nicholson, head of Dell Publishing's newly formed children's book division starting in the mid-1960s, led the industry in what was to prove to be one of its most important modern-day transformations. He recalled: "At that time there was a vast gulf between the literary trade children's publishing that Harper & Row was doing and the mass market publishing that Western was doing. There was a good deal of misunderstanding on both sides about the other."[55]

By the mid-1960s, the time seemed right to Nicholson and a few other innovators to challenge these old assumptions. Young Americans, the new argument went, had more pocket money than ever before and might be tempted to spend some of it on books of particular interest to themselves if they also felt they were getting a bargain.[56] The vastly increased Title 2 buying power of schools and libraries also figured largely in the calculus. Nicholson recalled:

Government funding resulted in massive, often indiscriminate buying [by institutions] because the money always had to be spent by a certain deadline. Rather than decide which of the twenty-seven available books about the North Pole was best, schools and libraries bought them all. Paperbacks were one of the best ways you could spend your money because you could get so much more for your dollar.[57]

Nicholson, who had begun his career as one of Albert Leventhal's Artists and Writers Guild protégés, brought to his new job many of the lessons that the founders of Golden Books had learned about sending great numbers of children's books out into the world at an affordable price.[58] At the time of his arrival at Dell, the highly profitable company — which had started out under George Delacorte as a publisher of glamour and crime magazines, pulp novels, and comic books — had recently launched the Dell Laurel Leaf Library of books for teens.[59] When the imprint proved to be an immediate success, Dell's president, Helen Meyer, decided to extend the experiment by adding an imprint of books for younger age groups. Nicholson's first task was to create what came to be called Dell Yearling Books for children in the lower grades (ages seven to thirteen). Yearling launched in the fall of 1967, winning instant respectability through shrewd marketing and by offering a wide range of fiction "by distinguished authors" in tasteful paperback editions that were faithful to the originals.

The first Yearling list featured E. B. White's *Charlotte's Web* and *Stuart Little;* five of Hugh Lofting's Doctor Dolittle fantasies; Louise Fitzhugh's *Harriet the Spy; The Saturdays* by Elizabeth Enright; and Lois Lenski's *Strawberry Girl.* Acquiring the rights to the two White books had proven to be the key that opened the door to everything else. Accomplishing this feat had taken all of Nicholson's considerable skills as a salesman and diplomat.

Nicholson had had to work his magic on two powerful skeptics, Harper's Ursula Nordstrom, publisher of *Stuart Little* and *Charlotte's Web*, and Katharine S. White, the author's wife and business manager. He had the advantage of unheard-of sums at his disposal to offer for the rights he sought, but Nicholson knew that money alone would not be decisive with the tough-minded, principled women. Nordstrom gave her assent only when she realized that Nicholson was probably correct in his insistence that the paperback editions of the White books would reach a new market of readers rather than cut into the current demand for the books in hardcover. She had also concluded that, for the time being at least, the venerable House of Harper would have no interest in entering the paperback market itself. Nicholson offered to pay a $37,500 advance against future royalties for a seven-year paperback license for the two books — this at a time when $500 or $1,000 was a typical author advance for a children's trade book.[60]

It then became Nordstrom's job to help persuade Katharine S. White. In a letter aimed at reassuring her, Nordstrom quoted at length from the comments of Virginia Olson of Harper's subsidiary rights department. White had expressed her concern about having her husband's work associated with the publisher of the likes of *Modern Romances* and *Dick Tracy*. Nordstrom, who could not have failed to see her point, attempted gamely to gloss over the question by citing Olson's assurances:

> I don't understand Mrs. White's question, "What does Harper think of the stigma left over from Dell's bad cheap start?" I don't remember any cloud over Dell's list. Years ago they simply did mysteries but as I remember, they were perfectly respectable mysteries. Within the past few years they have moved into the big time along with Pocket Books, Bantam, and Fawcett. Dell is doing the most creative job I've seen with books for young people. They are pouring a lot of money into this project, have titles at three age levels, and we are hoping that they will be extremely successful in reaching a new market and will be able to sell to children who don't have the price of the hardbound editions.[61]

Nordstrom then quoted Olson with regard to the common-wisdom fear of the time about the likely impact of paperback editions on hardcover sales: "It has been our experience with adult books that paperback editions don't cut into our sale at all and sometimes even make it grow. This has also been the experience with the only, up to now, publisher of paperback reprint editions of books for young people, namely Scholastic. We have checked their sales against ours time and time again to prove this point to ourselves. Libraries will continue to buy the hardbound editions and bookstores will continue to sell them." Nordstrom offered the further assurance that Harper would stipulate that Garth Williams's illustrations be retained in their original format. Finally the Whites accepted, and the paperback deal was made. A year after the Dell Yearling editions of the White books went on sale, Nicholson asked Nordstrom for and obtained a letter for circulation within the industry confirming the fact that the paperback editions had indeed not had a negative effect on the hardcovers. Nordstrom's letter, Nicholson later said, "completely broke the logjam with every other publisher."[62]

Nicholson did everything imaginable to allay teachers' and librarians' fears as well. Realizing, for example, that the format of the books would strongly influence their reception, Yearling "emphasized the fact that [in contrast to Pocket Books and other established paperback lines] the size of the type and the leading had not changed from the hardcover edition. It wasn't always easy to convince them [teachers and librarians]. . . . But as it turned out, we were publishing the right format at the right time."[63]

Nordstrom came to regret her decision to cooperate with Nicholson after the reports began to come in that showed the substantial profits Dell was reaping from the arrangement — or rather, what she regretted was that she had not been in a position to publish the paperbacks herself.[64] It was in fact with the details of Dell Yearling's stunning success that Nordstrom later built the case for her own department's foray into the paperback realm. There would be nothing coincidental about Harper's timing: the Harper Trophy imprint (Harper's answer to Yearling) debuted in 1974, just after Dell's licenses to publish *Charlotte's Web* and *Stuart Little* expired. For the second time in seven years, the White books headlined the launch of a major paperback venture.

By the end of the decade, the paperback book for children and teens had come to be seen as a democratizing influence. As publishers struggled to find ways to respond constructively to national events, the affordable format seemed an ideal means of putting books that addressed the issues of race and poverty into the hands of more of America's young people. As the competition for paperback rights to such books intensified, Avon reported paying Scribner $18,000 for rights to Kristin Hunter's *The Soul Brothers and Sister Lou.* Bantam paid M. Evans and Company $12,500 for *On City Streets* — a poetry anthology! — edited by Nancy Larrick.[65]

Meanwhile, in Washington, the Nixon administration, which came to power in January 1969, quickly went to work dismantling the provisions of Title 2 that had benefited schools, libraries, and the publishing industry. Amid the increasingly bitter national debate over the war in Vietnam and the growing realization that, as rich as America was, it could perhaps not afford both "guns and butter" after all, institutional funding for children's books began to dry up at every level. Commiserating with science writer and activist Millicent E. Selsam about the situation, Ursula Nordstrom observed: "The whole swing in the country is simply heartbreaking. . . . School bonds are defeated over and over again in communities across the country. The whole trend is away from everything we've believed in."[66] Not all Johnson-era support for children's literature, however, was withdrawn at once. Before 1969 was over, Charles S. Joelson, a New Jersey Democrat and member of the House Appropriations Committee, led a successful floor fight for an amendment that by adding $1 billion to President Nixon's education budget, spared forty thousand elementary and secondary school libraries from shutting down altogether.[67]

Despite the changed national climate and substantial decline in government support, publishers such as Harper's Ursula Nordstrom, Atheneum's Jean Karl, and Elizabeth R. Riley of T. Y. Crowell maintained their professional resolve and sense of social responsibility. Each of these women had managed her department's expansion with enough prudence and foresight to withstand the leaner times that now confronted them. One of the highlights of the fall 1969 Harper list was also one of the more provocative picture books that Nordstrom had ever published. Written and illustrated by another teen author, a nineteen-year-old African American from Brooklyn named John Steptoe, *Stevie* presented readers with a first-person account, in black street dialect, of an African American boy's ambivalent feelings about his life as a foster brother. Steptoe had gone to show Nordstrom his portfolio at the urging of his high school art teacher, and Nordstrom, who still prided herself on standing ready to "meet the next Mark Twain," had been moved and impressed not only by the intensity of Steptoe's Rouault-inspired paintings but also by the plainspoken eloquence of the young man himself. "You can certainly say something so that it stays said," she would one day tell him.[68] Nordstrom lived for such encounters, not least because, as in Steptoe's case, the gifted newcomer so obviously needed her guidance. She immediately went to work — engaging him in conversation in her office, asking for more detail to embellish a point, sympathizing, probing, praising, cajoling — whatever she could do to help him develop and craft the story that was needed to make a book from his paintings. When Steptoe finally sent her a handwritten first draft, Nordstrom typed it herself and returned it to him with her delicately worded suggestions, framed by the ardent declaration that any change she proposed was for the sole purpose of helping him to express in its most perfect form whatever it was that was "in your head."

Two years earlier, William Styron had taken considerable heat for having shown the effrontery — or courage, depending on one's politics — to write a historical novel for adult readers in the voice of an African American man, the leader of a failed rebellion against his slave masters. In the time of the Black Power movement, the awarding of a Pulitzer Prize to Styron for *The Confessions of Nat Turner* hardly put an end to the controversy about the propriety of cross-cultural appropriation. When *Stevie* came along, implicitly laying claim — in a book for younger grade-school children — to the very kind of authenticity that had rendered the Styron book so controversial, the national media were quick to seize upon the story. In August 1969, in the same number that carried its report of the Woodstock rock festival and featured Norman Mailer's *A Fire on the Moon* as its cover story, *Life* magazine profiled Steptoe and reprinted his first book in its entirety.[69] Grandiosely proclaiming that *Stevie* "ushers in a new era of realism in children's books," the piece went on to catch the modest, idealistic, sandal-clad young man sounding for one discordant moment like a militant. Asked whether white children would find the text of *Stevie* hard to follow, Steptoe had replied: "The story, the language is not directed at white children. I wanted it to be something black children could read without translating the language, something real which would relate to what a black child would know." As media interest in the book fed upon itself, the nineteen-year-old wunderkind from Bed-Stuy, Brooklyn, found himself the object of a media blitz worthy of a Pulitzer graybeard, even landing on the *Today Show*. For Nordstrom, however, the exhilaration of having set into motion yet another hugely promising career was to prove all too fleeting. Two more books and half a dozen years after their first meeting, Steptoe would break off all contact with the editor. For the rest of a sadly sporadic, twenty-year career marred by drug use and a profound sense of alienation, Steptoe would cling to the bitter belief that he had allowed himself from the first to be made a token of.

In 1970, in the greatest act of managerial folly since the firing in 1932 of May Massee by Doubleday, William Jovanovich dismissed Margaret K. McElderry as director of Harcourt, Brace, and Jovanovich's children's book division, having concluded, as the one-time salesman bluntly told her to her face, that the "wave of the future has passed you by." Atheneum seized the opportunity to offer McElderry a plum position. Eager to secure her services without ruffling in-place children's book director Jean Karl's feathers, Atheneum board chairman Pat Knopf proposed that McElderry be made the publisher of an autonomous imprint within the house, to be called "Margaret K. McElderry Books." Karl would continue to do all the things that she was justly celebrated for. Down the hall from her, so too would McElderry. The situation could not have been quite that simple, of course. The awarding of an eponymous imprint — the very first of its kind in American children's book publishing — had about it the glint and glitter of a coronation. For McElderry, the arrangement was particularly sweet. Having last worked at the house where the first such imprint had been established in an adult trade division — Harcourt's distinguished Kurt and Helen Wolff Books — McElderry rejoiced at the prospect not only of making publishing history by accepting Atheneum's generous terms, but of doing so in a way sure to leave William Jovanovich knee-deep in embarrassment.[70]

By the end of the "turbulent" 1960s, it had become a media truism that contemporary young people were maturing more rapidly than those of past generations. The proposition desperately called for qualification. Had not millions of young Americans been compelled by the exigencies of the Great Depression, to name just one trying period from the past, to experience extremes of privation and emotional and social stress years before they were equipped, from a purely developmental standpoint, to withstand such pressures? Yet an observation by Richard Jackson in a *Horn Book* essay that summarized the decade's trends in children's books was striking for what it revealed about the changing maturity rates of young people as readers and consumers of popular culture: "The 10-to-14 novel of a decade ago," Jackson reported,

> is today published for 8-to-12-year-olds. Children know more of life now, and writers and artists are showing them more in their books, through psychological fantasy, contemporary "realism," even through some very sophisticated nonfiction. . . . Living within constant earshot and eyeshot of TV, the telephone, films, and pop music, they are the most communicated-at generation in history. They need books that are different.[71]

Perhaps as the radical social theorist Paul Goodman had suggested at the start of the decade in *Growing Up Absurd: Problems of Youth in the Organized System,* disaffection within the ranks of the nation's young people was merely the inevitable consequence of life in a society increasingly organized on the model of the large, impersonal corporation. Certainly, as Ann

Durell's Bunky Bannister testified, the new, corporate style of management and culture at Harper & Row, Macmillan, and other houses had taken much of the "fun" out of publishing. The profitability of the junior departments having at last made an impression on the larger business world, a torrent of corporate buyouts and mergers seemed inevitable too. By the end of the decade the 1961 Caldecott Medal triumph of dark-horse illustrator Nicolas Sidjakov and the obscure, quixotic Parnassus Press — the upstart publisher, it turned out, had borrowed its lofty name from its Berkeley, California, street address — no longer seemed just improbable but otherworldly.

The Children's Book Week poster for 1969, the year that marked the celebration's fiftieth anniversary, featured a mop-headed child standing atop a tall stack of books to address a rally of placard-bearing youngsters. The children, it appeared, had gathered to demonstrate (innocently enough) for "Book Power." With an approving nod to the increasingly vocal women's rights movement, the artist responsible for the poster, Emily Arnold McCully, had taken care to leave indeterminate the sex of the youngster who led the rally. Boy or girl, the child wore a peace button that was too large to be missed by anyone. How different all this was from the days when the committee of editors who chose the annual Book Week rallying cry confined themselves to a menu of such hard-to-oppose sentiments as "Grow Up with Books" (1933), "Reading Is Fun" (1952 and 1953), and, just the previous year, "Go Places with Books" (1968). More than a few teachers and librarians around the country found the new poster offensive, while others felt that some such statement had been long overdue. To raise eyebrows — and questions — had clearly been McCully's and the Council's intention.

"'Is it for children?'" Richard Jackson wrote in *The Horn Book*, "is perhaps the decade's commonest, knottiest question. No child ever asks it, however. 'Too violent,' 'too abstract,' 'too suggestive' are perhaps the commonest criticisms — but who besides adults is critical of books for such reasons? Children find other reasons for liking or not liking books. And publishers can only guess at those reasons, for we" — and here, Jackson might have been speaking for the overwhelming majority of the nation's experts, from Dr. Spock on down — "are less certain than we were ten years ago about what being young or growing up means."[72]

The garden gate had at last been breached.

8

CHANGE AND MORE CHANGE
The 1970s

There is a new honesty in books for the young.[1]

— MARGARET K. MCELDERRY, in *The Horn Book* (1974)

There is real hope for a culture that makes it as easy to buy a book as it does a pack of cigarettes.[2]

— EDUARD C. LINDEMAN, educational theorist and publishing consultant

"IS THE PAPERBACK REVOLUTION DEAD?"[3] An editorial comment in the *New York Times Book Review* for February 16, 1969, posed this question at a time when for the people on the children's book side of the business, at any rate, the answer was clearly no. The *Times* piece marshaled a grab bag of supposedly ominous statistics to suggest that consumer enthusiasm for the low-priced format might indeed have begun to wane. The total number of paperbacks sold annually in the United States had risen only slightly in the past ten years, at a time when the population grew by 15 percent. The number of places at which paperbacks were sold had not increased during that same period either — although it had held steady at a hefty 100,000 newsstands, cigar stores, bookshops, and other outlets. Perhaps because juvenile publishing was not the focus of the article, the import of one cited statistic — that three-quarters of the nation's schools were now purchasing paperbacks for library or classroom use — had seemed beneath comment and somehow not undermining of the article's argument, though an increase as stunning as that might well have given the writer pause. The highbrow newspaper of record had done its grudging best to make a pop cultural phenomenon look like a fad. Yet before the year was out, the publishers of adult paperbacks would — along with their children's books colleagues — have ample reason to know that the obituary had been premature: in 1969 Bantam printed 4 million copies of Arthur Hailey's *Airport*, Delta sold more than 1 million copies of Eldridge Cleaver's *Soul on Ice*, and Avon sold 1.9 million copies of Israeli psychologist Haim Ginott's *Between Parent and Child.*[4]

The publishers of children's books entered the 1970s with a feverish determination to prove to their corporate overlords that they had as keen a purchase on current market trends as their colleagues in "adult trade" who had lately achieved such Olympian heights of commercial success.

In the spring of 1971, three major houses, Doubleday, Random House, and Holt, Rinehart and Winston, launched new juvenile paperback imprints, each drawing exclusively on titles from its own backlist.[5] Everyone, it seemed, had learned the lesson of the Harper/Dell Yearling experience and become eager to turn hardbound straw into paperback gold. Anticipating this development, George Nicholson and his colleagues at Dell began to invest more heavily in their own hardback imprint, Delacorte Books for Young Readers, as a feeder list for their thriving paperback lines. Even houses too small to get caught up in the frenzy benefited from it to some extent. In 1972, following the release of the Dell Yearling paperback edition of *Are You There God? It's Me, Margaret.* Bradbury Press, the small, independent publisher of the original clothbound edition, turned its first profit from the income it derived from the deal, and Judy Blume began her ascent as one of children's literature's bestselling authors — as well as one of its most controversial.[6]

Profitability was not the only reason for the paperback's newfound acceptance. The widely reported decline in childhood literacy rates and the popular suspicion that television was the chief culprit behind the decline were becoming matters of growing national concern. Nancy Larrick, once again sounding the industry alarm, reported in *Publishers Weekly* that by the end of high school the average American child had spent eleven thousand hours in school and fifteen thousand hours watching television.[7] While Larrick agreed that television's staccato rhythm and seductive capacity for instant gratification served to undermine the development of the reading habit in 1970s children, she believed that publishers, librarians, and teachers also deserved a share of the blame. Undue restrictions placed on library hours and on access to the advanced books for which some children were in fact ready; the tendency of teachers to turn the reading of the classics into a chore; and the tendency of publishers to cater to teachers' ill-conceived agendas by loading down more and more children's books with "ready-made tests" and other "joy-killers" — all were contributing to the decline in children's enthusiasm for reading. When it came to considering the possibilities for mitigating the problem, Larrick pointed with guarded optimism to the new outpouring of affordable paperbacks as a chance for young people to learn to associate books and reading with freedom of choice. "If we had faith in the children to choose their own books and revel in the pleasures of reading," Larrick concluded, "the future could be radiant. The children are ready, but most adults will have to be recycled."[8]

In a forward-looking gesture, the administrators of the National Book Awards in 1969 had added a new prize for "young people's literature" to the roster of their literary laurels.[9] Books of unassailable merit by Meindert DeJong, Isaac Bashevis Singer, and Lloyd Alexander had won the first three National Book Awards in the new category. In the fourth year, however, a firestorm of controversy erupted when the prize for 1972 went to Donald Barthelme for a picture book, the author's first, called *The Slightly Irregular Fire Engine, or, The Hithering Thithering Djinn*. Barthelme, a darling of the New York literary establishment, had illustrated the slender volume himself with collage illustrations cobbled together from recycled Victorian steel engravings, old postage stamps, and other "found" images. To readers with the proper art-historical background, Barthelme's pictures recalled the Surrealist collages of Max Ernst, but with a more antic, "Pop"-inflected spirit. Readers of Barthelme's fiction, which appeared regularly in *The New Yorker*, would also have been quick to note the affinity between the illustrations and the main body of his work — the witty postmodern short stories in which a collage of fragmentary scenes replaced continuous narrative as the organizing principle. All the same, his picture book struck some critics as self-indulgent, and children's librarians who cared about such matters would soon be pointing with scorn to Barthelme's exalted literary status as the only conceivable explanation for the book's triumph in a field of finalists that had also included Ursula K. Le Guin's *The Tombs of Atuan*, Virginia Hamilton's *The Planet of Junior Brown*, Robert C. O'Brien's *Mrs. Frisby and the Rats of NIMH*, and William Steig's *Amos and Boris*.[10]

As a National Book Awards judge that year, Paul Heins, the donnish critic who as the editor (since 1967) of *The Horn Book* was accustomed to having his literary opinions treated with extreme deference, for once had found himself in the minority. So vehemently did Heins object to the committee's choice that, in a break with NBA custom, he had demanded the right to voice his objections from the podium at the gala awards ceremony, where Flannery O'Connor and historian Allan Nevins were among the evening's other honorees. In the months that followed, letters poured in to *The Horn Book* praising him for his principled public stand and expressing bitter disappointment at what many in the field considered a lost opportunity. "Thank you for not letting hundreds of us down," wrote the influential Kansas librarian Ruth Gagliardo. "I was so pleased at your selection as juror, I was horrified at the choice of book. There is *such straining* in much of today's writing."[11] Author Julius Lester expressed the hope that the next year's committee would "know children's literature" and would therefore avoid the pitfall of being "impressed by cleverness and vapid New York cocktail party chic."[12] A reader from Texas, voicing a criticism that would be heard with increasing frequency about one book or another in the years to come, simply stated: "*The Slightly Irregular Fire Engine* is certainly not a book for children."[13]

That same year Temple University Press unveiled volume 1 of a new academic journal called, simply, *Children's Literature*. The plump paperback, running to just under two hundred pages, touted itself as a compendium of "essays emanating from The Modern Language Association Seminar on Children's Literature."[14] The editor's introduction revealed, at a minimum, that the central figure behind the venture was possessed of a sly sense of humor. Writing under the banner of "The Editor's High Chair," Francelia Butler, an English professor at the University of Connecticut at Storrs, took the occasion to explain why the critical study of children's literature needed to be pursued by "humanists" rather than only by "children's 'experts,'" by which she meant primarily educators and librarians. Butler offered three reasons for what she took to be a lamentable history of neglect — considering the literature's indisputable role in the transmission of culture — on the part of literary scholars: first, that "[the] simplicity [characteristic of some genres of children's literature] is too readily equated with triteness"; second, that children's literature "usually lacks the verbal sophistication and complexity with which people in higher education have traditionally been trained to deal," thus paradoxically rendering the subject an unusually hard one to teach; and third, that the category is a catch-all in which "good and bad tends to be lumped together."[15] With a lively flourish, Butler embellished this last point with the provocative suggestion that "perhaps the scorn of the literature on the part of the humanists is due to a confusion of terminology. Perhaps many current books should not be considered 'literature' but rather, cleverly disguised propaganda for moral or economic purposes."[16] Here was an incendiary thought not likely to be met in *The Horn Book*'s pages, at least not as stated in such blunt terms. Butler for her part wrote as if *The Horn Book* either did not exist or else was beneath her mention.

The essays collected in *Children's Literature* were wide-ranging, for the most part jargon-free, exploratory in the best sense, and surprisingly assured in tone considering the newness of the authors to their material. Here were taproots sent out in a multitude of promising directions. How interesting to learn that Lewis Carroll had been reading Charles Dickens's *Our Mutual Friend* while he was writing *Through the Looking-Glass* and to be presented with compelling evidence that in several small but significant ways the latter book bears the mark of Dickensian influence. Or to have John Ruskin's literary fairy tale *The King of the Golden River* pinpointed as a pivotal work in the influential Victorian author's transformation from art critic to social commentator. Or to be shown that early variants of so simple-seeming a story as "Red Riding Hood" reverberated with echoes of ancient mythology and could also be read as a reliable index of a wide range of "social attitudes toward children," and that one of the most effective approaches to understanding the tale was in terms of its erotic content.[17] In contrast, Paul Heins, in a review published in *The Horn Book* the previous year of Maurice Sendak's latest picture book, *In the Night Kitchen*, had sheepishly avoided all mention of Mickey's nudity even as he hailed the book as a "work of art" replete with "subconscious elements" that complicated and deepened the "storytelling and pictorialization."[18] Writing in the same issue of *The Horn Book* in his regular "Views on Science Books" column, Harry C. Stubbs with disarming candor acknowledged a

recent letter from a reader [who] asked, with justice, why this column had never discussed "facts of life" books. I had, and still have no good answer; it simply had not occurred to me. The subject does have both scientific and educational aspects. Now that I do think of it, a rather peculiar fact strikes me. Sex and death are the only subjects I can think of at the moment which have a basis in scientific fact, but on which a

sizeable body of competent and sincere people seriously consider ignorance to be better than knowledge — at least for children. I do not
agree with these people.[19]

The new 1960s-bred university critics were less diffident about sexual-
ity and about the underlying issue of children's books as a literature defined in good part by cultural taboos. Just as promisingly, they exhibited a
lightly held awareness of the potential usefulness for their purposes not
only of the writings of Freud and other psychologists but also of such researchers in the humanities as Philippe Ariès, the French statistician who
during the postwar period had helped to pioneer the elusive study of the
history of ordinary people's daily lives. In the years to come, Ariès's *Centuries of Childhood: A Society History of Family Life*, which first appeared in
translation in the United States in 1962, would become perhaps the most
widely cited work by scholars interested in approaching children's literature historically.

Even at a time when universities were redefining their academic standards, adding "creative writing" and other counterculture-inspired courses
to their curricula and becoming more receptive to such nontraditional in-
terdisciplinary approaches as those of "American Studies" and "Women's
Studies," the notion that children's books could and should be taught as literature aroused the deepest skepticism in more tradition-minded academics. It was much to the chagrin of her colleagues that Butler's University
of Connecticut undergraduate lecture course in children's literature had
quickly become the English Department's most popular offering. Such
was their resentment that her fellow professors — specialists in Shakespeare, Wordsworth, and other bankable mainstays of the canon — ex-
acted a heavy price in intradepartmental backbiting over the years. On re-
tiring from the university, Butler, in a pointed rebuke to her peers, gave her
substantial personal library of children's books not to the University of
Connecticut, as she might have been expected to do, but rather to Hollins
College, in Roanoke, Virginia, where an innovative summer master's program in children's literature, intended primarily for working teachers, had
recently been established. During her teaching years, Butler blithely presided over a lecture hall overflowing with undergraduates even on days
when she did not bring in one of her Connecticut artist friends — Maurice
Sendak or, a bit later, James Marshall — to regale the group, more than a

few of whom had come to regard Sendak's *Where the Wild Things Are* as the anthem of their rebellious generation.

To those who saw the unkempt, iconoclastic college students of the time as irresponsible latter-day Peter Pans, the attempt to elevate children's literature to the status of a scholarly discipline provided an ideal symbol for all that was topsy-turvy in contemporary university life. For that reason alone, the young scholars who gravitated to the new field — whether from backgrounds in Romantic or Victorian literature, or American or Renaissance studies, history, folklore, or sociology — were destined for a taste of the professional marginalization that the publishers of children's books had been living down since the years following World War I. Still, theirs would be far and away the milder form of the affliction, if only because having grown up during the postwar baby boom years amid a bounty of bicycles, Little Golden Books, Saturday morning cartoons, and toys, they took it for granted that childhood mattered and that childhood therefore must be a worthy subject for reflection. The new scholars would in fact ask why previous generations had not felt as they now did, and they would come to identify themselves with those rare older persons who, like Alice long after waking from her Wonderland dream, succeeded in keeping, "through all her riper years, the simple and loving heart of her childhood."

In the short run, the new critics had little impact on the publishers whose work they wished to put into a more meaningful cultural context. But by the mid-1970s, at least one observer of the field, herself not an academic but rather a freelance critic and historian, had crossed over to become the children's book editor of Parents' Magazine Press.[20] Selma G. Lanes had made her reputation as the author of a series of thoughtful essays published in the *New York Herald-Tribune*, the *New York Times Book Review*, and *Washington Post Book World*. Lanes had a fresh, unsentimental feeling for her subject, a healthy disregard for received pieties, and, much like the new academic critics, an impatience bordering on contempt for the insularity of past attempts at critical writing about the field. "With the possible exception of advertising and . . . film," Lanes would observe, "no popular art medium in our time has been as experimental, inventive and simply alive as children's books, particularly those for the younger age levels. . . . Yet, nothing approaching the seriousness with which we take films — or, for that matter, advertisements — has yet been bestowed upon the consideration of young children's books." Of *The Horn Book*, Lanes without quite naming names stated: "While there is one magazine of repute devoted in its entirety to children's books and their authors, surely its genteel prose and self-congratulatory tone often smack more of class notes in an alumni quarterly than the astringent and measured judgments that characterize critical writing in . . . *Partisan Review, The New York Review of Books* and *Film Quarterly*."[21]

At about this time, another group of historically minded writers and their artist and designer friends gathered in Peru, Illinois, to plan the launch of an ambitious literary magazine for children. *Cricket*, founder Marianne Carus hoped, would fill the void left by the passing of the great children's periodicals whose heyday had come a half-century or more earlier. Carus had done her homework, and despite the close to one hundred children's magazines of one kind or another that were then on the market, she believed the time was right for a new *St. Nicholas*. She started with a few distinct advantages. Her husband owned the Open Court Press, a small house known primarily for scholarly books in the fields of philosophy, education, and Eastern thought; Open Court would publish and distribute the magazine. Prior work for Open Court had brought Carus to the point of considering the new venture. A series of literature-based basic readers for the elementary school market that she had edited for the house had proven to be highly successful. Teachers had contacted her asking for more high-quality reading material for the classroom — the shorter the better they specified, given the difficulty of interesting children in reading. It occurred to Carus that the magazine was the ideal format for addressing the teachers' needs.[22]

The first editorial board meeting, held in November 1972 at the Starved Rock Lodge in northern Illinois, brought together a luminous group that included *Cricket*'s new senior editor, Clifton Fadiman, a figure well known to the nation's reading public as *The New Yorker*'s book critic and as a member of the Book-of-the-Month Club's august panel of judges; editorial advisory board members Lloyd Alexander, Isaac Bashevis Singer, Eleanor Cameron, Paul Heins, Kaye Webb (founder of Puffin Books and the doyenne of British publishers for children), Walter Scherf (director of the International Youth Library in Munich), Virginia Haviland (of the Library of Congress), and Sheila Egoff (Canada's leading authority in the field); and art director Trina Schart Hyman. Earlier that year, a prototype of the first issue had gone out to librarians, teachers, the media, writers, illustrators, and others for their comments. Heralding great things to come, it featured a special "greeting" to readers from Snoopy by Fadiman's old friend Charles Schulz. In January 1973, the inaugural issue went on sale. To stir up media and publishing industry awareness, Carus gave a lavish launch party at New York's St. Moritz Hotel, about which a guest commented afterward: "If a bomb had gone off during your party, the entire children's book world would've been wiped out."[23] Carus herself later recalled that the main question people had for her that evening was why her offices were not in Manhattan: "Nobody . . . could really understand how anybody in publishing could survive in the middle of Illinois cornfields, of all places!"[24]

While New York showed no sign of relinquishing its claim as the nation's publishing capital, the Open Court Press would soon be joined by dozens of other "small" or "alternative" press ventures based elsewhere and devoted to publishing work for children. Many of these presses were the pet projects of one or two individuals who had recognized a gap in the existing literature and had made it their mission to provide the needed book or type of book themselves. Although many of the presses were short-lived, others took root as viable mini-laboratories for an industry that seemed to grow more risk-averse in direct proportion to the consolidation of its ownership in fewer and fewer hands.

On November 24, 1972, a significant editorial career came to an untimely close with the death of Velma V. Varner, the managing director and editor of Viking Junior Books, of cancer, at the age of fifty-six.[25] Varner, a former librarian from Michigan, had joined the Viking department in 1964 under Annis Duff and succeeded her four years later in a transition far smoother than the one Duff herself had endured under May Massee. Varner might well have empathized with Duff, having herself assumed the directorship of Morrow Junior Books in the fall of 1954 only to realize that her predecessor, Elisabeth Hamilton, who had been retained as an adviser, was loath to surrender effective control of the department to her and was prepared to make her life miserable to establish the point. In two years' time, Varner beat a rueful retreat from Morrow to make way for Hamilton's "return" to her old job and then landed more happily at World, where she headed the department before moving to Viking.

It spoke well for both Duff and Varner that the latter woman had dared to argue the case for publishing S. E. Hinton's *The Outsiders* and that when the book became a media sensation Duff made certain that Varner received due credit for the discovery. The federal money that became available during the Johnson administration years for institutional book purchases had played to Varner's strength as an editor of nonfiction, especially of books about space travel and science.[26] It was also Varner who ushered Viking into the paperback era with the creation of the Seafarer imprint and who, with an eye for visual dash and sophistication that was very much in the May Massee tradition, had added artist Leonard Baskin and the Japanese-born illustrator Taro Yashima to the Viking list. Varner perhaps ranked second only to Margaret K. McElderry among the internationalists dedicated to exposing American children to books that shone a light on other world cultures. While at Putnam in the early 1950s, she had published *The Animal Frolic,* a picture-book adaptation of a twelfth-century Japanese scroll that was considered a Japanese national treasure.[27] At World she had introduced American children to the elegant paper-engineered picture books of Italian graphic designer and sculptor Bruno Munari.

Both Varner and McElderry became well-known figures at the annual Bologna Children's Book Fair, where since 1964 publishers from around the world had gathered each spring to display their new lists and negotiate the sale and purchase of foreign rights. Varner's chosen successor at World, Ann K. Beneduce, shared the older woman's internationalist outlook and deep curiosity about publishing opportunities abroad. When, in 1968, Beneduce was offered a picture-book project by an American artist that called for prohibitively expensive die-cuts and other special production work, she traveled to Japan in search of a printing company capable of manufacturing the book at a reasonable cost. Having found a suitable printer, she was able the following year to publish Eric Carle's *The Very Hungry Caterpillar.* The book quickly became a major commercial success, more so at first on the strength of its popularity with parents and preschool teachers than with librarians, who remained mistrustful of books with toylike elements. Carle's subsequent picture books, with their appealing animal heroes, sleek International Style graphics, novelty embellishments, and simple, fablelike texts proved to have such consistent appeal for children of other countries as well that from the early 1970s onward the annual breakfast that Beneduce hosted for publishers from around the world at the Bologna fair became one of the fair's highlights. Beneduce would arrive at breakfast with a mockup of Carle's latest work and unveil it before the assembled group. Each publisher would then be asked to say how many copies of the book he or she was prepared to order. The size of the first printing would be set based on the grand total for all the participating publishers.[28] The larger the print run of a book, especially one printed in full color with additional novelty effects, the lower the production cost per copy for all their houses; thus, in these "copublishing" arrangements, as the international partnering deals came to be called, it benefited everyone to opt for the largest reasonable order. Such was the enthusiasm for Carle's books year after year that by the end of breakfast Beneduce could usually relax in the knowledge that her trip had already paid for itself many times over.

Velma Varner had from time to time published her views on her changing profession. In her last such commentary, cast in language notably more diplomatic than Nancy Larrick's, she had argued for the need to encourage more writers and artists from minority groups to enter the field. At the same time, Varner had refused categorically to rule out the possibility that an author of one race might be capable of imagining his or her way into the experience of a person of another race, as Ezra Jack Keats had attempted to do. "Say it to me true and say what you mean in a way that will be meaningful to children, and I will publish it."[29] Varner then advanced the discussion begun by Larrick several years earlier in the *Saturday Review* by declaring that America's minority populations also needed significant representation within the ranks of the publishing houses themselves. In this regard, the nation's public libraries were somewhat ahead of their publishing counterparts: African Americans had achieved positions of authority in the children's services departments of the public library systems in New York City, Nassau County (New York), Philadelphia, and Chicago. As short a roster of reform as this was, it stood in positive contrast to that of America's publishers for children, which during the 1970s lacked even a single person of color in a high-level role.[30]

The early 1970s saw the first overall decline in sales of children's books during the postwar years. In preceding periods, annual sales had increased on a slow but steady trajectory: from $86.9 million in 1960 to $117.0 million in 1965 and $148.0 million in 1970. In 1975 the figure dipped to $124.6 million.[31] The reversal would prove short-lived, with the next five years making up for the loss many times over, culminating in an upward surge to $210.8 million by the end of the decade. The spectacular growth during the 1980s would dwarf even this achievement. In the meantime, however, publishers were realizing that they worked in an increasingly unpredictable economic environment in which rising inflation, the withdrawal of federal funding

for books, and the resulting contraction of school and public library service to children had lately converged to weaken the market upon which
they had been taught to depend. Only the Western Publishing Company,
publisher of Golden Books and a vast array of other lower-priced books,
novelties, and games, and its mass-market rivals seemed immune to the industry's economic woes. Western's growth continued unabated throughout
the troubled decade, with major expansions of its domestic direct marketing operation and its publishing activities in Australia, the signing of a
lucrative new long-term printing contract with Dell Publishing, and a corporate restructuring that transformed Western into a publicly traded company listed on the New York Stock Exchange.[32]

Western was hardly invulnerable, however. As its publishing business
faced increased competition, its hold on its leading authors and illustrators
grew more tenuous. Western had two standard publishing contracts for
freelancers: one that offered a "flat fee" for creating the text or illustrations
of a book, and one (reserved for the stars of the list) that provided for a
royalty on future sales — though a royalty pegged at a lower percentage
rate than that traditionally offered by trade publishers. The argument that
Golden Books co-creator Lucille Ogle and her colleagues had always made
was that because the twenty-five-cent books sold in huge multiples of the
printings typical of trade publishers, the financial reward to be reaped by
accepting the line's lower royalty was all but guaranteed to pay off in the
end. In the late 1960s, as the company prospered on an ever grander scale,
its most successful author, Richard Scarry, had begun to question the rationale for his having to accept below-industry-standard terms. Scarry hired
an attorney who, rather than simply negotiate a new contract on his behalf,
instead organized an auction for Scarry's next book in which Western
would have to bid against other houses for the project. In April 1967, after Western's president, Albert Leventhal, refused to match a substantially
higher offer made by Random House for Richard Scarry's *What Do People Do All Day?* the author signed a multi-book contract with the latter publishing company.[33] As the corporate mentality swept the industry,
long-standing relationships counted for less and talent went to the highest
bidder.[34]

The appointment of George M. Nicholson to succeed Velma Varner at Viking was notable not only for the fact that the new director was a man. The

citadel of the "book beautiful" would now take its instructions from a pub-lishing veteran who had served his apprenticeship at Golden Books and made his mark at Dell, publisher of paperbacks and comics.

Nicholson by then had begun to know the trade as well as the mass-market side of the business at first hand. More importantly, he had come to see the potential for blending aspects of the two approaches in promising new models for publishing. He arrived at Viking not directly from Dell, but from an intervening two-year stint as department head at Holt, Rinehart and Winston, the prestigious publisher of Newbery medalist Lloyd Alexan-der and Caldecott winner Evaline Ness. Holt by then was a property of CBS, and Nicholson's assignment there had been to make money for the parent company by bringing Holt's juvenile trade department into closer alignment with its school division.[35] At Viking he faced an equally daunting task: to preserve one of the industry's great backlists while expanding its reach into the paperback realm and building up Viking's relationship with its new British one-half owner, Penguin Books.

A Bologna regular, Nicholson found much to his liking on British publishers' lists and began to import the work of, among others, picture-book authors Janet and Allan Ahlberg, fantasy writer Joan Aiken, and poet Ted Hughes. He also published emerging American authors, including novelists Richard Peck and Rosa Guy, and in a sort of ultimate confirma-tion of karmic contact with the department's glory days, illustrator Gerald McDermott, the 1975 Caldecott Medal winner for *Arrow to the Sun*. Yet all was not as it once had been. Inflationary pressures now prompted once un-thinkable compromises in the physical makeup of new printings of even the most venerable backlist titles. In August 1974, in anticipation of the twenty-ninth reprint of *Make Way for Ducklings*, Viking's managing editor, Gertrude Shafer, wrote Robert McCloskey in fear and trembling to ask his permission to eliminate the dust jacket from his book and to replace the original cloth cover with a preprinted one and a reinforced binding. Shafer wrote the artist: "If we have to cut corners when we reprint 20,000 copies of a book, you can imagine some of the other problems we are running into these days."[36] McCloskey reluctantly consented to the changes, but was soured by the experience and by others like it that followed. While the "book beautiful" was far from dead, a greatly expanded, more complex, and less predictable market had reduced allegiance to the once-sacrosanct Massee ideal to one of a handful of competing considerations.

As revelatory of changes afoot in the industry as Nicholson's arrival at Viking was the unexpected departure from Harper, in the late winter of 1973, of Ursula Nordstrom. The announcement of Nordstrom's early retirement came as a shock to all but her closest friends in publishing. To her inner circle of authors, to whom she wrote privately in advance of the public announcement, she attributed the decision to the ever-increasing burden of administrative work that had steadily crowded out the chance to pursue her first love, editing. That was true, but not the whole story. Notwithstanding her extraordinary record of achievement and legendary status, Nordstrom had failed to maintain cordial relations with Harper's seniormost management. The triggering event seems to have been a slight leveled at Nordstrom at a Harper stockholders' meeting at which her name was mentioned but then not voted on for some honor (most likely an officer's position on the Harper board). It was arranged that, working from home, she would continue to edit her favorite authors and artists — Maurice Sendak, Mary Rodgers, Molly Stoltz, and a few others. A year later, as Nordstrom struggled to cope with the fresh indignities of overseeing a handful of projects at a cramped work table in her Connecticut bedroom, she wrote her longtime friend and ally Katharine S. White: "I've been working for over 40 years and the worst curse I could put on any man is: 'In your next life may you be born a talented and creative woman.'"[37]

Titles edited by her now originated under a new Harper imprint as "Ursula Nordstrom Books." In the past, Nordstrom had always made an elaborate show of shunning the limelight, and when the imprint was first offered to her she had bristled again. When at last she agreed to the plan, it was perhaps with the bittersweet thought that if her longtime rival Margaret K. McElderry could publish books under her own name, she might as well do the same. As for the rest, Nordstrom kept in touch with her old office with the help of her trusted New York–based assistant, Barbara A. Dicks — the fabled "BAD" of countless epic-length memos that flew back and forth between New York and Connecticut. The high-strung department Nordstrom had left behind, with its hothouse atmosphere so reminiscent of the boarding schools of her own childhood, was always good for a diverting story or two. As if to ensure that this would continue to be so, Nordstrom had taken care in handpicking her successor to choose a young staff editor, not because she was capable of filling her own shoes, but rather — or so it would later be whispered by other, perhaps envious Harper staffers — because she was not.[38]

Writing in *The Horn Book* in December 1973, McElderry recalled for the newcomers in the field her own first impressions of publishing a quarter of a century earlier. The post–World War II years had been a time, she wrote, of both uncertainty and hope, when publishers had felt a solemn duty to help satisfy the

> great hunger for knowledge about what had been happening elsewhere [in the world]. In the United States we were eager to know about books that had been published abroad — and the same kind of interest was evident in other countries. Thus began a period when books from other lands were eagerly scanned by publishers, and many were chosen for translation and publication both here and abroad.[39]

McElderry contrasted the late 1940s — the time of global institution building, when the International Board of Books for Youth and the International Youth Library had both come into being — with the present-day era of "gigantic and rapid upheavals and changes in our way of life." She noted with regret that "we in the United States [have] shifted our focus . . . to a much narrower one. We began concentrating on ourselves, trying to understand what was happening and why, how we could define and solve our problems. Naturally," McElderry added, "this shift in focus has greatly affected the publishing of books for children."[40] She cited the testimony of librarians who "again and again" told her that children wanted to read about present-day American life, and not about life elsewhere. Whatever the reasons for the children's reported preference, its meaning for publishers was clear enough: there would be fewer translations, at least for now. McElderry for her part was unwilling to abandon entirely what she considered the publishers' "responsibility . . . to try to make the best books from other parts of the world available."[41] Still, the new reality called for more prudence and greater selectivity than in the past. As she also wished to make clear in one of her first public utterances since her arrival at Atheneum, she did not, as William Jovanovich had accused her of doing, intend to live in the past.

The morning headlines only confirmed the need for Americans to know more about the world's diverse cultures and about global social and economic trends. With the growing assertiveness of the Organization of Petroleum Exporting Countries (OPEC), Americans were becoming aware as never before of the interdependent nature of the emerging global economy.[42]

Decisions taken in distant capitals could, it turned out, have repercussions for the publishers of children's books. OPEC's imposition of an oil embargo against the United States and its pro-Israel allies on October 17, 1973 — days after the start of the Yom Kippur War — precipitated the industrial world's first energy crisis and triggered widespread fears of inflation. At Viking Junior Books, as managing editor Gertrude Shafer later recalled, "we had [just] nervously okayed a 25,000 reprinting of *Blueberries for Sal,* projecting a price increase. Then the books arrived in our warehouse the day Nixon instituted price controls!" — thus locking the publisher in to a retail price that no longer made financial sense.[43]

The "new realism" in fiction for grade-schoolers and teens continued to be the most passionately debated topic when attention turned back from bottom lines to books. On its spring list for 1974, Pantheon, an imprint of Random House, published what was to become the decade's most controversial book for young readers, a novel by Robert Cormier called *The Chocolate War.* The son of a Massachusetts factory worker, Cormier earned his living as a reporter for the *Fitchburg Sentinel and Enterprise* in that state and wrote fiction in his free time. His first three novels, all published for adults, had appeared to scant notice, each from a different house.[44] On submitting his latest manuscript to his agent at Curtis Brown, Cormier had supposed that it too would be published, if at all, as adult fiction.

The agent to whom Cormier had sent *The Chocolate War* was a former schoolteacher from Iowa. Marilyn E. Marlow had a warm but unequivocal manner that inspired Cormier's absolute trust and confidence. In Marlow, he had, it seemed, found his ideal reader: a devoted admirer of the taut craftsmanship and advocate for the risky emotional intensity of his work. It appealed to them both that the writer's debut novel, *Now and at the Hour,* had been the very first manuscript that the agent had ever sold. Now, not quite a decade and a half later, both their careers were about to take another fateful turn.

A literature major with dreams of the big city, Marlow had tried teaching before deciding, in 1959, to leave Iowa for New York to make her way in the "nebulous world of publishing."[45] After a brief stint at Harcourt, Brace, where she was given the ill-fitting task of writing blurbs for biology texts, she found an entry-level job as a "first reader" in the adult trade department of the literary agency Curtis Brown. The following year Marlow was promoted to agent. In addition to handling the usual run of manuscripts like those by the unknown Robert Cormier, she was asked to develop children's literature as a new specialty within the firm. It amused her later to realize she had been chosen for the task on the dubious strength of her teaching experience — a bad time in her life that had done nothing to raise her awareness of the rapidly changing field. Always a self-starter, however, she seized upon the new opportunity with her usual alacrity and before long had a working knowledge both of the books then being published for young readers and of the people responsible for them.

Curtis Brown's newfound interest in the genre owed something to happenstance. The agency already represented a handful of writers — Rumer Godden, Phyllis McGinley, Ogden Nash — who produced children's books from time to time. This circumstance and the extraordinary growth of juvenile publishing during the Great Society years had combined to prompt the agency's expansion. The business potential in doing so certainly seemed great, provided publishers' hostility to agents could be overcome in a segment of the industry in which, up until then, comparatively few writers and artists had had representation. Another New York agency, Macintosh and Otis, appears to have been the very first one to assign an agent to the specialty — Mary Squire Abbot and later Caroline Sauer. A third New York office, Brandt and Brandt, had also showed some interest prior to the 1960s. They remained the exceptions, however. When news of Marlow's assignment became known to the industry, Sauer promptly telephoned her new rival to invite her to lunch, as much, it seems, in a gesture of high-minded collegiality as out of a desire to size up the competition. Thirty-five years later, Marlow could still quote Sauer's overture verbatim: "Miss Marlow? I think it's time we met: Stouffer's — the basement. Quarter to twelve. Don't be late. Dutch treat."[46]

Overall, the publishers of children's books resented — as well they might — the intrusion of agents and their machinations into their traditionally informal and often friendship-entwined relationships with authors. It was true, of course, that adult trade publishers had long since come to terms with this more businesslike way of doing business. One had to look back as far as the 1890s to find Holts, Scribners, and Putnams demanding to know, from the depths of their richly appointed, mahogany-paneled chambers, why anyone should have to come between themselves and an author in the making of arrangements that in the past had been sealed over cigars with a handshake.[47] If children's book publishing had until then remained an industry backwater, its immunity from the added financial pressures and competitive atmosphere that agents fostered and traded upon had had much to do with it.

By the time Cormier sent off his fourth novel manuscript to New York, Marlow, while still engaged in representing writers of literary fiction, was already well established in her new role, with S. E. Hinton (*The Outsiders*), Paul Zindel (*The Pigman*), and Jane Yolen (*The Emperor and the Kite*), among others, on her client list. Cormier had told her that the new book was based in part on an incident that had occurred at his son's Catholic boys' school. Responding enthusiastically by letter, Marlow, who shared Cormier's devout Catholicism, declared *The Chocolate War* "one of the most overwhelming manuscripts I have ever read." She then sounded a cautionary note: "I don't know how it's going to go in the publishing world. It is virtually unrelenting in its force."[48]

Marlow recognized that *The Chocolate War* belonged in the tradition of John Knowles's *A Separate Peace*, William Golding's *Lord of the Flies*, and J. D. Salinger's *A Catcher in the Rye*, all of which had been published as general trade books. But she also believed *The Chocolate War* was close in spirit to the best examples of the newly emerging genre of hard-hitting realistic teen and preteen fiction that included the work of Zindel, Hinton, Louise Fitzhugh, and M. E. Kerr. With this in mind, and after receiving Cormier's assurances that the category placement and marketing of the book did not matter to him, Marlow submitted the manuscript to Ursula Nordstrom, who, as the publisher of Fitzhugh and Kerr, had the most consistent reputation for risk-taking with the young adult genre. When the two women discussed *The Chocolate War* by phone, Nordstrom told Marlow that she "couldn't believe" that she was turning the book down, but that she felt she had to do so, having concluded that the novel was too violent for young readers.[49] Coming from Nordstrom, these words were enough to send a chill up an agent's spine. Marlow next showed the manuscript to Viking's Velma Varner, the publisher of *The Outsiders*. Varner's response to the book was exactly the same. Several more rejections followed, including two (following a temporary shift in strategy) from adult trade departments. Then Fabio Coen, head of Pantheon's juvenile division, accepted *The Chocolate War*. Coen was not without his own reservations. Marlow later had to persuade him to keep Cormier's original title, which the editor argued made the book sound like one intended for a younger audience. But this was a minor concern when weighed against the disturbing qualities of the book that had prompted such a worrisome early response.

The Chocolate War told the story of a tyrannical Catholic boys' school where the adults in charge made few concessions to democratic principles and where a student who refused to conform to the school's accepted norms was doomed to having his dissenting views savagely ridiculed, his reputation destroyed, and perhaps even to being beaten senseless by his classmates. Although hardly intended as an allegory of contemporary publishing, *The Chocolate War* and the emotional, industrywide debate it stirred came at a time when publishing employees were themselves having to face, with unaccustomed regularity, unsettling new questions concerning their relationship to their employers.

On June 17, 1974, members of the Association of Harper & Row Employees went out on strike in a dispute with management over the terms of a new three-year contract. The strike, which lasted for seventeen days, was marred by crossed picket lines and threats of mass firings. Ursula Nordstrom observed the situation from Connecticut, doubtless relieved not to have had to choose between her fierce loyalty to the House of Harper and her natural sympathy for the underdog. The conflict belonged to a different publishing world from the one to which for thirty years she had sworn her undying allegiance.

The Harper strike was the first employee walkout to affect the publishing industry since the days of the Great Depression. But it proved to be the first of two highly charged labor walkouts to take place that same year. On Monday, October 14, 1974, Macmillan, Inc., citing declining profits in a time of spiraling inflation, dismissed more than one hundred employees, or approximately 10 percent of the staff of its book divisions. The dramatic move, which came virtually without warning, was greeted with outrage and extreme skepticism by many at the firm who, as the *New York Times* reported the following morning, regarded the official explanation "as a subterfuge for an attempt to break a union organizing drive in the company."[50] The timing of the mass firings left little room for doubt about this. Local 153 of the Office and Professional Employees International Union had been engaged in organizing efforts in the company for seven months, and on the

previous Friday, the eleventh, the union had notified Macmillan's management that it had asked the National Labor Relations Board for a referen-
dum to determine whether or not Macmillan would become a union shop.
By then, more than half of the company's employees had informally indi-
cated their approval of the plan, making the outcome certain.

The wish for greater bargaining power in a notoriously underpaid
profession was not, however, the only issue propelling the crisis. A union
organizer told the *Times* that "the active women's movement within the
publishing division also was a factor in the dismissals." A month earlier, in
response to a complaint filed by Macmillan employees that alleged sex discrimination in the company's hiring and promotion practices, New York
State Attorney General Louis J. Lefkowitz had launched an investigation
into the matter. A week before the firings, three hundred of the company's
female employees met to discuss the situation further. Janet Schulman,
Macmillan's juvenile marketing director, was among the leaders of the
group, and among those let go on the fourteenth, along with five other
members of her department.

Three days earlier, on Friday, the eleventh, Susan Hirschman had
been summoned to a confidential meeting with Macmillan management at
which she was told to make immediate plans for the dismissal of half her
staff and for cutting her list by 50 percent. Rather than doing so, she spent
the weekend with two colleagues drawing up an alternative plan that called
for postponing some books and amortizing the cost of others over a period
of years with the ultimate goal of preserving the integrity of her department. Hirschman circulated her plan first thing Monday morning, but
when management, without responding to her, announced the company-
wide firings later that day, it became clear that no one had bothered to consider her ideas. Unwilling to associate themselves with the company's actions, Hirschman and her department's managing editor, Ada Shearon,
both resigned in protest the following day and prepared to consider their
options.[51]

A strike meeting was called for noon on Wednesday, the sixteenth.
Picketing began the following day. The strike proved to be brief and accomplished little from the employees' point of view.[52] The following January
the National Labor Relations Board, at the conclusion of a two-month-
long investigation, sided with management, finding no compelling evidence of union-busting in the company's decision to lay off so many of its

employees. Macmillan, it was concluded, appeared to have responded to economic pressures.[53] Few among those who had gone out on strike would have agreed, of course, and the legacy of anger and resentment left behind by the episode contributed its share to the emergence of a changed culture of publishing in the years to come: a culture marked by a loosening of the bonds of employee loyalty to a given house; by an increased tendency for employees, including senior editors, to change houses at least once during their professional lives; and, as a consequence of this more fluid situation, by a loss of institutional memory.

That October, *The Horn Book* marked its fiftieth anniversary with a retrospective issue featuring memory pieces and congratulatory messages by fantasy writer Susan Cooper, Grace Allen Hogarth (the former Houghton Mifflin editor, now retired and living in Maine), English novelist and critic John Rowe Townsend, and others. Townsend took the occasion to walk the ever less clearly delineated boundary line separating children's books from literature in general. Noting that it had become a sort of mantra of authors for the young to insist that they did not write for children but rather for themselves, Townsend went on to cite several cases of recent books that had found readers on both sides of the age divide. Some such books — for example, Alan Garner's historical fantasy *Red Shift* — had been published in the United States as juveniles, while others, including Richard Adams's bestselling animal fantasy *Watership Down*, had not. Townsend found the borderline to be not equally permeable from either side. It seemed that a book stood a somewhat better chance of crossing over if it started out life as one published for adults. If the publishing history of Adams's *Watership Down* did not entirely conform to this observation, it nonetheless illustrated the flux and fluidity of publishing categories. *Watership Down* had first seen the light of day as a children's book published in England, where it won two major literary prizes, including the 1972 Carnegie Medal, Britain's equivalent of the Newbery. Six years later, Macmillan released it in the United States as an adult trade book after Susan Hirschman had first acquired it for the firm's Department of Books for Boys and Girls. The prepublication change in departmental sponsorship came about after the president of Avon, a major paperback house, read the book and, recognizing its bestseller potential, paid a substantial sum for paperback rights. In light of that development, Hirschman had told Townsend, "it seemed only fair to the author and everyone else concerned to have it published on the general trade list where it could be given the broadest possible exposure."[54]

With the publication of the anniversary number, Paul Heins stepped down after seven years on the job as *The Horn Book*'s editor. In an almost antique counterpoint to the abrupt firings, resignations, and staccato comings and goings that now characterized employment at the major publishing houses, Heins's successor, it was announced in December, would not be some outsider brought in to prop up sales or market share, but Ethel L. Heins, the retiree's wife and a figure well known to the magazine's readers as a reviewer, librarian, and prize committee member. A small, emphatic, deeply knowledgeable woman with a rapid-fire conversational style that contrasted, comedically at times, with that of her mild-mannered husband, the new editor pledged herself, in her first editorial, to a "continuity of purpose and of zeal" — noble words resounding with echoes of *Horn Book* editors past. She then gave readers a taste of her own tough-minded candor: "We are living," Heins wrote,

> in an oppressive atmosphere of appalling revelations, ominous forecasts, and agonizing problems; and it has become the fashion to look back wistfully to a time when life, in retrospect, seemed to have been less catastrophic. But neither despair nor nostalgia is vitalizing. Those of us who are concerned with young people must be clear-eyed about the present.[55]

Susan Hirschman had resigned from Macmillan in October 1974 with reason to assume that some tempting new opportunity would come her way before long. Events soon proved her right. Even as Macmillan underwent a wholesale retrenchment, William Morrow and Company, a general trade house owned by the educational publisher Scott, Foresman, found itself in a position to expand. Morrow's general trade department was known primarily for its steady output of celebrity biographies and bestselling adult fiction — though it also published anthropologist Margaret Mead. The company's juvenile trade division, staid and reliable Morrow Junior Books, was an institutional mainstay, the publisher of a broad range of nonfiction in the sciences and social sciences — and of bestselling children's novelist Beverly Cleary. At a time when houses that could afford to do so were diversifying their operation, Scott, Foresman had already expanded its juvenile program once, with the acquisition of Lothrop, Lee, and Shepard, an old firm that in recent years had concentrated on series nonfiction intended for school library use. In 1968 Lothrop became the second juvenile imprint within William Morrow.

Now Hirschman was being asked to create what, to the amusement of her friends, she called "the Third Division." She agreed to do so when it became clear that she would be free to rehire the key members of her Macmillan staff. Apart from that consideration, what made Morrow such a good home for her was the fact that the Morrow Junior and Lothrop lists had so little to do with the kinds of books that she herself excelled at publishing — most especially picture books for preschoolers and fantasy fiction.

Finding a suitable name for the new imprint proved a challenge. After rejecting out of hand the suggestion that she publish under her own name, Hirschman proceeded to consider, and then think better of, several names that reflected her personal tastes: "Drumlin Books" for a type of glacial rock formation that had always interested her; "Austen Books" for the author of *Pride and Prejudice.* Whatever the initial appeal of "Harbor Books for Boys and Girls," it sounded too much like "Harper Books" — as Hirschman in a sort of Freudian epiphany realized to her chagrin. A more satisfactory choice presented itself in the title of a lyrical picture book by Elizabeth Coatsworth, *Under the Green Willow,* which Hirschman had published at Macmillan. "Greenwillow" linked up nicely not only with Hirschman's own publishing past but also, given Coatsworth's long association with Louise Seaman Bechtel, with the history of the profession. In 1969, while still riding high at Macmillan, Hirschman had paid tribute to Bechtel by publishing *Books in Search of Children,* a collection of her speeches and essays; the volume opened with Bechtel's dedication: "For Elizabeth Coatsworth Beston, with loving gratitude for the special friendship that has brightened every year since college." With the advent of Greenwillow Books, Hirschman announced her commitment to uphold the legacy created by those two remarkable women.[56]

With the imprint name set, new contracts could at last be drawn up. The logo — adapted by fellow Macmillan ex-pat art director Ava Weiss from an illustration in the Coatsworth book by Janina Domanska — quickly followed. Along with Weiss, valiant Ada Shearon (whose employment prospects, as an older person nearing retirement age, had been far less certain than Hirschman's when the two women resigned as a matter of principle from Macmillan) joined Greenwillow as the new imprint's executive editor. Completing the senior staff a year later would be another Macmillan (and one-time Harper) editor, Elizabeth Shub. As for the all-important inaugural list, acquiring books proved to be much less of a problem than one might have thought. Macmillan, on record as having planned to cancel large numbers of the department's contracts, bowed to the new reality and released projects by several longtime Hirschman authors and artists, enabling them to continue to work with an editor to whom they felt deeply loyal. Hirschman's British publishing colleagues held off selling the North American rights to books on their lists so that Hirschman could have them when she was ready. As a consequence, the first seventeen Greenwillow titles, published in the fall of 1975, included works by an enviable array of established figures, including Ezra Jack Keats, Anita Lobel, Tana Hoban, Pat Hutchins, Mary Q. Steele, and Elizabeth Coatsworth. From the very beginning, Greenwillow exhibited all the ripeness and depth of a publishing imprint in its prime.

The Greenwillow example showed that with strong editorial vision and a supportive management, highly individualized styles of publishing could still thrive within a corporate structure. Meanwhile, other, more quixotic responses to the furious wave of corporate consolidation that had become such a defining feature of the New York publishing scene were proliferating in the form of small, independent shoestring ventures, many of them based in nontraditional publishing locales such as northern California, the Pacific Northwest, and Toronto.

In San Francisco, Harriet Rohmer, a single mother with a young child enrolled in a Head Start program in the city's less affluent, multi-ethnic Mission District, was startled to realize that more than one dozen different national cultures were represented in her son's small group. It disturbed Rohmer that, at story time, no picture books could be found that reflected the cultural backgrounds of the majority of the youngsters. She decided to try, on a small scale, to provide such materials for the children and others like them. Rohmer had trouble, at first, raising even a small amount of start-up money. Then a substantial grant came through from the federal government's Department of Health, Education, and Welfare, and in 1975 Rohmer was able to launch the Children's Book Press with the goal of publishing bilingual picture books that addressed the cultural needs of minority children and their families like those living in her midst. Enlisting writers and illustrators to make books about their own cultures (among the artists were a number of Mission District Latino muralists), Rohmer published a first list of ten bilingual picture books of distinctive design that quickly attracted the notice of both booksellers and librarians. When the first orders trickled in, she and her skeleton staff had, quite suddenly, to learn to cope with success on a scale that, however modest, was nonetheless well beyond what they had anticipated. A second grant allowed them to issue a second list. The company, while continuing to experiment with the types of books it offered, grew judiciously, gradually making a permanent place for itself in the publishing landscape.[57]

Dozens of other small or "alternative" presses — the latter term had become a badge of honor to many of these self-starters, who saw themselves as stalwart emissaries of the 1960s "counterculture" — carved out specialty niches of one kind or another, whether in the area of crafts, regional history and culture, or such issues as concern for the environment. The Feminist Press, founded in 1970 to work toward the "eliminat[ion of] sexual stereotypes in books and schools, providing instead a new (or neglected) literature with a broader vision of human potential," brought out *Tatterhood*, a collection of little-known folktales featuring female heroes.[58] The book went on to reach a large, appreciative readership, in part thanks to its selection by the Book-of-the-Month Club. Based in northern California, another small company inspired by feminist concerns, the Volcano Press, published *Period.*, a landmark guide to menstruation for preteens.[59] In these two instances and many others, the alternative presses expanded the subject matter and audience for children's books in ways that the more cautious larger houses were not likely to have done at the time. The big houses would later bring some of these experiments into the mainstream, whether by acquiring paperback rights to books first published in hardcover by an alternative press or simply by imitating innovative work for which the smaller presses had shown there was a market.[60]

With so much attention focused on the "new realism" in fiction for grade-schoolers and teens, it was logical to wonder why so little attention was being paid to the ultimate literature of realism, nonfiction. In an essay called "Where Do All the Prizes Go? The Case for Nonfiction," a veteran contributor to the genre, Milton Meltzer, held the industry to account for its failure to recognize the artistry required to create memorable works of biography, history, or science. Marshaling an embarrassment of damning statistics and naive quotations, Meltzer made a compelling case for the underrepresentation at medal time of books belonging to this wide-ranging and ill-defined category. He cited Jane Langton, a novelist and awards judge who had freely acknowledged to him that to offset their confusion and guilt in the matter, she and her fellow committee members had finally settled on a single nonfiction title to include on their list of five finalists for an unnamed major annual prize. The judges had taken their decision, she recalled for Meltzer, out of "sheer naked prejudice and personal bias in favor of fiction."[61] Not every deep-seated prejudice that librarians and publishers had to think hard about concerned the issues of race and ethnicity. An entire class of books, and the people who wrote and illustrated them, were being discriminated against as well.

Even more provocative that year was psychoanalyst Bruno Bettelheim's *The Uses of Enchantment: The Meaning and Importance of Fairy Tales*, an ambitious meditation on the therapeutic value of traditional tales in work with emotionally troubled children, and more generally on the salutary role played by storytelling in human culture. Although Bettelheim made only fleeting reference to modern-day children's literature, his book in one stroke elevated the subject of children's literature to the level of earnest cocktail party conversation.

The core of Bettelheim's analysis concerned his practice of employing folktales such as "Red Riding Hood" and "Hansel and Gretel" as a therapeutic device for divining the submerged distresses and fears of patients too young to articulate them in the more usual ways. Bettelheim impressed many readers with his assertion that far from being childish and trivial stories, fairy tales were incomparably powerful distillations of humankind's most basic interior dilemmas. As such, *The Uses of Enchantment* might have served as a resounding validation of the work of the publishers and librarians for children, who had long championed folklore as foundation works of modern children's literature — had it not been for the blistering attack Bettelheim unleashed, in his introduction, on contemporary children's books as contrasted with the favored stories of old. Bettelheim wrote: "The deep inner conflicts originating in our primitive drives and our violent emotions are all denied in much of modern children's literature, and so the child is not helped in coping with them."[62] It was a curious argument to make at a time when books at every age level, from Sendak's *In the Night Kitchen* to Cormier's *The Chocolate War*, were drawing fire from critics for exhibiting precisely the opposite tendency. As Paul Heins aptly observed in his *Horn Book* review of *The Uses of Enchantment:* "His intention of helping adults to become more fully aware of the importance of folk tales is admirable, but his dismissal of the rest of children's literature as 'shallow in substance' is unfortunate. If he had investigated the significant accomplishments of writing for children during the last century — especially books of fantasy — with as much care as he has given to folk tales, he might have avoided making a snap judgment about what he terms 'so-called children's literature.'"[63] For Heins in particular it must have come as salt on the wound when *The Uses of Enchantment* was awarded the 1977 National Book Award in "Contemporary Thought."

Ironically, Bettelheim's polemic served to legitimize the work of fantasy writers such as Madeleine L'Engle, Lloyd Alexander, and Susan Cooper, who had come of age in the shadow of "new realism," and it also gave a quasi-scientific basis for the maverick suspicion, held by some of the field's new literary scholars, that "Cinderella" and *Harriet the Spy* perhaps had far more in common than anyone had previously dared to imagine. Bettelheim's lofty pronouncements also served to further burnish the already considerable reputation of Maurice Sendak, whose intense, Dürer-esque illustrations for *The Juniper Tree*, a collection of Grimms' fairy tales published by Farrar, Straus and Giroux three years earlier, now came into crisper focus as the visualization of Bettelheim's insights into the psychologically penetrating nature of the tales.[64] Such in fact was the impact of Bettelheim's book, as it was variously interpreted or even misinterpreted by children's book publishers, that those concerned primarily with books for younger children became far more open than in the past to less sunny, more psychologically probing approaches to storytelling and art. The decade would draw to a fitting close with the publication of Chris Van Allsburg's haunting first picture book, *The Garden of Abdul Gasazi*.

In 1978 George M. Nicholson moved from Viking back to Dell to direct a business that had grown dramatically in the last five years. Much of the growth in paperback sales that had occurred in the mean time was attributable to changes in bookselling. The rapidly expanding chain bookstores, led by B. Dalton, Waldenbooks, and Barnes and Noble, had vast expanses of shelf space to fill and the need to freshen their inventory each month in hopes of luring customers back.[65] Teens were among those who felt most comfortable in the cavernous new stores: adult customers might chafe at the lack of sales help, but for teenagers eager to elude the intrusive supervision of grownups, the arrangement could seem ideal. For these younger shoppers, the chains offered another advantage over more traditional sources of reading matter. As Nicholson recalled: "The basic philosophy of those chains was, 'No chatting up at the checkout counter.' Kids could buy anything they wanted, no questions asked, whereas a librarian might say to them, 'That's too old for you. You shouldn't be reading that book.' There was no judgment at the chains. All they wanted was your cash."[66] For publishers, the challenge was now to capture as much of that cash as possible.

Among the aftershocks of the decade's rampant inflation had been a catastrophic decline in funding for public libraries nationwide, with the result that large numbers of children's librarians lost their jobs and untold numbers of young people thought better of entering a field in free fall. Looking back on the period, the New York Public Library's Marilyn Iarusso would lament her profession's "lost generation."[67]

To the extent that the disaster could be said to have had a bright side, it revealed itself with the appearance of a new wave — the first since the 1920s — of independent bookstores specializing in children's books. Many of the new stores were owned or staffed by entrepreneurial former librarians. The densest concentration of them was to be found at first in California. At their best, they offered a level of service that the chain stores could not hope to match and quirkier, more thoughtfully chosen inventories. Many also became stopgap community centers, filling some of the same social needs — a place to take one's preschooler for story hour, a place for parents to meet and exchange useful information — once served by the libraries. Like the alternative presses whose books they sometimes made a point of championing, the "independents" started with the disadvantages of a David venturing into a marketplace dominated by corporate Goliaths. In this regard, the presses were by far the better off of the two upstart groups: B. Dalton or Waldenbooks might decide, if only to burnish their public image, to promote the list of one or another alternative press, but the chains had little use for the independent stores except as test-marketing fodder: the success of an independent targeted its neighborhood or area as a potential new store site for the ever-expanding chains. In the meantime, however, the small shops increased in number, slowly at first, and then in a cascading effect of explosive growth, and basked in the glow of the local goodwill and modest sales they generated. In 1973 about a dozen such stores were in business nationwide, including four in California. By the end of the decade, the number had jumped to eighty; a decade later there would be four hundred.[68]

In 1973 New York City got its first new children's bookstore in decades in a Brooklyn Heights storefront operated by two cousins, Cynthia Herbert and Nancy Foutz, the latter of whom had kept her day job as a librarian at Gulf + Western Industries. Located on the borderline between two affluent residential neighborhoods, Child's Play benefited from some street traffic but did the lion's share of its business with local nursery schools and day care centers. In an interview with *Publishers Weekly*, the owners noted that although they had observed that "grandmotherly types" were "not interested in paperbacks," it seemed important to stock a good supply of the less costly books anyway. "With a very small investment we can keep on hand all the classics such as *Twenty Thousand Leagues Under the Sea* and *Jane Eyre* — books that are not asked for frequently but you need to keep, just in case."[69] The two women were always on the lookout to avoid carrying books that perpetuated offensive racial and gender stereotypes. They were convinced that far too many books were being published. Relatively inexperienced though they were, they spoke for all their colleagues both then and in the years to come when, reflecting on the financial risk entailed in opening their store, they acknowledged: "Just how risky it was we didn't know."

Still another reverberation of the lavish critical acclaim accorded *The Uses of Enchantment*, which had won both a National Book Award and a National Book Critics Circle Award, was the bolstering of the argument made by scholar and editor Francelia Butler and her followers for children's literature as a serious field of study in the humanities. Scholars from sundry other disciplines who had made holiday excursions into the field by writing occasional articles for *Children's Literature* now began to produce full-dress, book-length studies. Some even reconsidered their academic career paths and looked for ways to make children's literature their declared specialty. Among the more noteworthy new books was one by Roger Sale, a professor of English at the University of Washington who had been one of the first contributors to *Children's Literature*. Sale's *Fairy Tales and After: From Snow White to E. B. White* was a collection of essays that ranged widely from the Grimms' and Andersen's fairy tales to *The Wind in the Willows* and *Charlotte's Web*. Once again, as with *The Uses of Enchantment*, Paul Heins was quick to pounce on Sale's effort for betraying an "oblivious[ness] of the background, range, and extent of contemporary children's literature," not to say of the critics (including those, of course, who wrote for *The Horn Book*) who had come before him.[70] Sale had not, however, set out to produce a comprehensive survey but rather to write with critical perspective about the books he remembered from childhood. Yet it was true that in doing so he had shown an irritating tendency to sound like someone who had stumbled upon virgin territory, where no thoughtful grownup had trod before. As in a fairy tale in which events are doomed to repeat themselves, it seemed that each new critic who now came along to write about children's books believed that he or she was doing so for the first time.

More potent in its impact on the publishing world than any critical reconsideration of the classics, however, was the U.S. Supreme Court ruling that came down in January 1979 in the case of *Thor Power Tool Company v. Commissioner of Internal Revenue*. The *Thor* case would have an immediate and transformative effect on the children's book publishing industry — notwithstanding the astounding fact that it had nothing directly to do with the book business. Its import lay in the tax implications of the new regime it established for valuing a manufacturer's inventory. By dramatically curtailing their ability to write off the unsold inventory left over in their warehouses at the end of the year, publishing executives suddenly lost their strongest business argument for keeping in print backlist titles with lackluster sales. In the past, it had made a certain kind of sense to the publishers of children's books in particular, whose institutional customers typically reordered backlist books year after year as the older copies became outworn, to keep such books in stock for as long as possible — this apart from the bedrock tradition among publishers for children, amounting almost to a moral imperative, that worthy books deserved to remain available. Other categories of publishing had by then become more ruthless about dropping books that did not justify their continuance by maintaining a set level of sales each year. But for the children's book world, the ruling resulted in a rather abrupt and wholesale abandonment of a cherished ideal.

As the unseemly slashing of once-sacrosanct backlists began, a downward recalibration of the standard first printings for future books helped to off-set increasingly wary publishers' jitters. Assertions of faith in a quiet or quirky book's ultimate success no longer counted for nearly as much at meetings where backlist titles came up for review. Commenting on this shift in publishing culture, Susan Hirschman would remark years later that had *Goodnight Moon* been published in later times, it most likely would have gone out of print before "children had [had] a chance to claim it for their own."[71] As an all-too-perfect postscript to the *Thor* bolt from the blue, just weeks after the high court issued its ruling, the massive Putnam warehouse in East Rutherford, New Jersey, was flooded during a severe storm, and a substantial portion of the company's inventory destroyed. Reporting the news, an alternative press science fiction journal gamely advised its readers: "If any of you own any recent (1978) Putnam/Berkley SF hardbacks, they are now worth a fortune. A flood at Putnam's warehouse has destroyed their entire 1978 hardback SF [inventory]! It is unlikely they'll be reprinted in this form again."[72] As for the juvenile publishing world, if the act of God was a portent, what it foretold was the swift coming of the day when a children's book, however well reviewed and honored, could no longer "live" — quaint, old-fashioned word — on its merits alone.[73]

9

SUITS AND WIZARDS AT THE
MILLENNIUM'S GATE

"Never Have So Few Published So Many"

— EDWIN MCDOWELL, "Media Business" headline,
New York Times (September 19, 1988)

"Here's Harry! Behind the Fastest-Selling Book in History"

— Cover story headline, *Newsweek* (July 17, 2000)

THE ELECTION, IN NOVEMBER 1980, of Ronald Reagan as president of the United States cast a pall over the industry, portending tax cuts at the federal, state, and local levels that in turn were bound to result in reductions in government support for school and public libraries. The anticipated damage could not, moreover, be measured entirely in dollars and cents. As Dutton's juvenile publisher, Ann Durell, accurately forecast:

> The influence of the Moral Majority and the conservative climate in the country will also mean that there will be a more conservative approach to education, with emphasis on the fundamental skills and the use of textbooks rather than trade books. Conservatives tend to distrust the freedom that a wide spectrum of reading gives a child.[1]

In response to the Reaganauts' sanguine assertions that a combination of private giving and corporate largesse would somehow take up the slack created by decreases in federal funding for social programs and education, *Publishers Weekly* cautiously noted that it was "too early to tell whether reduced government funds will lower the profits from [book sales to public and school libraries] or whether gifts from the 'private sector' will ensure continuing institutional sales."[2] Having watched the tide go out on their industry only a decade earlier following the withdrawal by Congress of Great

Society program funding for school and public library book purchases, publishers had ample reason for skepticism.

An early casualty of the new conservative climate was the commitment of publishers to expand the range and number of children's books that addressed the needs and aspirations of the nation's African American community. Having not long ago made a public show of the lessons they had learned from the civil rights movement and of their intention to do their part to right past injustices, publishers now showed a striking readiness to retreat from that goal. Evidence of the changed attitude was not hard to find. With sixteen well-received books to her credit, the African American poet Eloise Greenfield reported having to struggle, for the first time in years, to find a publisher for her next book, *Alesia*. Beryl Benfield, president of the Council on Interracial Books, ruefully observed that many of the children's books her organization had been championing since the mid-1960s — all of them examples of books that presented "positive images" of black children — were no longer in print. As one editor, who chose not to be identified, bluntly said in response to complaints from the African American community: "You're only 20% of the population. How can I be concerned with you?"[3]

Other types of books suited the new era better. In July 1981, one industry observer noted the "bemuse[ment]" as well as gratification of publishers over a historic shift, first registered a year earlier, in the market: "Traditionally," wrote Jean F. Mercier in *Publishers Weekly*

> schools and libraries have been the main customers of the 2,500 to 3,000 children's titles issued annually. Recently, however, sales in bookstores directly to the public have been increasing, despite higher cover prices. "We expect that 60% of our books will be [sold] to the general buyer within the near future," one editor assured *PW* — a remarkable switch from the 20% to 30% that used to be sold to the public.[4]

Books for babies and toddlers, for which librarians of past generations had had little or no use, now became a priority with publishers eager to reach young book-buying parents at the earliest possible moment. Board books with pages printed on durable cardboard stock capable of withstanding the exploratory tugs and bites natural to toddlers proliferated, often in sets of four, and by the rack load. Whether knowingly or not, those publishers who contributed to the revitalization of the board-book genre built on the decades-old experiments of early childhood education experts, especially those of the Bank Street School. While the lion's share of the new "baby books" amounted to little more than flash cards with a binding and had a decidedly down-market flavor, some were the work of two gifted illustrators — an emerging American talent named Rosemary Wells and the already famous British artist Helen Oxenbury — who demonstrated the minimalist genre's unsuspected potential for character and plot development, humor, and emotion and for giving the very young a first taste of the pleasurable experience of books.

Wells for her part had not deliberately set out to resurrect a neglected genre. As her editor, Phyllis J. Fogelman, recalled:

> The first book that Rosemary both wrote and illustrated for Dial, *Unfortunately Harriet* (1972), was small in format. Her books got younger and younger and less offbeat at Dial. Finally, she came in with a dummy for *Max's First Word* (1979). It was obvious to me that it should be a board book. We had both bemoaned the fact that when our children were babies, no board books had been available that told a simple, satisfying story. I asked her to do three other little books about Max, and of course she did.

Publishing for the newly emerging retail market was not for the risk-averse. "To keep the price reasonable," Fogelman recalled, it was necessary to order a first printing of the Wells board books of thirty-five thousand each, "a much bigger print run than I had ever ordered up till then."[5]

Hoping to offset the risk with income derived from the sale of foreign rights, Fogelman exhibited the books at Bologna, where they caught the eye of an ebullient Englishman named Sebastian Walker, who was just then setting up shop in London as an independent publisher devoted entirely to children's picture books. Walker passed up the chance to acquire British rights to the Wells books but took away a set of samples to show his own star illustrator. Helen Oxenbury was intrigued by the challenge of working in the deceptively simple format. Oxenbury's first set of board books appeared in 1982 on Walker's second list and were quickly taken for foreign editions in the United States and elsewhere. The little books' sweeping success single-handedly lifted the young firm to profitability.[6] The episode showcased the speed with which trends in children's books, and even certain individual titles, could now have an almost immediate impact across national borders.

The new focus on books for children of the youngest ages (and their book-buying parents) extended up the developmental ladder a rung to picture books that more closely resembled traditional bedtime fare than board books yet were "younger" in concept and design than the old standbys, like *Make Way for Ducklings* and *Mike Mulligan and His Steam Shovel*. The latter had been created for children capable of lasting through a folktale or other fully developed story. At Greenwillow, Susan Hirschman and her small, devoted staff thrived as demand rose for this younger type of picture book, which had been among their specialties since their Macmillan days a decade earlier. A Greenwillow picture book was instantly recognizable as such even from across a room. Less showy than much of the competition, it was nonetheless graphically crisp and contemporary-looking, emotionally focused, and inviting to the touch. Hirschman, having known her share of betrayal at both Harper and Macmillan, demanded undivided loyalty from her Greenwillow artists, in return for which she committed herself to the advancement of their long-term careers to an extent that was becoming increasingly rare elsewhere. She said on more than one occasion that she "published authors, not books." By the mid-1990s, Hirschman was not only still bringing out new work each year by members of her remarkably cohesive stable of illustrators but also publishing the first books of some of their grown children.[7]

Such continuity, however, was hardly the norm. At the opposite extreme from Hirschman's boutique-like up-market domain, the industry's largest single entity as measured in sales, the Western Publishing Company, was stumbling badly. The sole owner since the mid-1960s of the lucrative Golden Books franchise, Western struggled to regain its past glory in a vastly changed world in which the near-universal embrace of paperback publishing had rendered Golden's low-priced illustrated books less special than they had been for earlier generations. By 1980, the original group of visionary publisher-entrepreneurs — Albert Leventhal, Georges Duplaix, and Lucille Ogle, who had engineered the triumph of the Golden Books experiment — had all left the scene. Even before the company passed (for only a brief time, as it turned out) into the hands of the world's largest toy maker, Mattel, bureaucratization had begun to overwhelm the company's creativity, a problem exacerbated by the two-pronged organization of the company's top management, in offices located in New York and Racine.[8] In 1984, after an uneasy four-year relationship, Mattel sold Western to a group of private investors headed by Manhattan real estate executive Richard A. Bernstein, who took the company public two years later. Bernstein started with a top-notch editorial staff but undercut its authority both by hiring sales and marketing executives from other industries who lacked an understanding of the book trade and, on at least one occasion, by unwittingly generating adverse publicity through an ill-considered remark: "We're really not publishers," Bernstein told the *Wall Street Journal.* "We do a tonnage business."[9] The comment provided the children's book world's haughtier critics with all the ammunition they needed and severely hampered the efforts of Western's editors to revitalize and upgrade the reputation of their list, which many bookstores still refused to carry. Meanwhile, Golden's heavy dependence for its bread-and-butter income on licensed-character books was for the first time proving to be less than reliable. Stiff competition from Random House, the nation's leading publisher of general interest trade books, had begun to erode Western's longtime supremacy in this arena, which dated back to the company's decades-old exclusive licensing agreement with Disney and hand-in-glove relationship with Dell. Under its new chairman, Michael D. Eisner, Disney chose for the first time in half a century to loosen its ties to Western by opening its wide array of print licenses to competitive bidding. The decision epitomized the atomization of the publishing industry as a whole: long-standing relationships of all sorts increasingly stood for less, and a speculative, almost casino-like atmosphere infiltrated the once-gentlemanly culture of publishing. It would seem not so much amusing as apt that when the publishing world converged in 1990 for the annual American Booksellers Association convention, the meeting site was not New York or Boston or Chicago, but Las Vegas.

As the children of the baby boom came of age, entered the workforce, and started families of their own, some became keen to reflect on their childhood years as history and to look more closely at the books they had grown up on as literature and art. In the fall of 1980, Harry N. Abrams, the leading American publisher of art books, departed from the firm's familiar pattern of celebrating the work of museum-certified masters of the history of art to publish *The Art of Maurice Sendak,* a full-dress "coffee table" monograph on the preeminent contemporary practitioner of the art of children's book illustration. The author, Selma G. Lanes, was a critic of proven discernment, and the commentary she provided on the artist's work was wide-ranging and perceptive. Readers of the new volume soon realized, however, that access to the great man had come at a price. While Lanes's book offered fresh insights aplenty and a lavish sampling of art in reproduction, the tone of the discussion at times sounded cozily protective. There was something not quite grownup about the whole affair.

Still, there was no denying the power and virtuosity of the artwork put on view, or the claim that Sendak had long since taken his place in the Romantic visionary tradition that extended back to William Blake, Caspar David Friedrich, Otto Runge, and, more recently, Randall Jarrell, with whom Sendak had twice collaborated on books. The litany of Sendak influences and affinities hardly stopped there but rather grew in Lanes's reckoning to include not only pivotal figures in the history of illustration (Rowlandson, Lear, Tenniel, Caldecott, de Brunhoff) but also a broad swath of the "greats" of art history, from Rembrandt and Dürer to Picasso and Chagall. Equally telling was the documentation of Sendak's lifelong allegiance to pulp and celluloid pop-cultural influences — among them the raucous comic-strip art of Winsor McKay and the Big Little Books and Disney animated cartoons of the 1930s and 1940s — which earlier generations of critics had dismissed out of hand as unworthy of children and of the name of art. It was, of course, Sendak's reputation as one of the key contributors to the convergence of "high" and "low" culture that had sealed the case for art-book treatment in the first place. The *Wall Street Journal* may have proclaimed him the "Picasso of children's books," but Sendak was just as likely the field's Andy Warhol.[10]

Abrams for its part had spared no expense, encasing the massive volume in a modish, clear acetate dust jacket through which one of the rumpus scenes of *Where the Wild Things Are* could be limned. The first printing also featured an elaborate paper-engineered version of a mechanical wooden toy that Sendak and his brother Jack had cobbled together as poor but enterprising children in Depression-era Brooklyn, as well as a tipped-in facsimile of the artist's speculative first dummy, dating from 1955, for a picture book tentatively named "Where the Wild Horses Are."

The Art of Maurice Sendak could hardly have been better timed. As institutional budgets for children's books continued to decline, pop-up nov-

elties and other "toy books" aimed squarely at the retail trade were proliferating. As documented by Lanes, Sendak's devotion to kitsch and camp
culture seemed to confer the artist's imprimatur on the trend as a whole.

In a related development, and as a hedge against a further unraveling
of the institutional market, publishers spoke more approvingly than ever of
children's books with a potential crossover appeal for adults.[11] Houghton
Mifflin's Walter Lorraine, whose training at the Rhode Island School of Design had been in typography and graphic design, had emerged during the
1970s as an editor with an uncanny knack for publishing visual books that
had strong appeal for both young readers and adults. It was Lorraine who,
on seeing a workmanlike dummy by a recent RISD graduate named David
Macaulay, had sensed that the young artist was ready to do far better work
about a subject that interested him more. When pressed by Lorraine about
what subject that might be, David Macaulay had replied, "Cathedrals."
With the editor's encouragement, *Cathedral*, the first of Macaulay's oversized illustrated books about monumental manmade structures, was born.
Booksellers at first had as hard a time categorizing Macaulay's work — was
it fiction or not fiction? about architecture or history? for children or for
adults? — as they did shelving the tall, slender volume. *Cathedral* found its
audience anyway, and by the 1980s Macaulay's many books in the same vein
were seen as exemplary crossover material.[12]

So too were the darkly droll, surrealistic picture books of another
Rhode Island School of Design graduate and Lorraine discovery, Chris
Van Allsburg. Van Allsburg's swift rise to prominence confirmed Maurice
Sendak's genre-altering impact on a younger generation of illustrators.
Meanwhile, Sendak's own canonization by Abrams seemed at last to settle
the question of whether the cream, at least, of children's book illustrators
merited the undiluted attention of art critics, collectors, and historians.

Sendak, who as a young artist had left Brooklyn to make his reputation in Greenwich Village, now lived in relative seclusion in a sprawling old
house in the Connecticut woods. There, in June 1979, after a five-year struggle, he had completed the artwork for a picture book titled *Outside Over
There*. Sendak had hesitated for weeks about delivering the finished art to
Harper.[13] Before doing so, he made a pilgrimage to nearby Bridgewater to
show his new paintings to Ursula Nordstrom. Nordstrom wept at the sight
of the ravishing watercolors. Her tears that day would be her last editorial
comment to him, and *Outside Over There* the last book published under
her imprint.

When Sendak's latest picture book saw the light of day in the spring of 1981, the predictable ballyhoo greeted its arrival. Two details of its promotion caught the attention of industry insiders. As if to underscore the point that neither the artist himself nor a work of the caliber of *Outside Over There* needed any sort of puffery, both the front and back dust-jacket flaps of the book had been left completely free of copy and embellishment. Equally unusual, Harper presented Sendak's book on both its adult and junior lists. "I had waited a long time to be taken out of kiddy-book land," Sendak remarked somewhat ruefully not long afterward, "and allowed to join the artists of America."[14]

Notwithstanding this and a few other late-career high notes, Nordstrom, who was then in her early seventies, had much to feel bittersweet about. Decades of devoted, brilliant work for Harper had left her in shockingly straitened financial circumstances. It was doubtless partly with Nordstrom in mind that one of her authors, John Donovan, now executive director of the Children's Book Council, expressed his bewilderment and anger at the continued resistance in the publishing industry to giving talented, productive women their due. Writing in 1985, Donovan observed: "Perhaps there are now more women not quite getting to the top than there were more than a decade ago. That's a kind of progress, I guess. . . . [But] that the women who work in children's books — those who have made fortunes for publishers — have not ended up running some of those same companies is an astonishment."[15] Of Nordstrom's contemporaries, only Margaret K. McElderry remained at her job.

Other books joined *The Art of Maurice Sendak* on the growing shelf of critical reflections. In *Pipers at the Gates of Dawn*, Jonathan Cott presented a series of interviews with notable figures in the children's book firmament — Maurice Sendak (of course), Laurent de Brunhoff, Theodor Geisel, William Steig, Iona and Peter Opie, P. L. Travers, Astrid Lindgren, and Chinua Achebe. Cott's project had the feel of an Aquarian's quest for spiritual enlightenment, a sort of *Meetings with Remarkable Men* for college-educated baby boomers for whom sustained contact with one's "inner child" had come to seem one of life's worthiest goals. Notwithstanding what some critics took to be Cott's stifling self-absorption (or perhaps, for the cohort that would come to be known as the "Me Generation," because of it), the book struck a chord with readers, many of whom knew the writer's work from the pages of *Rolling Stone*, and it became a bestseller. The author had in fact made a tantalizing point: that the "counterculture" had deep roots in a "counterliterature" that had the curious distinction of being both everywhere — on the bookshelves in millions of families' homes — and nowhere — absent from nearly all serious considerations of literature. Had the children's books of the 1940s, 1950s, and 1960s done their part to inspire the student rebellions and cultural reevaluations of the years of youth rebellion? The popular success of Cott's book strongly suggested that they had.

Maurice Sendak's preeminent status in the field had long since freed him of the obligation to prepare his art for the printer by the tedious "preseparation" process that had been the norm for American illustrators for decades. Moreover, to make it more convenient for him to oversee the reproduction of his work on press, his books continued to be printed in Manhattan, long after much of the manufacturing business had shifted to less expensive printing firms in New Jersey and western Massachusetts. Then, in the early 1980s, two important developments — one legislative, the other technological — dramatically altered the economics of color printing, with immediate consequences not only for the publishers of picture books but also for artists less favored than the field's few established masters.

On the legal front, Congress in 1982 reversed a long-standing protectionist clause in the copyright law that had left American publishers with the untenable option of forfeiting their own and their author's copyright on any book they printed abroad. The lifting of this burdensome restriction allowed publishers to take their full-color printing jobs to companies in Asia, which charged substantially less for high-quality work than their American competitors. Going "on press" to oversee the printing of a book now became a rare luxury for the art director or production manager of a house, let alone for the illustrator. But the quality of color reproduction being achieved by printing houses in Hong Kong, Singapore, and elsewhere was such that the new arrangement had few detractors.[16] Greenwillow's art director, Ava Weiss, who now traveled to Asia twice a year, estimated that printing in Asia resulted on average in a hefty 20 percent saving.[17]

At the same time, advances in laser scanning technology rendered obsolete the difficult and time-consuming preseparation process for preparing color art for the printer. For all but the handful of illustrators who actually enjoyed preseparating their art, the news was a godsend. Color drum scanners made it possible for printers to create, at relatively low cost and with a high degree of accuracy, the series of plates needed for applying each of the four standard inks used in color reproduction. This meant in turn that illustrators were now free to work in a subtler palette and a broader, more finely nuanced range of styles. It also meant that, to the extent that cost had been a barrier in the past, beginning illustrators would no longer have to prove themselves by illustrating their first few books in black and white before being entrusted by the publisher with the luxury of "full color." Publishers seized upon the new technology to spur the creation of a new generation of picture books whose richly hued covers would be capable — especially if displayed face-out — of vying for attention on bookstore shelves with the brightness and allure of posters. To maximize the effect, the trim sizes of picture books — an issue once dealt with as a matter of aesthetics balanced against cost — began to increase, occasionally even to outlandish proportions. In an indication of the continuing erosion of editorial authority relative to that of the sales and marketing departments within the larger houses, it often hardly seemed to matter whether the larger format in a given case was the most appropriate one from a book-making standpoint. Picture books were becoming point-of-purchase advertisements for themselves.

The new circumstances favored a different breed of artists: those who arrived on the scene more or less fully formed, at least in terms of their technical facility. Gone were the days when one's first few books, rendered in black and white or perhaps in the limited palette of three colors, were regarded as an apprenticeship to which only the most modest commercial expectations were attached.[18] The largely self-taught Maurice Sendak had started his career in this way. As he observed the disappearance, both at Harper and elsewhere, of the workshop conditions under which Ursula Nordstrom had nurtured him, Sendak began to comment in interviews on the likelihood that had he attempted to enter the field thirty or more years later than he had, he might well have failed to make his mark.

Accustomed to regarding themselves as proud members of the technological rear guard, publishers (more than a few of whom held on to their manual typewriters long after desktop computers became the norm) were pleasantly surprised to find that new technologies and new media — as well as some that were no longer quite so new — might hold much good in store for their embattled world of books. In July 1983, the Public Broadcasting System aired the first in a new series of fifteen half-hour-long programs for children and their parents called *Reading Rainbow*. Timed to serve as a boon to stay-at-home mothers during the long months of summer vacation, each installment of the new show spotlighted a small selection of picture books through a blend of guest celebrity readings, animated segments, spots filmed "on location," and other features aimed at capturing the widest possible audience. There was even a segment during which on-camera child "critics" touted their favorite books to their peers. The picture books selected for full-dress treatment were often not the obvious commercial choices but rather those that happened to appeal most strongly to Dr. Twila Liggett, the program's executive producer (and a former schoolteacher), and her staff. Among the titles highlighted during the first season were a Kafkaesque slapstick comedy called *Louis the Fish* by the up-and-coming collaboration team of writer Arthur Yorinks and illustrator Richard Egielski and, from Bradbury Press (the maverick publisher that had introduced older readers to the provocative work of Judy Blume), Amy Schwartz's *Bea and Mister Jones*, with a winking commentary on the ups and downs of both kindergarten life and the corporate rat race. Publishers and wholesalers soon noticed that sales of the featured books jumped dramatically, on a consistent basis, as a direct result of exposure on the show. There were wrinkles to be ironed out, of course. Some independent booksellers had trouble at first coping with the sudden increase in demand, while publishers were sometimes caught short of inventory just as orders for a title surged. With the B. Dalton bookstore chain as the underwriter of the cost of broadcast transmission to local PBS stations nationwide, independents had cause to wonder whether they were not starting from a disadvantage when placing rush orders for featured books for which the publisher's inventory was low. Notwithstanding these problems, many in the children's book industry, after decades of warily eyeing the medium, now saw as realistic the possibility that television might indeed become a driving force not just for book sales but also for the cause of literacy.[19]

Along with the market shift toward retail had come a new climate of unpredictability for publishers and booksellers alike. As the annual number of juveniles dipped briefly in mid-decade — down from 1980 by as much as one-third, for a total of about two thousand titles in 1984 — the trend toward publishing what Jean F. Mercier called "dismissable books," issued "only with hopes of quick profits," was gaining ground. The roster of dubious offerings included "floods" of paperback romances for teens, assorted movie tie-ins, "so-so toy books," and formulaic "pick-your-own-plot items," among others.[20] The last reference was to Bantam Books for Young Readers' overwhelmingly successful "Choose Your Own Adventure" series, narrative page-turners with the novel element of multiple-choice endings, and to the imitations these books had spawned. By 1985, Bantam's bestselling juvenile series (which was then in its sixth year) had become so popular that the house had taken to issuing two new book-length installments every month. On the strength of that series' outsize performance, and in tandem with that of Francine Pascal's hugely popular "Sweet Valley High" teen romance series, Bantam doubled its juvenile business from 5 to 10 percent of total sales in the first half of the 1980s. Even more striking than the statistics was the complete overhaul the company acknowledged in its publishing philosophy. Bantam now considered children and teens, not their parents, its primary market.[21]

For Americans forced by circumstances in recent decades to rely on their local libraries, five-and-dime stores, and supermarkets as their primary sources of children's reading matter, it had never been easier to buy the latest award-winning books or to create an impressive home library for one's child. By 1983, the United States was home to approximately one hundred children's-only bookstores, up from only a dozen such stores a decade earlier. About three-quarters of the stores belonged to former librarians and teachers, many of whom had lost their jobs in the recession of the previous decade.[22] In 1985, as the trend continued to gain momentum, the owners of the independent stores formed the Association of Booksellers for Children (ABC) with the goal of sharing information, offering each other moral support, and, to the extent possible, countering the encroachment on their business by the chains. "Hand-selling" — the time-honored practice of personally recommending a book about which the bookseller felt strongly (regardless of whether it was one of the "lead" titles that its publisher had chosen for special treatment) — became a hallmark of the individualized service that customers came to expect from the stand-alone stores.

The independents gave their stores jaunty "literary" monikers — Toad Hall (Austin, Texas), the Red Balloon (St. Paul, Minnesota), the White Rabbit (La Jolla, California), the Cheshire Cat (Washington, D.C.), Eeyore's (New York City) — that underscored their owners' knowledge and love of the literature. Author and illustrator book signings became regular occurrences, as did story hours, holiday parties, and other promotional events aimed at building customer loyalty. The booksellers reached out as well to teachers, many of whom stocked their classrooms with the latest children's books at their own expense in an effort to mitigate the impact of government cutbacks on school and library funding.[23] In 1986 there were at least fifty independent children's booksellers in northern California alone. Like the school of little fishes memorialized in Leo Lionni's picture-book fable *Swimmy*, the independents banded together in a spirit of cooperation as their best chance for survival in an environment increasingly dominated by a few giants given to predatory behavior.[24]

The intensity of their concern was palpable, and for good reason. While the practice of opening a new chain branch store within blocks of a successful independent store was perfectly legal — and probably inevitable given the broadly based national trend toward "big-box" retail stores of all kinds — the consequences for both the reading public and the publishing industry were far more complex than was immediately apparent.

A survey conducted in 1981 with thirty-three independent children's booksellers from around the United States found that such stores rarely needed to make significant "returns" — the cumbersome practice of sending back quantities of unsold front-list books to the publisher, typically within a few months of their initial release, for a full refund. The independents, it seemed, often knew their customers well enough to gauge, with a high degree of accuracy, what they could and could not sell to them.[25] In contrast, the chains took a more scattershot approach, ordering substantial quantities of books, risk-free, in the expectation that some titles would find a readership and others would not. The typical size of these initial orders was large enough to impel publishers assiduously to court the chains' business and to pay close attention to the chain buyers' opinions and tastes. Fearful of being left behind in the burgeoning, highly competitive retail market, publishers saw no alternative but to take what they realized was an increasingly high-stakes gamble. With the initial "announced" sales figures for a book no longer assured of being anywhere close to the final ones, a major new element of flux thus entered into the publishers' already fragile calculus, causing a traditionally cautious industry to grow ever more so.

As publishers sought new ways to limit the risk, the larger houses quietly initiated the practice of inviting buyers from the major chains to attend internal meetings at which book projects then under consideration by the house were discussed. The practice inevitably served further to weaken editorial authority within a house, as the buyers' reactions now became an important, if not determining, factor in its decision for or against proceeding with a title. As a book project entered the design stage, the chain buyers might also be consulted about — and were sometimes even granted veto power over — the cover design. In this way, the largest booksellers assumed an informal yet significant role in the editorial process, a development whose closest historical parallel was to be found in the dominant influence during the decades preceding World War II of the small coterie of librarian critics led by Anne Carroll Moore. The major difference between these two examples lay, of course, in the librarians' scrupulous detachment from market considerations. In contrast, the logic of the new situation pointed to the likelihood that the largest booksellers would eventually seek to further limit the influence of publishers, as the market's middlemen, by becoming publishers themselves. By the early 1980s, that is precisely what Barnes and Noble had done.

In the mid-1980s, as the structure of the book publishing industry continued to morph and reconfigure itself, publishing executives were also beginning to ponder the ramifications of computer technology, both for the customers they served and for their own operations.[26] One of the first uses to which computers were put within the industry was for setting up daily, store-by-store inventory control for the big chains — a more accurate and timely accounting by far of the commercial fate of the tens of thousands of individual titles published each year than had ever before been achieved. One consequence of the innovation was that it gave the chains a more powerful tool with which to determine which books to return to the publisher after a disappointing initial sale. Unfortunately for the publishers, no comparable program for deciding what books to publish came along to balance out the retailers' newfound precision, nor did any such program seem likely to appear anytime soon. The predictable result was yet another shift toward caution in editorial decision-making.

On the more positive side of the advent of the bookstore chains, parents who found it intimidating to enter a traditional bookstore often welcomed the high degree of anonymity afforded by the larger, less heavily staffed chain stores. Displays of Caldecott- and Newbery-winning titles held out the promise of a fail-safe choice to those who roamed the shelves with no firm idea of what their child might benefit from reading. Discounts given on selected popular titles served as another powerful incentive to shop at the chains. Parents unsure about what their children should read naturally preferred paying less for the experiment.

Publishers — and the occasional enterprising author — meanwhile searched for effective new ways to promote their books. Theodor Geisel, an advertising artist before he gained fame in the late 1930s as Dr. Seuss, had perhaps been the first modern picture-book artist to fully grasp the marketing concept later termed "branding." During the late 1950s, Geisel had adapted his best-known character, the Cat in the Hat, as a logo not only for his own early reader titles but also for those he commissioned from others as publisher of the Beginner Books imprint. Such was the Seuss books' sales appeal that booksellers had been more than willing to go along with the publisher's scheme to display them on separate shelves. Three decades later, the "look" and format of the Seuss books continued to reinforce the desired impression of their iconic status — just as the uniform design of Little Golden Books had done for that popular line, from the war years onward. By the 1980s, another former advertising artist named Eric Carle was busy applying the same branding principles to a steady output of picture books. Carle typically incorporated some novelty feature as well, a practice that, by associating the book as much with the realm of toys as with that of literature and art, gave parents a persuasive, double-barreled rationale for making a purchase.

Old-fashioned series books — the successors to the pulp fiction published decades earlier by the Stratemeyer Syndicate — also worked especially well in the big new bookstores, where entire ranges of shelves could be dedicated to them in the expectation that young people eager for the latest installments of their favorites would return time and again to satisfy their craving. The frequency with which new titles were added to the most popular series (monthly releases were common) blurred the distinction between series books and magazines. Whatever one chose to call the cheaply printed, easily digested chapter books, the trend fed on itself. Ann M. Martin's "Baby-Sitters Club" books, introduced in August 1986 by Scholastic, won so many loyal preteen girl fans, and proved to be so lucrative for their author, that within four years' time a charitable foundation was spun off from the profits.[27] In 1989 R. L. Stine's "Fear Street" horror fiction series for teens made its first appearance, also published by Scholastic, to be followed in 1995 by the "Goosebumps" books for preteens. The latter series became such a factor in Scholastic's overall business that when sales of the books dipped precipitously in 1997 after a history-making run of popularity, the company's stock price plunged on the news.[28]

By the mid-1980s, Macmillan, the dominant juvenile publisher during the 1920s, was once again the industry behemoth. In 1983 the company acquired the Bradbury Press. A year later — the same year Macmillan acquired the whole of the Scribner Book Companies, reducing that firm, one of the nation's oldest publishers, to a subsidiary in a deal that took effect in June 1984 — Macmillan added Four Winds Press, the trade imprint of Scholastic, to its quiver. The Scribner announcement had come with the standard assurances that Scribner's editorial independence would be scrupulously preserved. As the *New York Times* noted, however, recent history had been mixed on this count. While Knopf had been allowed to operate unfettered by its acquiring company, Random House, the once-independent J. P. Lippincott Company virtually disappeared as a trade publisher on being absorbed by Harper & Row.[29] With the Scribner purchase, Macmillan's juvenile department thus annexed three more distinctive lists — Margaret K. McElderry, Atheneum, and Scribner — all of which had been joined since 1976 following the merger of the latter two imprints' parent companies. McElderry herself, the doyenne of the field, and Atheneum's Jean Karl, also something of a legend, would continue to work down the hall from one another, but now in the company of many others.

Simon & Schuster, a subsidiary since 1975 of Gulf + Western, now entered a frenzied period of expansion of its own, acquiring in 1984 alone a total of sixty companies, including Prentice-Hall, a major educational publishing house with a midsized children's trade list.[30] Meanwhile, the company's own juvenile division teetered — literally, in the upper reaches of a windswept Columbus Circle office tower that would later be found to be structurally unsound — as, decades after its brash, brilliant early period as the co-originator of Little Golden Books, it struggled to refashion its editorial identity. In 1985 Holiday House celebrated its fiftieth anniversary as an independent firm led by only its second owner in all that time, John and Kate Briggs, the latter of whom presided over the company's marketing efforts.[31] Such counterexamples to the overwhelming trend toward consolidation were, however, increasingly rare. Before the decade was out, every major American house would have changed hands at least once, and an industry survey conducted by the staff of *Books in Print* would find that "American book publishing figures resemble statistics showing land ownership patterns in many third world countries. Two percent of the nation's publishers are responsible for 75 percent of the titles, and the top 30 percent are responsible for 99 percent."[32]

In January 1985, speakers at the tenth annual meeting of the Educational Paperback Association, a group comprising sixty publishers and wholesalers, gathered in New York to survey major changes in publishing for the youngest readers, "from the perspective of educators and parents as well as publishers." Reporting on the event, a journalist noted that

> while it's not unusual for parents to want to foster a love for reading in their children, these new parents are remarkable in that this concern can sometimes border on what one panelist termed an "obsession" with early educational attainment. Two panelists, only half-jokingly, mentioned pregnant women who had asked them to recommend books that they could read to their children *in utero*.[33]

One reason for the anxiety felt by middle-class parents about their children's reading skills had to do with their own rising social and economic expectations as members of the nation's best-educated generation in history. Parents who had begun to reap the material rewards of a "good" education now wished to make certain, in an increasingly competitive economic environment in which both the father and mother now often had to work full-time to maintain their lifestyle, that their own children would do at least as well. The American dream had rarely felt so perishable. Those who had studied child psychology and group dynamics in college now wondered how such theories applied to the upbringing of their own sons and daughters. The joke around the neighborhood sandbox was that it was never too early to start preparing one's child for admission to Harvard. No children's books mirrored the parental mood more clearly than did Jill Krementz's bestselling series of photographic essays about precocious high achievers, starting with *A Very Young Ballerina*.[34]

Other social factors contributed to the near-crisis mentality. Because more middle-class mothers than in recent memory now worked outside the home, leaving a substantial portion of daytime child care to others, a new sense of urgency attached itself to the task of choosing the "right" books and recreational experiences for their youngsters, to say nothing of the selection (when this was an option) of the best possible schools, often starting from when the child was two or three. Parents with competing claims on their attention spoke fervently of the "quality time" they aspired to share with their children, a high-stakes proposition complicated, when reading was the activity of choice, by the sheer number of new children's books flooding the market and the limited information available for use in evaluating them.[35] In making their book selections, many parents turned hopefully to the roster of Caldecott and Newbery Medal winners. Some parents even paid their children to read these and other "classics."

In the face of all this parental confusion and concern, a Massachusetts journalist and artist named Jim Trelease recognized both a need and an opportunity. As a part-time volunteer in the Springfield public schools, Trelease had observed that many of the children he met considered reading a chore and that those who enjoyed books were most often the ones whose parents or teachers read aloud to them. Trelease's father had taken the time to read to him as a boy, and he continued the tradition with his own two children. Now the journalist began to wonder if he had stumbled onto an important discovery. Were children who were read to on a regular basis more likely than others to become lifelong readers? On finding a substantial body of supporting research in the educational literature, Trelease decided to make it his mission to popularize the notion. In 1982 (three years after the author's self-published version), Penguin published Trelease's *Read-Aloud Handbook*. The stout paperback guide — which offered advice and inspiration to parents and capsule reviews of hundreds of children's books — became a *New York Times* bestseller after "Dear Abby" praised the author's efforts in a February 1983 column. The following year, having proven himself to be a compelling motivational speaker (as well as something of a super-salesman), Trelease quit his job and embarked on a full-time crusade, hosting workshops and delivering exhortatory speeches to parents, booksellers, teachers, and community groups around the country. Always the message was the same: to turn children into readers, adults needed to make time in their busy day to read to and with the children closest to them.[36]

As reading children's books aloud became de rigueur in more and more American households, more people than ever, it seemed, also dreamed of creating the books themselves. In August 1984, at Santa Monica's Miramar Hotel, members of the Society of Children's Book Writers met for their tenth annual national conference amid signs that their rapidly expanding organization had entered a new, more grownup phase. Membership was up from 50 in the Society's first year to over 2,500, with more than thirty regional chapters in all parts of the continental United States and Canada.[37] At earlier, smaller meetings, the overwhelming majority of attendees had been hopefuls at publishing: a predictable mix of aspiring writers, librarians and teachers with a backlog of storytelling experience, and individuals with a new-age or therapy-driven desire to "reconnect" with their "inner child." What better way to realize that goal than to write the next *Goodnight Moon* or *Alice's Adventures in Wonderland* and just possibly strike it rich in the process? The conviction casually entered the lore of the new baby boom generation of high-achieving, book-minded parents that writing for children was somehow easier than writing for people one's own age. It was a myth well suited to a society increasingly preoccupied with celebrity culture: at least one route to instant fame lay open to all.

By 1984, however, the Society was already well on its way to becoming an organization more closely resembling a professional guild. Of the 220 paid registrants who had traveled to Los Angeles from all parts of the United States (all but 20 of them women) for the four-day-long event, not quite half had at least one publication to their credit.[38] As always the convention schedule was jam-packed with general sessions featuring stars of the profession, interlaced with smaller workshops and time for networking. Notwithstanding the speakers' occasional orphic pronouncements — "Avoid insects as main characters" was one that Eric Carle, for one, had certainly done well to ignore — the conference left participants with the confidence that the time was indeed right for writers with talent to pursue a beguiling dream that might one day also provide a good living. As sales of children's books doubled between 1986 and 1990 to cross the $1 billion mark for the first time ever, such hopes were hardly unwarranted.

John Steptoe, the African American picture-book artist who in 1969 had enjoyed a spectacular rise to prominence as the teenage creator of *Stevie*, had suffered for the next two decades from the suspicion that the magnitude of his success owed as much to the submerged racism of tokenism as it did to a legitimate regard for his talent. Steptoe died in 1989, just as the renewed concern of educators and librarians, spurred by a steady expansion of the African American middle class and of America's Asian and Spanish-speaking populations, made multiculturalism an issue — and a buzzword — that publishers for children could once again ill afford to ignore.[39]

In practice, the term referred almost exclusively to books about African American heritage. The Coretta Scott King Awards for the writing and illustration of books for young people, presented at the annual American Library Association convention at a ceremony separate from the one devoted to the Caldecott and Newbery Medals, provided a rallying point for those within the publishing and library communities who were determined not to allow past progress to fall by the wayside, as it had seemed, only a few years earlier, in danger of doing.[40] (One year an electrical failure and partial collapse of the ceiling during the King Awards ceremony was half jokingly taken by some as a reminder of the fragile nature of the effort.) At the Dial Press, Phyllis Fogelman, a protégée of Ursula Nordstrom, championed the work of illustrators Jerry Pinkney, Tom Feelings, and Diane and Leo Dillon and of the writers Julius Lester, Mildred Taylor, and others. In doing so, Fogelman for a time found herself in a distinct minority.

During the fallow period of mainstream publisher disengagement from social concerns, which coincided more or less precisely with the Reagan years, alternative presses with modest resources but a strong grass-roots commitment continued to step up to fill the void. Founded in 1988, Just Us Books of Orange, New Jersey, was one such independent, shoestring venture. Cofounder Wade Hudson came to publishing with public relations experience, while his wife and partner was a graphic designer with a background in textbook work. The Hudsons — at first with no longer-term plans in mind — achieved a credible one-shot success with their first self-published book, Cheryl Willis Hudson's *Afro-Bets ABC Book*, a project they had been unable to place elsewhere. Then came the decision to go into business, and the selection of a company name that good-naturedly summed up the unlikelihood of it all. Just Us proved to be one of the alternative presses' success stories. Within three years, the company had more than 360,000 books in print and annual revenues of $1.2 million.[41] As pressure mounted on the larger houses to address the issue of cultural diversity, Wade Hudson found himself much in demand as a consultant in the once-unbreachable precincts of corporate publishing.[42]

The Hudsons soon had company. Glenn Thompson was an African American expatriate who, while living in London during the 1970s, had cofounded Writers & Readers Publishing Cooperative as a publisher of books aimed at promoting cultural literacy among ordinary working people. In 1986 he had moved to New York and opened up shop in the city. Two years later, Thompson launched a juvenile imprint, Black Butterfly Children's Books, with the publication of *Nathaniel Talking*, a poetry collection written by Eloise Greenfield and illustrated by Jan Spivey Gilchrist. At awards time, the press's first effort did not go unnoticed. *Nathaniel Talking* received both a Coretta Scott King Award for its illustrations and a Coretta Scott King Honor for its text. Black Butterfly published several subsequent collaborations by Greenfield and Gilchrist, as well as work by Tom Feelings.[43] Then, in 1992, in response to the appearance of this new wave of worthy books on African American themes, three African American mothers, including the writer Toni Trent Parker, founded Black Books Galore! as a nonprofit organization dedicated to the books' promotion and distribution.

A broader definition of multiculturalism came into view when, in the spring of 1993, Philip Lee and Thomas Low, two Chinese Americans living in New York, announced their first list as partners in a small house devoted to publishing picture books inspired by a wide array of American society's underserved ethnic and racial minorities. With three titles on their inaugural list, Lee & Low Books epitomized the trend of "niche publishing," a strategy for parlaying smallness into strength by marketing a limited number of well-focused books of a kind otherwise lacking.[44] The chains responded positively to what the new company had to offer, realizing that to do so served their interest as a counter to their tarnished reputation as aggressive marketplace spoilers. To carry books such as those published by Lee & Low implied, at least in the abstract, that chain booksellers too had a social conscience.

It was not uncommon for parents who wandered into the big-box stores, often with restless small children in tow, to react with frustration at the bewildering array of children's books placed before them in row after row of floor racks and shelves. While the classics offered some of these shoppers a comforting fallback position, a survey of mothers' read-aloud preferences conducted by the Gallup organization for *Publishers Weekly* in May 1985 had revealed that the better educated the mother, the more likely she was to favor new books over remembered favorites.[45] The difficulty, of course, lay in knowing which of the thousands of new titles were the best choices.

Two new monthly magazines that launched within months of each other in the mid-1980s, each with an initial circulation of 200,000, set out to nourish the aspirations and allay the fears of the new parents of the better-educated group. *Child* magazine, a subsidiary of Milan-based Taxi Publishing, emphasized high-end children's fashion. *Parenting*, a joint venture of Time, Inc., and San Francisco-based entrepreneur Robin Wolaner, proposed instead to become the "*New Yorker* of the women's service magazines" by offering an ambitious menu of short fiction, humor, investigative journalism, and stylish graphics, along with the standard nuts-and-bolts service pieces.[46] Surprisingly for a magazine in its category, *Parenting's* top editors had been recruited from *American Photo* and *Esquire*. Launching under a name that initially sounded awkward to some, *Parenting* in short order helped to introduce a new gender-neutral gerund into the language. The novel assumption behind the name — short-lived though it proved to be as a road map for the magazine's editorial direction — was that liberated fathers, unafraid of their "feminine side" and keen on sharing the hard but satisfying work of child rearing with their wives, would take to the monthly with equal fervor. A photo of a well-groomed mother, a preschooler in overalls, and a hipster dad wearing a fake nose and glasses made the launch issue's all-important cover statement. In less than a year's time, dads were off the magazine's cover for good.

In a bid to win the loyalty of their demographically most desirable subscribers, both new monthlies gave over substantial space to reviews of children's books in every issue. In striking contrast to the new arrivals, *Parents* magazine, the long-dominant category leader with a circulation of 1.5 million, made room for children's books only at holiday time. Other traditional service magazines such as *Redbook* and *Ladies' Home Journal* had as little, or less, to say about children's books and reading. Setting aside their customary caution, a few of the larger book publishers even experimented with advertising in the new magazines, which experienced rapid growth along with the rise in the birthrate. The publishers' experiment soon ran its course, however, as within a year's time both new monthlies crossed the 400,000-subscriber threshold and advertising rates became prohibitive. To their credit, both *Child* and *Parenting* continued to review books in every issue anyway. Before long, *Parents* felt compelled to do so as well.

Stunning developments in world affairs and the unprecedented ease of air travel were changing the way children's book publishers did business, and with whom. In 1984 Phyllis Fogelman traveled to the Soviet Union — an unthinkable destination just a few years earlier — and returned with an agreement to publish in America the first children's book in memory by a living Soviet artist: a picture book called *Once There Was a Tree,* by Natalie Romanovna, with illustrations by a young artist named Genady Spirin, whose exquisitely rendered naturalistic paintings seemed surrealistically to rise out of a Tolstoyan time warp. In September 1987, Ann K. Beneduce, one-time protégée of internationalist Velma Varner and now publisher of Orchard Books, attended the Moscow Book Fair and came home with the upbeat assessment that *"glosnost* is real!"[47]

The Bologna International Book Fair — welcomed from its inception in the 1960s as a rare chance for publishers from around the world to converge and do business in convivial surroundings — now came to be viewed as just one of many points of rendezvous along a continuum of year-round global contacts carried on by mail, telephone, fax, and in person. The Japanese illustrator, philosopher, and television personality Mitsumasa Anno, known for his adroitly witty wordless picture books (several of which he tailored specifically for the Western market), now joined the field's pantheon of international superstars, a select club that also included Maurice Sendak, Richard Scarry, Eric Carle, the Netherlands' Dick Bruna, and a few others. A sense that the British and American markets were beginning to merge from a sales and marketing perspective was reflected in the decision in the fall of 1989 to simultaneously release bestselling young-adult novelist Robert Cormier's *Fade* in the United States (by Delacorte) and in the United Kingdom (by Victor Gollancz). "To my knowledge," Delacorte's publisher George Nicholson told *Publishers Weekly,* "this hasn't ever been done in children's books."[48] The practice was already a common one in the world of adult trade bestsellerdom. As the 1990s unfolded, the comment that children's book publishing was becoming more and more like the adult side of the business would be repeated with ever-greater frequency.

Meanwhile, the ill-defined concept of multiculturalism was severely put to the test when in the fall of 1990 Alyson Publications, an independent press dedicated to providing books that explored the life experiences of children of gay and lesbian parents, released its first two picture books: *Heather Has Two Mommies* and *Daddy's Roommate.*[49] Together, the two books incited the greatest public uproar over a picture book since Garth Williams's *The Rabbits' Wedding,* with its supposed depiction of a biracial marriage, and prompted numerous book challenges and bannings at schools and libraries around the nation. The controversy surrounding the books came to a head when by a 63–36 majority the U.S. Senate agreed to deny federal funding to schools that "implement or carry out a program that has either the purpose or the effect of encouraging or supporting homosexuality as a positive lifestyle alternative."[50] The episode typified the increasingly well-coordinated and aggressive opposition of Christian fundamentalist groups to aspects of contemporary American culture deemed by them to be objectionable.

During the 1980s, as censorship of children's books intensified, Judy Blume, the decade's most censored American author for young people, reluctantly stepped into the public role of advocate for writers' First Amendment rights. In Blume's estimate, censorship cases had quadrupled during the Reagan presidency.[51] Noting that the number of such cases had already taken a marked upturn a year or so before Reagan's election, Judith F. Krug, director of the American Library Association's Office of Intellectual Freedom, observed: "The same factors that led to the increase in censorship also led to the election of Reagan." What the Reagan administration had done was "to create an atmosphere that [was] conducive to censors, be they in or out of government."[52]

While Jerry Falwell's Moral Majority was a major instigator of challenges to children's books in schools and libraries, other objections to books were (or appeared to be) of local origin. In November 1984, the trustees of the Peoria, Illinois, school district voted to ban three novels by Blume from the city's school libraries on the ground that the books' strong language and sexual content were inappropriate for children under thirteen who might gain access to them. With Blume due in Chicago later that month to receive the Carl Sandburg Freedom to Read Award given by the Friends of the Chicago Public Library, the Peoria school board's action drew the attention of the Associated Press and other news media. Caught in a whirlwind of embarrassing national publicity, Peoria's trustees reversed their decision in early December.[53] But their action did little to take the chill out of the air.

During the 1990s, children's book publishing became the fastest-growing area of the American publishing industry. In 1994 an estimated five thousand new titles were published, more than double the number of a decade earlier.[54] The sheer magnitude of the sector's latest growth spurt thrust the field into the media limelight as never before. Children's literature was becoming impossible to ignore. In 1996, in one of countless indications of the rising status of "kids' books," the National Book Foundation, administrator since 1988 of the prestigious National Book Awards, revived the award in the "young people's literature" category after a lapse of thirteen years. On the whole, the feeling within the industry was that the cultural and economic mainstreaming of juvenile publishing was a most welcome development, and long past due.

A hip, irreverent picture book by Jon Scieszka and Lane Smith, *The Stinky Cheese Man*, served as the unofficial anthem of the new era. Scieszka and Smith — and their unseen third collaborator, designer Molly Leach, who had come to the project with a background in magazine work — flaunted their merry disdain for old-fashioned sweetness and sentiment as they showed their respect for their young audience by suggesting that contemporary children were as worldly-wise, if not also as cynical, as their parents. College students had a major hand in making *The Stinky Cheese Man* a bestseller. It had been with this crossover market in mind that the publisher had taken the extraordinary step of advertising the book on NBC's *Late Night with David Letterman*.

Publishers with little or no past connection to the juvenile field now looked for any reasonable way to ride the overall growth trend. John Wiley and Sons, a longtime publisher of scientific and technical books, now introduced a paperback science series for grade-schoolers. As museums around the nation discovered the money to be made by stocking high-end children's gift books in their shops, Harry N. Abrams, publisher of *The Art of Maurice Sendak* and a vast catalog of other art books, realized it was ideally positioned to publish picture books of its own and began to do so in 1999.

The Disney Company, which since the 1930s had been reaping profits from the licensing of its iconic cartoon characters to book publishers, finally decided that it might make even more money if it published some of the books itself. In 1991 the entertainment giant set up a publishing division in New York with a mandate that encompassed but also far exceeded the realm of Disneyana. When it came time to staff the new operation's juvenile trade division, which it named Hyperion Books for Children, Disney repeatedly raided Harper, perhaps hoping eventually to find its way to the crown jewels of that venerable print-era magic kingdom, foremost among them being the work of Maurice Sendak.[55]

In a whirl of Brownian motion, publishers once known only for hardcover books added paperback lines to their list, while paperback houses expanded in the opposite direction. In 1985, after more than sixty years as a publisher of educational magazines and three decades of a near-monopoly on the school paperback book club and book fair markets, Scholastic inaugurated a hardbound trade imprint; seven years later, the company introduced Cartwheel Books, an imprint dedicated to board books and other novelties for the youngest children.[56] Heading the imprint was one of the industry's only African Americans in an executive position, Bernette Ford. A company long considered down-market by the publishers whose authors and artists won all the prizes, Scholastic was rapidly becoming the avatar of the new publishing era: a market- and media-savvy house with a list that ran the gamut from mass-market to high-end trade and with a culture that rewarded experimentation.

Countless permutations now played themselves out. Hoping to revive its flagging fortunes, the Western Publishing Company, publisher of Golden Books, drifted briefly into the business of selling other publishers' bestsellers when in 1992 it formed an alliance with the international retailer Toys 'R' Us.[57] Under the arrangement, Western agreed to operate boutique-like bookshops housed within a select number of the toy retailer's megastores, the number to increase rapidly over the course of a few years. Other publishers, most notably archrival Random House, expressed discomfort at the notion of Western assuming even limited control over the sale of its own titles. Smaller houses and independent booksellers criticized the deal as a competition-stifling combination of giants. For Western, a big business that had become ever more administratively top-heavy after decades of nimble growth, the venture simply proved in the end to be too costly.

Wariness of publishing giant-ism did seem in order just then. In 1994 Simon & Schuster acquired the Macmillan Publishing Company, only to be absorbed later that same year (along with the rest of its parent company, Paramount Communications, the successor to Gulf + Western) by Viacom. In this way, once unimaginably large houses were now routinely dwarfed by still larger corporate entities. Four years later, the German publishing megalith Bertelsmann, whose portfolio of American holdings already included the combined might of Bantam, Doubleday, and Dell/

Delacorte, added Random House to its portfolio and merged the four once proudly freestanding enterprises into a single — there was no other word for it — super-publisher.

The concurrent consolidation of publishing and bookselling increasingly put independents in both businesses at a major disadvantage, creating bad feeling and arousing suspicions of foul play at every turn. In the fall of 1995, Dial published Tom Feelings's *The Middle Passage*, a lavish, oversized illustrated book that had been more than twenty years in the making. Twenty years earlier, the publisher would have had to struggle to get a book chronicling the experiences of enslaved Africans during their forced voyage to America into the hands of its audience. By the mid-1990s, conditions were more favorable: illustrated books honoring the history of African Americans had become an accepted part of the publishing mainstream.[58]

Yet the timing of the release of Feelings's book had its unfortunate side as well. Dial's parent company, Penguin, was just then one of a small group of major houses to have been singled out by the American Booksellers Association in a lawsuit accusing the publishers of systematically giving preferential treatment to their chain-store customers. Penguin, which traditionally spent lavishly on exhibition-hall display space at the ABA's annual conventions, retaliated by boycotting the event, held that year in Chicago. That June, without a booth at which to showcase her fall list, Fogelman flew to Chicago on her own and ronin-like wandered the convention floor with a large black bag over her shoulder. Inside the bag was a complete set of unbound page proofs of *The Middle Passage*. The publisher, who knew everyone in the industry, proudly produced Feelings's magisterial work for anyone who would look at it.

The Middle Passage arrived in stores that fall with a retail price of $40 — an unheard-of "price-point" for a children's book, but not for an art book. Fogelman's gamble — that the book would make its way to some extent in both markets — was an extreme case of publishers' growing preoccupation with "crossover potential" as a strategy for increasing a book's chances in the perplexing world of shrinking shelf lives and tidal-wave returns. Certain types of books — most notably nonfiction — seemed to hold special promise in this regard. In the past, children's books about science, history, foreign cultures, and the like had sold overwhelmingly to schools and libraries. Purchased on the strength of the information they storehoused and their timeliness in filling perceived gaps in the literature, such books had rarely been showered with the most sumptuous design and illustration treatments possible but had tended rather to be given the look of the thing they were destined to become: required reading. By the 1980s, however, the rise of the retail market for children's books, combined with advances in color printing technology and Americans' growing sense that theirs was a "visual culture," had prompted a reconsideration of both the look and market of the once graphically dreary category.

The field was ripe for enterprise. An agile science writer and former teacher, Seymour Simon had become enthralled with the spectacular space photographs being beamed back to earth by NASA and was aware that many of these government-generated pictures passed directly into the public domain. Morrow Junior Books, long a leader in the institutional nonfiction market, entered a new, more retail-friendly phase when it published Simon's *Saturn* and *Jupiter*, the first two picture books to showcase the extraordinary color images, in 1985. The sleekly designed, oversized books were printed on heavy, high-gloss paper and made striking use of white type set against bold black backgrounds. The generous trim size gave the already dramatic images a heightened big-screen impact. Booksellers who in the past would have had little shelf space for an astronomy title were happy to display face-out books as enticing as these, which looked like gifts and sold briskly.

Other writers found new uses for photography. A former journalist named Russell Freedman published dozens of workmanlike, well-reviewed children's science books before turning to history for subject matter, and to historical archives as a source of photographs with the power to bring the past to life for children of the television age. Freedman coined the term "photo-biography" to describe the book about Abraham Lincoln for which he won the 1988 Newbery Medal. It had been more than forty years since a work of nonfiction last won the big prize, though just one year earlier a Newbery Honor had been given to another photographically illustrated work of nonfiction, Patricia Lauber's *Volcano: The Eruption and Healing of Mount St. Helens*. Both winning titles combined the visual appeal of gift books with the solid substance needed for schoolwork. Both books were also engaging enough to be enjoyed by adults who for recreation in decades past might have leafed through the pages of *Life* magazine and who now watched public television shows like *Nature* and *American Masters*.

Nowhere was the new popularity of children's nonfiction more evi-

dent than in the overwhelming public response to a cleverly written and illustrated series of science-based picture books, the "Magic School Bus" series published in hardcover by the Scholastic Press. The author, Joanna
Cole, had scores of children's science books to her credit when *The Magic
School Bus at the Waterworks* made its debut on bookstore shelves in the
fall of 1986. In the past, it had been a rare and wonderful day when Cole
spotted one of her books on the shelves of a retail store. Now she watched
with amazement as quite suddenly, all across America, parents and children
lined up around the block for bookstore autographing sessions with her
and Bruce Degen, the book's illustrator. Degen, a former New York City
high school teacher with his own yard-long list of modest commercial successes behind him, recalled: "It was absolutely wild. We felt almost like the
Beatles."[59]

A star system had indeed begun to emerge. As publishing houses combined and expanded, but without increasing their staffs proportionately to
cope with the new bulge in their lists, it made increasing sense to the executives in charge to concentrate their marketing and sales efforts almost entirely on the relative handful of front-list books that seemed likeliest to
earn serious money. For the authors and illustrators who qualified as members of the elite group, the house provided individualized services comparable to those of a private bank. In stark contrast to life at this highest tier,
the vast majority of authors were left to fend for themselves, their books
having been budgeted in advance, in the elaborate ritual entailed in the
preparation of profit-and-loss statements, or "P-and-Ls," to at least break
even for the publisher. Each season a few books by unknowns or by long-
unsung "midlist" veterans did break through, lifting the status and fortunes
of their creators. As for the rest, publishers showed no reluctance (especially post-*Thor*) about putting books out of print after a year or two; in
fact, from a budgetary point of view, it served their interest to do so.

The transfer of a significant measure of authority from the editorial
to the marketing executives at the major houses proceeded at a furious
rate. Publishers now "repackaged" backlist "classics" — the "Little House"
books, *The Tale of Peter Rabbit, Curious George*, "Narnia," *Madeline* — as
"brands" and proceeded to "extend" those brands to the breaking point and
sometimes beyond. The ultimate expression of the trend was the embrace
of the "celebrity" picture book, a phenomenon that gathered momentum
following forays into the field during the early 1990s by pop singer Carly Si-

mon and actress Jamie Lee Curtis. Celebrities, the logic went, had ready access to television airtime on the shows of the talk-show hosts whose good word sent book buyers flocking to the stores. Baby boomer parents, unsure of what book to buy for their young children, might very well choose one created by a performer they admired.

More publishers were themselves becoming stars after a fashion. Within the trade houses, single-editor imprints, many bearing that editor's name, proliferated: Laura Geringer Books (1990) and Joanna Cotler Books (1995), both at Harper; Bonnie Verburg's Blue Sky Press (1992) and Arthur A. Levine Books (1997) at Scholastic; Walter Lorraine Books (1995) at Houghton Mifflin; and Michael di Capua Books, a uniquely fungible enterprise that reconstituted itself in succession at Farrar, Straus and Giroux (1987), Harper (1991), Hyperion (1999), and Scholastic (2006); among others.[60] Apart from whatever the trend revealed about "celebrity culture" and the newfound need of editors to share billing with their authors, it was also an adaptive response to the worst aspects of the corporate publishing culture. Imprint heads reclaimed for themselves some of the old freedom to publish what they wished without first having to answer to committees of business-head overlords. The imprints operated as semi-autonomous states within an imperial domain: editorially independent yet still in a position to take full advantage of the central authority's vast sales and marketing apparatus. For those editors fortunate enough to have earned this enviable status, it often seemed the best of both worlds.

Meanwhile, new houses were once again opening their doors, hinting at a search for correctives to the excesses of the current system. Handprint Books, the venture of a former head of Penguin's children's book division, occupied space in a Brooklyn, New York, brownstone. In Cambridge, Massachusetts, Candlewick Press, the American outpost of the United Kingdom's Walker Books, launched its inaugural list in the spring of 1992. Front Street Books, a start-up founded by a former juvenile publishing director at Farrar, Straus and Giroux, opened for business in 1994 in Asheville, North Carolina. With Federal Express and the Internet at everyone's beck and call, it perhaps no longer mattered where a publisher was headquartered.

The man behind Candlewick was a roguish English visionary of considerable personal charm. Sebastian Walker also brought to his work a high sense of purpose and keen eye for art and design. In 1978, with a loose patchwork of sales and editorial experience as prologue, Walker had set up shop in London with a small staff and (thanks to the charm) one of England's most celebrated illustrators, Helen Oxenbury, already committed to working with him.

From the start Walker envisioned an up-market house that would make its way by the artful organization of lucrative international co-editions of its list of graphically distinguished picture books. Walker estimated that England accounted for only 15 percent of his potential market. America was the big prize. As he told a reporter: "When a book is right for the States, you are suddenly aware that this is the richest, most powerful economy in the world."[61] It was doubtless with this idea in mind that he hired two Americans, David Ford and Amelia Edwards, as the firm's managing director and art director. The company had its shabby-genteel offices in a former sweatshop situated above an Indian restaurant on a side street off unfashionable Tottenham Court Road. Access was by an iron fire escape on which bowls of curry were sometimes left out to cool.[62] In deference to the value he placed on the American editors who came to visit, such as Atheneum's Margaret K. McElderry and Random House's Janet Schulman, the publisher was said to have made a point of sweeping the fire escape clear of rotting fish heads and the occasional dead rat. For the conquering Americans, visits to the offbeat establishment were considered good publishing fun and were generally worth the effort. Among the prizes that McElderry came away with was the quintessential bedtime book of the 1990s, Michael J. Rosen and Helen Oxenbury's *We're Going on a Bear Hunt*. Schulman snapped up Oxenbury's first board books.

To fuel the company's rapid expansion, Walker risked alienating England's booksellers by creating a small, customized list of picture books to be sold at half the standard retail price exclusively at Britain's largest supermarket chain, Sainsbury's. Always at his most persuasive when playing the visionary gadfly, Walker had a ready response for critics who accused him of betraying the trust of the traditional bookselling community and perhaps even of acting in violation of Britain's "retail price maintenance system": "There is a vocal minority of booksellers who hate us," he dryly observed. " . . . Luckily, most booksellers applaud us for taking a limited range of titles to the widest possible public; they see, as we do, that once children's books have become common currency in every home, then parents will want *more* children's books."[63] In deciding to offer parents high-quality picture books at below-market prices, and then in choosing supermarkets as his sales and marketing partners in the venture, Walker had taken a leaf from postwar American juvenile publishing's single most remarkable success story: Little Golden Books.

When the time at last seemed right to establish offices in the United States, Walker brashly offered the job of launching the operation to Janet Schulman, then editor in chief of Random House's vast juvenile department — and to *her* boss, publisher Gerry Harris. Schulman was impressed enough by the super-salesman from London not merely to "laugh at the idea, [but]" she recalled, "we didn't take the offer terribly seriously . . . either."[64]

Against a backdrop of corporate mergers and buyouts, David Ford introduced the imprint's inaugural catalog with a rousing statement of principles that harkened back to the pioneering era of the 1920s and 1930s: "Candlewick Press," he declared,

> is an independent children's book publisher. We are not part of a large corporation; we are not controlled by investors, shareholders, or financial officers. We publish children's books, and that is all we do. We do it because we believe that children need and demand the very best books, and that we can produce the best books only by giving them our undivided attention.[65]

In the fall of 1994, as the publishing and library worlds prepared to celebrate the seventy-fifth anniversary of Children's Book Week, Random House Books for Young Readers fired several members of its senior staff, including the flagship Knopf imprint's distinguished art director, the department's veteran director of library and school promotion, and Frances Foster, the quietly effective longtime editor who while at Knopf had championed the work of such writers as Louis Sachar and Philip Pullman and a roster of illustrators led by the Czech émigré artist Peter Sís.[66] A combination of factors, among them an internal power struggle, had precipitated the purge, but the main rationale management offered to explain the bizarre house-cleaning was the argument that with the retail market for juveniles as strong as it was, the department no longer needed to cater to the needs of libraries and schools.[67] As had been the case in past decades with the firings (from Doubleday) of May Massee and (from Harcourt, Brace) Margaret K. McElderry, one publisher's loss was another one's gain. Within days of her dismissal, Foster accepted the offer of an imprint at Farrar, Straus and Giroux, one of the few remaining independent trade houses. Among the first books she published at her new professional home was Louis Sachar's *Holes*, a novel that went on to win both the Newbery Medal and the National Book Award.[68]

Turmoil in the industry continued. In the fall of 1997, the News Corporation combined HarperCollins and another of its properties, the weekly magazine *TV Guide*, under a new organizational umbrella called News America Publishing Group. As it did so, company executives briskly denied rumors that HarperCollins was up for sale and that negotiations were already under way with the German media conglomerate Bertelsmann.[69] As it turned out, Harper remained a property of Rupert Murdoch's Australian-based media empire, the News Corporation. But the following year Bertelsmann bought Random House.

During the 1990s, historian Steven Mintz has observed, "marketers coined the word *tween* to describe the demographic group from eight to twelve, which had not yet reached the teen years but aspires to teenage sophistication. In an era of niche marketing, the tweens — whose average weekly income rose from $6 to $22 a week during the 1990s — became one of the most popular markets for clothing manufacturers and record companies."[70] One children's bookseller described this volatile stage as a time when "[readers] go from Dr. Seuss to Madonna in one great leap."[71] Tweens would soon flex their muscle in both the economic and literary sphere by making J. K. Rowling's Harry Potter fantasy series the bestselling books, after only the Bible, in history.

In the summer of 1998, at the American Library Association convention in Washington, D.C., publicity staffers at the Scholastic exhibition-hall booth were busy handing out bound galleys of the first volume of a British fantasy series that they said had a large, enthusiastic readership in the United Kingdom, not only among middle-grade school children but also (this was the surprise) among college students. The book in question, the work of a first-time author from Scotland named J. K. Rowling, had already garnered considerable industrywide media attention as a result of Scholastic's having acquired North American publication rights at auction for the then-unprecedented sum (for a children's book) of $100,000. Industry observers took the news as, if nothing else, the latest sign that children's book publishing was indeed becoming more like the high-stakes adult side of the business.

What followed could not have been predicted by anyone. Driven largely at first by independent bookseller enthusiasm, old-fashioned word of mouth, and a hearty endorsement from the hip new online bookseller Amazon.com, *Harry Potter and the Sorcerer's Stone* became a runaway bestseller. In its first year, by which time the first sequel had also appeared in the United States, the two books had combined American sales of more than five million copies and had been translated into twenty-eight languages. As of September 19, 1999, the first book, then in its thirty-eighth week on the *New York Times* fiction bestseller list, occupied the top spot, with the second title, *Harry Potter and the Chamber of Secrets*, ranked at number three.[72] A *Time* cover story appeared just days after the third installment went on sale in the United States, this time only two months after its appearance in the United Kingdom rather than a full year later, as had been the case with the two earlier Potters. To its dismay, Scholastic had discovered that it was losing sales from avid fans who, rather than endure the wait, were going to the trouble of ordering the latest book from Britain.

The arrival of the third Potter book set off grumblings among adult trade publishers who feared losing yet another slot on the *Times'* all-important bestseller list. Within months of Harry's appearance on the cover of *Time* over the banner headline "The Magic of Harry Potter: Hero of Three Best Sellers, He's Not Just for Kids," the *New York Times*, in an effort to make the world safe for Danielle Steele and Tom Clancy, moved to isolate Rowling by introducing a separate list devoted to juveniles.[73] Children's book advocates generally praised the decision, noting that the new list was sure to give greater public exposure to many other less widely heralded but equally worthy books in addition to Rowling's. But to some, the move seemed an embarrassing face-saving exercise and a final refusal to concede that children's books might in fact occupy a significant place in the cultural mainstream.

The outsized success of the books made them a lightning rod for attacks from many quarters. In the wake of the *Times'* announcement, Harold Bloom, writing in the pages of the *Wall Street Journal*, offered a damning critique of an author whose books, surreally, he boasted of not having actually read in their entirety. "Taking arms against Harry Potter, at this moment," Bloom began, "is to emulate Hamlet taking arms against a sea of troubles." Four columns of fine print later, the Yale professor concluded: "The cultural critics will, soon enough, introduce Harry Potter into their college curriculum, and *The New York Times* will go on celebrating another confirmation of the dumbing-down it leads and exemplifies."[74]

The predictable backlash also included public library challenges initiated by fundamentalist Christian groups, who objected to the author's references to witchcraft, and at least one baseless legal claim that Rowling had stolen the idea for the series from the obscure works of another writer.

Meanwhile, scholars did (as Bloom had predicted) begin to offer undergraduate courses, convene conferences, and publish their proceedings. In circles of ambitious parents everywhere, the secular equivalent of medieval miracle tales made the rounds, with improbable reports of the precocious four- or five-year-old who had somehow mustered the concentration and stamina to read one of the Rowling tomes cover to cover independently. The author's tales of preternaturally capable young wizards and rapacious Death Eaters living in their midst well suited an age of fantastically high parental expectations and equally exaggerated parental fears.

The "Potter Phenomenon," as it came to be called in the media, discredited some of the adult world's most basic assumptions about young people's reading habits. Until then, it had been widely assumed by publishers, librarians, and educators that few boys cared to read works of fantasy; that few preteen boys were truly avid readers in any genre; and that none but the "special" child of either sex would voluntarily tackle a book of any description that was much more than two hundred pages long.

As Scholastic left increasingly little to chance (by the third book, no advance review copies were made available to the media, thereby eliminating the possibility of negative criticism prior to the actual sale date), other publishers wondered how best to capitalize on the excitement. Greenwillow, a longtime publisher of British fantasy, took the opportunity to reissue several of the earlier works of Diana Wynne Jones. More than a few houses became newly willing to entertain proposals for multibook fantasy series — the longer the book, it now seemed, the better. News that a Potter film deal was in the works stoked the fire of what, after a time, had clearly assumed the character of a craze, a publishing bubble to rival the 1990s stock-market bubble generated by Internet-based new technologies.

Yet there was still something genuinely touching about the public response to the Potter books themselves. During the early days of the summer of 2000, in the run-up to the release of the fourth volume, *Harry Potter and the Goblet of Fire*, bookstores all around the country (both independents and chains) announced plans for late-night book parties to be held on the strictly controlled official release date (in the United Kingdom as well as in the United States) of Saturday, July 8, when copies of the book would go on sale at precisely one minute past midnight. Children dressed as their favorite character arrived at the stores to be greeted by booksellers in dark robes and tall, pointy hats, in retail spaces temporarily transformed into festive wizard halls through the addition of faux cobwebs, buckets of mist-producing dry ice, and tables of refreshments. "Not since *Gone with the Wind* has a best-selling book swept the nation the way Harry Potter has," the *Times* wrote later that day. Barnes and Noble reported having sold 114,000 copies of the new book in the first hour.[75] With the first of the feature films still more than a year off and Potter products just beginning to flood the market, supposedly under the author's strict supervision, it was not unreasonable to wonder how much longer the passion for the books could last, as well as how much of that passion was now attributable to peer pressure or marketing hype, rather than sheer love of the books and their doughty young hero.

Still, the great success of the book parties, which collectively counted as the most widely observed celebration of reading in the nation's history, seemed a bright spot in an otherwise grim time of politicians' dubious professions of concern for childhood literacy and corporate America's relentless drive to make consumers of even the youngest children. At 732 pages, Rowling's fourth installment was also the longest one by far, yet eight-, nine-, and ten-year-olds eagerly lined up for the chance to rise to the challenge. If there was no magic in any of this, it was nevertheless an extraordinary moment, one that none of the experts in children's literature past or present — librarians, publishers, educators, booksellers, or critics — could have imagined, let alone planned. The gatekeepers of culture and commerce had been taken by storm. Children, it seemed, had once again made their choice.

Acknowledgments

During the 1980s, while researching my biography of Margaret Wise Brown and serving as a *Parenting* magazine contributing editor, I was fortunate to have the chance to meet many of the leading figures of the American children's book world, including several whose careers extended back to the 1930s and 1940s. The present book benefited greatly from my conversations with Augusta Baker Alexander, Dorothy A. Bennett, Lucienne Bloch Dimitroff, John Donovan, Josette Frank, Morell Gipson, Virginia Haviland, Clement Hurd, Edith Thacher Hurd, Ruth Krauss, Claudia Lewis, Virginia Mathews, Robert McCloskey, John G. McCullough, J. P. Miller, Ursula Nordstrom, Lucille Ogle, Harriet F. Pilpel, Beatrice Schenk de Regnier, William R. Scott, Art Seiden, Maurice Sendak, Marc Simont, Esphyr Slobodkina, William Steig, Alvin Tresselt, Leonard Weisgard, Garth Williams, and Charlotte Zolotow.

Over the fourteen years that this book was in preparation, I worked on a great many other, related projects, the research for which did double duty as background and material for the present history. I am especially grateful to Anita Silvey and Roger Sutton, who, as editors of *The Horn Book* magazine, commissioned a series of interviews with editors and other publishing figures who made lasting contributions to children's literature. I am also fortunate to have had the opportunity to write histories of Morrow Junior Books and Golden Books and to edit the professional correspondence of Harper's visionary editor Ursula Nordstrom.

My thanks to those who sat for interviews, responded to research queries, or provided research leads or original source material for the present book: Sue L. Alexander, Charles Antin, Marc Aronson, Bud Baker, Kate Barnes, C. A. P. Barron, Ann K. Beneduce, Judy Blume, Eunice Blake

319

Bohanan, John Briggs, Dorothy S. Briley, Donna Brooks, Caren Chapman, Jane Claes, John Y. Cole, Robert Cormier, Mary Cosgrave, Claire Counihan, Etienne Delessert, Tomie De Paola, Barbara A. Dicks, Tim Ditlow, Connie Epstein, Peggy Farber, Phyllis Fogelman, Frances Foster, Suzanne M. Glazer, Tzofit Goldfarb, Ian Graham, Elizabeth Graves, Dorothy Haas, Regina Hayes, Susan Hirschman, Grace Allen Hogarth, Johanna Hurwitz, Marilyn Iarusso, Gary Ink, Richard Jackson, Sybille Jagusch, Sandra Jordan, Norton Juster, Mimi Kayden, John Keller, Andy Laties, Walter Lorraine, Marilyn Malin, Marilyn E. Marlow, John Mason, Margaret K. McElderry, Steven Mooser, William C. Morris, David Mowery, Diane Muldrow, Lee Kingman Natti, George M. Nicholson, Andrea Pinkney, Paula Quint, David Reuther, Margret Rey, Elizabeth M. Riley, Diane Roback, Harriet Rohmer, Morton Schindel, Miriam Schlein, Terri Schmitz, Ian Schoenherr, Janet Schulman, Henrietta M. Smith, Tracy van Straaten, Jean Vestal, William Weiss, Refna Wilkin, and Lauren Wohl.

I wish to thank the librarians and archivists at the following institutions for their help in navigating the collections in their care: Bank Street Collection of Education Archive, R. R. Bowker Library; Clara Whitehill Hunt Collection, Brooklyn Public Library; Katharine S. White Collection, Bryn Mawr College; Oral History Project, Columbia University; May Massee Collection, Emporia State University; Harcourt Archive; HarperCollins Archive; Houghton Library, Harvard University; Museum of the City of New York; New-York Historical Society Library; Central Children's Room and Rare Books and Manuscripts Division, New York Public Library; Newberry Library; George Peabody Library; Penguin USA Archive; Scribner Archive, Princeton University; Random House Archive; Maurice Sendak Collection, Rosenbach Museum and Library; *Horn Book* Archive, Simmons College; Society of Children's Book Writers and Illustrators; Kerlan Collection, University of Minnesota; Maine Women Writers Collection, University of New England (Portland); Lucille Ogle Collection and Jane Werner Watson Collection, University of Oregon (Eugene); De Grummond Collection, University of Southern Mississippi; Louise Seaman Bechtel Collection, Vassar College; Betsy Beinecke Shirley Collection, Yale University.

I undertook this project at the suggestion of Norma Jean Sawicki. My sincere thanks to her for her belief that such a book was wanted, and for her faith in my ability to write it. I am grateful for the assistance given and patience shown by the editors at Houghton Mifflin with whom I worked at later stages of the project, and most particularly for the encouragement and guidance provided by Deanne Urmy, who did so much to help bring this book to completion.

Thanks as always for the support and understanding shown by my wife, Amy Schwartz, and by my son, Jacob, who shares the dedication with the man for whom he is named, a builder of bridges, world traveler, and inspiration to me from earliest memory.

NOTES

1. PROVIDENCE AND PURPOSE IN COLONIAL AMERICA AND THE YOUNG REPUBLIC

1. Quoted in Steven Mintz, *Huck's Raft: A History of American Childhood* (Cambridge, Mass.: Belknap/Harvard University Press, 2004), 10.

2. William Cardell, *Story of Jack Halyard,* 3rd ed. (Philadelphia: Uriah Hunt, 1825), x, quoted in Anne Scott MacLeod, *A Moral Tale: Children's Fiction and American Culture, 1820–1860* (Hamden, Conn.: Archon, 1975), 20.

3. Quoted in Edmund S. Morgan, *The Puritan Family: Religious and Domestic Relations in Seventeenth-Century New England,* rev. and enlarged ed. (New York: Harper & Row, 1966), 88.

4. David D. Hall, "Readers and Writers in Early New England," in Hugh Amory and David D. Hall, eds., *A History of the Book in America,* vol. 1, *The Colonial Book in the Atlantic World* (Chapel Hill: University of North Carolina Press/ American Antiquarian Society, 2007), 119–21.

5. Gillian Avery, *Behold the Child: American Children and Their Books, 1621– 1922* (Baltimore: Johns Hopkins University Press, 1994), 26. Avery quotes from *The School of Good Manners,* a work by Boston schoolmaster Eleazar Moody dating from 1715.

6. John Tebbel, *Between Covers: The Rise and Transformation of American Book Publishing* (New York: Oxford University Press, 1987), 5–6.

7. Ibid., 29.

8. Paul Leicester Ford, ed., *The New-England Primer: Its Origin and Development* (New York: Dodd, Mead, 1897), 10, 12.

9. Hall, "Readers and Writers," 43; John Rowe Townsend, *John Newbery and His Books: Trade and Plumb-Cake for Ever, Huzza!* (Metuchen, N.J.: Scarecrow, 1994), 151.

10. Ford, *The New-England Primer,* 27–28.

11. Ibid., 29.

12. Ibid., 31.

13. Ibid., 47.

14. Mintz, *Huck's Raft*, 27.

15. Avery, *Behold the Child*, 31.

16. Bernard Wishy, *The Child and the Republic: The Dawn of Modern American Child Nurture* (Philadelphia: University of Pennsylvania Press, 1968), 55.

17. Ibid., 47.

18. Leonard W. Labaree, Ralph L. Ketcham, Helen C. Boatfield, and Helene D. Fineman, eds., *The Autobiography of Benjamin Franklin* (New Haven: Yale University Press, 1964), 110.

19. Elizabeth Carroll Reilly, "The Wages of Piety: The Boston Book Trade of Jeremy Condy," in William L. Joyce, David D. Hall, Richard D. Brown, and John B. Hench, eds., *Printing and Society in Early America* (Worcester, Mass.: American Antiquarian Society, 1983), 96.

20. Labaree et al., *Autobiography of Benjamin Franklin*, 128.

21. Fowle's brother Daniel opened his own Boston print shop in partnership with Gamaliel Rogers in 1740 and enjoyed a far better reputation for press-work than his brother. Like many of his peers, Daniel Fowle ran afoul of the authorities as the publisher and distributor of satirical material deemed offensive to the British Crown. Fowle is credited with publishing what Gillian Avery has described as the "earliest known storybook for children published in America, *A New Gift for Children*," which, according to d'Alté Welch, may have been first issued in Boston in 1756. If the dating is correct, Fowle's signal contribution to juvenile literature arrived in the same year that the printer himself, having recently served jail time for his political transgressions, left Massachusetts for New Hampshire and presumably calmer surroundings. See Avery, *Behold the Child*, 48; and Henry Walcott Boynton, *Annals of American Bookselling, 1638–1850* (New Castle, Del.: Oak Knoll, 1991), 81–82.

22. Tebbel, *Between Covers*, 8–13; Boynton, *Annals of American Bookselling*, 121; M. A. McCorison, preface to Isaiah Thomas, *The History of Printing in America, with a Biography of Printers & an Account of Newspapers*, 3rd ed. (New York: Weathervane, 1970), xi.

23. Boynton, *Annals of American Bookselling*, 122.

24. Among the books featured in Newbery's advertisement in the Pennsylvania newspaper was *A Museum for Young Gentlemen and Ladies, or A private tutor for little Masters and Misses*, in which pages of curious facts and bits of advice about correct behavior culminated in a selection of "Dying Words and Behaviour of Great Men, when just quitting the Stage of Life; with many other useful Particulars, all in a plain familiar Way for the Youth of Both Sexes."

25. Avery, *Behold the Child*, 40–41.

26. John Rowe Townsend, *Written for Children: An Outline of English-Language Children's Literature*, 3rd ed. (New York: J. P. Lippincott, 1987), 21–22.

27. Townsend, *John Newbery*, 153.

28. Ibid., 151–52. According to Townsend, the very first American Newbery reprint, an edition of the *Royal Primer*, appeared in 1753 under the Philadelphia imprint of James Chattin. *Goody Two-Shoes* had its first American edition in 1775 under the venerable New York imprint of Hugh Gaine. As Townsend also notes, prior to the American Revolution, "children's books were undoubtedly imported [to the thirteen colonies], but it is impossible to say which titles or in what numbers."

29. James Raven, "The Importation of Books in the Eighteenth Century," in Amory and Hall, *History of the Book*, 183–98.

30. Boynton, *Annals of American Bookselling*, 125.

31. Avery, *Behold the Child*, 48.

32. Boynton, *Annals of American Bookselling*, 2.

33. Warren Chappell, *A Short History of the Printed Word* (Boston: Nonpareil/David R. Godine, 1980), 163–66.

34. David D. Hall, "Introduction: The Uses of Literacy in New England, 1600–1850," in Joyce et al., *Printing and Society in Early America*, 28–29.

35. Boynton, *Annals of American Bookselling*, 127–28.

36. Lewis Leary, *The Book-Peddling Parson: An Account of the life and works of Mason Locke Weems, patriot, pitchman, author and purveyor of morality to the citizenry of the early United States of America* (Chapel Hill, N.C.: Algonquin, 1984).

37. Boynton, *Annals of American Bookselling*, 131–32. Weems had studied medicine for three years in London and Edinburgh prior to the start of the American Revolution. He took orders in the Church of England in 1784 and served as rector of a Maryland parish for five years before finding his true calling and pulpit in the book trade.

38. Quoted in Leary, *The Book-Peddling Parson*, 79–80.

39. Quoted in ibid., 82–83.

40. Quoted in ibid., 84.

41. Ibid., 96. Leary quotes Weems as having identified the source of the famous anecdote as an "aged lady, who is a distant cousin [of Washington], and when a girl spent much of her time in the family."

42. Ibid., 143.

43. Labaree et al., *Autobiography of Benjamin Franklin*, 10.

44. Leary, *The Book-Peddling Parson*, 144.

45. Quoted in ibid., 151.

46. Jill Lepore, "Noah's Mark," in *The New Yorker* (Nov. 6, 2006): 86.

47. Ibid., 78, 85; Labaree et al., *Autobiography of Benjamin Franklin*, 10.

48. Linda F. Lapides, "For Amusement and Instruction: Children's Books in Bygone Baltimore," checklist for the exhibition of the same name (Baltimore: Johns Hopkins University, George Peabody Library, December 6, 2000–January 31, 2001), 4.

49. Charles A. Madison, *Book Publishing in America* (New York: McGraw-Hill, 1966), 35.

50. Alexander Anderson, *Autobiography of an Early American Wood Engraver* (New York: Traders Press, 1968), unpaged. See also Mahlon Day, *New York Street Cries in Rhyme: Facsimile of the "Copyright 1825" Edition*, ed. Leonard S. Marcus (New York: Dover, 1977), xx.

51. Alice M. Jordan, *From Rollo to Tom Sawyer, and Other Papers* (Boston: Horn Book, 1948), 11.

52. Harry B. Weiss, "Mahlon Day, Early New York Printer, Bookseller, and Publisher," in *Bulletin of the New York Public Library* 45, no. 12 (December 1941): 1011. The steady demand for Day's business publications attested to the chaos in the monetary system that preceded the introduction of a uniform national paper currency in 1861.

53. Harry B. Weiss, "Solomon King, Early New York Bookseller," *Bulletin of the New York Public Library* (September 1947): 531.

54. Harry Weiss estimated that between 1800 and 1830 at least sixty-eight New York bookseller-printer-publishers had some involvement in the publishing of juveniles. During these years, Weiss noted, the city's population more than quadrupled, from 60,000 to 242,000. See Weiss, "The Printers and Publishers of Children's Books in New York City, 1698–1830," *Bulletin of the New York Public Library* (August 1948): 387.

55. Weiss, "Solomon King," 1008.

56. For an account of childhood life across the economic and social spectrum in New York City from the early to the mid-nineteenth century, see Leonard S. Marcus, "Small Souls: Children's Lives in Lower Manhattan, 1825–1860," *Seaport* (Fall 1979): 22–27.

57. Karen Beall, *Kaufrufe und Strassenhändler: Cries and Itinerant Trades* (Hamburg: Dr. Ernst Hauswedell, 1975).

58. Day, *New York Street Cries*, xxi.

59. Ibid., xviii.

60. Everett F. Bleiler, ed., *Mother Goose's Melodies: Facsimile Edition of the Munroe and Francis "Copyright 1833" Version* (New York: Dover, 1970), ix–x.

61. Leonard S. Marcus, "*Parley's Magazine: For Children and Youth*," in *Children's Periodicals of the United States*, ed. R. Gordon Kelly (Westport, Conn.: Greenwood, 1984), 347.

62. Boynton, *Annals of American Bookselling*, 143–44.

63. Eugene Exman, *The House of Harper: One Hundred and Fifty Years of Publishing* (New York: Harper & Row, 1967), 13.

64. Alice B. Cushman, "A Nineteenth-Century Plan for Reading: The American Sunday School Movement," *The Horn Book* (February 1957): 61–71; (April 1957): 159–66. In part 1 of her essay, Cushman reports: "The staggering production of the Union is claimed to have been 6,000,000 volumes by 1830!" — which is to say, just six years after the Union's founding.

65. Carol Gay, "Jacob Abbott," in *Dictionary of Literary Biography*, vol. 42 (Detroit: Gale Research, 1985), 3–6.

66. Jacob Abbott, *Rollo's Vacation* (Boston: Thomas Webb, 1839), 123.

67. Jacob Abbott, *Beechnut: A Franconia Story* (New York: (Harper & Brothers, 1850), 149.

68. Edwin G. Burrows and Mike Wallace, *Gotham: A History of New York City to 1898* (Oxford: Oxford University Press, 1999), 632.

69. Exman, *The House of Harper*, 41–42, 46.

70. Quoted in Gay, "Jacob Abbott," 10.

71. Barrows Mussey, "Introduction to the Dover Edition," in Peter Parley, *The Tales of Peter Parley About America* (1828; New York: Dover, 1974), vi.

72. Samuel Griswold Goodrich, *Recollections of a Lifetime*, vol. 1 (New York: Miller, Orton, 1857), 172.

73. Ibid., 166–70.

74. Quoted in Mussey, "Introduction to the Dover Edition," xvi.

75. Ibid., 9.

76. Eager to be remembered as one of American literature's first champions and tastemakers, Goodrich later claimed to have invited Hawthorne for an interview. But Hawthorne's biographer, Brenda Wineapple, thinks it more likely that her subject made the overture on the urging of his Bowdoin classmate, the Reverend George B. Cheever. See Brenda Wineapple, *Hawthorne: A Life* (New York: Knopf, 2003), 74.

77. Ibid., 74–75.

78. In a letter from Samuel Goodrich to Nathaniel Hawthorne, dated May 31, 1831, Goodrich said that the latter's stories were "as good, if not better, than anything else I can get." Quoted in Wineapple, *Hawthorne*, 77.

79. Mussey, "Introduction to the Dover Edition," xvii–xviii.

80. Ibid., v.

81. Michael Joseph, "Old Comic Elton and the Age of Fun: Robert H. Elton and the Picture Book," *Children's Literature Association Quarterly* 28, no. 3 (Fall 2003): 162–63.

82. Quoted in Mussey, "Introduction to the Dover Edition," xix.

83. *Parley's Magazine* (March 16, 1833) (specimen number), inside front cover.

84. Marcus, "*Parley's Magazine*," in Kelly, *Children's Periodicals*, 348–52.

85. Ruth K. MacDonald, "*Merry's Museum*," in Kelly, *Children's Periodicals*, 295.

86. Caroline M. Hewins, *Caroline M. Hewins: Her Book* (Boston: Horn Book, 1954), 30.

87. Joseph, "Old Comic Elton and the Age of Fun," 159.

88. Ibid., 162.

89. Mussey, "Introduction to the Dover Edition," xxii.

90. Jordan, *From Rollo to Tom Sawyer*, 70.

91. Labaree et al., *Autobiography of Benjamin Franklin*, 10.

92. Samuel Griswold Goodrich, *Recollections of a Lifetime, or, Men and Things I Have Seen: In a Series of Familiar Letters to a Friend*, vol. 2 (New York: Miller, Orton, 1857), 333–34.

93. Goodrich, *Recollections*, vol. 1, 110–14.

94. Quoted in Wishy, *The Child and the Republic*, 53–54, from "Books for Children," *Living Age* 1 (June 15, 1844): 301.

95. Quoted in Amy Weinstein, *Once Upon a Time: Illustrations from Fairytales, Fables, Primers, Pop-ups, and Other Children's Books* (New York: Princeton Architectural Press, 2005), 1.

96. Hewins, *Caroline M. Hewins*, 39.

97. Susan Bivin Aller, "Hartford's First Lady of the Library," *Hog River Journal* (Summer 2007): 28.

2. WONDER IN THE WAKE OF WAR

1. William T. Adams, "Books for Boys and Girls," *Oliver Optic's Magazine* (March 1872): 206.

2. Samuel Osgood, "Books for Our Children," *Atlantic Monthly* 16 (December 1865), quoted in Gillian Avery, *Behold the Child: American Children and Their Books, 1621–1922* (Baltimore: Johns Hopkins University Press, 1994), 121.

3. *The Student and Schoolmate* was published by Robinson & Richardson, Boston, and Calkins and Stiles, New York (1855–56); James Robinson & Co., Boston (1857–58); Robinson, Greene & Co., Boston (1859); Messrs. Galen James & Co, Boston (1860–62); and Joseph H. Allen, Boston (1863–72). *Merry's Magazine* had a succession of publishers, including I. C. and J. N. Stearns, New York (1841–44); S. T. Allen, New York (1845); I. C. and J. N. Stearns, New York (1846); G. W. and S. O. Post, New York (1847–48); D. MacDonald, New York (1849–50); S. T. Allen, New York (1850–55); J. N. Stearns, New York (1855–66); and Horace B. Fuller, Boston (1867–72). *Our Young Folks* was published by Ticknor & Fields, Boston (1865–68) and its successors, Fields, Osgood, Boston (1866–70) and James R. Osgood, Boston (1871–73).

4. Quoted in James Marten, *The Children's Civil War* (Chapel Hill: University of North Carolina Press, 1998), 35.

5. Ibid., 32–33.

6. Osgood, quoted in Steven Mintz, *Huck's Raft: A History of American Childhood* (Cambridge, Mass.: Harvard University Press, 2004), 186.

7. *Putnam's Magazine* 2 (December 1868): 760, quoted in Richard L. Darling, *The Rise of Children's Book Reviewing in America, 1865–1881* (New York: R. R. Bowker, 1968), 9.

8. Quoted in Darling, *The Rise of Children's Book Reviewing*, 8.

9. Ticknor & Fields's roster of authors included Ralph Waldo Emerson, Henry David Thoreau, Henry Wadsworth Longfellow, Nathaniel Hawthorne, Harriet Beecher Stowe, and Mark Twain.

10. Quoted in John Morton Blum, ed., *Yesterday's Children* (Boston: Houghton Mifflin, 1959), xiv. See also Joan Brest Friedberg, "*Our Young Folks: An Illus-*

trated *Magazine for Boys and Girls*," in *Children's Periodicals of the United States*, ed. R. Gordon Kelly (Westport, Conn.: Greenwood, 1984), 329–41.

11. Friedberg, "*Our Young Folks*," 331.

12. Homer had his first magazine illustrations published in the 1 August 1857 issue of *Harper's Weekly*. The images were of Harvard student life; an article on this theme was then commissioned to accompany the pictures. See Eugene Exman, *The House of Harper: One Hundred and Fifty Years of Publishing* (New York: Harper & Row, 1967), 104–6.

13. David Tatham, *Winslow Homer and the Illustrated Book* (Syracuse, N.Y.: Syracuse University Press, 1992), 90–91.

14. Carol Gay, "William Taylor Adams (Oliver Optic)," *Dictionary of Literary Biography*, vol. 42 (Detroit: Gale Research, 1985), 16.

15. Darling, *The Rise of Children's Book Reviewing*, 15–16.

16. Ibid., 14.

17. Ibid. For information about the origin of the pseudonym Oliver Optic and for the fullest account of Adams's publisher, Lee & Shepard, see Raymond L. Kilgour, *Lee and Shepard, Publishers for the People* (Hamden, Conn.: Shoe String, 1965).

18. Darling, *The Rise of Children's Book Reviewing*, 16.

19. Harriett R. Christy, "*The Student and Schoolmate*," in Kelly, *Children's Periodicals*, 430.

20. Ellen B. Ballou, *The Building of the House: Houghton Mifflin's Formative Years* (Boston: Houghton Mifflin, 1970), 102–7.

21. Ibid., 110.

22. Ibid., 110–12.

23. Christopher Camuto, "Roberts Brothers," in *Dictionary of Literary Biography*, vol. 42 (Detroit: Gale Research, 1985), 393–98.

24. Ballou, *The Building of the House*, 113. Dutton took over the prestigious address in late 1865 following the death of William D. Ticknor, who had been traveling at the time with his author and friend, Nathaniel Hawthorne. The latter died only weeks later. See John Tebbel, *Between Covers: The Rise and Transformation of American Book Publishing* (New York: Oxford University Press, 1987), 61.

25. Ballou, *The Building of the House*, 115.

26. Ibid., 116.

27. Horace E. Scudder, "Books for Young People," *Riverside Magazine for Young People* 1 (January 1867): 44.

28. Frank Luther Mott, *Golden Multitudes: The Story of Best Sellers in the United States* (New York: Macmillan, 1947), 309–12.

29. In November 1868, Lyman Abbott, the third son of Jacob Abbott, became *Harper's Monthly*'s book critic. Reviews of children's books figured prominently in the department he directed through the mid-1870s. Abbott did not hesitate to comment on books written by his own brother, Edward, or by

their father, whom he frankly proclaimed to be "at his best, the very best living writer for youth." See Darling, *The Rise of Children's Book Reviewing*, 93.

30. Darling, *The Rise of Children's Book Reviewing*, 217–19.
31. Ballou, *The Building of the House*, 117.
32. Quoted in ibid., 123.
33. Ibid., 124.
34. Horace E. Scudder, "Andersen's Short Stories," *Atlantic Monthly* 36 (November 1875): 601.
35. Quoted in Ballou, *The Building of the House*, 119.
36. David L. Greene, "The *Riverside Magazine for Young People*," in Kelly, *Children's Periodicals*, 367–70.
37. Scudder to Andersen, October 25, 1866, in *The Andersen-Scudder Letters: Hans Christian Andersen's Correspondence with Horace Elisha Scudder*, ed. Jean Hersholt and Waldemar Westergaard (Berkeley: University of California Press, 1949), 7.
38. Helge Topsöe-Jensen, "The Background of the Letters," in ibid., xx.
39. Horace Scudder to Hans Christian Andersen, October 25, 1866, in ibid., 7–8.
40. Hans Christian Andersen to Horace Scudder, April 21, 1868, in ibid., 10–11.
41. Ruth K. MacDonald, "*Merry's Magazine*," in Kelly, *Children's Periodicals*, 293–300.
42. The magazine's name by then had become *Merry's Museum for Boys and Girls*.
43. Ednah D. Cheney, ed., *Louisa May Alcott: Life, Letters, and Journals* (New York: Gramercy, 1995), 131.
44. Helen L. Jones, "The Part Played by Boston Publishers of 1860–1900 in the Field of Children's Books," *The Horn Book* (February 1969): 24.
45. Martha Saxton, *Louisa May Alcott: A Modern Biography* (New York: Farrar, Straus and Giroux, 1995), 295.
46. MacDonald, "*Merry's Magazine*," 298.
47. Quoted in Saxton, *Louisa May Alcott*, 301–2.
48. Camuto, "Roberts Brothers," 397.
49. Horace Scudder to Hans Christian Andersen, November 21, 1870, in Hersholt and Westergaard, *Andersen-Scudder Letters*, 85–86.
50. Greene, "The *Riverside Magazine for Young People*," 369.
51. Tebbel, *Between Covers*, 42.
52. Quoted in Marilyn H. Karrenbrock, "Mary Mapes Dodge," *Dictionary of Literary Biography*, vol. 42 (Detroit: Gale Research, 1985), 152.
53. Alice M. Jordan, "Horace E. Scudder," *The Horn Book* (May–June 1929): 37–42.
54. Ballou, *The Building of the House*, 163.
55. Darling, *The Rise of Children's Book Reviewing*, 213.
56. Richard W. Clement, *Books on the Frontier: Print Culture in the American West, 1763–1875* (Washington, D.C.: Library of Congress), 94–103.
57. Karrenbrock, "Mary Mapes Dodge," 153.

58. Ibid.

59. For a fascinating, detailed account of the tensions that characterized the three magazine editors' working relationship, see Ballou, *The Building of the House*, 170–72.

60. Karrenbrock, "Mary Mapes Dodge," 155.

61. Ibid., 147.

62. Ibid., 156–57.

63. Jens Andersen, *Hans Christian Andersen: A New Life*, tr. Tiina Nunnally (New York: Overlook Duckworth, 2005), 495–96.

64. Alice M. Jordan, *From Rollo to Tom Sawyer* (Boston: Horn Book, 1948), 114.

65. Fred Erisman, "*St. Nicholas,*" in Kelly, *Children's Periodicals,* 378. See also Anita Moss, "Kate Douglas Wiggin," in *Dictionary of Literary Biography,* vol. 42 (Detroit: Gale Research, 1985), 383.

66. *Appleton's Journal* 14 (November 6, 1875): 601, quoted in Darling, *The Rise of Children's Book Reviewing,* 37.

67. Unwilling to permit the unsatisfactory first run of just under two thousand copies to be bound and sold to English book buyers, the author, Charles Dodgson, and illustrator, John Tenniel, had agreed that crude Americans were unlikely to notice or care about the deficiencies in the printing. For this reason, they sanctioned the sale to Appleton. See Morton N. Cohen, ed., *The Letters of Lewis Carroll,* vol. 1 (New York: Oxford University Press, 1979), 77–79 (note).

68. *Scribner's Monthly* 11 (April 1876): 897, quoted in Darling, *The Rise of Children's Book Reviewing,* 37.

69. William T. Adams, "Sensational Books," *Oliver Optic's Magazine* 18 (September 1875): 718.

70. Gay, "William Taylor Adams," 16.

71. Saxton, *Louisa May Alcott,* 328–29.

72. Jones, "The Part Played by Boston Publishers," 22–26.

73. Tebbel, *Between Covers,* 81.

74. Charles A. Madison, *Book Publishing in America* (New York: McGraw-Hill, 1966), 26.

75. Exman, *The House of Harper,* 139–41.

76. Quoted in ibid., 116.

77. Henry C. Pitz, *The Brandywine Tradition* (New York: Weathervane, 1968), 52–53.

78. Ian Schoenherr, telephone interview with the author, June 28, 2007. Schoenherr generously shared many details of his research into the professional life and world of Pyle.

79. Amy Weinstein, *Once Upon a Time: Illustrations from Fairytales, Fables, Primers, Pop-ups, and Other Children's Books* (New York: Princeton Architectural Press, 2005), 5.

80. "McLoughlin Brothers Materials Added to De Grummond Collection," *Juvenile Miscellany* (Fall 1997): 1.

81. Ibid., 1–2.

82. See Darling, *The Rise of Children's Book Reviewing*, 20–21.

83. Pitz, *The Brandywine Tradition*, 81.

84. C. H. Cramer, *Open Shelves and Open Minds* (Cleveland: Case Western Reserve University Press, 1972), quoted in Paul Dickson, *The Library in America: A Celebration in Words and Pictures* (New York: Facts on File, 1986), 36.

85. Mildred Batchelder, "The Leadership Network in Children's Librarianship: A Remembrance," in *Stepping Away from Tradition: Children's Books of the Twenties and Thirties*, ed. Sybille A. Jagusch (Washington, D.C.: Library of Congress, 1988), 76–77.

86. Ibid., 71–72.

87. Frances Clarke Sayers, *Anne Carroll Moore: A Biography* (New York: Atheneum, 1972), 276. The roundtable had no official status at first with the American Library Association. But within a few months' time, the ALA formally invited the group to act as the organization's Children's Librarians' Section, with Moore as president.

88. Ibid., 113.

89. Richard W. Clement, *Books on the Frontier: Print Culture in the American West, 1763–1875* (Washington, D.C.: Library of Congress, 2003), 18.

90. Ibid., 122–23.

91. Helen L. Jones, "The Part Played by Boston Publishers of 1860–1900 in the Field of Children's Books" (part 3), *The Horn Book* (June 1969): 334.

92. Madison, *Book Publishing in America*, 70; Exman, *The House of Harper*, 171–73.

93. Exman, *The House of Harper*, 180–83.

94. "The St. Nicholas League," *St. Nicholas* (October 1910): 1146. The young poet left out the "St." from her middle name.

95. Michael Patrick Hearn, ed., *The Annotated Wonderful Wizard of Oz: Centennial Edition* (New York: W. W. Norton, 2000), xxxii.

96. David Dzwonkoski, "George M. Hill Company," in *Dictionary of Literary Biography*, vol. 49, ed. David Dzwonkoski (Detroit: Gale Research, 1986), pt. 1, 201.

97. Katharine M. Rogers, *L. Frank Baum, Creator of Oz: A Biography* (New York: St. Martin's, 2002), 64–68.

98. Dzwonkoski, "George M. Hill Company," 201.

99. Rogers, *L. Frank Baum*, 109.

100. Karrenbrock, "Mary Mapes Dodge," 159–60.

101. Quoted in ibid., 160.

3. INNOCENCE LOST AND FOUND

1. Effie L. Power, "Books of Fiction for the Borderland Age," *The Publishers' Weekly* (October 20, 1923): 1368.

2. Bertha E. Mahony, "The First Children's Department in Book Publishing," *The Horn Book* (August 1928): 3–4.

3. See, for instance, an item in *The Publishers' Weekly* (February 26, 1916): 686, which quotes author and *St. Nicholas* editor Tudor Jenks as having recently told the *New York Times:*

   > The modern boy knows that the circulating library, with its thousands of volumes, is pathetically imploring him to take advantage of it, and that in a corner of it is the special children's table, piled high with books. But the largeness of it and the quantity of books it presents to his notice overwhelm him, and he no longer counts the reading of a book as a pleasure. . . . It is a pity that the number of our books, and specially the number of our children's books, cannot be arbitrarily limited. What our children's books need is an improvement in quality, and considerable decrease in quantity, and possibly a sort of specialization — an adaptation, so that a different sort of book would be written for the town boy than that written for the country boy. It seems to me that some sort of specialization like this is inevitable.

4. Anne Carroll Moore, "Viewing and Reviewing Books for Children," reprinted in Moore, *My Roads to Childhood: Views and Reviews of Children's Books* (Boston: The Horn Book, 1961), 49.

5. Louise Seaman Bechtel, "May Massee: Publisher," *The Horn Book* (July 1936): 211.

6. Moore, "Viewing and Reviewing Books for Children," 46.

7. Ibid., 46–47.

8. For the story of the origins and history of Children's Book Week, see Leonard S. Marcus, *Seventy-five Years of Children's Book Week Posters: Celebrating Great Illustrators of American Children's Books* (New York: Knopf, 1994).

9. Franklin K. Mathiews, "The Boys Want More Books," *The Publishers' Weekly* (May 24, 1919): 1437.

10. At the 1919 American Booksellers Association convention, Frank K. Reilly of Chicago, who proposed the creation of "Patriotic Book Week," quoted a forthcoming book by Emerson Hough: "We must remake America. We must purify the source of America's population and keep it pure. We must rebuild our whole theory of citizenship in America. We must care more for the safety of America's homes and the safety of the American ideal. We must insist that there shall be an American loyalty, brooking no amendment or qualification."

    For a detailed account of the xenophobia and atmosphere of fear that spread through the nation in the wake of World War I, see Ann Hagedorn, *Savage Peace: Hope and Fear in America, 1919* (New York: Simon & Schuster, 2007).

11. Clara Whitehill Hunt, *What Shall We Read to the Children?* (Boston: Houghton Mifflin, 1915), 6.

12. Franklin S. Hoyt, "Problems in the Production of Books for Children," address to the convention of the American Library Association, reprinted in *The Publishers' Weekly* (August 2, 1919): 345.

13. Rowe Wright, "Women in Publishing," *The Publishers' Weekly* (July 28, 1928): 318.

14. George P. Brett, "The Macmillan Children's Book Department," *The Horn Book* 4, no. 3 (August 1928): 25.

15. Ibid., 26.

16. Charles Morgan, *The House of Macmillan (1843–1943)* (London: Macmillan, 1943), 163–64.

17. Mahony, "The First Children's Department," 5.

18. Peggy Farber, "Louise Seaman Bechtel: A Biographical Study," master of science in education dissertation (New York: Bank Street College of Education, 1992), 49.

19. Brett's father, George Edward Brett, had directed the American office of Macmillan, which served at first only as a sales outlet for books published in London and then expanded to originate titles by American authors as well, from 1869 to 1890.

20. Stephens's editorial correspondence, which Marc Aronson first called to the author's attention, is housed in the New York Public Library's Manuscripts and Archives Division. While in some letters Stephens merely relays the wishes of "Mr. Brett" to an author, on other occasions, as in the following letter to Frank Stockton, she shows at the least that her employer trusted her to handle a delicate editorial matter with suitable aplomb:

> My dear Mr. Stockton: —
>
> Since I enclosed to you the sample pages for the Pirate Stories we have been recalling the history of a book of our house that had a name not unlike — at least to the public ear — the heading of these tales. That was a book of ill-luck, and the superstition natural to sea stories prompts us to want to use another name. We have therefore taken the liberty to ask the printer to set up "Buccaneers and Pirates of Our Coasts" in place of "Pirates of the American Coasts."
>
> We hope this change will not be unagreeable to you. You will, I am sure, instantly understand how commercial interests prompt and in a degree force us to a variation.

Kate Stephens to Frank R. Stockton, New York, N.Y., March 19, 1898, Macmillan letterbooks, vol. 118, p. 27, New York Public Library.

21. Farber, "Louise Seaman Bechtel," 43–44; John Tebbel, "For Children, with Love and Profit," in *Stepping Away from Tradition: Children's Books of the Twenties and Thirties*, ed. Sybille A. Jagusch (Washington, D.C.: Library of Congress, 1988), 18.

22. Muriel Fuller, "Eunice P. Blake," *The Publishers' Weekly* (July 4, 1936): 30–31. Gertrude Blumenthal, who was Seaman's secretary and for a time her only departmental colleague, was a dancer.

23. Louise Seaman Bechtel, "When a Publisher Makes a Catalog," reprinted in Bechtel, *Books in Search of Children: Speeches and Essays by Louise Seaman Bechtel* (New York: Macmillan, 1969), 16.

24. Ibid., 13.

25. Elizabeth Coatsworth to Louise Seaman, Arles-sur-Rhône, undated (spring

or summer 1920), Louise Seaman Bechtel Collection, box 7, folder 116, Vassar College Library.

26. Louise Seaman to Elizabeth Coatsworth, New York, N.Y., December 8, 1919, Elizabeth Coatsworth Collection, folder 164, Maine Women Writers Collection, University of New England.

27. Marian Cutter, "Does the Librarian Make a Good Bookseller?" *The Publishers' Weekly* (October 23, 1920): 1249.

28. "Business Notes," *The Publishers' Weekly* (November 15, 1919): 1234.

29. "A New Book-Shop for Children," *The Publishers' Weekly* (October 23, 1920): 1236.

30. George P. Brett, "The Macmillan Children's Book Department," *The Horn Book* (August 1928): 26.

31. Elizabeth Coatsworth to Louise Seaman, North Africa, May 18, 1922, Louise Seaman Bechtel Collection, box 7, folder 116, Vassar College Library.

32. Bechtel, "Books in Search of Children," 191.

33. Louise Seaman Bechtel, "'A Rightful Heritage,'" reprinted in Bechtel, *Books in Search of Children: Speeches and Essays by Louise Seaman Bechtel* (New York: Macmillan, 1969), 24.

34. Barbara Bader, *American Picturebooks from Noah's Ark to the Beast Within* (New York: Macmillan, 1976), 26–27. According to Bader: "The prescription called for a black key drawing, with tissue overlays for the additional colors, the colors to be flat, with no Ben Day tints and a minimum of overprinting, the books to be printed in groups of four using the same colors."

35. Bechtel, "'Berta and Elmer' and Their Picture Books," reprinted in Bechtel, *Books in Search of Children: Speeches and Essays by Louise Seaman Bechtel* (New York: Macmillan, 1969), 64.

36. Quoted in Bader, *American Picturebooks*, 26.

37. Edna Ferber, *So Big* (Garden City, N.Y.: Doubleday, Page & Co., 1924), 229.

38. John Tebbel, *Between Covers: The Rise and Transformation of American Book Publishing* (New York: Oxford University Press, 1987), 156, 303, 306; Ann Douglas, *Terrible Honesty: Mongrel Manhattan in the 1920s* (New York: Farrar, Straus and Giroux, 1995), 14.

39. Virginia Haviland, "Louise Seaman Bechtel," introduction to Bechtel, *Books in Search of Children: Speeches and Essays by Louise Seaman Bechtel* (New York: Macmillan, 1969), xix.

40. Dianne Johnson-Feelings, ed., *The Best of the Brownies' Book* (New York: Oxford University Press, 1996), 12; E. Wendy Saul, "The Brownies' Book," in R. Gordon Kelly, *Children's Periodicals of the United States* (Westport, Conn.: Greenwood, 1984), 62.

41. Quoted in Hagedorn, *Savage Peace*, 3.

42. Katharine Capshaw Smith, *Children's Literature of the Harlem Renaissance* (Bloomington: Indiana University Press, 2004), 26–27.

43. Johnson-Feelings, *The Best of the Brownies' Book*, 335–36.

44. Ibid., 336–37.
45. Saul, "The Brownies' Book," 63–64; Johnson-Feelings, *The Best of the Brownies' Book*, 347.
46. Irene Smith, *A History of the Newbery and Caldecott Medals* (New York: Viking, 1957), 37.
47. Association for Library Service to Children, *The Newbery and Caldecott Awards: A Guide to the Medal and Honor Books* (Chicago: American Library Association, 1996), 1.
48. Smith, *A History of the Newbery and Caldecott Medals*, 38.
49. Ibid., 36.
50. Ibid., 35.
51. Ibid., 48–50. The document drafted by Frederic Melcher, dated November 9, 1922, summarized the purpose of the award, the scope of the authority granted to the ALA to devise the process for selecting the annual recipient, and Melcher's own role as the donor of the medal.
52. Moore, "Viewing and Reviewing Books for Children," 47.
53. Smith, *A History of the Newbery and Caldecott Medals*, 40.
54. Tom Dardis, *Firebrand: The Life of Horace Liveright, the Man Who Changed American Publishing* (New York: Random House, 1995), 125–28, 264, 291, 313, 341.
55. Austin Hay, "Another Outline of History," *New York Times Book Review and Magazine* (January 8, 1922), 14.
56. Frances Clarke Sayers, *Anne Carroll Moore: A Biography* (New York: Atheneum, 1972), 215.
57. Moore, "Holiday Books," reprinted in Moore, *My Roads to Childhood: Views and Reviews of Children's Books* (Boston: Horn Book, 1961), 159.
58. Smith, *A History of the Newbery and Caldecott Medals*, 45.
59. Ibid.
60. Ibid., 43.
61. Ibid., 62; Frederic G. Melcher, "The Child's Own Reading," *The Publishers' Weekly* (July 22, 1922): 181.
62. "The Story of an American Publishing House," *The Publishers' Weekly* (June 22, 1918): 1922.
63. Louise Seaman Bechtel, Macmillan Department of Books for Boys and Girls catalog for 1930, 58, Louise Seaman Bechtel Collection, box 17, folder 206, Vassar College Library.
64. Tebbel, "For Children, with Love and Profit," 19; Louise Seaman Bechtel, "May Massee, Publisher," *The Horn Book* (July–August 1936): 208–16.
65. Elizabeth Gray Vining, "May Massee: Who Was She?" in George V. Hodowanec, ed., *The May Massee Collection: Creative Publishing for Children, 1923–1963: A Checklist* (Emporia, Kans.: Emporia State University, William Allen White Library, 1979), v.
66. Bechtel, "May Massee," 213.

67. George Hendrick quotes Sandburg in his foreword to Carl Sandburg, *More Rootabagas*, ill. Paul O. Zelinsky (New York: Knopf, 1993).

68. Carl Sandburg to May Massee, Elmhurst, Ill., September 3, 1921, May Massee Collection, reprinted in Hodowanec, *May Massee Collection*, 287.

69. Frederic G. Melcher, "May Massee: As Seen by the Booksellers," *The Horn Book* (July–August 1936): 246–47.

70. Tebbel, "For Children, with Love and Profit," 19.

71. Douglas, *Terrible Honesty*, 14.

72. Ibid., 4.

73. Louise Seaman Bechtel, "The Art of Illustrating Books for the Younger Readers," *New York Times Book Review*, November 10, 1940, reprinted in Bechtel, *Books in Search of Children: Speeches and Essays by Louise Seaman Bechtel* (New York: Macmillan, 1969), 43.

74. Peter J. Schmitt, *Back to Nature: The Arcadian Myth in Urban America* (New York: Oxford University Press, 1969), 31.

75. Tebbel, "For Children, with Love and Profit," 19.

76. Harold R. Willoughby, "C. B. Falls and His Influence on American Poster Art," *The Poster* (April 1923): 9.

77. May Massee, "Acceptance of [AIGA] Medal," *The Horn Book* (August 1959): 275–77.

78. Anne Carroll Moore, "The Creative Spirit in America," reprinted in Moore, *My Roads to Childhood: Views and Reviews of Children's Books* (Boston: Horn Book, 1961), 193.

79. Nicholson first made his name as one-half of the "Beggarstaff Brothers," a short-lived but hugely influential fin-de-siècle British team of poster artists. He went on, working solo, to create several sets of popular prints depicting London types, famous personages of the day, and hunting scenes before turning his hand to children's-book illustration. In 1923 Massee published the American edition of Margery Williams's *The Velveteen Rabbit*, for which Nicholson contributed the still-well-known original illustrations.

   Nicholson met Massee's appreciation of his work with something less than gratitude. British scorn for the upstart Americans is palpable in a series of marginal notes written by him in a copy of the Doubleday edition of *Clever Bill*, now in the collection of Donnell Central Children's Room, New York Pubic Library, detailing his displeasure at the printing.

80. May Massee to Charles Buckle Falls, Garden City, N.Y., March 7, 1924, May Massee Collection.

81. Elizabeth Cleveland Miller, "May Massee: As the Authors of Her Books See Her," *The Horn Book* (July 1936): 222.

82. Bechtel, "May Massee, Publisher," 213.

83. Moore, *My Roads to Childhood*, 249.

84. Louise Seaman to Elizabeth Coatsworth, New York, N.Y., December 8, 1919, Coatsworth Collection, folder 164, Maine Women Writers Collection.

85. Mahony, "The First Children's Department," 22.

86. Louise Seaman to Elizabeth Coatsworth, New York, N.Y., October 1919, Coatsworth Collection, folder 164, Maine Women Writers Collection.

87. Louise Seaman to Elizabeth Coatsworth, New York, N.Y., November 1919, Coatsworth Collection, folder 164, Maine Women Writers Collection.

88. Sayers, *Anne Carroll Moore*, 231–33.

89. The reformist Union was dedicated to aiding and safeguarding the rights of working women.

90. Quoted in Barbara Bader, "Realms of Gold and Granite," *The Horn Book* (September–October 1999): 526.

91. Bertha E. Mahony, editorial, *The Horn Book* (October 1924): 1.

92. Alice M. Jordan, "The Bookshop from the Outside," *The Horn Book* (October 1924): 12–15.

93. Quoted in Bader, "Realms of Gold and Granite," 527.

94. [Bertha E. Mahony], "The Crossword Puzzle Book," *The Horn Book* (October 1924): 11–12.

95. For a detailed account of Lucy Sprague Mitchell's education, thoughts about books for children, and impact on the field, see Leonard S. Marcus, *Margaret Wise Brown: Awakened by the Moon* (Boston: Beacon, 1992; New York: Harper Perennial, 1999), 42–69, 77–96, 101–2.

96. Moore, "Viewing and Reviewing Books for Children," 53.

97. Lucy Sprague Mitchell, *Here and Now Story Book*, ill. Hendrik Willem van Loon (New York: E. P. Dutton, 1921), 15–16, 18.

98. Ibid., 1.

99. Haviland, "Louise Seaman Bechtel," xiii.

100. Ibid., 26.

101. Bechtel, "'A Rightful Heritage.'" According to Bechtel, the rise to power of Mussolini presented an obstacle to American publication when the Italian dictator diverted the nation's publishing resources for use by his government's propaganda machine. Further delays resulted from the Italian publisher Bemporad's refusal to pay for the proofreading services of a British national living in Florence.

102. Winifred Howard, "Preparing to Make Children's Books," *The Horn Book* (February 1930): 44.

103. Frank Schick, *Trends in American Book Publishing* (Urbana: University of Illinois, Graduate School of Library Science, 1958), 220.

104. Marilyn S. Greenwald, *The Secret Life of the Hardy Boys: Leslie McFarlane and the Stratemeyer Syndicate* (Athens: Ohio University Press, 2004), 39.

105. Ibid., 37–38; Tebbel, "For Children, with Love and Profit," 14–17.

106. Greenwald, *The Secret Life of the Hardy Boys*, 20.

107. Ibid., 20–21. Howard Garis, a former journalist and the future author of the Uncle Wiggily books, coined the expression during his apprenticeship as one of Stratemeyer's most reliable freelancers.

108. "'For It Was Indeed He,'" *Fortune* (April 1934): 87.

109. Barbara Bader, "Only the Best: The Hits and Misses of Anne Carroll Moore," *The Horn Book* (September–October 1997): 528.

110. Douglas, *Terrible Honesty*, 33.

111. Edmund Wilson, *The Twenties: From Notebooks and Diaries of the Period*, ed. Leon Edel (New York: Farrar, Straus and Giroux, 1975), 44–45.

112. Dorothy Parker [Constant Reader], "Far from Well," review of A. A. Milne, *The House at Pooh Corner*, ill. Ernest Shepard, *The New Yorker* (October 20, 1928): 98.

113. Mahony, "The First Children's Department," 3.

114. Bader, "Realms of Gold and Granite," 527.

115. Louise Seaman Bechtel, "The Giant in Children," reprinted in Bechtel, *Books in Search of Children: Speeches and Essays by Louise Seaman Bechtel* (New York: Macmillan, 1969), 145.

116. Ibid., 144.

4. Sisters in Crisis and in Conflict

1. Louise Seaman Bechtel, "May Massee, Publisher," *The Horn Book* (July 1936): 214.

2. "Children's Book Departments Are Facing a Crisis," *The Publishers' Weekly* (October 22, 1932): 1623–25.

3. According to the Department of Health and Human Services, National Center for Health Statistics, in 1925, 2,909,000 live births were recorded in the United States; in 1930 the number declined to 2,618,000, and in 1935 to 2,377,000. According to Steven Mintz, during the Depression, "for the first time in American history, the birthrate dropped below the replacement level." Steven Mintz, *Huck's Raft: A History of American Childhood* (Cambridge, Mass.: Belknap/Harvard University Press, 2004), 237.

4. Ibid., 1623; John Tebbel, *Between Covers: The Rise and Transformation of American Book Publishing* (New York: Oxford University Press, 1987), 299.

5. Muriel Fuller, "Louise Raymond," *The Publishers' Weekly* (October 17, 1936): 1598–99.

6. "Suppose It Had Been Books," *The Publishers' Weekly* (November 29, 1930): 2466.

7. Bertha Mahony Miller, "Criticism of Children's Books," *The Horn Book* (May 1946): 175, 224.

8. Katharine S. White, "Books for the Babies," *The New Yorker* (December 1, 1934): 89.

9. Quoted in Scott Elledge, *E. B. White: A Biography* (New York: W. W. Norton, 1984), 254.

10. The gist of Moore's letter may be inferred from E. B. White to Anne Carroll

Moore, North Brooklin, Maine, February 15, 1939, reprinted in Dorothy Lobrano Guth, ed., *Letters of E. B. White* (New York: Harper & Row, 1976), 192–93.

11. For further details of the contretemps occasioned by Moore's reaction to *Stuart Little*, see the account of the book's publication in Chapter 5, 175–77.

12. Herbert Hoover, address to the White House Conference on Child Health and Protection, November 19, 1930, available at www.presidency.ucsb.edu/ws/index.php?pid=22442.

13. "Books at the Conference," *The Publishers' Weekly* (November 29, 1930): 2466–67.

14. "Publishing and Selling Children's Books" (excerpts from the "Report of the Committee on Reading"), *The Publishers' Weekly* (November 29, 1930): 2454, 2458.

15. Ibid., 2453.

16. Ibid., 2456.

17. Ibid., 2458.

18. Louise Seaman Bechtel, "Books in Search of Children," reprinted in Bechtel, *Books in Search of Children: Speeches and Essays by Louise Seaman Bechtel* (New York: Macmillan, 1969), 191–214. Bechtel delivered this speech, the tenth R. R. Bowker Memorial Lecture, at the New York Public Library in 1946.

19. Marion Fiery, "What Makes a Children's Book Permanent?" *The Publishers' Weekly* (October 2, 1932): 1612.

20. Roosevelt appears to have been paraphrasing the sixteenth-century French philosopher Michel de Montaigne's observation, "The thing I fear most is fear," in *Essays*, book 1, ch. 18.

21. Fuller, "Louise Raymond," 1598.

22. Among the Artists and Writers Guild's other clients at the time were Little, Brown, Grosset & Dunlap, and Simon & Schuster.

23. Leonard S. Marcus, *Golden Legacy: How Golden Books Won Children's Hearts, Changing Publishing Forever, and Became an American Icon Along the Way* (New York: Random House, 2007).

24. Warren I. Susman, *Culture as History: The Transformation of American Society in the Twentieth Century* (New York: Pantheon, 1984), 27–38.

25. In February 1929, Seaman married Edwin de Turck Bechtel, an attorney for the American Express Company, but continued to use her maiden name as a Macmillan employee until her resignation from the house in January 1934.

26. Louise Seaman Bechtel, "Finding New Books for Boys and Girls," reprinted in Bechtel, *Books in Search of Children: Speeches and Essays by Louise Seaman Bechtel* (New York: Macmillan, 1969), 4.

27. Louise H. Seaman to Elizabeth Coatsworth, New York, N.Y., November 27, 1931, Elizabeth Coatsworth Collection, "Literary Correspondence to ECB Folder," folder 222, Maine Women Writers Collection, University of New England.

28. "Children's Book Departments Are Facing a Crisis," *The Publishers' Weekly* (October 22, 1932): 1623.

29. Peggy Farber, "Louise Seaman Bechtel: A Biographical Study," master of science in education dissertation (New York: Bank Street College of Education, 1992), 89.

30. Anne Carroll Moore to Louise Seaman Bechtel, New York, N.Y., January 10, 1934, Louise Seaman Bechtel Collection, box 32, folder 468, Vassar College Library.

31. Louise Seaman Bechtel, "May Massee, Publisher," *The Horn Book* (July 1936): 214.

32. May Massee to Ingri and Edgar Parin d'Aulaire, New York, N.Y., undated (fall 1932), May Massee Collection, Emporia State University.

33. May Massee to Ingri and Edgar Parin d'Aulaire, New York, N.Y., undated (late 1932), May Massee Collection, Emporia State University.

34. May Massee to Bertha E. Mahony, undated (spring 1933), Horn Book Archive, Simmons College.

35. In 1933 the same architect, Eric Gugler, designed the White House Oval Office.

36. Elizabeth Gray Vining, "May Massee: Who Was She?" in *The May Massee Collection: Creative Publishing for Children, 1923–1963: A Checklist*, ed. George V. Hodowanec (Emporia, Kans.: Emporia State University, 1979), viii.

37. William C. Morris, interview with the author, tape recording, New York, N.Y., October 15, 1994.

38. The editing of the famed Scribner Illustrated Classics series, featuring art by N. C. Wyeth, Maxfield Parrish, and others, had been a side responsibility of *Scribner's* magazine's art director, Joseph Hawley Chapin. See David Michaelis, *N. C. Wyeth: A Biography* (New York: Knopf, 1998), 216, 271–73.

39. Quoted in Sophie C. Silberberg and John Donovan, "Fifty Years of Children's Book Week: Fifty Years of Independent American Children's Book Publishing," *The Horn Book* (December 1969): 705.

40. Ibid., 705.

41. Alice Dalgliesh, "Improvement in Juvenile Books During the Last Ten Years," *The Publishers' Weekly* (October 25, 1930): 1970–73.

42. Alice Dalgliesh, *Along Janet's Road* (New York: Scribner, 1946), 70.

43. Ibid., 69.

44. A. Scott Berg, *Max Perkins: Editor of Genius* (New York: E. P. Dutton, 1978), 267–68.

45. Ibid., 268.

46. Ibid., 266.

47. Frances Foster, 2002 Ethel Heins Memorial Lecture, Children's Literature New England conference, Harvard University.

48. Founded in 1881, Stokes published Stephen Crane, Louis Bromfield, and Edna Ferber, as well as such luminaries of the children's book world as Frances Hodgson Burnett, Gelett Burgess, Helen Bannerman, Eleanor Farjeon,

and Hugh Lofting, and it was among the first houses to exploit the possibilities of three-color printing for art books and juveniles. If Stokes had been singled out by the trade journal as an exemplar of publishing stability, however, the choice proved an ironic one, as just six years later the house was absorbed by J. P. Lippincott.

49. Muriel Fuller, "Doris S. Patee," *The Publishers' Weekly* (August 29, 1936): 710–11.

50. Melanie Rehak, *Girl Sleuth: Nancy Drew and the Women Who Created Her* (New York: Harcourt, 2005), 123–23. In a lengthy obituary, the *New York Times* noted that "until his illness [pneumonia] began a week ago, Mr. Stratemeyer worked every day at his office at 24 West Twenty-fifth Street, Manhattan, usually dictating his stories." "Funeral Tonight for E. Stratemeyer," *New York Times* (May 12, 1930): 21.

51. "Laura Harris," *The Publishers' Weekly* (April 18, 1936): 1596–97.

52. Ludwig Bemelmans, quoted in "Massee: As Her Author-Illustrators See Her," *The Horn Book* (July–August 1936): 231.

53. Milton B. Glick, quoted in "May Massee: As Seen by Publisher and Designer," *The Horn Book* (July–August 1936): 244.

54. Frederic G. Melcher, "May Massee: As Seen by the Booksellers," *The Horn Book* (July–August 1936): 246.

55. Alice M. Jordan, "May Massee: The Librarians' Point of View," *The Horn Book* (July–August 1936): 236.

56. Bertha Mahony married William D. Miller in 1932.

57. Lee Bennett Hopkins, "Munro Leaf," in *Pauses: Autobiographical Reflections of 101 Creators of Children's Books* (New York: HarperCollins, 1995), 117.

58. Anne Carroll Moore, "The Three Owls' Notebook," *The Horn Book* (January 1938): 31.

59. B. R. Crisler, "Ferdinand Makes His Screen Debut," *New York Times* (October 23, 1938): 165.

60. Hopkins, "Munro Leaf," 116–17.

61. Ibid., 116. In his retellings of the story of *Ferdinand*'s genesis, Leaf varied the time it had taken him to write the story; his estimate here of forty minutes was on the high side.

62. Muriel Fuller, "May Massee of Viking Press," *The Publishers' Weekly* (March 11, 1950): 1339.

63. Frances Clarke Sayers, *Anne Carroll Moore: A Biography* (New York: Atheneum, 1972), 233.

64. "Women Editors in London," *The Publishers' Weekly* (October 17, 1936): 1587.

65. Russell Freedman, *Holiday House: The First Fifty Years* (New York: Holiday House, 1985), 9.

66. Helen Gentry, "Fine Books for Children, Too," *The Horn Book* (July 1935): 213.

67. Quoted in Freedman, *Holiday House*, 4.

68. John Tebbel, "For Children, with Love and Profit: Two Decades of Book Publishing for Children," in *Stepping Away from Tradition: Children's Books of the Twenties and Thirties*, ed. Sybille Jagusch (Washington, D.C.: Library of Congress, 1988), 33.

69. Vernon Ives, quoted in Freedman, *Holiday House*, 8.

70. Ibid., 14.

71. Ibid., 15.

72. Ibid.

73. For information about the founding of William R. Scott, Inc., see Leonard S. Marcus, *Margaret Wise Brown: Awakened by the Moon* (Boston: Beacon, 1992; New York: Harper Perennial, 1999), 88–89, 92–96, 99–102.

74. Ibid., 48. Mitchell recalled her father's attitude toward her childhood passion for writing in Lucy Sprague Mitchell, "Pioneering in Education," an oral history conducted in 1960 by Irene Prescott, University of California at Berkeley, General Library, Regional Cultural History Project, 1962, 155.

75. Late in life, Mitchell would tell her former student and friend Margaret Wise Brown: "I sometimes wonder — now that my chance has passed — whether I could have made words magical if my civic conscience had been less domineering?" Quoted in Marcus, *Margaret Wise Brown*, 256.

76. Ibid., 67–69.

77. Bertha E. Mahony, "*Another Here and Now Story Book*," *The Horn Book* (May–June 1937): 166.

78. Anne Carroll Moore, "The Three Owls' Notebook," *The Horn Book* (May–June 1937): 168.

79. See, for example, Louise H. Seaman, "Not Only in Spring," *Atlantic Monthly* (April 1929): 33–37.

80. Anne Carroll Moore, "The Three Owls' Notebook," *The Horn Book* (March 1937): 79.

81. Bertha Mahony Miller, "Artists Triumph," *The Horn Book* (July 1938): 206.

82. Irene Smith, *A History of the Newbery and Caldecott Medals* (New York: Viking, 1957), 64.

83. Clara W. Hunt to Frederic G. Melcher, Brooklyn, N.Y., June 24, 1937, *Publishers Weekly* Library, New York, N.Y. In his reply to Hunt the following day (also found in the R. R. Bowker Library), Melcher reaffirmed his wish that the medal be named for Randolph Caldecott.

84. As Moore cautioned: "Prizes and medals have started something, something not always easy to reconcile with creative art. Prizes and medals are good only so long as judgments remain sound and untouched by adventitious circumstances." Anne Carroll Moore, "The Three Owls' Notebook," *The Horn Book* (January 1938): 32.

85. Melcher once again turned to the sculptor and decorative artist who had created the design for the John Newbery Medal. The work of New York–based artist René Paul Chambellan could also be seen at New York's Rockefeller

Center, for which he had created a series of Triton, Nereid, and dolphin sculptures as part of the Center's Promenade fountains.

86. For information about Disney's early involvement in the realm of character licensing for books and merchandise, see Robert Heide and John Gilman, *Disneyana: Classic Collectibles, 1928–1958* (New York: Disney Editions, 1994); Robert Heide, John Gilman, et al., *Mickey Mouse: The Evolution, the Legend, the Phenomenon* (New York: Disney Editions, 2003); and Marcus, *Golden Legacy.*

87. Anne Carroll Moore, "The Three Owls' Notebook," *The Horn Book* (January 1938): 32.

88. Anne Carroll Moore, "The Three Owls' Notebook," *The Horn Book* (March 1938): 92.

89. The closest rival to comic books was the Big Little Books line of comics compilations published by Whitman, the publishing imprint of the Western Printing and Lithographing Company, starting in 1932. The Big Littles had a diminutive trim size, a page count running into the hundreds, and garish movie poster–style cover art. At ten cents each, they sold in the hundreds of thousands at five-and-dime stores and other retail outlets.

90. Dorothy P. Lathrop, "Caldecott Medal Acceptance," *The Horn Book* (July 1938): 214.

91. Miller, "Artists Triumph," 202–3.

92. Frederic G. Melcher was quick to recognize the significance of the new photographically illustrated magazines for book publishing. In his editorial for the May 29, 1937, issue of *The Publishers' Weekly,* Melcher concluded: "From the current blaze of new experiment we can learn much."

93. In *Five Years of Children's Books* (1936), Bertha Mahony Miller included mention of Mary Steichen Martin and Edward Steichen's *First Picture Book* and its sequel, but noted: "However fine the pictures, the photographic picture books have less space for the workings of a child's fancy and are sooner exhausted than imaginative pictures." Quoted in Barbara Bader, *American Picturebooks from Noah's Ark to the Beast Within* (New York: Macmillan, 1976), 103.

94. See Helen Hammett Owen, "Photographic Picture Books," *The Publishers' Weekly* (October 24, 1931): 1923–24; "'Orbis Pictus,'" *The Nation* (October 16, 1935): 426; Bader, *American Picturebooks,* 100–114, 585.

95. Anne Carroll Moore, "High Roads to Children," reprinted in Moore, *My Roads to Childhood: Views and Reviews of Children's Books* (Boston: Horn Book, 1961), 348.

96. Bertha Mahony Miller, "Wayfarers All," *The Horn Book* (May–June 1938): 141. For more on the initial critical reception of *The Hobbit,* see Humphrey Carpenter, *J. R. R. Tolkien: A Biography* (Boston: Houghton Mifflin, 1977), 186.

97. Quoted in Susman, *Culture as History,* 233.

98. Ibid., 222.

99. Robert McCloskey, interview with the author, tape recording, Weston, Conn., February 11, 1991.
100. Susman, *Culture as History*, 220.
101. Ibid., 226.
102. Ibid., 228–29.

5. WORLD WAR AND MASS MARKET

1. Anne Carroll Moore, "The Three Owls' Notebook," *The Horn Book* (July 1940): 265.
2. Frances Clarke Sayers, *Anne Carroll Moore: A Biography* (New York: Atheneum, 1972), 220–21.
3. Judy Taylor, Joyce Irene Walley, et al., *Beatrix Potter, 1866–1943: The Artist and Her World* (London: Frederick Warne/National Trust, 1987), 30.
4. Moore, "The Three Owls' Notebook," *The Horn Book* (July 1940), 265.
5. Brooke was in good company. Other children's room festival days celebrated the birthdays of Hans Christian Andersen, Walter de la Mare, and William Shakespeare.
6. Moore, "The Three Owls' Notebook," *The Horn Book* (July 1940), 265.
7. "Children's Book Illustrations Sold for British Relief," *The Publishers' Weekly* (October 26, 1940): 1692.
8. Russell Baker, *Growing Up* (New York: Congdon & Weed, 1982), 206.
9. Louise Seaman Bechtel, "The Comics and Children's Books," *The Horn Book* (July 1941): 297.
10. Ibid., 296.
11. Grace Allen Hogarth, "The War and Reading," *New York Times Book Review* (November 2, 1941): 1.
12. "The Hunt Breakfast," *The Horn Book* (March–April 1941): 72.
13. Bechtel, "The Comics and Children's Books," 296.
14. Ibid., 298.
15. Peter Schwed, *Turning the Pages: An Insider's Story of Simon & Schuster, 1924–1984* (New York: Macmillan, 1984), 2.
16. William W. Parish, "The Story of Little Golden Books," *The Westerner* (March 1951): 12.
17. Philip B. Kunhardt Jr., *The Dreaming Game: A Portrait of a Passionate Life* (New York: Riverhead, 2004), 220–24.
18. Grace Allen Hogarth, unpublished memoir, collection of Grace Allen Hogarth, 103.
19. Ibid., 104.
20. Grace Allen Hogarth to H. A. Rey, Boston, Mass., November 4, 1940, Rey Collection, Houghton Library, Harvard University.
21. When *Curious George* was first published in England, in 1942, the title had to be changed again, this time to *Zozo*, George being the name of the sitting king of England and "curious," in Britain, being a code word for "gay." For

more information about the creation of the Reys' best-known book, see Leonard S. Marcus, introduction to *The Original Curious George* (Boston: Houghton Mifflin, 1998); Louise Borden, *The Journey That Saved Curious George*, ill. Allan Drummond (Boston: Houghton Mifflin, 2005).

22. Helen Jones contributed the section on the 1940s to Sophie C. Silberberg and John Donovan, "Fifty Years of Children's Book Week: Fifty Years of Independent American Children's Book Publishing," *The Horn Book* (December 1969): 707.

23. Records in Houghton Mifflin's files charting the annual sales of its children's books indicate that *Curious George* sold an average of just over three thousand copies annually through 1944. Sales for 1945 were listed as "negative six," suggesting that the book was out of stock and could not be reprinted that year. Sales slowly returned to their former levels in the following few years before experiencing an upward spike in 1953 that proved to be the start of a long-term trend of growing demand for the book.

24. Virginia Lee Burton, "Symphony in Comics," *The Horn Book* (July 1941): 307–11; Grace Allen Hogarth, "Virginia Lee Burton, Creative Artist," *The Horn Book* (July 1943): 221.

25. Burton, "Symphony in Comics," 308.

26. Catherine Barron to the author, Oxford, U.K., December 5, 1993, author's archive.

27. In a 1950 reissue of *Calico*, Burton restored "Stinker" as the name of the story's chief bad guy.

28. Robert Lawson, "The Caldecott Medal Acceptance," *The Horn Book* (July 1941): 282.

29. Ibid., 279.

30. Ibid., 277.

31. Review of *Homer Price*, *Saturday Review* (October, 16, 1943), quoted in Gary D. Schmidt, *Robert McCloskey* (Boston: Twayne, 1990), 29.

32. Josette Frank, quoted in Helen Hoke, Leo Lerman, and Evelyn Hamilton, "The Problem Book," *The Publishers' Weekly* (October 18, 1941): 1154–55.

33. Ibid., 1154.

34. Bradford W. Wright, *Comic Book Nation: The Transformation of Youth Culture in America* (Baltimore: Johns Hopkins University Press, 2001), 34; Josette Frank, interview with the author, handwritten notes, New York, N.Y., April 13, 1985.

35. Anne Carroll Moore to Rachel Moore Warren (early 1941), quoted in Sayers, *Anne Carroll Moore*, 260.

36. Ibid.

37. Ibid., 268.

38. May Massee to Bertha Mahony Miller, New York, N.Y., July 2, 1943, Horn Book Archive, Simmons College, Boston.

39. Bertha Mahony Miller to May Massee, Ashburnham, Mass., July 13, 1945, Horn Book Archive.

40. Roni Natov and Geraldine DeLuca, "Discovering Contemporary Classics: An Interview with Ursula Nordstrom," *The Lion and the Unicorn* (Spring 1979): 120.

41. Ibid.

42. Ibid., 126.

43. For more on Ursula Nordstrom's publishing philosophy and the professional environment in which she worked, see Leonard S. Marcus, ed., *Dear Genius: The Letters of Ursula Nordstrom* (New York: HarperCollins, 1998).

44. For accounts of the creation of *Make Way for Ducklings*, see Schmidt, *Robert McCloskey*, 76–93; Leonard S. Marcus, introduction to *Make Way for McCloskey: A Robert McCloskey Treasury* (New York: Viking, 2004).

45. Ursula Nordstrom to Georges Duplaix, New York, N.Y., October 10, 1942, reprinted in Marcus, *Dear Genius*, 6.

46. Leonard S. Marcus, *Golden Legacy: How Golden Books Won Children's Hearts, Changed Publishing Forever, and Became an American Icon Along the Way* (New York: Random House, 2007), 4–7.

47. Ibid., 10–15.

48. Lowe, who had risen in the company to become president of Whitman Publishing, resigned in 1940 to found a rival publishing house, the Samuel E. Lowe Company, in Kenosha, Wisconsin, with additional offices in New York and London. Lowe preferred being his own boss and found it increasingly difficult to execute his more unconventional ideas as part of the growing bureaucracy that was Western. See ibid., 36–37.

49. For information about Western's long and profitable association with the company founded by George Delacorte and later headed by Helen Meyer, see "Ding Dong Dell," *The Westerner* (May 1949): 11–14; and "Four Billion Comic Books," *The Westerner* (February 1958): 16.

50. Barbara Bader, *American Picturebooks from Noah's Ark to the Beast Within* (New York: Macmillan, 1976), 26–30, 278.

51. Perhaps the main reason Simon & Schuster was the ideal partner for the project — for which production manager Tom Bevans suggested the inspired name of Little Golden Books — was that the company had a storehouse of relevant experience by virtue of its having entered into a similar partnership in the late 1930s, in a venture that had culminated in the launch of the first modern mass-market paperback line for adults — Pocket Books. The introduction in June 1939 of the twenty-five-cent line had an immediate and lasting impact on the way books were bought and sold in the United States. (Supremely confident from the first, Simon & Schuster's business partner Robert de Graff had wanted the full-page launch-day advertisement that ran in the *New York Times* for June 19, 1939, to read: "Out Today — The New Pocket Books That Will Transform New York's Reading Habits." His partners, wishing not to appear too cocky, had insisted on changing "Will" to "May.") Consumers snapped up the compact budget editions of bestsellers

and classics such as James Hilton's *Lost Horizon* and Thornton Wilder's *The Bridge of San Luis Rey* from custom-designed wire racks in train stations, drugstores, five-and-dime stores, and other heavily trafficked locales not necessarily associated with bookselling. This was precisely what had to happen for Little Golden Books to succeed.

52. Mitchell had been in discussions with Georges Duplaix and Lucille Ogle as early as 1943 about the possibility of a special Bank Street series of Little Golden Books, written by members of Bank Street's Writers Laboratory. Wartime shortages had delayed the launch of the series until 1946. The first two titles appeared that year: Lucy Sprague Mitchell's *The New House in the Forest*, illustrated by Eloise Wilkin; and *The Taxi That Hurried*, coauthored by Mitchell, Irma Simonton Black, and Jessie Stanton, with illustrations by Tibor Gergely.

53. "A Memorandum to the Trade from Simon and Schuster About The Little Golden Books," text for the eight-page color insert advertisement that ran in the September 19, 1942, issue of *Publishers' Weekly* under the title "A Statement About the How's, Why's and Wherefores of Little Golden Books." Random House Archive.

54. Dorothy A. Bennett, interview with the author, El Cerito, Calif., April 23, 1984.

55. Garth Williams to the author, Santa Fe, N.M. (postmarked), February 14, 1983, author's archive.

56. Tenggren, who had contributed concept paintings for *Snow White*, *Pinocchio*, *Fantasia*, and other major Disney feature animations, had left Los Angeles for New York in 1939. After the war, he introduced his friends Alice and Martin Provensen, the latter of whom was a Disney alumnus, to the Guild's editors. Among the other former Disney artists who joined the Golden stable after the war were J. P. Miller, Mary Blair, and Aurelius Battaglia.

57. Steve Santi, *Collecting Little Golden Books: A Collector's Identification and Price Guide*, 5th ed. (Iola, Wisc.: Krause, 2003), 2.

58. Bernard Grun, *The Timetables of History: A Horizontal Linkage of People and Events* (New York: Touchstone/Simon & Schuster, 1982), 517.

59. Margaret Lesser, "The Impossible Is Happening," *Publishers' Weekly* (August 28, 1943): 687. Note that as of the issue of August 8, 1942, the journal of record of the book publishing industry dropped the "The" from its name.

60. William M. Tuttle Jr., *"Daddy's Gone to War": The Second World War in the Lives of America's Children* (New York: Oxford University Press, 1993), 112–33.

61. Louise Seaman Bechtel, "Children in a World at War," *The Horn Book* (March 1942): 89.

62. Grace Allen Hogarth, in *Bulletin of the New Hampshire Libraries* (September 1943), quoted in *Library Journal* (October 15, 1943): 835.

63. Tuttle, *"Daddy's Gone to War*," 125. See also the advertisement for Leaf's book in *The Horn Book* (July–August 1943): 285.

64. Jack Matthews, *Toys Go to War: World War II Military Toys, Games, Puzzles, and Books* (Missoula, Mont.: Pictorial Histories, 1994), 106, 109.

65. During the war years the Main Library of Toledo, Ohio, carried out a fascinating experiment, selectively purchasing comic books for the library's Boys' and Girls' Room on a temporary, noncirculating basis. The comics, reported Toledo's supervisor of work with children, Ethel C. Wright, in the October 15, 1943, issue of *Library Journal*, were "placed in the center section of a floor rack with a poster above saying: 'This Is an Experiment. Ask the Librarians for Information about It.' Popular books of mystery and adventure, fun and laughter, in clean bright covers were kept in the sections on either side. Our purpose was to observe how children reacted to Comics when exposed to them in an environment of attractive children's books which equaled in story interest, on the child's own plane of experience, the adult experiences found in the Comics." Wright reported that after several weeks of making available these special offerings, the results had been inconclusive. The children had not (as hoped) rejected comics in favor of the nearby books. A few of the comics were stolen. The librarians had found that some comics were more objectionable than others, making generalizations about content inadvisable. Most baffling to the libraries that took part in the experiment were the reasons for the comics' undeniable popularity with children. "It was difficult," wrote Wright, "to understand how the second- and third-graders could be interested when one considered the very poor print and confusing sequences. There seemed to be a contagious attraction about the magazines for all ages of children, which spread like wildfire as soon as a Comic appeared in the hands of a child. A few first-grade children even sat quietly for a time, poring over the pictures and turning the pages slowly. One wondered what continuity of thought or meaning they could get from the pictures alone." See Ethel C. Wright, "A Public Library Experiments with the Comics," *Library Journal* (October 15, 1943): 832–35.

66. Grace Allen Hogarth, unpublished memoir, 108–9.

67. Eunice Blake, "How Will Children's Books Look in 1944?" *Library Journal* (December 15, 1943): 1039.

68. Lesser, "The Impossible Is Happening," 687.

69. Howard Pease, "Without Evasion: Some Reflections After Reading Mrs. Means' *The Moved-Outers*," *The Horn Book* (January 1945): 17. For the background of this book, see Suzanne Rahn, "Early Images of American Minorities: Rediscovering Florence Crannell Means," *The Lion and the Unicorn* (April 1987): 98–115.

70. "The Ten-Cent Juvenile," *The Publishers' Weekly* (November 10, 1934), 174–75.

71. Muriel Fuller, "Mary Alice Jones of Rand McNally & Company," *Publishers' Weekly* (March 26, 1949): 1416–17.

72. Ibid., 1417.

73. In April 1944, Grace Allen Hogarth had returned with her two children to her home in England. See "The Hunt Breakfast," *The Horn Book* (May 1945): 138.

74. Leonard S. Marcus, "An Interview with Margaret K. McElderry — Part 1," *The Horn Book* (November–December 1993): 694.

75. The situation was not all grim. "A few people," McElderry later recalled, "had held off to wait and see what would happen, notably Eleanor Estes. Carolyn Haywood was very sweet and fair. She had one new book on the list which she left behind, though she could have broken her contract. Stephen Meader . . . was very loyal to Harcourt." Nonetheless, McElderry had been unnerved. "Basically," it had seemed at the time, "I was presented with a clean slate, and I didn't know what to do." Ibid., 696.

76. "Morrow Opens New Juvenile Department," *The Publishers' Weekly* (July 26, 1941): 245.

77. Leonard S. Marcus, *Morrow Junior Books: The First Fifty Years* (New York: William Morrow, 1996), 1–2.

78. Connie Epstein, interview with the author, tape recording, New York, N.Y., June 16, 1995.

79. Marjorie Hill Allee, "Books Negro Children Like," *The Horn Book* (March 1938): 85.

80. See, for example, Eleanor Weakley Nolen, "The Colored Child in Contemporary Literature," *The Horn Book* (September 1942): 348–55.

81. Ellen Tarry, interview with the author, New York, N.Y., July 25, 1984.

82. Massee published the best known of Tarry's children's books, a photographically illustrated story of contemporary Negro urban life called *My Dog Rinty*, coauthored by Marie Hall Ets, photographed by Alexandra and Alexander Alland (New York: Viking, 1946).

83. Garth Williams, interview with the author, by telephone, November 13, 1989; Leonard S. Marcus, "Garth Williams: An Interview," *Publishers Weekly* (February 23, 1990): 200; Joan Brest Friedberg, "Garth Williams," in *Dictionary of Literary Biography*, vol. 22, ed. John Cech (Detroit: Gale Research, 1983), 367–75.

84. Quoted in Scott Elledge, *E. B. White: A Biography* (New York: W. W. Norton, 1984), 263.

85. E. B. White to Frances Clarke Sayers, North Brooklin, Maine, November 24, 1945, reprinted in *The Letters of E. B. White*, ed. Dorothy Lobrano Guth (New York: Harper & Row, 1976), 270–71. White, who considered the rumor-mongering of gossip columnists distasteful, wrote to assure Sayers that he had no intention of instigating any such "to-do."

86. Quoted in ibid., 267.

87. See, for example, Katharine S. White to Louise Seaman Bechtel, New York, N.Y., September 12, 1961, a letter written at the time that Frances Clarke Sayers was starting work on Anne Carroll Moore's biography. White comments:

> I'm interested . . . in your contribution to the biography of Anne Carroll Moore. . . . It isn't only because of that letter to me begging me to persuade Andy to withdraw "Stuart Little" from publication because it would hurt his reputation. It is as much because of the false sentimentality she taught the children's li-

brarians. I really saw it in action over several years at the Candlelight meeting at the N.Y. Public Library. Much as she did for children's books and their illustrators at the start of her career, I can't help feeling her influence was baleful on the whole. Am I wrong? I wish you and not Mrs. Sayers were going to write the book.

Louise Seaman Bechtel Collection, box 43, folder 660, Vassar College Library.

88. Louise Seaman Bechtel to Bertha Mahony Miller, January 1947, Horn Book Archives, Simmons College.

89. "*Blueberries for Sal*: A Story for Children," *Life* (December 27, 1948): 69.

90. "The Tell-Well Press Promotes Juveniles Through the Department Stores," *Publishers' Weekly* (October 30, 1948): 1878–81.

91. Leonard S. Marcus, *Seventy-five Years of Children's Book Week Posters: Celebrating Great Illustrators of American Children's Books* (New York: Knopf, 1994), xvi.

92. "Year-round Agency to Promote Children's Books," *Publishers' Weekly* (March 3, 1945): 1006. In addition to the Association of Children's Book Editors, the Council began its life with sponsorship from a long roster of organizations with an interest in education, including the American Library Association, the National Education Association, the U.S. Office of Education, the National Congress of Parents and Teachers, the Child Study Association, the Jewish Education Committee, the National Association of Negro Business and Professional Women, the Catholic Library Association, Boy Scouts of America, and Girl Scouts of America.

93. Elizabeth Riley, "Book Week — A Nation-Wide Promotion Program," *Publishers' Weekly* (June 12, 1948): 2464.

94. Margaret McElderry, "Children's Books: A Growing Market," *Publishers' Weekly* (June 12, 1948): 2463.

95. Louise Seaman Bechtel, "From Dr. Dolittle to Superman: New Trends in Children's Books," reprinted in Bechtel, *Books in Search of Children: Speeches and Essays by Louise Seaman Bechtel* (New York: Macmillan, 1969), 221.

96. For details of Lepman's able efforts, see her memoir, Jella Lepman, *A Bridge of Children's Books* (Dublin: O'Brien Press, IBBY Ireland, and USBBY, 2002).

97. "Children Want Realism in Books, Authors Guild Told," *Publishers' Weekly* (October 29, 1949): 1895.

98. Ibid.

99. Ibid., 1896. By the late 1940s, Golden Books no longer had the mass-market side of the picture-book trade to themselves. By then, Samuel Lowe had launched his Bonnie Books imprint in direct competition with the Little Goldens; Chicago-based Rand McNally had introduced its similar line of Elf Books; and most significantly in terms of sales, Grosset & Dunlap, in partnership with the Curtis Publishing Company, had inaugurated its Wonder Books line.

100. Ibid., 1896.

101. Connie Bruck, "The Monopolist," *The New Yorker* (April 21 and 28, 2003): 141.

102. Bechtel, "From Dr. Dolittle to Superman," 217–18.

103. Louise Seaman Bechtel, "The Children's Librarian," reprinted in Bechtel, *Books in Search of Children: Speeches and Essays by Louise Seaman Bechtel* (New York: Macmillan, 1969), 233.

104. Ibid., 238.

6. Fun and Fear

1. William S. Gray and May Hill Arbuthnot, *Fun with Dick and Jane* (Chicago: Scott, Foresman, 1940).

2. J. D. Salinger, *The Catcher in the Rye* (Boston: Little, Brown, 1951), 3.

3. E. B. White, "Here Is New York," reprinted in *Essays of E. B. White* (New York: Harper & Row, 1977), 132.

4. Ann Hulbert, *Raising America: Experts, Parents, and a Century of Advice About Children* (New York: Knopf, 2003), 229.

5. Martha Wolfenstein, "The Emergence of Fun Morality," *Journal of Social Issues* (1951): 22.

6. Theodor Geisel (Dr. Seuss), *The Cat in the Hat* (New York: Random House, 1957), 18.

7. Quoted in Elizabeth Diefendorf, ed., *The New York Public Library's Books of the Century*, ill. Diana Bryan (New York: Oxford University Press, 1996), 209. In citing Salinger's book as one of America's seminal works of fiction, the New York Public Library staff noted that *The Catcher in the Rye* was considered a "shocking" book at the time of publication.

8. Margaret A. Edwards of the Enoch Pratt Free Library in Baltimore was among the first critics to note the emergence of this new, distinctively American genre. See Michael Cart, *From Romance to Realism: Fifty Years of Growth and Change in Young Adult Literature* (New York: HarperCollins, 1996), 13–15; Margaret A. Edwards, "The Rise of Teen-Age Reading," *Saturday Review* (November 13, 1954): 88–89; and Patty Campbell, *Two Pioneers of Young Adult Library Services* (Lanham, Md.: Scarecrow, 1998).

9. *This Fabulous Century, 1950–1960* (New York: Time-Life, 1985), 58–59, 62–63.

10. See Leonard S. Marcus, *Golden Legacy: How Golden Books Won Children's Hearts, Changed Publishing Forever, and Became an American Icon Along the Way* (New York: Random House, 2007), 138–75.

11. Bennett Cerf, *At Random: The Reminiscences of Bennett Cerf* (New York: Random House, 1977), 157–58.

12. Leonard S. Marcus, *Margaret Wise Brown: Awakened by the Moon* (Boston: Beacon, 1992; New York: Harper Perennial, 1999), 125.

13. Smith & Haas was de Brunhoff's first American publisher, but Random

House became associated with the Babar books before the merger with Smith & Haas by publishing lower-priced "flat" editions that sold for one dollar each as compared with three dollars for the more handsomely produced original editions.

14. Muriel Fuller, "Louise Bonino of Random House," *The Publishers' Weekly* (October 28, 1939): 1684–86.

15. Cerf, *At Random*, 158. Random House later made much of this point in its promotional materials for Landmark Books, as did the Book-of-the-Month Club. As a sales and marketing strategy it left many in the children's book industry understandably chagrined. Harper author Meindert DeJong clipped the following passage from a BOMC brochure and tacked it to the wall in front of his typewriter as "a goad and an irritant" — a reminder, as he wrote his editor Ursula Nordstrom, of the respect denied him and his colleagues simply because they chose to write for young people: "Parents made the happy discovery that the quality of the writing was immeasurably higher (in Landmark Books) than that of the vast majority of children's books being published. Landmark Books are written, not by the usual run of 'juvenile' writers, but by outstanding contemporary authors who have made their reputations in the field of serious adult writing." Quoted in Meindert DeJong to Ursula Nordstrom, Grand Rapids, Mich., January 23, 1953, reprinted in Leonard S. Marcus, *Dear Genius: The Letters of Ursula Nordstrom* (New York: HarperCollins, 1998), 62–65.

16. Cerf, *At Random*, 158.

17. "The Landmark Story," *Publishers' Weekly* (July 30, 1956): 460.

18. Ibid.

19. Cerf, *At Random*, 158.

20. Louise Bonino, "The Landmark Story," *Publishers' Weekly* (July 30, 1956): 460–62.

21. Ibid., 460.

22. Ibid., 462.

23. Marcus, *Dear Genius*, xxiii.

24. "Take a Bow, Lucile Pannell," *Publishers' Weekly* (April 2, 1949): 1510–11.

25. Lucy Tompkins, "National Children's Book Week — A Report," *Publishers' Weekly* (December 12, 1953): 2305–11.

26. Ibid., 2305–6.

27. Ursula Nordstrom to Janette Sebring Lowrey, New York, N.Y., April 14, 1954, reprinted in Marcus, *Dear Genius*, 76–77.

28. Leonard S. Marcus, "An Interview with Margaret K. McElderry — Part II," *The Horn Book* (January–February 1994): 34–37.

29. *This Fabulous Century 1950–1960*, 117.

30. Fritz Eichenberg, "Artist's Choice: *The Two Reds*," *The Horn Book* (July 1951): 239.

31. More than forty years later, Margaret K. McElderry was able to quote the re-

view from memory. See Leonard S. Marcus, "An Interview with Margaret K. McElderry — Part I," *The Horn Book* (January–February 1994): 35.

32. Marcus, "An Interview with Margaret K. McElderry — Part II," 35–36.

33. Ellen Levine, interview with the author, tape recording by telephone, March 22, 2007. By far the most detailed elaboration of the subject is found in Julia L. Mickenberg, *Learning from the Left: Children's Literature, the Cold War, and Radical Politics in the United States* (New York: Oxford University Press, 2006); but see also Barbara Bader's thoughtful critique of this study, "*Red, White, and Blue?*" *The Horn Book* (July 2006): 477–81.

34. Marcus, "An Interview with Margaret K. McElderry — Part II," 36.

35. Ursula Nordstrom to E. B. White, New York, N.Y., March 19, 1951, reprinted in Marcus, *Dear Genius*, 35–36.

36. Ursula Nordstrom to E. B. White, New York, N.Y., October 23, 1952, reprinted in Marcus, *Dear Genius*, 55–56.

37. For details of McElderry and Norton's working relationship, see Leonard S. Marcus, foreword to Mary Norton, *The Borrowers: Fiftieth Anniversary Gift Edition*, ill. Diana Stanley (San Diego: Harcourt, 2002).

38. L. M. Boston, *Memory in a House* (New York: Macmillan, 1974), 102–3.

39. Leonard S. Marcus, "An Interview with Frances Foster," *The Horn Book* (September–October 2003): 545–60.

40. Marcus, *Golden Legacy*, 147–48.

41. In September 1959, after nine years at Viking, Bell left the comparatively small literary house for the publishing colossus comprising the newly consolidated Random House, Pantheon, and Knopf.

42. Dan Wakefield, *New York in the Fifties* (Boston: Houghton Mifflin/Seymour Lawrence, 1992), 275.

43. Lowrey was best known as the author of *The Poky Little Puppy*. In all likelihood it was Nordstrom who had put Lowrey in touch with her publishing friend Lucille Ogle when the latter was planning Little Golden Books' inaugural list. Nordstrom was happy to help an author she cared about; as a publisher, she was interested in Lowrey primarily as a writer of fiction for older girls.

44. That year, 1954, was a grim one for congressional assaults on the protections guaranteed to Americans under the Bill of Rights. It was then that psychiatrist Fredric Wertham, in his bestselling *Seduction of the Innocent*, assailed the comic-book genre as a root cause of both illiteracy and juvenile delinquency. Wertham's authoritative pronouncements prompted a round of Senate hearings led by Estes Kefauver, the Tennessee Democrat and vice-presidential running mate of Adlai Stevenson. By October 1954, in response to these fast-moving developments, the publishers of comic books had adopted the self-censoring Comics Code, thereby preempting harsher restrictions that Congress might otherwise have imposed. Among comics aficionados, the chilling influence of the Comics Code is generally regarded as having

been powerful enough to eviscerate the genre for years to come. For a detailed account of these events, see David Hajdu, *The Ten-Cent Plague: The Great Comic-Book Scare and How It Changed America* (New York: Farrar, Straus and Giroux, 2008).

45. Judith and Neil Morgan, *Dr. Seuss and Mr. Geisel: A Biography* (New York: Random House, 1995), 162.

46. Marcus, *Golden Legacy*, 132–36. Richard Simon, who masterminded the *Doctor Dan* campaign, prided himself on his marketing flair and took the lead in assembling a staff capable of implementing his aggressive, showmanlike approach to publishing. Historian John Tebbel has observed: "In the fifties there seemed to be no end to [Simon & Schuster's] arsenal of merchandising methods, and of the men and women to make them work. In 1954, for example, the house conducted what was probably the most extensive campaign of mail-order selling the book business had ever seen up to that time; nearly 4,500,000 pieces of direct-mail advertising were distributed across the United States on behalf of the two Golden Book lines." John Tebbel, *Between Covers: The Rise and Transformation of American Book Publishing* (New York: Oxford University Press, 1987), 395.

47. "Ding Dong School, TV Show, Has Taken the 3-to-5-Year-Olds by Storm," *Publishers' Weekly* (April 4, 1953): 1508–10; Daniel J. Wakin, "Frances R. Horwich, 93, Host of 'Ding Dong School' in 50s," *New York Times* (July 26, 2001): B9.

48. Richard Severo, "Bob Keeshan, Creator and Star of TV's 'Captain Kangaroo,' Is Dead at 76," *New York Times* (January 24, 2004): A13.

49. Terri Payne Butler, "Moving Pictures: Morton Schindel Revisited," *The Horn Book* (September–October 1998): 558–59.

50. Morton Schindel, "Making Films for Children," in *Films for Children, with 1965 Supplement* (pamphlet) (New York: Educational Film Library Association, n.d.), author's archive.

51. *Captain Kangaroo* did air Weston Woods films for a time during the early 1960s. Butler, "Moving Pictures," 559.

52. Richard Schickel, *The Disney Version: The Life, Times, Art, and Commerce of Walt Disney* (New York: Simon & Schuster, 1968), 306–7.

53. Marcus, *Golden Legacy*, 148–51.

54. Clement Hurd, interview with the author, Starksboro, Vt., July 13–14 1982; Leonard S. Marcus, "Le Tout premier des livres, ou comment *Bonsoir Lune* devint un classique," *La Revue des Livres pour Enfants* (June 2000): 1–9.

55. Random House priced *The Cat in the Hat* at $2.00, but soon afterward reduced the price to $1.95. Sales of the book had passed the 200,000 mark by May 1958 and had reached 300,000 by November of that year. See Phil Nel, ed., *The Annotated Cat in the Hat: Under the Hats of Seuss and His Cats* (New York: Random House, 2007), 10.

56. John Hersey, "Why Do Students Bog Down on the First R?" *Life* (May 24, 1954): 148.

57. Morgan and Morgan, *Dr. Seuss and Mr. Geisel*, 154.

58. Ursula Nordstrom to Else Holmelund Minarik, New York, N.Y., December 28, 1956, reprinted in Marcus, *Dear Genius*, 88–89.

59. For details of Nordstrom's editing of *Danny and the Dinosaur*, see Marcus, *Dear Genius*, 103–10.

60. Barbara Bader, *American Picturebooks from Noah's Ark to the Beast Within* (New York: Macmillan, 1976), 312.

61. Morgan and Morgan, *Dr. Seuss and Mr. Geisel*, 157.

62. Stan and Jan Berenstain, "The Bear Beginnings," *Publishers Weekly* (October 7, 2002): 29.

63. Ibid., 31.

64. "The One and Only Dr. Seuss and His Wonderful Autographing Tour," *Publishers' Weekly* (December 8, 1958): 12–15.

65. "Knowledge Is Power," *Time* (November 18, 1957): 21.

66. Ibid., 23.

67. Muriel Fuller, "Elizabeth Riley of Crowell," *Publishers' Weekly* (March 10, 1951): 1263.

68. Franklyn M. Branley, "Franklyn M. Branley," in *Something About the Author Autobiography Series*, vol. 16, ed. Joyce Nakamura (Detroit: Gale Research, 1993), 24.

69. Franklin Watts, "A Publisher Looks at Series," *Library Journal* (January 15, 1962): 264.

70. Mickenberg, *Learning from the Left*, 152–58.

71. "David Riesman, Sociologist Whose 'Lonely Crowd' Became a Best Seller, Dies at 92," *New York Times* (May 11, 2002): A18.

72. David Riesman, with Nathan Glazer and Reuel Denney, *The Lonely Crowd: A Study of the Changing American Character*, abridged ed. (New York: Doubleday Anchor, 1953), 128–31.

73. Douglas Martin, "Emily W. Reed, 89, Librarian in '59 Alabama Racial Dispute," *New York Times* (May 29, 2000): B6. In response to the first objections to *The Rabbits' Wedding*, Garth Williams issued a statement through Harper in which he insisted that he had created the book without anything like a political agenda in mind: "I was completely unaware that animals with white fur, such as white polar bears and white dogs and white rabbits, were considered blood relatives of white human beings." As a further disclaimer, he noted that *The Rabbits' Wedding* "was not written for adults, who will not understand it because it is only about a soft, furry love and has no hidden messages of hate."

74. Robert McCloskey, "Caldecott Acceptance Speech," *The Horn Book* (August 1958): 245.

75. *This Fabulous Century*, 168.

76. "A.I.G.A. Medal to May Massee," *The Horn Book* (August 1959): 275.

77. Johanna Hurwitz, interview with the author, tape recording, Great Neck, N.Y., May 2, 1997; *Staff News*, New York Public Library (January 26, 1961): 13.

7. Shaken and Stirred

1. Quoted in Nancy Larrick, "The All-White World of Children's Books," *Saturday Review* (September 11, 1965): 63.

2. Bess Furman, "Busy Week Ahead for Youth Parley," *New York Times* (March 27, 1960): 71.

3. Emma Harrison, "Aims Set in War on Delinquency," *New York Times* (March 29, 1960): 27.

4. Bess Furman, "Eisenhower Fears Softness in Youth," *New York Times* (March 31, 1960): 26.

5. Ruth Hill Viguers, "Golden Anniversary White House Conference on Children and Youth: An Interpretation," *The Horn Book* (June 1960): 234. Viguers had become *The Horn Book*'s third editor in 1958, succeeding Jennie D. Lindquist, who had taken over for Bertha Mahony Miller in 1951.

6. Emma Harrison, "Youths at Capital Conclave Move to Support Negroes on Sit-ins," *New York Times* (March 30, 1960): 24.

7. Harper & Brothers published the original edition of *Profiles in Courage* in 1956. Cass Canfield Sr. had acquired the book and worked with then-Senator Kennedy to expand the manuscript into its final form. The Young Readers' Edition was sponsored by the Department of Books for Boys and Girls, but Ursula Nordstrom seems not to have worked on it.

8. That March, librarians, booksellers, and others around the country learned that an unknown Latvian-born Russian émigré artist named Nicolas Sidjakov had won the Caldecott Medal for 1961 for *Baboushka and the Three Kings*, a picture book published by the equally obscure Parnassus Press of Berkeley, California. The artist, it emerged, was the son of Russian expatriates who had fled their homeland during the time of the Bolshevik Revolution. As a young man, Sidjakov had made his way to Paris, where he studied painting; by the late 1940s he had experienced his first success as a poster artist for the reviving postwar French film industry. From France, he had gone to live in the United States. Sidjakov's pro-Western, anti-Communist credentials seem to have sufficed to spare him the minor uproar that had swirled about Nicolas Mordvinoff less than a decade earlier.

9. M. E. E., "Do We Need More Market Research?" *Publishers' Weekly* (February 15, 1960): 145.

10. Selma Lanes, "Fifty Years of Viking Junior Books," *Publishers Weekly* (February 18, 1983): 70.

11. Leonard S. Marcus, "An Interview with William C. Morris," *The Horn Book* (January–February 1995): 43.

12. John Tebbel, *Between Covers: The Rise and Transformation of American Book Publishing* (New York: Oxford University Press, 1987), 374.

13. Ibid.

14. Eden Ross Lipson, "Jean Karl, 72; A Publisher of Books for Children," *New York Times* (April 3, 2000): B8.

15. Simon Michael Bessie, interview, Columbia Oral History Project, vol. 2, 192.

16. A sampling of titles on Abingdon's 1960 spring list indicates the range of Karl's program: *Treasured Tales: Great Stories of Courage and Faith* by Laura Cathon and Thusnelda Young, illustrated by Mary E. Young; *Jane Addams, World Neighbor* by Miriam Gilbert, illustrated by Corinne B. Dillon; *The Hawaiian Box Mystery* by Alice Cooper Bailey; and *Science, Science Everywhere!* by Ruth Cromer Weir, illustrated by Gloria Stevens. For further details, see the Atheneum Books for Children advertisement in *The Horn Book* (April 1960): 92.

17. Leonard S. Marcus, "An Interview with Dorothy Briley," *The Horn Book* (November–December 1998): 693–94. The imprint's name was changed to Atheneum Books for Young Readers in the fall of 1994.

18. "News About Atheneum Books for Children" (four-page press release), n.d. (1962), author's archive.

19. To show that the imprint understood library and school buyers' concern for durability, the press release noted: "Institutional bindings, to be known as Atheneum Spartan Bindings, feature side sewing, drill cloth reinforcement, heavy binding board, and a sturdy, washable, damp proof binding cloth."

20. Henrietta M. Smith, interview with the author, tape recording by telephone, November 8, 1996. The George C. Hall Branch of the Chicago Public Library opened in January 1932.

21. Augusta Baker Alexander, interview with the author, New York, N.Y., January 31, 1985.

22. "A Tribute to Augusta Baker" (program for "A Symposium in Honor of Augusta Baker"), Donnell Library Center, New York Public Library, June 9, 1998, author's archive.

23. Augusta Baker, "Books About Negro Life for Children" (New York: Bureau for Intercultural Education, 1946), 4.

24. Augusta Baker, "Books About Negro Life for Children," rev. ed. (New York: New York Public Library, 1963), 6–7.

25. Ibid., 7.

26. Sandra Jordan and George M. Nicholson, interview with the author, New York, N.Y., April 27, 2007.

27. Ezra Jack Keats, "Caldecott," from "Collage: The Memoirs of Ezra Jack Keats" (unpublished manuscript), excerpts published in *The Lion and the Unicorn: Humor and Play in Children's Literature* 13, no. 2 (December 1989): 73.

28. In the Columbia Oral History Project, see, in addition to the comments of Atheneum's Simon Michael Bessie on this subject, those of Thomas H. Guinzburg of Viking. Asked whether Viking children's books accounted for a "fairly sizeable percentage" of the company's business, Guinzburg told an interviewer in 1981: "Yes. You've got to understand that every publishing house

has something, some bedrock that allows them to go on being a viable business even in years when they don't have any books that sell." See interview with Guinzburg, Columbia Oral History Project, vol. 1, 95–96.

29. Frances Clarke Sayers, report to Dr. Luther H. Evans, Librarian, Library of Congress, August 6, 1952, quoted in Julie Cummings, "'Let Her Sound Her Trumpet': NYPL Children's Librarians and Their Impact on the World of Publishing," *Biblion* 4, no. 1 (Fall 1995): 103.

30. Similar collections were later established: the University of Southern Mississippi's de Grummond Children's Literature Collection (1966); the Baldwin Collection of Historical Children's Literature (1977); and the University of Connecticut's Northeast Children's Literature Collection (1983).

31. Peggy Sullivan, "A Tale of Washington's Irvin," *The Horn Book* (June 1961): 288–89.

32. The allure of predictable, series-generated profits had apparently cast its spell even on the iconoclastic editor. Perhaps this was a further sign of increased pressure from above following the merger of Harper with Row, Peterson. As to the ethics of proceeding with a new Nutshell set without Sendak, Nordstrom argued that the concept of a boxed set of four miniature volumes had been as much her own idea as Sendak's and that therefore she was within her rights to develop the concept editorially as she saw fit.

33. Leonard S. Marcus, ed., *Dear Genius: The Letters of Ursula Nordstrom* (New York: HarperCollins, 1998), 157–58.

34. Sendak had first produced a dummy for a book with this title in 1955. For accounts of the making of *Where the Wild Things Are*, see Selma G. Lanes, *The Art of Maurice Sendak* (New York: Abrams, 1980), 85–107; and Leonard S. Marcus, *A Caldecott Celebration: Six Artists and Their Paths to the Caldecott Medal* (New York: Walker, 1998), 19–25. Sendak's many manuscript drafts, preliminary sketches, dummies, and final art for *Where the Wild Things Are* may all be seen at the Rosenbach Library and Museum in Philadelphia.

35. After helping Sendak navigate various legal matters that arose from time to time, attorney Sheldon Fogelman became his agent.

36. Marcus, *Dear Genius*, 166–67. *Where the Wild Things Are* was one of two books illustrated by Sendak to be honored by the *Times* that year. The other book, published by Holt, was *The Griffin and the Minor Canon* by Frank R. Stockton.

37. *Where the Wild Things Are* led the list of Harper books featured in a smaller display ad published in the December 1963 issue of *The Horn Book*.

38. Nordstrom believed the most serious competition of 1963 to be *Swimmy*, a picture book by former *Fortune* magazine art director Leo Lionni, published by Pantheon. *Swimmy* was chosen one of the year's three Caldecott Honor books.

39. Richard Jackson, "WE," *The Horn Book* (May–June 1993): 297.

40. Jackson, interview with the author, New York, N.Y., May 8, 1995.

41. Leonard S. Marcus, "An Interview with Susan Hirschman — Part I," *The Horn Book* (March–April 1996): 160–61.

42. Marcus, "An Interview with Susan Hirschman — Part II," *The Horn Book* (May–June 1996): 282–83.

43. Leonard S. Marcus, "Make Way for Marketing," *Publishers Weekly* (September 17, 2001): 33.

44. Nancy Larrick, "The All-White World of Children's Books," *Saturday Review* (September 11, 1965): 63–65, 84–85.

45. Whitney M. Young Jr. titled his column for August 6, 1964, "A Visit to the Children's Zoo." The reference was to a Little Golden Book of the same name — written by Barbara Shook Hazen, illustrated by Mel Crawford, and published in 1963 — which depicted a typical day at New York's Central Park Zoo, but with an all-white cast of characters. For a detailed discussion of Young's criticisms and their impact on publishing, see Leonard S. Marcus, *Golden Legacy: How Golden Books Won Children's Hearts, Changed Publishing Forever, and Became an American Icon Along the Way* (New York: Random House, 2007), 282–86.

46. Among the first winners of the Council's annual prize was an aspiring writer then employed as an editor at the Bobbs-Merrill educational publishing company, Walter Dean Myers. Myers won in the picture-book category for *Where Does the Day Go?* Parents Magazine Press published the book in 1969, with illustrations by Leo Carty. The author made his debut under the name Walter M. Myers. Mildred D. Taylor was another important writer who received crucial early encouragement from the Council.

47. Ruth H. Viguers, "A Pinch of This and a Dash of That," *The Horn Book* (February 1966): 19.

48. Keats's letter to the editor is quoted in Brian Alderson, *Ezra Jack Keats: Artist and Picture-Book Maker* (Gretna, La.: Pelican, 1994), 184.

49. Ann Durell, "IF THERE IS NO HAPPY ENDING: Children's Book Publishing — Past, Present, and Future — Part I," *The Horn Book* (February 1982): 29–30.

50. In 1963 eight Golden Press books — a record number — were selected by the American Institute of Graphic Arts for its exhibition of outstanding children's books published during the previous two years. Two years before, Mary Blair had become the first Golden artist to receive a prestigious *Herald-Tribune* Children's Spring Book Festival honor award, for *I Can Fly*, a Little Golden Book written by Gelolo McHugh. Western sales soared. In 1961 annual sales (for both printing and publishing) reached $124 million, a company record. In 1965 sales rose past the $137 million mark and in 1969 reached $169 million. For further details, see the publisher's in-house magazine, *The Westerner: Commemorative Issue* (Winter 1982).

51. C.B.G., "A Big Business, a Big Problem," *Publishers' Weekly* (February 21, 1966): 159.

52. Ursula Nordstrom to Russell Hoban, New York, N.Y., June 20, 1966, reprinted in Marcus, *Dear Genius*, 220–21.

53. Eden Ross Lipson, "Harlin Quist, 69, Publisher of Children's Books," *New York Times* (May 20, 2000): B11.

54. Jackson, interview with the author, May 8, 1995.

55. Sally Lodge, "Yearling Turns 25," *Publishers Weekly* (October 11, 1991): 41.

56. This hunch would be repeatedly borne out in the years to come. On acquiring the paperback rights to S. E. Hinton's *The Outsiders*, for example, Dell at first offered the novel on its adult list, where it languished. In 1968, when Dell moved *The Outsiders* to the Laurel Leaf list aimed at teens, it became a runaway success, achieving sales exceeding 6.5 million as of 1991. See ibid., 43.

57. Leonard S. Marcus, "An Interview with George M. Nicholson," *The Horn Book* (March–April 2007): 133.

58. Leventhal himself had recommended Nicholson for the job at Dell, which had a close working relationship with the Golden Press's parent company, Western. As the exclusive printer of Dell's paperback books, Western profited greatly from the relationship.

59. The first Laurel Leaf list appeared in 1962.

60. Nicholson made industry news several years later when he paid an advance of $1 million for the paperback rights to ten Winnie the Pooh books by A. A. Milne.

61. Ursula Nordstrom to Katharine S. White, New York, N.Y., October 27, 1966, HarperCollins Archive.

62. Marcus, "An Interview with George M. Nicholson," 131–32.

63. Lodge, "Yearling Turns 25," 42–43.

64. Ibid., 42.

65. Paul Nathan, "Exploding Market," *Publishers' Weekly* (January 6, 1969): 48.

66. Ursula Nordstrom to Millicent E. Selsam, New York, N.Y., June 19, 1969, reprinted in Marcus, *Dear Genius*, 274.

67. Wolfgang Saxon, "Charles S. Joelson, 83, Congressman Who Saved School Libraries," *New York Times* (August 21, 1999): A10.

68. Ursula Nordstrom to John Steptoe, New York, N.Y., August 25, 1970, reprinted in Marcus, *Dear Genius*, 300–301.

69. "Stevie," *Life* (August 29, 1969): 54–59.

70. The Wolffs' Harcourt imprint, established in 1961, specialized in publishing serious literary work in translation by modern European authors.

71. Quoted in Sophie C. Silberberg and John Donovan, "Fifty Years of Children's Book Week: Fifty Years of Independent American Children's Book Publishing," *The Horn Book* (December 1969): 710–11.

72. Ibid., 711.

8. Change and More Change

1. Margaret K. McElderry, "The Best of Times, the Worst of Times: Children's Book Publishing, 1924–1974," *The Horn Book* (October 1974): 92.

2. Quoted in Kenneth C. Davis, *Two-Bit Culture: The Paperbacking of America* (Boston: Houghton Mifflin, 1984), 337. Lindeman's distinguished career en-

compassed pioneering advocacy in the field of adult education. He served as an editorial consultant to Penguin Books and New American Library.

3. "The Ten-Year Plateau," *New York Times Book Review* (February 16, 1969): 1.

4. Davis, *Two-Bit Culture*, 337.

5. Publishers did not all go about this in the same way. Doubleday's new Zephyr line featured both picture books and middle-grade fiction, with pricing ranging from 75 cents to 95 cents. Random House's Windward Books specialized entirely in middle-grade material, all culled from the combined hardcover lists of its Random, Knopf, and Pantheon imprints. Holt's Owlet Books, all picture books, sold for $1.25 to $1.95. See "Doubleday, Random, Holt Enter Juvenile Paperback Field," *Publishers' Weekly* (February 22, 1971): 120.

6. Richard Jackson, "WE," *The Horn Book* (May–June 1993): 300.

7. Nancy Larrick, "Will Children Still Read Children's Books?" *Publishers Weekly* (April 10, 1972): 122. Note that as of the January 17, 1972, issue (its one-hundredth anniversary issue), the journal dropped the apostrophe from its name to become *Publishers Weekly*.

8. Ibid., 123.

9. The National Book Awards categories added during the 1960s included: arts and letters (nonfiction); history and biography; science, philosophy, and religion; and literary translation.

10. The other books in contention that year included Jan Adkins's *The Art and Industry of Sand Castles*, John Donovan's *Wild in the World*, June Jordan's *His Own Where*, Chela Duran Ryan's *Hildilid's Night*, Marilyn Sachs's *The Bear's House*, and Clyde Watson's *Father Fox's Pennyrhymes*.

11. Ruth Gagliardo, in "Letters to the Editor," *The Horn Book* (October 1972): 501.

12. Julius Lester, in ibid., 501. Lester had been a recipient of a Newbery Honor in 1969 for *To Be a Slave*.

13. Mrs. Lewis A. Waddell, in ibid., 501.

14. From the title page of Francelia Butler, ed., *Children's Literature*, vol. 1 (Philadelphia: Temple University Press, 1972).

15. Ibid., 7.

16. Ibid., 8.

17. Lee Burns, "Red Riding Hood," in ibid., 32.

18. P. H., review of *In the Night Kitchen* by Maurice Sendak, *The Horn Book* (February 1971): 44–45.

19. Harry C. Stubbs, "Views on Science Books," *The Horn Book* (February 1971): 69.

20. Lanes's writings from this time were collected in *Down the Rabbit Hole: Adventures and Misadventures in the Realm of Children's Literature* (New York: Atheneum, 1971). She became editor in chief of Parents' Magazine Press in 1974.

21. Lanes, *Down the Rabbit Hole*, v–vii.

22. Marianne Carus, ed., *Celebrate Cricket: Thirty Years of Stories and Art* (Chicago: Cricket, 2003), 2.

23. Ibid., 13.

24. Ibid.

25. Muriel Fuller, "Velma Varner of World Publishing Company," *Publishers' Weekly* (July 27, 1959): 163–64; "Velma Varner, 56; Viking Press Editor," *New York Times* (November 25, 1972): 34.

26. Selma Lanes, "Fifty Years of Viking Junior Books," *Publishers Weekly* (February 18, 1983): 70.

27. Varner had first seen the scroll on display at New York's Metropolitan Museum of Art, where it was on loan as part of a national touring exhibition organized by the Japanese government as a postwar goodwill gesture to the United States.

28. Only the black line step of the printing process was left to each of the participating houses, an arrangement that allowed for the insertion of text in any language.

29. Velma Varner, "Thoughts on Children's Books, Reading, and Tomorrow," in *Reading, Children's Books, and Our Pluralistic Society*, ed. Harold Tanyzer and Jean Karl (Newark, Del.: International Reading Association, 1972), 71–77.

30. Evelyn Diggs was perhaps the *only* African American employed in the field. Diggs did library promotion work at Little, Brown during the 1970s and for some years before that at William R. Scott, Inc.

31. Diane Roback, "Children's Book Sales: Past and Future," *Publishers Weekly* (August 31, 1990): 30.

32. Western went public on the New York Stock Exchange in 1973. See *The Westerner: Commemorative Issue* (Winter 1982): 14.

33. Walter Retan and Ole Risom, *The Busy, Busy World of Richard Scarry* (New York: Abrams, 1997), 69–71.

34. For an author with as lucrative a backlist as Scarry's, changing publishers was no simple matter, however. Once emotions cooled, it became clear to Scarry as well as to Leventhal that it was in their mutual interest to maintain some sort of active business relationship. In order to sustain booksellers' interest in the older Scarry titles published by Western, it was felt that Western needed from time to time to have something new by the author to offer as well. With this in mind, Western's editors went to work devising new formats and other "repurposed" uses for Scarry material from his early work-for-hire days. Then, in 1971, Scarry, in an agreement tailored not to conflict with his flourishing relationship with Random House, signed a new two-book contract with Western. Ibid., 109.

35. Leonard S. Marcus, "An Interview with George M. Nicholson," *The Horn Book* (March–April 2007): 134–35.

36. Gertrude Shafer to Robert McCloskey, New York, N.Y., August 29, 1974, Penguin USA Archive.

37. Ursula Nordstrom to Katharine S. White, Bridgewater, Conn., June 26, 1974, reprinted in Marcus, *Dear Genius*, 356–57.

38. Ellen Rudin succeeded Nordstrom as director of Harper Junior Books.

39. Margaret K. McElderry, "The Hazards of Translation," *The Horn Book* (December 1973): 565.

40. Ibid.

41. Ibid., 566.

42. OPEC was founded in 1960 with five charter members: Iran, Iraq, Saudi Arabia, Kuwait, and Venezuela. Membership expanded throughout the 1960s and afterward to include a total of fourteen nations around the world.

43. Lanes, "Fifty Years of Viking Junior Books," 71.

44. Cormier's first three novels were *Now and at the Hour* (Coward, 1960), *A Little Raw on Monday Mornings* (Sheed, 1963), and *Take Me Where the Good Times Are* (Macmillan, 1965).

45. Marilyn E. Marlow, interview with the author, tape recording, New York, N.Y., April 22, 1994.

46. Ibid.

47. Donald Sheehan, *This Was Publishing: A Chronicle of the Book Trade in the Gilded Age* (Bloomington: Indiana University Press, 1952), 74–78.

48. Marilyn E. Marlow, in "Robert Cormier Remembered," *Publishers Weekly* (January 1, 2001): 38.

49. Ibid.

50. Paul L. Montgomery, "Macmillan Book Divisions Sharply Cut Their Staffs," *New York Times* (October 15, 1974): 1, 45.

51. Eleanor Blau, "Two Editors Quit Macmillan in Protest," *New York Times* (October 16, 1974): 40; Leonard S. Marcus, "An Interview with Susan Hirschman — Part II," *The Horn Book* (May–June 1996): 287–88. Shearon, who was nearly of retirement age, relinquished her Macmillan pension rather than stay on the job under the circumstances. Hirschman urged her not to do so but to no avail, and she promised to bring Shearon along with her if and when she landed elsewhere. Within a year's time, Hirschman made good on her pledge when she invited Shearon to join her on the staff of a new Morrow imprint, Greenwillow Books.

52. John Tebbel, *Between Covers: The Rise and Transformation of American Book Publishing* (New York: Oxford University Press, 1987), 366.

53. "Briefs on the Arts: N.L.R.B. Declines to Cite Macmillan," *New York Times* (January 4, 1975): 12.

54. Quoted in John Rowe Townsend, "An Elusive Browser," *The Horn Book* (October 1974): 39.

55. E. L. H., "'An Expectancy of Triumph,'" *The Horn Book* (December 1974): 663.

56. Marcus, "An Interview with Susan Hirschman — Part II," 289.

57. Harriet Rohmer, interview with the author, tape recording, San Francisco, Calif., July 21, 1989.

58. Quoted from the publisher's mission statement, as reprinted in Ethel John-

ston Phelps, ed., *Tatterhood and Other Tales*, ill. Pamela Baldwin Ford (New York: Feminist, 1978).

59. The story behind this book is told in Patricia Holt, "'Period.' — A Book for 'Normal' Girls," *Publishers Weekly* (February 29, 1980): 120.

60. There are numerous instances of the alternative presses' impact on the major trade houses. Morrow Junior Books acquired paperback rights from Canada's Kids Can Press to *Cat's Cradle Owl's Eyes* by Camilla Gryski, illustrated by Tom Sankey, and several sequels in a popular series about string games. Farrar, Straus and Giroux acquired paperback rights from the Dog Ear Press of Maine to Mary Beth Owens's *A Caribou Alphabet*. Scholastic and Holt led a wave of bilingual picture-book publishing by mainstream houses that was largely inspired by the work of Harriet Rohmer's Children's Book Press.

61. Milton Meltzer, "Where Do All the Prizes Go? The Case for Nonfiction," *The Horn Book* (February 1976): 23.

62. Bruno Bettelheim, *The Uses of Enchantment: The Meaning and Importance of Fairy Tales* (New York: Knopf, 1976), 10.

63. Paul Heins, review of *The Uses of Enchantment* by Bruno Bettelheim, *The Horn Book* (June 1976): 301–2.

64. Bettelheim's appreciation of Sendak's work was erratic at best. One might have thought that Bettelheim would have hailed *Where the Wild Things Are* as just the kind of fantastic yet emotionally bracing tale that young children needed in order to come to terms with their innermost drives. Yet, to the surprise of many observers, Bettelheim had lashed out at Sendak's Caldecott Medal–winning book in his regular column in *Ladies' Home Journal* for March 1969, chastising the author for having raised the specter of a child's worst fear — desertion — while also failing "to understand . . . the incredible fear it evokes in the child to be sent to bed without supper . . . by the first and foremost giver of food and security — his mother." Quoted in John Cech, *Angels and Wild Things: The Archetypal Poetics of Maurice Sendak* (University Park: Pennsylvania State University Press, 1995), 111.

65. Waldenbooks began as a Depression-era lending library in Bridgeport, Connecticut. By the late 1940s, the company had fifteen locations. It opened its first bookstore in 1961. By 1981, it had become the first bookseller to have at least one store in every state.

    Barnes and Noble first went into business as a printing company in 1873. The firm opened its first bookstore in 1917. Leonard Riggio took over the company in 1971, at a time when it was struggling, and began the aggressive expansion campaign that transformed it into the nation's largest bookseller.

    The newest of the chains was B. Dalton, which the Minneapolis-based department store company, Dayton Co., created in 1966 with the goal of servicing well-educated, affluent young suburbanites. By 1968, there were 12 B. Dalton stores in 7 states. Six years later, 125 stores were in operation, and by 1976 the number had jumped again to 360 stores.

66. Marcus, "An Interview with George M. Nicholson," 133.

67. Iarusso, who was then assistant coordinator of the Office of Children's Services of the New York Public Library, made this comment in a talk given at the conference "Children's Literature and the Baby Booms: Continuity and Change, 1945–1990," New School for Social Research, New York, October 20, 1990. Other participants included Margaret K. McElderry, Milton Meltzer, Joanna Rudge Long, Margaret M. Coughlan, Terri Schmitz, Selma Lanes, Marc Simont, and Ann Flowers. The conference was organized and moderated by the author.

68. "A Bookstore Grows in Brooklyn — New York's First for Children Only," *Publishers Weekly* (July 16, 1973): 100. Veteran bookseller Andy Laties supplied information about the number of independent children's-only stores in 1980 and 1990.

69. Ibid.

70. Paul Heins, review of *Fairy Tales and After: From Snow White to E. B. White* by Roger Sale, *The Horn Book* (February 1979): 82.

71. Marcus, "An Interview with Susan Hirschman — Part II," 292.

72. Somtow Sucharitkul, "News," *Washington Science Fiction Association Journal* (March 1979), available at www.wsfa.org/journal/j79/3/index.htm.

73. Marlow, interview with the author.

9. Suits and Wizards at the Millennium's Gate

1. Ann Durell, "Children's Books in the '80s: Gutenberg or Götterdämmerung?" *Publishers Weekly* (February 26, 1982): 82–83.

2. Jean F. Mercier, "Coming Up Roses," *Publishers Weekly* (July 23, 1982): 73.

3. Sandra Roberts, "Books for Black Children by Black Writers: A Passing Fancy?" *Publishers Weekly* (July 23, 1982): 82–83.

4. Jean F. Mercier, "Fall 1981 Children's Books Special," *Publishers Weekly* (July 24, 1981): 89.

5. Leonard S. Marcus, "An Interview with Phyllis J. Fogelman," *The Horn Book* (March–April 1999): 159.

6. Mirabel Cecil, *Sebastian Walker, 1942–1991: A Kind of Prospero* (London: Walker, 1995), 80.

7. In the mid-1990s, Hirschman published the first picture books by Nina Crews, daughter of Greenwillow illustrator-authors Donald Crews and Ann Jonas, and a number of books written by Miela Ford, daughter of Greenwillow regular Tana Hoban, whose photographs illustrated Ford's texts.

8. Mattel owned Western from 1979 to 1984. See Leonard S. Marcus, *Golden Legacy: How Golden Books Won Children's Hearts, Changed Publishing Forever, and Became an American Icon Along the Way* (New York: Random House, 2007), 202–4.

9. Randall Smith, "Western Publishing Gets Renewed Attention, but Some Who Recall the '86 Drop Are Wary," *Wall Street Journal* (July 27, 1987): 1.

10. For the comparison to Picasso, see Rodger Ricklefs, "Scary Stories: Maurice Sendak's Pen Strips Children's Books of Their Innocence," *Wall Street Journal* (December 20, 1979): 26, 68, 70.

11. Viking Junior Books' efforts in this regard epitomized the shift at the trade houses toward novelty and other traditional mass-market types of books. Viking's facsimile reprints of the nineteenth-century master of the movable book, Lothar Meggendorfer, had, for instance, proven a wild success. Selma Lanes, "Fifty Years of Viking Junior Books," *Publishers Weekly* (February 18, 1983): 68–72.

12. Leonard S. Marcus, "An Interview with Walter Lorraine," *The Horn Book* (March–April 1998): 176–77.

13. Selma G. Lanes, *The Art of Maurice Sendak* (New York: Abrams, 1980), 235.

14. Ibid.

15. John Donovan, "My Say," *Publishers Weekly* (February 22, 1985), 160.

16. Marcus, "An Interview with Phyllis J. Fogelman," 158.

17. Marianne Yen, "Printing Overseas," *Publishers Weekly* (February 21, 1986): 99–100.

18. Leonard S. Marcus, "An Interview with Susan Hirschman — Part II," *The Horn Book* (May–June 1996): 293–94.

19. Susan Schwartzman, "*Reading Rainbow* TV Series Gains Momentum for a Second Season," *Publishers Weekly* (February 24, 1984): 120–23.

20. Jean F. Mercier, "The Children's Special: Fall 1984," *Publishers Weekly* (July 27, 1984): 83.

21. Ann Martin, "Bantam's Books for Young Readers: Coming of Age in 1985," *Publishers Weekly* (July 26, 1985): 108–9.

22. Caron Chapman (director, Association of Booksellers for Children), interview with the author, by telephone, Minneapolis, Minn., September 1, 1993.

23. Sonja Bolle, "Innovative Promotions from Children's Booksellers," *Publishers Weekly* (July 26, 1985): 147–48.

24. Barbara Karlin, "Children's Booksellers: New Spirit of Cooperation, Not Competition," *Publishers Weekly* (July 25, 1986): 112–15.

25. Daisy Maryles and Diane Roback, "The Problems and Rewards (Mostly the Latter) of Running Bookstores for Children," *Publishers Weekly* (July 25, 1986): 131–36. Half of the booksellers surveyed estimated annual returns of from 1 percent to 3 percent; a substantial majority stated that they considered returns to be "virtually no problem."

26. Herbert R. Lottman, "Getting Ready for Bologna," *Publishers Weekly* (February 22, 1985): 88. Lottman reported that computers for use in education had first been exhibited at the fair the previous year and that in 1985 a vastly expanded international exhibition of "New Information Technologies in Education" was one of the fair's highlights.

27. The Ann M. Martin Foundation was established in 1990 to provide financial support to literacy and education initiatives, programs benefiting the homeless, and other projects intended to improve the lives of children.

28. David Pauly, "Goosebumps Report Chills Blood of Scholastic Investors," *Bloomberg News* (February 25, 1997). The decline in sales of Goosebumps books was given as the major factor, along with reduced sales for Scholastic's school book clubs, for a spectacular one-day drop in the company's share price of 24¾ to 36¾. Analyst Alexander Paris of Barrington Research forecast that Scholastic sales might not recover for three or four quarters. Paris also questioned the company's credibility: "Either they didn't tell us everything they knew," he concluded, "or they didn't have the information they needed." See also Christopher Byron, "In Big Stock Plunge, Scholastic Investors Get the Goosebumps," *New York Observer* (March 31, 1997): 1, 23.

29. Herbert Mitgang, "Macmillan Acquires Scribner," *New York Times* (April 26, 1984): C17.

30. See "A Brief History of Simon & Schuster," available at www.simonsays.com/content/feature.cfm?feature_id=1631&tab=1.

31. Russell Freedman, "Holiday House: The First Fifty Years," *Publishers Weekly* (February 22, 1985): 98–101.

32. Edwin McDowell, "Never Have So Few Published for So Many," *New York Times* (September 19, 1988): D14.

33. Diane Roback, "Wholesalers and Publishers Look at the Changing Preschool Market," *Publishers Weekly* (February 22, 1985): 141–43.

34. Jean Mercier, "'Doing Things No One Else Was Doing': Jill Krementz Shoots 'em Young," *Publishers Weekly* (July 26, 1985): 103–4. By the 1980s, Krementz, while continuing to add to the series, had launched a second series of photographically illustrated books with a bibliotherapeutic focus. The first of these new books was *How It Feels When a Parent Dies* (Knopf, 1981).

35. Roback, "Wholesalers and Publishers," 141.

36. Biographical information appears on Trelease's extensive website: www.trelease-on-reading.com/bio.html.

37. Sue L. Alexander, interview with the author, tape recording by telephone, June 14, 2007.

38. Peter Seymour, "Avoid Insects as Characters," *Publishers Weekly* (February 24, 1984): 80–81.

39. Glenn Fowler, "John Steptoe, 38, Illustrator, Dies; He Also Wrote Children's Books," *New York Times* (September 1, 1989): D17.

40. The Coretta Scott King Awards were established in 1969 to honor the memory of the late Dr. Martin Luther King Jr. and the continuing work on behalf of the civil rights movement of his widow. During their first decade the awards recognized excellence on the part of African American writers for young people, and they were extended in 1979 to honor African American illustrators as well.

41. Kathleen T. Horning, "The Contributions of Alternative Press Publishers to Multicultural Literature for Children," Library Trends (January 1, 1993), reprinted in HighBeam Encyclopedia, www.encyclopedia.com/printable.aspx?id=1G1:13208343. In this excellent article, Horning draws on the exten-

sive holdings of alternative press materials in the collection of the Coopera-
tive Children's Book Center at the University of Wisconsin in Madison.
Among the other presses she features is one that preceded Just Us Books —
Chicago's Third World Press. Founded in 1967 by the poet Haki R. Madhubuti,
Third World has published a variety of books for adult and young readers.

42. The Just Us Books website provides a good capsule history of the house. See
www.justusbooks.com/modules/content/index.php?id=2.

43. Horning, "The Contributions of Alternative Press Publishers."

44. For information about Lee & Low's first lists and publishing philosophy, see
Philip Lee, Thomas Low, et al., *Lee & Low Books: A Tenth Anniversary Celebration of Multicultural Publishing* (New York: Lee & Low, 2003).

45. Leonard A. Wood, "Children's Books: Part II — What Mothers Read to Their
Children," *Publishers Weekly* (October 4, 1985): 21.

46. *Child* magazine launched in October 1986; *Parenting* followed in January
1987. The account of *Parenting*'s beginnings is based on the recollections of
the author, who was hired as *Parenting*'s children's book reviewer during the
summer of 1986.

47. Diane Roback, "Bologna 1988: Weak Dollar No Barrier to Business," *Publishers Weekly* (May 20, 1988): 42.

48. Ibid., 41.

49. Lesléa Newman, *Heather Has Two Mommies*, ill. Diane Souza (Boston: Alyson,
1990); Michael Willhoite, *Daddy's Roommate*, ill., author (Boston: Alyson,
1990).

50. Steven Mintz, *Huck's Raft: A History of American Childhood* (Cambridge,
Mass.: Harvard University Press, 2004), 365–66.

51. Mark I. West, *Trust Your Children: Voices Against Censorship in Children's Literature* (New York: Neal-Schuman, 1988), 7.

52. Ibid., 127–28.

53. Associated Press, "Peoria, Ill., Bans Three Books from School Libraries," *New
York Times* (November 11, 1984): 35; Associated Press, "Peoria School Board
Restores Three Judy Blume Books," *New York Times* (December 5, 1984): A16.
The three books in question were *Then Again Maybe I Won't, Deenie,* and
Blubber.

54. "Program Report on Selling and Marketing," *Society of Children's Book
Writers and Illustrators Bulletin* (February–March 1994): 1.

55. Sendak did illustrate some picture books for Hyperion. The best of these,
Brundibar, a collaboration with Tony Kushner, was published in 2003 under the Hyperion imprint of Sendak's longtime editor, Michael di Capua.
Sendak had first worked with di Capua decades earlier, when the latter was
Randall Jarrell's editor at Macmillan. In later years, di Capua had had imprints at Farrar, Straus and Giroux, and from 1991, at HarperCollins, where
Lisa Holton was the marketing director. In 1996 Holton left Harper to become publisher of Hyperion Books for Children and Disney Press; three
years later, she brought di Capua to Hyperion, again with an eponymous im-

print. Sendak published books with di Capua at each of the houses with which the editor was associated.

56. Scholastic annual report (1992), 5.

57. Eben Shapiro, "Now It's Books 'R' Us as Toy Giant Expands," *New York Times* (September 28, 1992): D6.

58. Michael Thomas Ford, "The Cult of Multiculturalism," *Publishers Weekly* (July 18, 1994): 30–34. Fogelman expresses the view that children's books on African Americans have entered the mainstream.

59. Quoted in Leonard S. Marcus, *Side by Side: Five Favorite Picture-Book Teams Go to Work* (New York: Walker, 2001), 55.

60. "Scholastic Launches Blue Sky Imprint," *Publishers Weekly* (March 22, 1993): 26; "New Hats in the Ring," *Publishers Weekly* (July 17, 1995): 145.

61. Cecil, *Sebastian Walker*, 75.

62. Ibid., 73–74.

63. Ibid., 70–71. See also Amanda Smith, "'The Pursuit of Literacy,'" *Publishers Weekly* (February 21, 1986): 101–2.

64. Cecil, *Sebastian Walker*, 117.

65. David Ford, introduction to the spring 1992 Candlewick Press catalog (inside front cover).

66. At the time of her dismissal, Foster had on her desk the manuscript for Pullman's *The Golden Compass*.

67. Within three years, Random House had reversed itself, hiring a new institutional marketing staff while also contracting out for advice from the marketing director it had fired, Suzanne M. Glazer, who had gone into business as a marketing consultant.

68. Foster's sweet revenge was to prove short-lived, however, at least where Sachar was concerned. In a sign of the times, the author put up for auction the sequel to *Holes* rather than simply place the book on Foster's list, as might have been expected in the past. The Delacorte imprint of Random House outbid Foster to become the publisher of *Small Steps* (2006). Random's Dell imprint was already Sachar's paperback publisher.

69. Doreen Carvajal, "News Corp. Unit Will Fuse HarperCollins to TV Guide," *New York Times* (September 24, 1997): D9.

70. Mintz, *Huck's Raft*, 348.

71. "Children's Book Publishing in the Nineties," *Society of Children's Book Writers Bulletin* (November–December 1992): 1.

72. Paul Gray, "Wild About Harry," *Time* (September 20, 1992): 68.

73. Dinitia Smith, "The Times Plans a Children's Best-Seller List," *New York Times* (June 24, 2000): B12.

74. Harold Bloom, "Can 35 Million Book Buyers Be Wrong? Yes." (editorial page), *Wall Street Journal* (July 11, 2000): A26.

75. David D. Kirkpatrick, "Harry Potter Magic Halts Bedtime for Youngsters," *New York Times* (July 9, 2000): 14.

INDEX

Abbott, Jacob: advice books for parents, 4; background, publishing history, 18–21

ABC Book (Falls), 94–95

The ABC Bunny (Gág), 115

academic scholars/critics: analyses of children's books as literature, 253–55, 277–78, 314; books about authors and illustrators, 284–86

Acheson, Dean, 193

Action Comics, 137

Adams, Richard, 269

Adams, William Taylor ("Oliver Optic"), 32, 37–38, 57–59, 105

The Adventures of Huckleberry Finn (Twain), 43, 122

The Adventures of Pinocchio (Collodi), 103–4

The Adventures of Tom Sawyer (Twain), 43

adventure stories, 37, 57, 60, 122. *See also* series books

African Americans: *The Brownies' Book* magazine for, 83–85; as characters in children's books, 235–37; among children's book authors, 213, 237; children's books for, 174–75, 212–15, 236–37, 241, 306; Coretta Scott King Awards for writing and illustration, 299; dialect stories, debates about, 175, 245–46; in illustrations, 225–26; among librarians,

224–25, 259; paperbacks for, 244–45; presses owned by, 299–300; among publishing executives and editors, 305

Afro-Bets ABC Book (Hudson), 299

Agassiz, Elizabeth, 36

agents, literary, 91–92, 264–66

Ahlberg, Janet and Allan, 261

Aiken, Joan, 261

Airport (Haley), 250

Alcott, Louisa May, 47–49, 55–60

Alcott, William, 25–26

The Alderman's Feast, 27

Aldrich, Thomas Bailey, 36

Alexander, Lloyd, 251, 256, 261, 275

Alexander and the Terrible, Horrible, No Good, Very Bad Day (Viorst), 224

Alfred A. Knopf: children's division, 104, 110; Random House acquisition of, 222, 295

Alger, Horatio, Jr., 38, 105

Alice's Adventures in Wonderland (Carroll), 58, 79

Allee, Marjorie Hill, 175

All Falling Down (Zion and Graham), 195

almanacs, 5–6, 30

Along Janet's Road (Dalgliesh), 121

alphabet books, 3, 13, 299. *See also* schoolbooks/primers

alternative presses. *See* independent publishers and presses